A CRITICAL HISTORY OF KANNADA LITERATURE

CRITICAL HISTORIES OF INDIAN LITERATURES

The series presents *critical* histories of Indian literary traditions. Each volume examines the literary history and canon of a particular language and traces the sociopolitical forces that have shaped its literature. In the process, it addresses:

- the contexts, debates, and cultural influences and negotiations that inform the zeitgeist of each stage of its development
- texts, authors and traditions that have been marginalised in canon formation
- the reception of writings by Dalit, women, minority and subaltern authors through its history
- multiple manifestations of the 'literary', such as the 'oral', 'performative' and 'devotional'
- the role played by translation and cross-cultural negotiations in the formation of regional literary traditions
- the transactions between sociopolitical movements and literary/cultural movements through the development of the language and literature.

Series Editors

E. V. Ramakrishnan is a well-known critic in Malayalam and English, besides being an Indian English poet and translator. He is a former Professor and Dean as well as Professor Emeritus of Central University of Gujarat. He is a recipient of Kerala Sahitya Akademi Award (1995), Odakkuzhal Award (2018) and Kerala Sahitya Akademi's Vilasini Award (2018). He received the Sahitya Akademi Award (2023) for his Malayalam work, *Malayala Novelinte Deshakaalangal.*

M. Asaduddin is an author, critic and translator. He has been a Fulbright Scholar-in-Residence at Rutgers University, New Jersey, USA, and a Charles Wallace Trust Fellow at the British Centre for Literary Translation at the University of East Anglia, Norwich, UK. He was formerly Professor of English and Dean at Jamia Millia Islamia. His translations have received the Sahitya Akademi Award, the Katha and A. K. Ramanujan awards for translation, the Crossword Book Award and the Urdu Academy (Delhi) Award.

A CRITICAL HISTORY OF KANNADA LITERATURE

RAJENDRA CHENNI

Orient BlackSwan

A CRITICAL HISTORY OF KANNADA LITERATURE

ORIENT BLACKSWAN PRIVATE LIMITED

Registered Office
3-6-752 Himayatnagar, Hyderabad 500 029, Telangana, India
Email: centraloffice@orientblackswan.com

Other Offices
Bengaluru, Chennai, Guwahati, Hyderabad,
Kolkata, Mumbai, New Delhi, Noida, Patna

First published 2026

ISBN 978 93 6973 635 5

042552

Typeset in Adobe Garamond Pro 10.5/13 *by*
K. Divya, Hyderabad 500 060

Printed in India at
Ashwin Printing Agency

Published by
Orient Blackswan Private Limited
3-6-752, Himayatnagar
Hyderabad 500 029, Telangana, India
Email: info@orientblackswan.com

Contents

Series Editors' Preface

As an interdisciplinary area of study, literary historiography has moved to the centre stage in recent decades. Literary history is now seen as a site of contending ideologies and conflicting narratives. The early histories of Bhasha literatures made their appearance in the late nineteenth and early twentieth centuries, closely following the colonial models of historiography. In the context of colonial modernity, India had become an object of study. Disciplines like Indology tended to equate 'India' with the 'classical India' of antiquity, and this privileged Sanskrit over the 'vernacular' (read Bhasha) literatures. Several of the binaries we encounter in the study of Indian literatures, such as oral/written, tradition/modernity, elite/subaltern, exclusive/inclusive, major/minor and great/small, were the products of the historiography of this period. That 'classical India' was a construct of certain discourses is now grasped in the light of recent postcolonial and poststructuralist criticism. Critical theory has cleared a space for recovering Bhasha literatures, which were earlier seen as minor and marginal.

It is now recognised that Bhasha literatures have a history that goes back to the beginning of the second millennium, or in some cases, as in the case of Tamil, even earlier. The early literary histories of these literatures, which were written in modern Indian languages, replicated the canon shaped by the Orientalist narratives of the nineteenth century. With the emergence of feminist, Dalit and subaltern critical perspectives, the homogenising tendencies of classical aesthetic traditions could no longer be sustained. Discursive formations which are rooted in the oral traditions of communities have their separate histories which are performative and political. Obviously, the idea of the 'literary' has undergone a change in the wake of the resurgence of the 'marginal' voices in Bhasha literatures. Terms such as the 'author', 'text' and 'reader' are no longer stable identities, but relationships which change with sociopolitical contexts.

These changing cultural contexts have prompted us to initiate a series of critical histories of Bhasha literatures, which will explore aspects that were ignored earlier. The fact that multilingualism is a marked feature of Indian literatures has meant that a text may have multiple sub-texts pointing to different cultural or linguistic sources. Intertextuality, not influence, is what defines the nature of cultural exchanges between Bhasha literatures. This is illustrated by the Bhakti tradition which moved across India from

Tamil to Punjabi, crossing several languages, creating a common heritage of symbols, images and discourses. Also, literary translation which has a long history in India, hardly finds any mention in the existing literary histories.

These critical histories do not propose to present a linear history of texts and authors, chronicling the 'progress' of a singular literature. The idea is to move away from the 'colonial' discourses of historiography. The authors are under no compulsion to exhaustively tabulate or document every text and author. They may choose to identify those traits in a genre which have a bearing on the culture as a whole. They may use the insights of recent theoretical developments to examine the nature of power relations that animate a text. Translations; multilingual echoes; hybridity as a cultural phenomenon; the relations between politics and culture as seen through migrations of ideas, people and texts; the issues of gender and caste; echoes from a remote past or from transnational texts—some of these may figure in each of these critical histories. As we enter a posthuman world, an anthropocentric perspective of literature will no longer be tenable. Climate change alters our scale of time and forces us to look for alternate means of relating to the world around us. Authors who never spoke to us may now make more sense, and their voices may sound more urgent and immediate. As we come close to our own times, the cultural scene becomes more complex and varied. Social media and virtual worlds mediate our reception of the written word. We feel that a critical history of this kind will provoke fresh thinking on certain texts, authors or periods, or unearth new texts which were marginalised and forgotten. It may also function as a source book of ideas for those who work in the field of culture.

Our objective is to reclaim literary history as part of cultural history, where literature speaks to other knowledge systems, manifestations of human creativity and representations of human and non-human experience.

E. V. Ramakrishnan **M. Asaduddin**

Introduction

The present work was planned as part of Orient BlackSwan's series of critical histories of literatures in the Bhashas. The concept note by the series editors and the later discussions made it clear that these critical histories would focus on the contexts, the debates and the major preoccupations in the literary traditions. They would of course deal with the canonical texts, but also look closely at the processes of exclusion and marginalisation. Every literary history has to be a chronological narrative in some way or the other, but it should not end up as a mere catalogue of texts and events. Each book in the series was planned to address readers who may not be from the language community.

When I set out to write the critical history of Kannada literature, within these parameters and the word limit suggested, I realised that I would need to both employ a chronological framework and include the accepted canon. In dealing with a vast and heterogeneous body of works in a literary tradition composed over a millennium, it would be necessary to map its contours and development, while at the same time see the literary itself as historically and politically constructed, and literary texts as conditioned by the social structures as well as the discourses. The greater challenge was to make the history accessible to the non-expert reader.

This work is a *critical* introduction to the Kannada literary tradition from the early phase of literisation to the present. As such it does not attempt to offer comprehensive readings/interpretations of the major texts. The focus is on drawing attention to the way in which the texts enter into a complex dialogue with the socio-historical contexts. There are continuities and disjunctures, conformity and dissent—inevitable when a regional (local) literary culture has to confront the larger pan-Indian religious, political and aesthetic frameworks. The effort has been to understand how the literary in Kannada has always been a conflictual site with negotiations with *dharma*, temporal powers, political structures, and notions of gender, *Varna* and caste. There have also been seminal cross-cultural encounters with other indigenous traditions as well as with colonialism. I hope I have at least partially succeeded in avoiding the pitfalls of essentialising the Kannada tradition and of attributing a false universality to the major texts. I am aware of the number of texts I have not even been able to mention. My purpose has been to offer a critical introduction to what, in my view, are the major preoccupations in the Kannada literary tradition, which were in the first place, responses to the contexts in which its texts were created.

The present work begins with a critical review of the existing literary histories, the theoretical frameworks embedded in them and the areas opened up by them for the study of Kannada literature. This is followed by a brief introduction to the Kannada language, its relationship with the Dravidian family of languages, and its development as a vehicle of literary expression. The major part of the work takes the reader from the ancient period, through the contribution of the twelfth-century *Vachanakaras* to the medieval period. From Chapter Six ('Towards Modernity') onwards, the work focuses on the Kannada renaissance, the period of modernity and the postmodernist phase. There are also independent chapters on drama, theatre and women's writing. The development of Dalit writing and literary criticism are also examined at length. Folk literature and popular literature are also analysed in relation to what has been conceptualised as 'mainstream', canonical Kannada writing. The attempt has been to discuss major literary texts in the context of their complex negotiations with the sociocultural, political and ideological factors shaping them.

My purpose has been to provide a critical introduction to Kannada literature to contemporary readers, and to suggest, however briefly, its significance among the Bhasha literary traditions which constitute 'Indian literature'. The anonymous composer of the famous 'Song of the Cow' in Kannada begins by saying that his village is the centre of the earth. I believe every Bhasha literature, including Kannada literature, is one of the many centres from where one could begin to explore Indian literature.

Rajendra Chenni

Prolegomena

There comes in the history of every literary tradition a moment of an effort at self-recognition—of trying to articulate what the tradition is even while the tradition is in the making. Later this moment becomes the mythical moment of origin, at times leading to the error of essentialising the tradition and of foregrounding some elements in it so that they become hegemonic enough to marginalise the other elements. Despite this, the moment is of great significance even as the point from which to deviate and perhaps to deconstruct its centrality itself.

The Kannada work of aesthetics *Kavirajamarga* (The Royal Way of the Poets, 850 CE), described by Sheldon Pollock (2006) as the first book of aesthetics in a vernacular language anywhere in the world, inaugurates such a moment in the history of the Kannada literary tradition (Sundaram et al. 2017; Sitaramaiah 1994). The book in itself is mostly a translation and adaptation of the poetics of Bhamaha and Dandin. It closely follows the major conceptualisations of these works and also the modes of listing the appropriate and the inappropriate (*dosha*) in poetic practice. But what makes the work significant is the fact that it was intended to play a powerful role in the cultural politics of the time. Though there is dispute about the authorship, it is now generally agreed that it was composed by Srivijaya, either patronised by or in collaboration with Nrupatunga, the great emperor of the Rashtrakuta dynasty (Sitaramaiah 1994). In any case, the text itself declares in many places that what is being said has been approved or authorised by the king.

The Rashtrakuta empire occupied an important geopolitical territory and was one of the largest and more enduring of the 'empires' that existed before the emergence of the Vijayanagara empire. In Pollock's words, it was a 'vernacular polity'—a term which works on both the political and cultural planes. Pollock sees it as a political formation supported by the unleashing of the energies which had also ushered in the vernacular millennium in South Asia. There is no doubt that the author of *Kavirajamarga* was fully aware of the political purpose of the book of aesthetics. He demonstrates this first by drawing out the territorial boundaries of the *Kannadanādu* (*nādu* means land, kingdom, administrative unit, or place) as stretching from the Kaveri to the Godavari. The impact of this statement, and of mapping the *Kannadanādu*, can be estimated by the fact that this line is probably the only one from Old Kannada poetry quoted by all popular pro-Kannada movements in the twenty-first century. This drawing up of political boundaries not only aimed at transforming a 'place of affect' (an imagined, emotionally charged concept) into a real political space, thereby garnering the support of the people who occupied it. It was also a political strategy because there is no evidence to show that the *Kannadanādu* was inhabited by only speakers of the Kannada language. In fact, two factors which had dominated the history of this part of South India had always made a multilingual, multi-cultural context inevitable. The first was the geo-cultural contiguities which made the region a linguistic palimpsest. The second, the continuous shifting of boundaries of various kingdoms as well as the linguistic loyalties of the ruling dynasties. (For example, M. M. Kalburgi had to argue, with inscriptional evidence, that Krishnadevaraya, the popularly imagined founder of the Kannada empire, was a patron and writer of works in Telugu.) Therefore, for a work of aesthetics like *Kavirajamarga* to make a magisterial statement that the *Kannadanādu* stretched from the Kaveri to the Godavari was intended at once to reinforce the territory of the patron's empire and also to create an imagined community in which speakers of many languages and many dialects of Kannada (at least some of them mutually unintelligible) coexisted as subjects of a vernacular polity. Therefore, Sheldon Pollock (2006) translates '*Visaya*' and '*Nādu*' as 'culture land'. This 'culture land' is described as unique and distinctive (*Visesa*)—so are the people who are described as literate and well-versed in poetic practices so that they are capable of appreciating the nuances of poetry without a specialised/intensive reading.

However, *Kavirajamarga* also records the fault lines of an imagined community constructed on the notion of a dominant language. It includes an interesting discussion of the many regional dialects of Kannada which are so many that they outnumber the many tongues of the mythical *Adishesha* (the primordial serpent on which the Brahma reposes). 'The *Adishesha* (Vasuki) is tired / frustrated trying to explain the errors in the *Desis*', says *Kavirajamarga*. Added to this untenable plenty are the diachronic variations of the Kannada language which has already by then passed through the phase of *Poorva Halegannada* (the variation preceding *Halegannada* or Old Kannada). *Poorva Halegannada* is only a construct that linguists have tried to describe, but *Kavirajamarga* is emphatic about at least the previous form of Old Kannada which has now changed but which lesser poets continue to use in their works.

Since the political effort to create a linguistic polity inevitably involves the construction of the notion of a standard dialect, *Kavirajamarga* also speaks about *Tirulu Kannada*, the real, 'kernel', Kannada and goes on to identify the dialectal regions where this is spoken, namely Kopana, Puligere, Okkunda (*Kavirajamarga*, Chapter I). Interestingly, about a century later, Pampa, the first major poet of Kannada (902–75 CE), also identifies the same dialectal regions as the location of 'pure' or 'kernel' Kannada. If we draw on the information provided by inscriptions from the fifth century, when the first Kannada inscription at Talagunda was carved, it is obvious that the development of the Kannada script from the Brahmi script and its standardisation, must have contributed to the stabilisation of the 'standard' Kannada dialect. (For a detailed discussion see the second chapter.) The political ambition of firming up the *Kannadanādu* was supported by the declaration of the standard dialect in *Kavirajamarga*.

However, the fault lines do not end with this. While Pollock talks about the vernacular shift from the Sanskrit cosmopolis, historians such as S. Settar have highlighted the presence of the Prakrit cosmopolis which lasted for nearly a millennium in South India (Settar 2018)—not only its presence but also the fact that it was the chosen language for preaching and proselytising the laity for the two major religions, Jainism and Buddhism. The linguistic policies of these religions did not remain uniform and the changes majorly affected the status of Kannada. On par with various forms of Shaivism, Jainism was the most dominant religion in *Kannadanādu* and many influential royal dynasties adopted it. Jainism chose Kannada as the language of the people and thereby inaugurated what is traditionally known as the 'Jaina Age' in Kannada literature. From the first extant work of prose, *Vaddaradhane* (c. ninth century CE), to the major works until the fourteenth century, Jainism was the driving force behind literary creativity in Kannada. But there is ample evidence to suggest that Sanskrit continued to be the language of scholarship and was a prestige language. The great Jaina poets like Ranna and Ponna had among their sobriquets '*Ubhaya Kavi*', the bilingual master poet writing in Kannada and Sanskrit. It would not be wrong to assume that some form of Prakrit was spoken by the people of *Kannadanādu* (Settar 2018).

Therefore, the historical evidence supports the existence of 'an incorrigibly plural' *Kannadanādu* in the period in which *Kavirajamarga* speaks with royal authority about an unambiguously Kannada land with its boundaries marked by two rivers. The present work therefore does not subscribe to essentialist notions of a *Kannadanādu* or Kannada tradition. On the other hand, it does talk about continuities which are historically and politically conditioned. When we discuss *Kavirajamarga*, we are discussing not the mythical emergence of a Kannada tradition but a political phenomenon which happened under the rubric of larger historical interventions such as the emergence of vernacular polities, the formation, dissolution and re-formation of large polities (sometimes called empires), and the masked conflicts between the regional and the cosmopolitan or the pan-Indian. Even at the risk of sounding too squeamish, the present author would place 'regional' and 'pan-Indian' *sous rature*, as problematic terms especially in the pre-modern context being discussed.

The other important question is: Does *Kavirajamarga* enunciate a distinctively Kannada aesthetics? There have been at least three responses by scholars to this question.

1. No. *Kavirajamarga* is almost wholly a translation of the Sanskrit aesthetics as codified by Bhamaha and Dandin. This argument is supported by pointing out the literal translations in *Kavirajamarga* from the two authors.
2. Though the author of *Kavirajamarga* takes a more accommodative approach to Sanskrit aesthetics (say unlike the authors associated with *Sangam Tamilagam*), he does demonstrate how Kannada poetic practices deviate from the Sanskrit norms (as in the case of *Yati Bhanga)*.[1] He also mentions certain genres and prosodic units which can be shown to be distinctively Kannada (such as *Chattana* and *Bedande*).
3. The most interesting arguments have come from critics who consider *Kavirajamarga* to be a political statement in the guise of a book of aesthetics. In the Kannada context, these have come from K. V. Subbanna, D. R. Nagaraj and Ki. Rum. Nagaraj.

K. V. Subbanna refers to the 'imperial project' submitted by Nebrija to Queen Isabella of Spain, arguing that as significant as Columbus's intercontinental voyage was, so too was the cultural project of creating an authentic (standardised) state language, supported by an official grammar, which he saw as a precondition for the establishment of an empire (Subbanna 2000). He sees this project as foreshadowed in India by Koutilya's *Arthashastra* (c. third century CE) and the invention of the Brahmi script by Asoka as the medium of his empire. Subbanna is of the

[1] *Yati* refers to the caesura which according to traditional prosody is expected to occur at a predefined position in a line. Kannada poetry has consistently transgressed this norm. The deviation is known as *Yati Bhanga*.

view that the foundation of an empire is generally preceded by a major shift in the linguistic domain. He places *Kavirajamarga* as one such repetition of a historical pattern, this time accompanying the establishment of a Kannada linguistic polity. He also considers *Kavirajamarga* as the culmination of a long process which had seen Kannada go through literarisation and had also witnessed much reflection on language, culture and polity. He believes that *Kavirajamarga*, in this sense, is a composite text comprising layers of historical developments. Subbanna elaborates these ideas in a later monograph, *Kaviraja Marga Mattu Kannada Jagattu* (2000), wherein he developed the idea of a Kannada tradition characterised by certain central beliefs and values. Unfortunately, the two texts he discusses as examples of the Kannada tradition, though extremely popular and influential, turned out to be controversial. The first one, *Kerege Hara* (Sacrifice for the Pond), is a folk song celebrating the 'self-sacrifice' of the younger daughter-in-law of a feudal family to bring rains to fill up the local pond. Her distraught husband follows her by jumping into the pond. The song transparently suggests that the daughter-in-law was pressurised to sacrifice herself by her in-laws and abandoned by her parents. It could easily be read as a text about the victimisation of a woman in a feudal society. I shall be discussing the other folk song chosen by Subbanna later with reference to the Dalit interrogation of the universalist/essentialist notions of Kannada culture and values. The lesson is that the ideas of *Kannadaness* and Kannada values need to be discussed with reference to the historical, political and cultural contexts in which they appear from time to time.

Apropos the tribute Durgasimha (eleventh century) pays to Srivijaya, the author of *Kavirajamarga*, by saying 'Srivijaya is god', D. R. Nagaraj, while discounting the exaggeration, says, 'Srivijaya is god indeed for Kannada literary culture, in fact he virtually created that culture'. His following comments deserve scholarly attention: 'The *Kavirajamārga* is a fascinating text inviting global comparison, perhaps especially in its demonstration of the intimate tie between power and culture. It can be treated as a paradoxical occasion for both mourning and celebration: it is at once the statist rejection of a certain indigenous form and the beginning of a magisterial institution called literature' (2012, 47–48). Nagaraj is discussing how the idea of the literary, so crucial to a courtly culture, becomes formalised and institutionalised by excluding a number of cultural expressions in society. There is ample evidence from archaeological finds as well as from various *sastric* works that there were already many forms of expression which involved language, apart from the folk performative arts which also included songs and poetry. *Kavirajamarga,* the magisterial statist work, firmly established the idea of the literary which excluded these forms of expression.

Nagaraj argues that despite its accommodative stance vis à vis Sanskrit poetics, *Kavirajamarga* also foregrounded the idea of *Desi* which, along with *Mārga*, has been considered a distinctive characteristic of Kannada aesthetics and poetic practice. The two terms are the most discussed and debated in the Kannada tradition: 'If Sri Vijaya was sometimes overly fault-finding, or, worse, subordinated local practices to high theory, many prominent theorists of Kannada feel grateful for his critical genius since he tried to address the problem of *Desi* in a decisive fashion for the tradition' (Nagaraj 2012, 47–48).

A few explanations are in order here. There is a school of scholars who argue that *Mārga* and *Desi* are two modes of literary (poetic) expression and as such are part of the rhetoric of poetry and the verbal texture of a poem or a part of a poem. These scholars do not agree that the terms have implications beyond these domains. However, the tenor of the debates around the two terms has always indicated a different and broader conceptualisation. On the one hand, *Desi* is treated as an umbrella term for the folk, oral–aural traditions of expression. As Nagaraj suggests, these traditions did not have the onus of negotiations with the Sanskritic, classical and formalised traditions. *Mārga* on the other hand, is the sophisticated, literary mode with well-established conventions and stylised verbal strategies. To use a popular Kannada distinction, *Mārga* poetry is poetry for the eye, for reading (*Odu Gabba*); *Desi* poetry is for the ear (*Kelugabba*). The oral–aural goes with the performative tradition. This has to be recorded because, for instance, thousands of written scripts of *Yakshagana* (a prominent performative art form of coastal and Malnad Karnataka) disappeared for not being 'literature'. The same is also true of the scripts of commercial theatre in Karnataka which was the only medium to reach the general audience for the first four decades of the twentieth century. The disappearance of such texts is a phenomenon repeatedly seen in the Kannada tradition, especially when the literary rejuvenates its domination. However, to return to the argument, there is a fair amount of theorisation on *Mārga* and *Desi* as expressions of diverse life-worlds, of the hegemonic and subaltern social classes, and of the Vedic-brahminical and Shudra world views. Long before the theorisation took place, the sharp differences between the literary epics and the folk epics seemed to reinforce such a distinction.

Mārga and *Desi* have also been used to describe the pan-Indian Sanskritic models and the local-regional models of expression, respectively. This in turn is related to the powerful notion that like all Bhasha literary traditions, Kannada tradition secured its distinctive identity by confronting the pan-Indian Sanskritic model. It was Ki. Rum. Nagaraj (2012) who argued forcefully that the Kannada literary tradition continuously subverted the pan-Indian Sanskritic models in order to create space for the expression of a regional sensibility. Ki. Rum. Nagaraj, one of the finest scholars of old and medieval Kannada literature, worked out a theoretical model to explain the 'originality' of the Kannada works which were intended to be retellings of the Sanskrit or Prakrit originals. He examines Pampa's *Aadipurana* (934 CE) which borrows heavily from the original *Mahapurana*, the Jaina Sanskrit work written by Jinasena and Gunabhadra. It does not need much effort to see how closely Pampa follows the original. However, Ki. Rum. Nagaraj points out how the celebrated editor of Pampa's work, L. Basavaraju, draws our attention to the subtle modifications, elisions and additions through which Pampa creates his own epic. Ki. Rum. Nagaraj argues that Pampa's effort was towards transforming what was dry, mechanical and scholastic in the original into the living, vibrant and human. Adducing the example of the other great epic of Pampa, *Vikramarjuna Vijaya* (934 CE) which allegorises the *Mahabharata* story to make Pampa's patron King Arikesari, Arjuna, Ki. Rum. Nagaraj reiterates his argument that the great works of Kannada were expressions of a regional politics and a regional sensibility, even while they used a Sanskrit model. We shall be returning to this argument in a later chapter.

The issue is, did *Kavirajamarga* inaugurate the theorisation of *Mārga* and *Desi* in such a way that it would shape the later works as expressions of a local-regional world view? The present writer feels that *Kavirajamarga* does not really enter into such a fertile theorisation of the *Desi*. Yes, it does acknowledge its presence. What has this done with the historiography of Kannada literature? Kannada literary history has not obliged the historian by providing examples of either a pendulum-like oscillation between *Mārga* and *Desi* in different periods, nor has it provided a heart-warming narrative of resistance to the *Mārga* traditions. In fact, there are disruptions, disjunctions and multiple continuities in the tradition. What have been present are the inevitable exclusions, and subjugation of many things which constitute Kannada. While a literary historian cannot hope for the 'insurrection of subjugated knowledges' (Michel Foucault), he/she can try to record both conformity and resistance.

ONE

Existing Literary Histories and Their Problems

1

For a literary tradition with a continuous history of over eleven centuries, it is surprising that the number of Kannada literary histories is so small and that there is little theorising on the construction of the historiography of Kannada literature. Unless we fall back upon the stereotypes about the South Asian indifference to history or the lack of data, there is no acceptable explanation for this paucity. A number of existing literary histories have been included in the bibliography of this volume, but most of them are chronological narratives with highly subjective and impressionistic evaluations of major literary works. They also suffer from the characteristic defect of extolling the literary or ethical values of literary works and demonstrating little 'sense of fact' or attention to the multiple socio-historical and political factors which are inscribed into the texts themselves. There are also persistent confusions and disagreements about dates and places. (As Sheldon Pollock wryly comments [2006], even the location of Manyakheta, the capital of the Rashtrakuta dynasty, was not known to scholars for a long time.) Till date, we do not know with certainty the century to which Kumara Vyasa (also known as Gadugina Naranappa), one of the greatest of Kannada poets, belonged.[1] There are some arguments put forward by way of explaining this lack of a sustained interest in the history of literature. One argument may be described as the 'impersonality' theory. It is argued that notions of authorship and authorial rights were alien to the Kannada literary tradition. The author merged himself/herself with the tradition and believed that he/she was only a medium through which the text realised itself. As Kumara Vyasa says in the prefatory verses of his retelling of the *Mahabharata*, Veeranarayana (his deity) is the author, and he is only a scribe. He is of course referring to the myth that it was Lord Ganesha who was the scribe to Vyasa and wrote down the original *Mahabharata*. Like Kumara Vyasa, Pampa too in the prefatory verses of his retelling of the *Mahabharata* (*Vikramarjuna Vijaya*) describes himself as 'audacious' in trying to swim 'the ocean of Vyasa' (and his work)

[1] For a discussion on several issues relating to the date of Kumara Vyasa's work, see Rahamat 2004. Also see Mugali 1956/2018.

and promises to renarrativise the original without 'deforming its body'. While much could be said about the 'death of the author' in pre-modern Kannada tradition, the argument comes up against many contradictions. In *Aadipurana*, Pampa describes his genealogy, the conversion of his father from brahminism to Jainism and his own appearance, and also appends a list of the *nādus* to which his mistresses belonged. We also know the year when his two epics were completed. In other poets of the tradition, there are the conventional claims about their poetic achievements, such as they have 'vanquished the poems of the past'. They also mention the titles and soubriquets and make detailed mention of their patrons (as in the case of Ranna the Jain poet who wrote *Sahasa Bheema Vijayam*).[2] What is missing is the attempt to keep records of these texts in the public domain. There is need to pay some attention to the material conditions of the production of literary texts and their circulation in the pre-modern Kannada social world. There is little doubt that the production of texts—both literary and *sastric*—took place under the patronage either of a ruler (as in the case of Pampa patronised by Arikesari, a feudatory lord [*samantha*] under the Chalukya dynasty), or of the wealthy aristocracy (as in the case of Ponna who was patronised by Attimabbe, a remarkable woman from an illustrious and influential Jaina family).[3] Though Pampa speaks dismissively of the system of patronage saying, 'What can others give / What can they do (for you)' (Basavaraju 2002, 7; translation by the author), elsewhere he acknowledges profusely the liberal patronage he received from Arikesari.

The approval of the literary circle consisting of poets, authors, the cognoscenti known as *budhajana* (the wise/the well-informed, with literary training) and the *sahrudaya* (sensitive, empathetic) readers/listeners ultimately decided the worth of a work. Despite fabulous and exaggerated stories about the liberal patronage received by scholars and writers, it has to be assumed that their circle, at any point of time, was small. There is also the absence of data on whether anything resembling the systematic patronage and large poets' meets of the kind we find in the Moghul courts, existed in the South before the Vijayanagara empire. The author of *Kavirajamarga* speaks of the Kannada people as capable of sensitively responding to poetry

---

[2] Ranna was a tenth-century poet from Mudhol (now in North Karnataka) and was one of the three *Ratnas* of the Kannada poetic tradition. His work *Sahasa Bheema Vijayam* is a retelling of some episodes from the *Mahabharata*.

[3] Ranna eulogises Attimabbe in his work. Several inscriptions also describe her munificence. See R. V. Kulkarni, ed. *Sahasa Bheema Vijayam* (Bengaluru: Sahitya Parishat, 1998).

even without literary training, but he also says that no one who was not trained in the *sastras*, aesthetics and the literature of the past could dare to enter Nrupatunga's court. Therefore, it can be safely assumed that a knowledgeable and well-versed court circle of scholars and fellow authors existed in the capitals of the 'kingdoms' of the pre-modern period. Large number of inscriptions also record the gift of '*agraharas*' (landholdings) to brahmin scholars, many of whom could have been authors of *sastric* or literary works. Recent studies of the system of patronage in the Jaina context have also thrown light on some details of the patronage and the system of gift-giving.[4]

The other equally important part of the patronage was the copying of the manuscripts of literary works by scribes. Attimabbe is said to have supported the preparation of several hundred copies of Chavundaraya's work. These were preserved in the religious monasteries when the works were either hagiographies or overtly religious in their themes. The editor L. Basavaraju points out that of the two epics by Pampa, *Aadipurana*, the epic hagiography of the first *Thirthankara* Vrishabhanatha, survived in many copies in the Jaina monasteries, while the other secular retelling of the *Mahabharata* did not. Since the monasteries were also places of learning, it can be assumed that the 'books' inscribed on palmyra leaves were read and recited, though there must have been restrictions on reading out certain passages with erotic content which were part of the hagiographies too. Both the original *Mahapurana* and Pampa's *Aadipurana* do contain a number of erotic descriptions.

The circulation of the 'books'/works in the pre-modern period was limited and depended on both secular/courtly and religious patronage. This tradition is powerfully dislocated and disrupted by the *Vachanakaras* of the twelfth century led by Basava. There are references to a *Vachanakara* Shantharasa who was a *Vachana bhandari*, or treasurer and keeper of the *Vachanas*, though details are not available. Obviously, the *Vachanakaras* were opposed to royal patronage and rejected it. However, the *Vachanas* ('the spoken') participated in a collective oral–aural system of communication and did not need the traditional patronage.

These systems of patronage meant two things. One, that literary works survived in copies maintained by religious monasteries and aristocratic houses. But with political disruptions and social changes, it also meant that

[4] See Hampa Nagarajiah's analysis in *Vaddaradhane: Ondu Adhyayana* (Bengaluru: Kannada Pradhikara, 1992).

the texts 'disappeared' and became the 'lost texts' of the tradition until they were rediscovered at a much later stage. Some texts retained their 'aura' and 'cult value', as Walter Benjamin defines the terms, and had better chances of survival. For example, it is believed in rural Karnataka even today that the recitation of the canto *Virata Parva* from Kumara Vyasa's work can prevent famine and therefore the recitation is a socio-religious ritual.

The circulation of literary texts also took place through the art of recitation known as *Gamaka* (still very popular in many regions across Karnataka). Though details regarding the *Gamakis* are not adequately available, there is no doubt that this mode of communication is unsurpassed in its immediacy and intensity of effect on the listeners. Rendered by highly knowledgeable and trained reciters, this mode of collective listening took the canonical works to the common people. Kuvempu's novels record how the classics, especially Lakshmeesha's retelling of the *Mahabharata*, were read out in the feudal houses of the *Okkaliga* landlords to all and sundry.

One more equally powerful means of literary communication was the adoption of literary works into the folk-performative arts of *Yakshagana* and *Talamaddale*. Large sections of Kumara Vyasa's work were used in these performances, though the audience may not have recognised the author.

The brief details provided in the preceding passages support the existence of both systems of patronage and circulation of texts. But, in a paradoxical way, this was also probably detrimental to the development of literary histories in any form. The circulation of texts ensured the contemporaneity of the texts rather than their historicity. As there was a continuum in which the texts flowed from the written/inscribed to the oral/aural and the performative domains, their historicity was probably the least of the considerations. Most of the major pre-modern Kannada works were translations or transcreations, and thereby entered into the overpopulated field of retellings and re-narrativisations of myths, legends and past renderings. Kumara Vyasa says that there was such an overcrowding of retellings of the *Ramayana* that there was no space even to find a footing, and therefore he chose the *Mahabharata* for his retelling (Kuvempu and Iyengar 1958). By entering into the overcrowded field, the texts lost traces of authorship and the historicity of their being written. This of course is a reasonable conjecture. This should be considered along with the fact that modern notions of authorship, individuality of texts, etc., have little significance in the pre-modern literary-social world.

The Archives for Literary Histories

A brief note on the nature of the archive for history writing in Karnataka is in order here. The major 'documents' are the inscriptions. In Sheldon Pollock's view, *Kannadanādu* is probably the densest in the world in terms of the number of inscriptions found (2006). Approximately 25,000 inscriptions have been collected and read to date. However, the largest number of them are official documents such as those relating to land grants, and have little bearing on cultural matters except indirectly. For example, these grants throw light on the economic power of the donors—kings, feudal lords or wealthy men. They also help us understand the socio-cultural status of the grantees. A fascinating detail emerging from Settar's work (2018) on the artisan class in Karnataka is that the scribes who engraved or etched the stone and metal inscriptions were gifted landholdings, sometimes equalling similar grants made to brahmins. Thus the actual nature of the social hierarchies can be inferred from such inscriptions. Some of the longer inscriptions do provide us details of contemporary life, but very few mention anything about the literary world. It is the literary works themselves which contain such details in the *stuti kavya* (tributary verses), either independent ones or parts of larger literary works. With such paucity of data in the archival material, preparation of literary histories has been a daunting task.

This situation is further complicated by the 'loss of texts'. Going by the references in the surviving texts, what we now have as the corpus of Kannada literature is probably a very small portion of what was actually produced. The classic instance is *Kavirajamarga* which mentions a number of *poorva suris*, or master poets and authors of the past, such as Asaga and Vinayaditya. None of their works have survived. The present author does not subscribe to the view that a culture allows those texts to survive which it considers worthy of survival, since the view is obviously a little too idealistic. The literary canon is always a truncated and diminished entity. As a consequence, even the traditional canon-centred literary history—so disparaged at present—is itself a product of a lack and absences. The pre-modern canon of Kannada literature is small and meagre if we exclude the *Vachanas*. Unfortunately, we do not have a historical work on the pre-modern period which among other important things makes a mention of the works and authors of the tradition.

What should not be ignored is the acknowledgment of the debt to the *poorva suris* figuring in many of the pre-modern works. Mention has already been made of Pampa acknowledging Vyasa. He also refers to the works he drew upon in composing his *Aadipurana*. Using such references, one could even prepare a list of the acknowledged but lost works in the Kannada tradition.

From Pampa onwards there is evidence of canon-formation in the tributes paid to the past masters by poets. Use of honorifics and titles also suggests this ongoing process. The notion of the three *Ratnas* (Pampa, Ranna and Ponna), and the honorific for Pampa as the *Adikavi* (the archetypal/first poet) are not of modern origin. As in all cases of canon-formation, cultural policies and religion did play a role in this incipient canon-formation. We have already seen how the emergence of the literary led to the exclusion of many other forms of expression. The formation of the canon led to a hierarchisation even among the works of a single author. This happened in the case of Janna and Ponna.[5] It has also led to the wrenching away of literary texts from their contexts, in order to relocate them in a rarefied, universalist framework of 'great works of literature'. As we shall discuss later, this has been and continues to be the bane of literary history writing in Kannada.

The Colonial Origins of the Modern Literary History in Kannada

Modern literary history of the Kannada tradition is the contribution of Western missionaries, administrators and scholars who took ample help from their native collaborators. This involved two primary stages. The first stage involved the rediscovery of the lost texts, which meant the locating of manuscripts preserved in monasteries and by individuals, and bringing them to the public domain through print technology which itself was introduced by the missionaries in Karnataka. The history of print technology is a chequered one in Karnataka. William Carey (1761–1834) had prepared a grammar of the Kannada language and had created the fonts to print it at Srirampur in Bengal as early as in 1817. But an accidental fire is said to have destroyed both (Srinivas 1974). This Scottish missionary had learnt Kannada with the help of a *Munshi* and had printed the book himself. Thereafter several missionaries at various places in Karnataka such as Bellary, Bengaluru, Mangaluru and Dharwad had pursued publication in Kannada. Among them, the Wesleyan Press (originally at Bengaluru and later at Mysore), the Catholic Kodiyalbail Press (at Mangaluru) and Herrmann Friedrich Moegling's own press (at Mangaluru) laid a sound

[5] Most Kannada critics are sceptical about the literary merit of Ponna's works in comparison to Pampa's works.

foundation for printing technology and print culture in Karnataka. Among other things, the missionaries edited and brought out print versions of old Kannada works such as *Channabasava Purana, Basavapurana, Torave Ramayana,* and Kumara Vyasa's *Bharata*, as well as anthologies of poetic passages and folk poems. A little later, the Bibliothica Carnatika project was initiated and it led to the publication of major texts of Kannada in authoritative editions.

R. Narasimhachar, who co-authored the massive three-volume *Karnataka Kavi Charite*, is probably the first historian of Kannada literature. Gottfried Weigle, Moegling, Ferdinand Kittel and B. L. Rice had all contributed long essays attempting an overview of Kannada literature. These works belong to the first phase of the discipline of the modern literary history in Kannada literature. All these authors admit that the paucity of data has prevented them from writing a more comprehensive history of a literary tradition whose antiquity they are convinced of and which they partially admire. The story of the intellectual adventures of these Western missionaries who drew up the outlines of the history of Kannada literature is a fascinating one but sadly outside the purview of the present work.

To what extent was the work of these missionaries a part of the colonial production of knowledge? How did their understanding of the history and culture of the *Kannadanādu*, shaped by the colonial perceptions of India, lead them to the conceptualisation of an Orientalist history of Kannada literature? To what extent did this conceptualisation continue to frame the later histories of Kannada literature, with some questionable consequences?

It was Ferdinand Kittel (1832–1903), the greatest lexicographer of Kannada, who in his German and English writings proposed the periodisation of Kannada literature into ages named after the dominant religions of the period.[6] He seems to have begun with a more neutral chronological periodisation into the early period (800 CE to 1300 CE) to the late period (1300 CE to 1827 CE). But he then subdivided the later period into the Lingayat and Shaiva period (1400 CE to 1500 CE), and Vaishnava, Lingayat and Shaiva period (1500 CE to 1872 CE) (Harish 2014). B. L. Rice, in his three essays contributed to the *Journal of Royal Asiatic Society* (JRAS) (1882, 1883 and 1890), also reiterates a similar periodisation. According to him Jaina writers dominate the period from the beginning to 1300 CE, Lingayat and Shaiva writers dominate from 1300 CE to

[6] For a discussion of the works of Kittel, see Havanur Srinivas, *Hosagannadada Arunodaya* (Bengaluru: Kannada Pustaka Pradhikara, 1974). Also see several articles in G. B. Harish, ed. *Mumbelagu* (Bengaluru: Sahitya Parishat, 2014).

1500 CE, and brahmin and Vaishnava writers from 1500 CE onwards. These attempts are in line with the Orientalist perception of Indian history as dominated by religions. The periodisation ignores the multiple and complex factors which have shaped Kannada literature. Was Pampa a product of the hegemony of the Jaina religion in *Kannadanādu* of the tenth century, or was he a product of the turbulent, uncertain politics of his times? How is it that his *Aadipurana*, a Jaina hagiographic work, turns out towards its end to be a devastating critique of the very martial values he had extolled in his patron ruler Arikesari in the other epic he wrote?

The work of the missionary scholars coincided with the period when Kannada was being made the medium of instruction in the teacher training colleges (then known as Normal Schools) and the MA programme in Kannada was being introduced at Bombay University. Initially the list of texts was sketchy and dominated by translations of Sanskrit works in the pedagogical courses. Later, when the establishment of colleges and universities initiated the institutionalisation of the discipline of Kannada literature, companions (such as the justly famous Kannada *Kaipidi* in two volumes, published by Mysore University) and official literary histories began to be produced. But what did not change was the periodisation of Kannada literary history. It continues to be the foundation of the academic study of Kannada literature today. Interestingly, the missionary scholars had shown a keen interest in forms of expression beyond the literary—such as folklore and *Yakshagana*—which was excluded from the academic field of Kannada literature. It was only much later that optional courses in folk literature were introduced in the postgraduate departments of Kannada studies, and even later that separate departments of folk literature were established. These seemingly non-serious facts have been brought in here because the writing of literary histories of Kannada has rarely happened outside the academia till today. It is these academic histories we shall be examining in the next section.

2

We have seen in the previous section how the idea of a Kannada literary tradition was the contribution of Christian missionaries, scholar–administrators and the native scholars who collaborated with them. The same could be said of the history of Karnataka too. Huge projects of archaeological explorations and the collection and reading of the inscriptions laid the foundation of the writing of Karnataka history. Colin Mackenzie, Walter Elliot and B. L. Rice played an extraordinary role in these projects (Srinivas 1974). It would be easy to describe these projects as Orientalist–imperialist. However, a more nuanced description would be as a project planned and carried out under the rubric of the Orientalist–imperialist framework with the declared or undeclared purpose of employing the knowledge thus gained to 'discipline' the subject people. But these intentions and imperial commands were heavily modulated by an intellectual curiosity and the rigour of the European education these individual participants had received. Elliot was imprisoned during the first battle which the British waged against Kittur Chennamma, the legendary leader of the first rebellion against the British rule in North Karnataka. After the eventual British victory and his release, Elliot devoted himself to the cause of Kannada and Karnataka by petitioning the British administration to consider Kannada (and not Marathi) as the vernacular language of the people of the region, and receiving no encouraging reply, went on to privately fund a Kannada vernacular school (Srinivas 1974). He began to collect inscriptions, which made a considerable contribution to the knowledge about Karnataka's past. Mackenzie collected a fabulous number of inscriptions and also funded the writing of hundreds of *Kaifiyats* (partly individual testimonials but also records and narratives of contemporary history) which remain extraordinary sources of non-formal history (Kalburgi 1994). Recent scholarship has demonstrated how these imperial projects were carried out with the active collaboration of native scholars and assistants. In any case, the two projects—Bibliotheca Carnatika and Epigraphia Carnatika—along with essays contributed to the *Journal of the Asiatic Society* and *The Antiquary* became the cumulative archive for the construction of Karnataka's history and the history of Kannada literature. They provided the material on which the modern discipline of Kannada studies was institutionalised.

The Influence of the *Ekikarana* Movement

The institutionalisation of Kannada studies took place in an intellectual–emotional environment which was shaped by the convergence of the nationalist movement, the Kannada sub-nationalist *Ekikarana* (unification of Karnataka) movement, and the socio-religious reform movements which had begun much earlier in India but continued to impact Karnataka from the last quarter of the nineteenth century to the first decades of the twentieth. These movements drew their energy from the great churning known as the Indian Renaissance. So powerful was the emotional charge of the metaphors of Renaissance and the reawakening that the literary-cultural movement in Karnataka, which also converged with the first phase of modern Kannada literature, was named *Navodaya* (the new rise, the new awakening). The socio-political energies of these movements were released by the unification movement which had many epicentres (Rao 2017). The movement was a historical and cultural necessity because when it began, the Kannada-speaking people were scattered over twety-nine fragments spread over two presidencies, British India and many small principalities. One large fragment was part of the dominion of the Nizam of Hyderabad and another was in the Mysore principality. Except in Mysore principality, Kannada was neither the medium of education nor the language of administration; nor was it a prestige language. These facts need to be emphasised because contemporary theories of linguistic identity and linguistic states consider such movements as products of atavistic, primordial identities in an unholy alliance with bastard forms of Euro-centric nationalism. The movements are also summarily treated as centred around the political-cultural aspirations of the native elite class under the tutelage of Westernised pedagogy. Such theoretical formulations become an excuse for the denial of history. Though the *Ekikarana* movement in Karnataka could be explained away within such theoretical models, a hard core of historical facts would still remain unexplained. As a later chapter shall deal with the unification movement, we need here to only analyse how 'Kannada' became a cementing factor to patch up the many fault lines which were the consequence of the fragmentation of the Kannada-speaking community. The movement obviously had no support from the imperial government, and the native elite was neither organised nor empowered. It had to be a cultural movement energised by the nostalgic narratives of a *Kannadanādu*, stretching from the Kaveri to the Godavari, and the 'Lost Glory of Karnataka' (the title of a famous essay by Aluru Venkata Rao, the 'high priest' of the unification movement) (1912). The leaders in the initial phase of the movement came from the brahminical upper middle class who were also active in the Congress-led freedom movement. An important supporting factor was Gandhiji's support for linguistic states and even Nehru, until he became the prime minister, did not oppose it. S. Chandrashekhar (2005) has analysed in detail how the idealistic movement had to negotiate with the hard political calculations by the two dominant castes—Lingayats and Okkaligas—about the possible demographic balance if Karnataka were to be united. However, the movement created an emotionally charged public register in which images of 'Mother Karnataka', 'Bhuvaneshwari' (the presiding goddess of

Karnataka), proliferated (Govindraju 2006). Therefore, modern Kannada literature of the *Navodaya* period had the cultural function of creating the *Kannadanādu* now conceptualised as a linguistic state called Karnataka. There had also been a long hiatus of the eighteenth century during which there were no major works in Kannada literature. There were also writers' groups and associations such as the *Geleyara Gumpu* (Friends' Group) led by Bendre, which made Kannada a concern of the civil society. The 'enthusiasm of the age' (a phrase used by the mystic/*Vachanakara* Allama, for another context) greatly impacted the ideas about Kannada literature of the past and the incipient attempts to write the history of Kannada literature.

Existing Histories and the Myth of a Pluralist *Kannadanādu*

A great deal of energy was invested in proving the antiquity of the Kannada language and its literary tradition. R. Narasimhacharya's *Karnataka Kavi Charite* (1961) begins with a comparison of the Kannada literary tradition with those of Tamil, Telugu and Malayalam, to demonstrate that except probably Tamil, Kannada had the longest surviving literary tradition. He also discusses the Dravidian origin of the Kannada language but emphatically argues that Kannada was a branch of the proto-Dravidian and not of Tamil. Like all literary historians of Kannada, Narasimhacharya also pays the obligatory tribute to the first Kannada inscription found at Halmidi (dated fifth century CE) and to *Kavirajamarga* (1961, 2020). He concludes correctly that the Kannada language had matured into a medium of literary expression centuries before the Halmidi inscription, and that there was a long line of lost texts and authors preceding *Kavirajamarga*.

This sets the tone for the later academic histories of Karnataka. The notions of the antiquity of the Kannada language and literature, the idea of a *Kannadanādu* and at least two Kannada 'empires', became the central, hegemonic frameworks monitoring the history of Kannada literature. These were supported by the notions of the 'Kannadiga tolerance' for and acceptance of different faiths and languages. There was a lot of political sense behind this last notion, because the unified Karnataka had to be a patchwork of a plurality of languages, religions and lifestyles. This made it an overriding concern to cull out from the canonical literary texts, statements of faith in a liberal and accommodative world view. Two such statements from *Kavirajamarga* and Pampa became (and continue to be) the hallmarks of the essentially liberal and pluralist Kannada tradition:

> Isn't it gold(en) to show tolerance to other faiths. (*Kavirajamarga*)
> Isn't the human race one? (Pampa)[7]

This construction of the Kannada literary tradition runs counter to the history of the violent conflict between the Jaina and Shaiva religious sects, which had been an undercurrent in Kannada society over a long period of time. The conflicts are reflected in various forms in the major texts but are generally elided in literary histories. The works of the Vaishnava *Dasas*, who were also major poets, are also held up in literary histories for their anti-caste and anti-*varna* declamations. However, later research has unravelled the ambiguities of their location in a caste society with a powerful institutionalised religious sect. It would not be wrong to argue that Kannada literary histories were constructed on the foundation of an imagined community called *Kannadanādu* whose tolerant and liberal ideologies successfully balanced the conflicts based on caste, class and gender. It was only great poets like Bendre (who also composed songs celebrating the *Kannadanādu* when the occasion demanded!) who created the counter image of the 'demon mother' who regrets having birthed not children but only labour pains. In this imagery, the demon mother also demands the sacrifice of life from the cowardly representative of the Kannadigas (Bendre 1960).

The strong point of the Kannada scholarship of the *Navodaya* period was the thorough and comprehensive inwardness of the scholars with the philological and poetic practices of the past and with the Old Kannada language. Sheldon Pollock (2006) praises them as philologists of global excellence. Every scholar and poet had an impeccable knowledge of traditional aesthetics and practices. Employing the models of Western scholars' skills of editing and emendations, these scholars prepared authoritative editions and commentaries on major works. Since most of these scholars seem to have subscribed to an artificial separation between textual scholarship and criticism, their excellent work remains confined to the 'purification of the text'.

The major critical mode throughout the *Navodaya* period was '*Rasa Vimarshe*' which in practice meant addressing the empathetic reader and drawing his/her attention to the positive and finer literary/aesthetic aspects of the text. This co-existed with the assumption that there was consensus on a set of core values accepted by the critic and the reader, and that the function of criticism was to demonstrate the presence of these values in literary texts. From a sociological–cultural perspective, this consensus depended on the

[7] All translations from the Kannada are by the author unless specified otherwise.

hegemony of the elite class. The class was part of the educated middle class, generally from the upper castes. Though predominantly brahminical it had been brought up on a loosely liberal education. It is surprising that during the historically turbulent period of colonial modernity, freedom struggle and the radical anti-brahminical movements in the neighbouring states of Tamil Nadu and Maharashtra, the literary class in Karnataka remained unperturbed. According to S. Chandrashekhar (2006) and other historians, it was the 'modern', 'welfare' state of Mysore (Mysore principality) which was largely responsible for this cultural consensus. The principality suppressed the anti-British peasant uprisings quite brutally and also managed to control the Congress-led freedom movement. Under the leadership of some forward-looking *diwans*, the principality encouraged industrialisation, large-scale irrigation, hydroelectric projects as well as women's education. In 1919 it accepted the Justice Miller Committee's Report which had recommended a considerably high reservation for all non-brahmin castes in state services. (The Report recommended half of the higher posts and two thirds of the lower appointments in each grade of the service for communities other than brahmins, to be implemented in seven years.) The Maharaja of Mysore, Krishnaraja Wodeyar IV, was among rulers like Shahu Maharaj of Kolhapur and the Gaikwads of Baroda who supported the backward classes (Chandrashekhar 2006). The overall consequence of such measures was the powerful myth of Mysore being a 'model' state which had also established a Prajamandali (people's council) of nominated members from the dominant classes but with the veneer of a democratic institution. The state thus remained free from any form of radical socio-religious reform movements.

The readers of the *Navodaya* period comprised the middle class and upper-caste educated individuals of such a society. The epicentre of the institutionalisation of Kannada literature was Mysore; and the most important scholars of Kannada studies were from the famous Maharaja College and (later) from Mysore University. When the Central College campus was established at Bengaluru, it was these academics who were transferred to the campus. B. M. Sri, A. R. Krishnashastri, T. S. Venkannaiah, D. L. Narasimhachar and T. N. Shreekhantaiah were all members of the academia which defined Kannada studies, formulated the curriculum, and set up the academic agenda. The idea of the Kannada literary tradition as a 'composite' stream to which all religions contributed without sectarian strife and upholding the values of tolerance and acceptance, was the construction of this class. The energies of writers and scholars in North Karnataka were invested in the *Ekikarana* movement and in securing a foothold for Kannada. Historically, North Karnataka and Hyderabad Karnataka had always been multilingual, multi-religious and open to several mystical–spiritual traditions such as the Sufi and the *Tatwapadakar* traditions.[8] The cultural homogeneity of the Mysore principality was unimaginable in these provinces.

This should explain why the literary historiography which developed in the Mysore academic circles conceptualised a non-conflictual, assimilative and accommodative Kannada literary tradition. As explained earlier, it was also politically expedient during the unification movement to imagine a similar culture and society.

After the early phase of Kannada literary historiography, we see a considerable expansion in terms of the literary works that are authoritatively edited, remarkable commentaries and companions. The *Navodaya* period also witnessed enormous creative activity with the introduction of the new, 'modern' genres such as the novel, the short story and the lyric. Drama and theatre also flourished. However, two things did not happen—the development of modern criticism and theorisation on literary history. The two major projects aimed at writing a multi-volume history of Kannada literature were launched at Mysore University (in 1974) and Bangalore University (in 1972). (The first volume was published in 1974.) The contributors were reputed scholars from all over Karnataka. The volumes were compilations of essays by individual scholars on selected topics. Though generally competent, they do not add up to a clearly defined intellectual project based on the necessary theorisation.

Surprisingly, the Bangalore University literary history does not carry an elaborate introduction to the project. A brief preface by G. S. Shivarudrappa, the chief editor, makes the following statements: 'Though honest attempts have been made in the last half century to examine, scrutinise and reconstruct the history of Kannada literature with a millennium long tradition, it can be said that no comprehensive attempts have been made to place Kannada literature against its historical, cultural contexts and examine it critically' (Shivarudrappa 1974, i). 'This [project], instead of making poets or religions the basic criterion, has divided Kannada literature into various chronological periods' (ii). The statement is not supported by the allocation of topics to the contributors. They do not differ very much from the topics discussed in the previous histories.

---

[8] See Amaresh Nugadoni, *Tatwapada-Sahitya Adhyayana* (Hampi: Kannada University, 2014).

The same is true of the Mysore University project of Kannada literary history. As suggested earlier, the separation of literary historiography from literary criticism seems to be the reason for the extreme poverty of theorisation in these literary histories. Scattered in many essays and notes by writers and scholars are significant insights into the major texts of the past. For example, the essays by Kuvempu, now collected in two volumes edited by Shivareddy (2004), show his extraordinary ability to subject major texts to close textual analysis, though employing terms and concepts taken from ancient Indian aesthetics. So do the essays and notes by D. L. Narasimhachar. However, these volumes suffer from a strange refusal to theorise on the basis of close readings, and the subtle discrimination and evaluation accompanying them.

3

The *Navodaya* and *Navya* Movements, and the Writing of Literary History

There is a case to be made out for arguing that, for reasons not very clear, literary historiography was not a priority for the major writers of the *Navodaya* period. Primarily, they saw themselves as participants in a literary-cultural renaissance, a period of innovation, experimentation and creativity. There were—somewhat limited—uses of the past for the present creativity, though the primary significance of the literary past was that of a monument which could energise the present. Despite this refusal to theorise on the past, the major *Navodaya* poets through their close readings reinforced the idea of the canonical texts of the past. For example, in a footnote to his preface to the abridged version of Pampa's *Aadipurana* (934 CE), Kuvempu speaks metaphorically of the 'great peaks' of Kannada literature (Shivareddy 2004). The two towering peaks are Pampa and Naranappa (Kumara Vyasa), and the two other smaller but no lesser peaks are Harihara and Raghavanka. There is a third one, much smaller but adding to the beauty of the landscape, Ratnakaravarni, the Jaina poet who wrote *Bharatesha Vaibhava* (Shivareddy 2004). The curious absences are Basavanna and the *Vachanakaras*. Kuvempu did write a tribute to Basavanna but did not seem to have rated him very high as a poet. One of the reasons is that the *Vachanas* had to be 'rediscovered' in the twentieth century and it took time for many to realise that the *Vachanas* were not aphoristic philosophical statements or gnostic sayings but poetry of the highest order. Ta. Su. Shamaraya also objected to another literary historian R. S. Mugali naming the period starting in the twelfth century as '*Basava Yuga*'. More will be discussed about this phenomenon in the chapter on the *Vachanakaras*.

In another essay, *Draupadiya Srimudi*, Kuvempu analyses the way in which major Kannada poets have dealt with the untying and tying up of Draupadi's plait of hair. The comparison also becomes a subtle evaluation of the poets through close reading of the relevant passages. Similarly, in *Sarovarada Sirigannadiyalli*, he takes up the famous episode of Duryodhana hiding himself in the Vaishampayana lake and compares its depiction in two major poets. The comparison is a complex analysis of retellings and intertextuality in a tradition as well as of diverse poetic practices. Kuvempu analyses the two contrasting styles of Pampa and Kumara Vyasa as *Sanskrita* (urbane, sophisticated, learned) and *Gramya* (folk, not urbane, earthy), but asserts that the two are equally powerful modes of expression. He also makes brilliant comments on the long 'biography' of Draupadi's pleat of hair in Kumara Vyasa who describes how it was ritually washed and purified on the occasion of her marriage to Arjuna, and how at the end of the game of dice the menstruating Draupadi was dragged to the court hall by her hair. That humiliation was the seed of the end of all Kauravas. For Pampa, Dushyasana's dragging of Draupadi by the hair was a misdemeanour and a crime, and deserved the punishment and more. In the other essay, Kuvempu analyses Pampa's magnificent description of the Vaishampayana pond when Duryodhana is about to enter it. The creatures and birds whose habitat the pond and its surroundings are, loudly protest against Duryodhana defiling the peacefulness of the pond and possibly destroying it along with himself. They express their fear that Bhima, who is sure to pursue Duryodhana here, will, in his uncontrolled rage, destroy them too. The pond itself is described in images of impending terror—'This is the door to the netherworld'. Kuvempu who advised the rebel poets (*Bandaya* poets) in 1980 that 'tradition is a family heirloom which you don't throw away because you don't like its shape. Rather you would smelt it and remake it into jewellery of your taste', immersed himself in the tradition without compromising his radical anti-*varna* and anti-caste beliefs. His prolific prose writings contain in them a critical history of the Old Kannada tradition. This is further strengthened by his radical reworking of myths in his plays which led to an interesting, and acerbic, public debate with Masti Venkatesha Iyengar. Masti questioned the freedom of the writer to rewrite the traditional myths, whereas Kuvempu considered it a writer's fundamental task. The debate formed a nucleus around which many of the arguments regarding the relationship of the writer with tradition developed in the 1980s and 90s. Here, in these essays under discussion, Kuvempu conceptualises reading of tradition as a critical revaluation. Unfortunately, this perspective did not inform the literary historiography in Kannada.

Da. Ra. Bendre (Dattatreya Ramachandra Bendre), the greatest poet of the *Navodaya* period, had a very different relationship with tradition. His poetry has stronger roots in the aural–oral folk traditions as well as in a whole world of subaltern mystical sects and folk rituals. He was equally powerfully grounded in the Sanskritic and Vedic knowledge systems, poetry and aesthetics. In an extraordinary passage, he describes the two major categories of poets in the Kannada tradition (Bendre 1974). One is the tradition of *Sahitya* poetry, by which he refers to the literary, scholarly mode of writing which in his view, is lacking in immediacy and the pulse of life. The other is described by him as the category of *Bhakta* poets who are able to 'make their own life a great work'. The densely written passage has the following to say:

> A *Sahitya* poet uses the social *Rasas* and enhances the vision of the *Samajikas* [individuals as members of a society]. But in this large-heartedness there is some hiding, some show . . . there is a topicality. . . . In the *Purana kavyas* of the Jaina poets there is none of the intimacy we find in their worldly poems. There is little of the [truly] otherworldly (*Aloukika*). This is the weakness of the *Sahitya* poets. The power of our *Bhakta* poets is greater than that of the *Sahitya* poets. The *Vachanakaras* who transformed their life into a work of the divine and composed *Vachanas* as though it was their breath, and our *Dasas*, they are more powerful. The creation of the *Sahitya* poet is the illusion (*Mayê*) of words. Though their *Loukika* poems are full of life, for them it is only like the *Vachana Sahitya*. . . . (195–97)

This is indeed a devastating critique of the *Sahitya* poets. The poets, who emerged from the literary elite, belonged to the court circle and were well-versed and erudite. They did not have any problems in negotiating with the *Mārga* or the pan-Indian Sanskrit tradition. The *Bhakta* poets had access to an altogether different world of knowledge and experience through the mystical–spiritual traditions. Interestingly, this is the aesthetics which emerges from the *Vachanakaras* who believed in *Saja* (*Sahaja*)—the naturalness and spontaneity of utterance as against the learned, artificial poetic modes. Allama described the poets of the past as 'parrots'. It is significant that Bendre should be categorising Kannada literary tradition on the basis of *Sahitya* and *Bhakti*.

Decades before the term and concept of the 'postcolonial' came into currency, Kuvempu had said that 'Kannada aesthetics had always been a shadow of Sanskrit. Now it looks as though in the future it will be a shadow of Western aesthetics; that would be perhaps far more dangerous' (Shivareddy 2004, 737). Such dialogues with tradition were disrupted in the period known as the *Navya* (modernist) period in Kannada, beginning with the late 1950s. The disruption reflected the alienation from tradition felt by the new school of writers. In fact, *Navya* defined itself as emancipation from tradition. Irwing Howe has described modernism as the rejection of the immediate past (Howe 1967). For the *Navya* writers the immediate past was the *Navodaya* tradition. Howe had made his statement guardedly, because both Eliot and Pound, the leaders of the Anglo-American literary modernism, while rejecting the immediate past, had no problems with the earlier traditions. In the case of Kannada, though Gopalakrishna Adiga, the founder of the *Navya* school, returned to his own version of the reconstructed Indian traditions, there was no longer the sense of a relationship with the past. U. R. Ananthamurthy declared that the contemporary writer needs to know only the modern European writers like Albert Camus and Sartre and probably the *Vachanakaras*, to become a writer. There was no need to 'read' the past anymore. It is not that Ananthamurthy's slogan shut out the past for the Kannada writer. There were many factors which led to this disjunction. One of the consequences was the emergence of a distinctive formalist–culturalist literary criticism for which literary history was not a priority. Though the two major academic projects of literary history began in the 1970s—in the heyday of literary modernity in Kannada—the projects had no connection with the *Navya* school.

4

Navya Critics and Literary Historiography

Govindaray H. Nayak began as a rigorous formalist critic with a Leavisian adherence to undeclared criteria which were both aesthetic and ethical. His critical practice involved close reading and verbal analysis based on intensive reading of the major texts of the Kannada tradition. He also wrote about his contemporary modernist writers with the same rigorous standards. His long introduction to an anthology of Kannada poetry brought out by the National Book Trust provides a critical overview which could easily form the basis of a history of modern Kannada poetry

(Shivareddy 2004). Like F. R. Leavis, Nayak also questioned some of the established reputations and accepted interpretations of texts. In his essay on Pampa, he subjects a famous passage spoken by Bahubali in *Aadipurana* to close analysis. The generally accepted interpretation is that having defeated Bharata, his brother, he suddenly experiences an epiphany discovering the utter uselessness of victory. He decides to give away the temporal power he had symbolically won by defeating Bharata. Nayak's close reading brings out the irony and the many ambiguities which reveal the 'impurity' (*Manakashaya*—a Jaina term describing the hidden, unconscious negative emotions) in Bahubali for which he needs to do penance. The analysis has a spiralling effect on the Jaina theological edifice of Pampa's epic poem. Does the truth of poetry conflict with the theology the poet intends to defend? The question is related to the great problematic which the Kannada Jaina poets had formulated—namely, the relationship between *Dharma* and *Kavyadharma*. It is such unresolved complexities which are elided in literary histories that tend to generalise the 'Jaina Age' as a homogeneous unproblematic phenomenon. In other essays, Nayak also raised pertinent questions about the poetry of Kuvempu and Bendre.

M. G. Krishnamurthy, probably the finest formalist critic of the *Navya* period, argued that *Malegalalli Madumagalu* (The Bride of the Hills, 1965) by Kuvempu, considered as the greatest novel in Kannada, was lacking in a 'centre', an organising principle bringing coherence to its vast, sprawling density of detail. He questioned whether the celebrated 'lifelike richness' and regional realism of the novel had distracted critics from noticing the absence of an integrating centre. Many later critics have disagreed with Krishnamurthy but not without responding to his arguments. This is another example of the sharp interrogation of received opinions by the *Navya* critics. However, as pointed out earlier, the divergence between literary history and literary criticism impoverished both in the Kannada context.

Mugali's *History of Kannada Literature*, and Other Projects

R. S. Mugali's *History of Kannada Literature*, originally written in Kannada in 1957, and then translated into English with a few modifications as part of a Sahitya Akademi project, remains till today the most popular academic literary history of Karnataka. In his preface to the English translation, the author refers to the guidelines provided by the Akademi which suggested that it should be a survey avoiding too many details. The work is a fairly comprehensive survey carried out sensitively by avoiding bias and prejudices, and aiming at drawing attention to the positive achievements of Kannada authors. It is done with the assumption that there is an autonomous space called 'literature' which is self-evolving and self-regulating. There may be excesses, lapses of taste, and weaknesses in style and expression among writers, which need to be identified. The literary works of a tradition exist in a liberal humanist abstract space which is impacted by the socio-cultural context, but then this context itself can be accommodated in the space called literature. There is no awareness in such a literary history that the discourse of literature is itself produced along with others in a material socio-cultural context. Mugali's literary history would have us believe that there are no unresolved conflicts either in Kannada society or Kannada literature.

Some of these issues are addressed in the two volumes of *Kannada Sahitya: Charitrika Belavanige* (Kannada Literature: Historical Development, 1986, 2011) by C. Veeranna. The author had planned to write a five-volume literary history but managed to write only two, bringing the discussion up to the medieval period in the second volume. The declared intention of the author is to examine Kannada literature as the product of historical developments which are in turn analysed from a broadly Marxist perspective. The work is probably the first literary history of Kannada to focus on the exclusions from the 'literary' in social contexts with a hierarchically organised class structure. The first volume was written long before the studies by Burton Stein and David Washbrook on South India became known to the Indian academic world; nor does the second volume show any familiarity with this scholarship. Veeranna employs the orthodox Marxist analysis of the feudal state supported by a Vedic brahminical priest-class and the kshatriya classes. He looks closely at the gifts of land to brahmin priests and pundits as well as to religious monasteries and institutions. He observes that the kings maintained a pragmatic policy of supporting all religions but the gift of land played a decisive role in organising the power of the state. He considers the literature of the period as the expression of a small elite patronised by the court and with readers/listeners from the elite, cultivated class. Veeranna makes useful comments on the oral and performative traditions (of *Haadu Gabbas,* or songs) referred to marginally in *Kavirajamarga* and in the inscriptions, which were excluded from the domain of the literary. He also makes brief comments on the many dialects of Kannada and their exclusion from the 'standard' dialect. The first volume centres around Pampa and the second one around the *Vachanakaras*. Veeranna proposes and supports his thesis that the *Vachanakara* movement was a movement of the labour class (class of artisans). This proved to be a necessary corrective to the interpretations which had leaned heavily on the *bhakti* and mystical elements of the *Vachanas*. It also supported the later subalternist readings of the *Vachanas*.

Kannada University, Hampi, has introduced a project of great significance to literary historiography, though it was planned as a series of revaluations of the major texts of the Kannada tradition. The project was titled *Samskritika Mukhamukhi*, or cultural interface. Leading scholars were invited to present papers and talks on major texts and participate in free and wide-ranging discussion, which were recorded and compiled in the form of books. Eighteen such seminars have been held and fifteen books have been published. The presentations and discussions have been eclectic, cutting across varied theoretical approaches. The series was in many ways the fruitful consequence of the several oppositional critiques which had developed in the Kannada context in the late 1970s and 80s. These have continued, though more sporadically and less intensely.

These critiques were products of the anti-brahminical, anti-caste, pro-farmer and Dalit movements of the 1970s and 80s. A detailed analysis of the movements shall be provided in a later chapter. These were vibrant, open-ended movements with a large popular base, and were powerful enough to impact the politics of the times. The major events that inspired these movements were the establishment of the *Barahagarara Okkuta* (Association of Writers) in 1980, Dalit Sangharsha Samiti (DSS) in 1974, and the Karnataka Rajya Raita Sangha (Farmers' Association or KRRS) in 1980. The Dalit and farmers' movements as well as the Kannada movement (known as the Gokak Movement) led to what is probably the most significant churning of ideas since the *Navodaya* movement. Marxist, Lohiaite and Ambedkarite ideologies with a mix of anti-brahminical and pro-backward-class ideologies led to a radical interrogation of tradition, culture, literature and politics. This continues to be the intellectual atmosphere even now, despite the decline and collapse of the movements themselves. The Dalit Sahitya movement and the *Bandaya Sahitya* (rebel/protest literature) movement developed powerful critiques of the existing literature and tradition. This has impacted the domain of literary criticism almost irreversibly. One of the main concerns has been rethinking tradition with particular reference to marginalisation of communities.

The Kannada University project has steered clear of allegiance to any particular ideology. But the discussions and the books recording them have raised fundamental questions about Kannada literary and cultural traditions. For instance: is *Vaddaradhane* (ninth century CE), a work of tales purportedly meant to help the pursuit of liberation by Jaina devotees, merely a work which uses the literary resources of Kannada to propagate a theology without any living relationship with the Kannada aesthetics? Or is it the work of a cultivated elite subscribing to a pan-Indian Sanskrit literary culture? Why among many similar works of translation of English poetry, B. M. Sri's *English Geetegalu* (1922) is said to have heralded the *Navodaya* poetry in Kannada? Does English Romanticism have anything to do with Kannada *Ramya* poetry of the *Navodaya* period? Did the egalitarian leader of the *Vachanakaras*, Basavanna, subscribe to gender stereotypes? Wasn't the trial of Akka Mahadevi an act of gender violence? Regrettably, Kannada University has not planned a project on the literary history of Karnataka where all such questions can be addressed. The present work intends to address some of these questions.

TWO

The Kannada Language

The Kannada language, in its long history, has never found itself in a monolingual context. It has always been negotiating with cross-linguistic relationships, not to speak of the internal variations including regional dialects and sociolects. It has had to adopt a whole set of strategies ranging from accommodation and acceptance to a nuanced rejection, in order to retain its identity. The term 'identity' here is unrelated to the politics of identity but is used to refer to the boundaries beyond which a language cannot stretch and yet remain an independent language. The multilingual context Kannada had to confront was a consequence of the language policies of major religions and ruling dynasties, and also of the material conditions of trade, commerce and political relationships across territories.

Kannada is one of the southern Dravidian languages and is said to have a history of about 2500 years (that is, including the stages of literisation and literarisation), though the first Kannada stone inscriptions have been dated to the fifth century CE. However, there are dependable evidences from references in the *Mahabharata*, and texts and inscriptions in other languages, to support its claims to antiquity. It is certainly younger than Tamil and older than Telugu and Malayalam, the other major Dravidian languages. Mention has already been made of the efforts to glorify its antiquity which were produced by the wave of Kannada subnationalism during the unification movement. More recently there has been another round of similar efforts to secure for Kannada the status of 'classical language'. Linguistic movements in India enjoyed a certain limited legitimacy before the reorganisation of (linguistic) states because speakers of the Bhashas were scattered over political territories and administrative units, some of which were irrational as in the case of Kannada. But some of the constitutional and state-centric measures have had the unfortunate effect of creating a linguistic politics which at times is fought over symbols and empty recognitions. There are scholars who believe that the eighth schedule of the Constitution (which 'recognises' 22 languages) created a hierarchy which deprived hundreds of mother tongues of the status of 'languages'. Similarly, the nomination of an official and administrative language may be a pragmatic necessity, but it is also an instrument of hierarchisation and exclusion. In the contemporary world, linguistic identities are not 'primordial' but political. They are caught in the matrix of linguistic subnationalisms, othering of communities and, at times, racial prejudices. However, this cultural politics is not of modern origin. This is borne out by the history of the Kannada language where we can trace the historical and continuous presence of cultural politics.

We have no detailed knowledge of the origin and emergence of Kannada in its earliest phases. All we can say for certain is that at some point of time, it branched out from Proto-Dravidian and evolved its separate identity. The debate whether it emerged from Tamil has been settled by experts who believe that Kannada branched out from Proto-Dravidian like the sister languages of South India, though it continued to maintain a strong relationship with Tamil. There are considerable syntactic and phonological similarities as well as an overlapping lexis between these two languages. So great was the grip of the myth of Aryan superiority and of Sanskrit being the 'mother of all languages' that a number of scholars rejected the notion of the Proto-Dravidian language. They also overplayed the presence of Sanskrit in Kannada. Strangely enough, the victim of these biased debates was Prakrit. It is ironical that a committee constituted by the Sahitya Akademi twice refused to consider the classical status of Prakrit which held sway for nearly half a millennium (Settar 2007). Kannada developed through a double negotiation with Sanskrit and Prakrit as well as continuous relationships with the Dravidian languages.

The evidence provided by inscriptions and textual sources suggests that Kannada had become a mature vehicle of poetry and prose well before the earliest inscriptions discovered at Halmidi and Talagunda (fifth century CE). One important point to note is that accomplished poets also doubled as writers of such inscriptions. Of course, the choice of the language used depended on the language policies of the major religions and of the rulers. The narrative constructed by Settar and others claims that Ashoka introduced both Prakrit and the Brahmi script to *Kannadanādu*. The Buddha is said to have taken the decision to preach his religion in the language used by common men and women, which led to the major Buddhist writings in Pali. But the proselytisation had to be done in one of the Prakrits. Though some Sanskrit scholars like Patanjali and Panini derided Prakrit as '*gramyalapa*', 'impure' or 'inefficient', the many varieties of Prakrit played a far more significant role in the lives of the people than Sanskrit. Prakrit, dubbed as 'the language of the snakes', was a major influence on Sanskrit, and not a distorted version of Sanskrit (Ollett 2017).

Panini also distinguished between two categories—the *Chanda* or *Kavya* language, and the *Loka*—obviously placing Prakrit in the latter category. It was argued that Prakrit could not be a vehicle of *Kavya* or *Sastra*. These prejudices have to be juxtaposed with the historical fact that from the third century BC to third century CE, Prakrit played a dominant role. Settar (2018) describes the phenomenon as 'Prakrit Cosmopolis'.

The Buddhist religion made Prakrit its medium, though historians have not been able to locate Kannada literary texts which can be described as Buddhist. It is in the rock edicts of Ashoka that Prakrit dominates. Several sites of Buddhist influence have been discovered across Karnataka evidencing the spread of the religion (Settar 2003; Narasimhacharya 1961). Since the rock edicts and inscriptions were public documents, it has to be assumed that Prakrit was the language of the people in the period. Though Jaina inscriptions are curiously absent in Karnataka during the early period, a number of leading Jaina scholars belonged to the land. Shravanabelagola was a major centre of learning, and a legend (with no proven historicity) associates it with the group of Jaina monks who accompanied Chandragupta to the area. Later on, Jaina religious leaders took the decision to use Kannada as the language of proselytisation as it was the language of the people. The result was the Jaina age in Karnataka, approximately from the eighth century to the twelfth century and beyond, because it survived the *Vachanakara* movement. The greatest poets of the age were the Jaina poets who wrote both *Loukika* and *Āgamika* (religious and theological) poetry. Though both Buddhist and Jaina scholars turned to Sanskrit as an inevitable consequence of the brahminisation of the two religions, they left an indelible mark on the Kannada language. Traditional aestheticians and grammarians from Srivijaya (the author of *Kavirajamarga*) onwards accepted Sanskrit words into Kannada, either in the *Samasanskrita* form (also known as the *Tatsama* form) or in the Kannadised *Tadbhava* form. In fact, Srivijaya spends considerable time explaining the rules governing the adaptation of Sanskrit words without leading to semantic errors. What he practically ignores is the large vocabulary loaned from Prakrit. He does not mention any rules for adapting these words into Kannada. R. Narasimhacharya, who wrote *Karnataka Kavicharite* and published a monograph on the history of the Kannada language, provides a list of such words (Settar 2007). Most of these are part of the modern Kannada language spoken today. In his many writings on the artisans of the Buddhist period, Settar provides a long list of architectural terms used by them, a majority of which are Prakrit words. Again, these words are part of the common vocabulary today and are used by artisans even today (for example, *kamba* [pillar]) (M. B. Neginhal in Settar 2017). It is therefore important to keep aside the myth of Sanskrit almost wholly shaping the Kannada language. Scholars like Neginhal have pointed out the impact of Prakrit on the pronunciation of individual words including the terminal sounds in Kannada.

From a sociolinguistic point of view, there is need to further explore the nature of bilingualism and multilingualism in *Kannadanādu*. Was it Prakrit which created a reading public in the ancient period? Was Sanskrit the language of the intellectual makeup of the Kannadiga of the time? What was the relationship between Prakrit and the derivative languages which grew out of Kannada such as Kodava, Toda and Badaga? What was their sociocultural status? Answers to these questions have a bearing on the linguistic politics in Karnataka today. On the one hand, the hegemony of Kannada is weakening the position of the other languages in Karnataka. For example, Urdu, which has the second largest number of speakers in Karnataka, has almost disappeared from the mainstream educational system in the state. Tulu is flourishing because of the strategies of cultural pride visibly employed in the public domain. But many other mother tongues are dying (Narayana, K. V. 2018; Devy 2014–25).

Though the literary elite and the court circles in the past readily accepted the supremacy of Sanskrit and Sanskrit aesthetics, the artificiality of the cultivated, highly Sanskritised poetic style alienated the people. The erudite *Champu* genre and style (using both prose and verse) was violently disrupted in the twelfth century by the *Vachanakaras*. Literary conventions were thrown aside and poetry was reconceptualised as speech, as the spoken word. Though Raghavanka of the thirteenth century opted for the regular stanza *shatpadi* and so did Kumara Vyasa, Kannada poetry never again went back to the cultivated, ornate Sanskritised style and idiom.

Nor was this only a question of style. It was also a question of the authority of the Sanskrit conventions. This authority must have been firmly entrenched because such conventions marred the works of highly original poets like Pampa and Raghavanka. The eighteen descriptions (*Ashtadashavarnanas*) which were epic conventions and included the description of the city and the city quarters occupied by prostitutes (*veshyavatike* or *sulegeri*) are an example of this. This convention was obviously intended as an opportunity to introduce the erotic element into the narrative, such as the description of the water games and the stroll in the parks, as well as of the royal hunting episodes. These descriptions are usually so stylised and mechanical that they jarringly contrast with the sense of purpose marking the other sections of the epic. A case in point is Raghavanka's *Harishchandra Kavya*, the thirteenth-century epic. As G. S. Shivarudrappa points out, the first eight *sargas* or cantos of the work have to be tolerated with extraordinary patience by the readers until the poet completes paying his obeisance to the epic conventions. The impeccable narrative of the trials of Harishchandra begins from here (Shivarudrappa 1993). There are also questions of propriety. For example, the long-drawn-out erotic descriptions of Bharata's sexual games with his queens and palace maids in *Aadipurana*, a hagiography, weaken the structure of the epic. L. Basavaraju points out that the original *Mahapurana* also contains these elements, and they are more crudely done than in Pampa's retelling. The original is attributed to two revered Jaina saint–scholars. We need to learn more about the literary circles and the functions they expected poetry to perform, to understand why the conventions were so strictly adhered to. The conventions were also closely related to the gender notions of the patriarchal society which encouraged the male gaze at the eroticised body of the woman. For instance, Kanaka Dasa (sixteenth century), a cult figure among the *Dasa* poets for his powerful anti-caste rhetoric, has no qualms about describing women erotically in his *Mohana Tarangini*, a conventional work quite different from his songs and *kirtanas* (a genre popularised by the *Dasas*, Vaishnavite Bhakti poets; compositions that were sung out to the common people) he composed. Similarly, in *Vikramarjuna Vijaya*, Pampa uses the conventional visit of the hero to the prostitutes' quarter by providing extraordinary portrayals of the lives of the common people in pursuit of pleasures. The passages in this section introduce us to the rhythms of the everyday speech of his time. However, the section has nothing to do with the main narrative.

There is a need to re-examine the much-extolled accommodative stance of the Kannada poetic tradition towards Sanskrit literary conventions. In his *Sangam Tamilagam Mattu Kannada Nādu Nudi*, Settar demonstrates how Tamil Sangam poetry evolved its own aesthetics and eschewed the patriarchal ideas of the erotic (Settar 2007). Meanwhile one also has to steer clear of orientalist notions of all Indian poetry as sensuous and erotic in the negative sense of the words. That the pre-modern aesthetic norms cannot be understood through the lens of the modern literary frameworks should alert us to the possible pitfalls in our reading of the traditional texts.

We have already discussed the attempt to construct a standard, literary Kannada dialect in *Kavirajamarga*. Indirectly, the attempt throws light on the highly variegated nature of Kannada speech during the period. The author points out that many incompetent poets, believing that poetry should be written in *Halegannada* (Old Kannada), write in what they believe to be *Halegannada* without understanding that it has changed. Most scholars believe that as *Kavirajamarga* is itself written in *Halegannada*, the author is referring to *Poorvada Halegannada*—that is, the previous or earlier form of *Halegannada*. Linguists have not been able to reconstruct it and have only pointed out some phonological features which changed in the *Halegannada* phase.

More important is the author's reference to the many dialects of Kannada. They are so many and so varied that Vasuki or Adishesha is frustrated and unable to decide what is correct or acceptable. The construction of a standard dialect necessarily involves notions of 'non-standard' variations, and Vasuki's frustration is understandable because there are no legitimate criteria for deciding what is non-standard in the variegated motley world of parole or actual speech. Elsewhere the author almost draws up the boundaries of a standard Kannada dialect (*tirulgannada*) by referring to places like Kopana, Puligere, Okkunda, etc., as locations where the dialect is spoken. At best this could be described as arbitrary. The futility of choosing a standard dialect was witnessed centuries later when the modern standard Kannada dialect had to be chosen. By then the dialect spoken in and around the places mentioned in *Kavirajamarga* was known as the 'North Karnataka dialect' which appeared unsophisticated and crude to the Kannada speakers in Mysore and Bangalore regions who were politically dominant. It was common in popular culture, especially in popular films, to use farcical characters speaking the north Karnataka dialect. This was in no way different from the cultural context of ancient Indian theatre in which upper-class men spoke Sanskrit and women, thieves, drunkards and criminals spoke one of the designated Prakrit dialects. Though linguists argue that the criteria of normativity and standardisation are unavoidable in the post-print cultural world, there is a need to understand how in the pre-modern world, there were processes that excluded certain Kannada dialects since a vernacular polity required a standard dialect. This is true of the other forms of expression known as 'folk' and derided as 'vulgar', 'crude' and 'unsophisticated'. The author of *Kavirajamarga* mentions *Chattana* and *Bedande*, two forms of folk origin, which have no place in the literary. Such derision of folk forms and folk speech continues in the later poets and aestheticians.

However, this did not mean a wall of prohibition keeping out the colloquial forms of speech and expression. The concepts of *Mārga* and *Desi* created a space for these, though they had to enter the literary as conventions. But in the actual practice of great poets like Pampa and Raghavanka, the entire continuum of speech including the colloquial, works as a free linguistic landscape to explore. In his epic, Raghavanka provides a catalogue of about fifteen varieties of traps and nets used to catch animals in words which were probably never heard even in the backyards of the palaces. The gradual diminution of this continuum with standardisation can be evidenced by comparing the words listed in Kittel's dictionary with the present-day Kannada vocabulary.

The issues relating to the speech variations of Kannada and their use in literary works return to the Kannada context with the rise of the novel in the last quarter of the nineteenth century. In the first social novel, *Indira Bai* (1899) by Gulavadi Venkata Rao, the author allows certain characters to speak in Konkani and Tulu and provides translations (Rao 1899). The narrative also shows an awareness of the heterogeneity of speech reflecting that of the social world in the novel. Interestingly, the opening passage describing the city is highly conventional and could have been part of the obligatory eighteen descriptions referred to earlier. In *Indira*, a novel by Kerura Vasudevacharya who was from North Karnataka, there are sudden dialectal shifts when the woman protagonist speaking in an unnaturally conventional language slips into an interjection (*Avvayya*) characteristic of the Madhva Brahmin Kannada sociolect which the author himself spoke in Bagalkote where he lived. There is a similar code-switching in the novels of Venkatesh Galaganatha (1869–1942), the popular author of historical romances that were based on the model of the novels of H. N. Apte, the Marathi writer whose works Galaganatha also translated. He switches from a conventional Sanskritised literary dialect to an extremely colloquial form of North Karnataka speech. A much-debated question is why does Kuvempu, writing decades later, indulge in a similar code-switching in his novels. While authentically reconstructing a rich earthy world of the many sociolects of the Malnad region (hilly and forest regions of Karnataka), he switches over to a grandiloquent highly Sanskritised Kannada which no Kannadiga has spoken in the past two thousand years of its existence.

These are not merely linguistic issues. As in the case of all Bhashas in India, dialects and sociolects are inalienably bound up with social locations. The deeply entrenched hierarchies have created islands of caste worlds with no communication among them. (The metaphor is from

U. R. Ananthamurthy.) Naturally, each caste group has evolved a sociolect, and migrations of labourers have also added dialectal features to the sociolects. In Kuvempu's novels, the labourers from 'below the *ghat*' (that is, from the coastal belt) speak a distinctive language variation. In a more recent novel, *Gandhi Banda* (2011) by H. S. Nagaveni, there is an interesting description of caste hierarchies characterising the architecture of the house of the brahmin landlord. From the inner quarters and kitchen to the fence and beyond, there are designated social spaces for various castes, so that when the wife of the landlord passes down a leaf full of pickle for a pregnant untouchable woman waiting far away from the fence, the pickle makes a social journey across these spaces. These social spaces are marked by distinctive sociolects.

In such a sociolinguistic scenario, it would be difficult to decode the thin line between literary aesthetic criteria and caste-centric prejudices. When Devanoora Mahadeva published his novella *Kusumabale*, written entirely in the Dalit sociolect of the Nanjangudu region, the reaction of some leading writers like Chandrashekhar Patil was to ask for a translation of the work in Kannada (or 'standard' Kannada). The Dalit poet Siddalingaiah used curse words from non-standard Kannada in his poetry, like the Marathi Dalit writers did in their life narratives. All this reaffirms the fact that Kannada is not just a language but a complex social matrix in which contestations take place continually.

Some Kannada scholars have recently addressed the issue of language loss and language death *vis-à-vis* the hegemony of the dominant language/s. The People's Linguistic Survey of India (PLSI) led by Ganesh Devy has documented the threat posed to the survival of smaller languages owing to many factors. Devy has argued that the loss of a language, however small, is the loss of a life-world, and thereby a significant loss to culture.

As long as we are preoccupied with the unitary notions of Kannada and *Kannadanādu*, we shall not be able to understand the seriousness of such cultural loss. *Kannadanādu* is not the land of Kannada speakers alone. In the real sense of the word, 'Kannada' itself is a group of languages including Tulu, Toda, Iruliga, Badaga and Kodava. Though these languages possess distinctive identities of their own, there are indelible kinship relationships among them. Historically, especially when provincial and 'state' boundaries were far less clearly drawn and were always shifting, communities speaking these languages shared historical and political experiences encoded into their languages. There are also repositories of oral histories and other forms of cultural memories bound up with these languages. Unless these are acknowledged and preserved, Kannada would be an impoverished entity. Questions have been raised whether the solution lies in the museumisation of these languages when the speakers of the languages are themselves being assimilated through the processes of modernisation. As in the case of most indigenous languages across the globe which are disappearing, there is need to thoroughly document and preserve them even if the possibility of keeping them alive becomes weaker by the day.

There have been two phases in Kannada literature when attempts were made to introduce the dialectal and other variations into fiction. The first was the period of realism from its beginning (in the last quarter of the nineteenth century) to approximately the fourth decade of the twentieth century. The multiple factors shaping realism included the modes of the realistic novel in English introduced through colonial education, the deep influence of the Gandhian social imagination which motivated Kannada writers to look closely at the realities of the rural Indian society, and the social-reformist urge which also made a similar impact. Most importantly, many gifted writers (like Shivaram Karanth and Kuvempu) turned away from the pseudo-historical romance popularised by Galaganatha with its revivalist model of history. They evolved and enriched the local or provincial novel focusing on the community rather than on the nation (Chenni 2011). The attempt to achieve an authentic realism in fiction led to the introduction of the dialectal and other speech variations. Though the attempt was criticised as 'anthropological' by later critics, for the first time, speech variations of Kannada entered the domain of the literary.

The next phase was the period of the *Pragatisheela* (progressive) literature. The major novelists of this period were Niranjana, Basavaraj Kattimani, Aa. Na. Kra. and Ta. Ra. Su. The progressive movement entered late into Kannada and had a short-lived, problematic tenure, in comparison with Hindi and Urdu. Though most of the popular progressive novelists used the familiar Kannada register of their middle-class readers, some of them also attempted to introduce the non-standard variations of speech.

The third phase was the period of the Dalit–*Bandaya* movements from the late 1970s onwards. We have already discussed the experiments by the leading Dalit writers to introduce the Dalit sociolects of Kannada into fiction. When these experimental writings are juxtaposed together, one relives the sense of the 'many Kannadas' that the author of *Kavirajamarga* was talking about in the ninth century. An interesting feature of Kannada fiction since the 1990s has been the emergence of community-centred novels which seek to document the past and present of local communities.

Gopalakrishna Pai's *Swapna Saraswatha* (2017) which won the Sahitya Akademi award, is an epic novel tracing the history of the Konkani-speaking Saraswat community, beginning well before its great exodus owing to violent oppression by the Portuguese. Na. Mogasale's novel *Ullanghane* (2008) is about the Banta or Nadava community in Dakshina Kannada. He also wrote a novel about the Havyaka community, *Mukhanatra* (2018), in the Havyaka dialect. Such works of fiction have also created space for the 'many Kannadas'.

The latest entrant is 'Kanglish' (Kannada + English) or a cosmopolitan Kannada in the works of Vasudhendra and Nagaraj Vastare who have written about the post-liberalisation cosmopolitan Kannada communities. Vastare has argued that modern Kannada has not been able to assimilate the radically new experiences of the so-called IT/BT cosmopolitan class, because these experiences are bound up with English (Vastare 2019). It makes no sense to prudishly adhere to the modern standardised Kannada. He describes his own experiments as a 'work in progress'. Nearly three decades of the transformation of Bengaluru into a cosmopolitan city and an international hub, with largescale migrations of young professionals from all parts of Karnataka, has led to two contradictory phenomena. One is the emergence of the new cosmopolitan Kannada that Vastare has advocated. The other is the audible presence of the major regional dialects of Kannada in Bengaluru owing to the migration of young professionals. At long last, the dialects are claiming Bengaluru though one has to await its impact on Kannada fiction.

THREE

Ancient Kannada Literature

One of the most significant practices in ancient Kannada literature (which has continued in the later periods in some form or the other) is the categorisation of literary works into *Loukika* and *Āgamika*. *Loukika* refers to 'this-worldly', the social or the historical, and to the temporal. *Āgamika*, with its other equivalent terms, refers to the religious, the transcendental and the spiritual. The earliest reference to the categorisation can be found in *Kavirajamarga* which suggests that the poetic practice of writing in the two domains existed earlier, though many works mentioned are lost. The author of *Kavirajamarga* uses the term *Samayika* derived from *samaya* (religious sect). It has been suggested that for many poets like Pampa and Ranna the two categories were necessary to reconcile or integrate the dualities of their individual lives. Pampa—whose father, born in a priestly brahmin family, had converted to Jainism—wrote his first epic, *Aadipurana*, on the life of the first Jaina *Thirthankara*, and claimed that writing a Jaina hagiography would bring him greater fame and everlasting spiritual wealth than any patronage. However, Arikesari, the feudatory ruler, not only offered him a stupendous patronage but also commissioned him to write a poem which would ensure fame for both the patron and the poet. Pampa wrote *Vikramarjuna Vijaya*, a retelling of the *Mahabharata*, allegorising the patron king as the brave Arjuna. He describes this epic as *Loukika* though it is a retelling of the Sanskrit epic (Veeranna 1986).

The ancient period pitted writers like Pampa in the conflict between the temporal and the religious, because it was a period which saw endless wars and battles between the dominant royal dynasties such as the Rashtrakutas, Gangas and Chalukyas. Pampa's patron, Arikesari, for instance, was a participant in the kaleidoscopic alignments, re-alignments, aggression and re-conciliations that marked the political domain of the period. Being poets, scholars and soldiers, Pampa and Ranna could not isolate the aesthetic from the political. In the realm of religion, royal patronage favoured one of the dominant religions of the time (Jainism, Shaivism and Vedic brahminism). Ranna, a Jaina, was part of the court of Iriva Bedanga who patronised the Vedic religion. But he also enjoyed the patronage of Attimabbe, a renowned Jaina aristocratic woman. Like Pampa, Ranna wrote *Sahasa Bheema Vijayam*, a retelling of episodes from the *Mahabharata* allegorising his patron as Bheema. Though one has to scrupulously avoid imposing modern conceptual categories on pre-modern South Indian history, Kannada literary texts of this period were written in the context of deep conflicts in both the political and religious domains. As Rajaram Hegde points out, despite the attempted separation between the *Loukika* and *Āgamika*, Jaina ritualistic practices, architecture, theology and poetry were a simulacrum of the socio-political world (Hegde 2001). Jainism had to accommodate several deviations from its earliest principles in order to convert the later laity. Jaina *Thirthankaras* had to be ascribed a godlike status and the iconography began to include female supernatural beings such as Jwalamalini and *Yakshis* (Hegde 2001). Though it was a religion valorising renunciation of the worldly, Jaina literature, including Pampa's *Aadipurana,* provides highly sensuous, even erotic, descriptions of the pleasures enjoyed in the afterworld. As Hegde argues, the afterworld was imagined as a mirror image of the hierarchical world of political power; the two main figures in the Jaina literature are the king and the brahmin. Thus, Jainism gradually incorporated feudal and patriarchal values of the society.

These are the factors which make *Vaddaradhane*, a collection of Jaina tales, such a great but contradictory text. For a long time since its modern publications in the 1930s, the title of the work had been '*Vaddaradhane*' and its author was believed to be Shivakotacharya from the Bellary region, though many scholars and editors believed that both were latter-day constructions. There now seems to be a consensus that the actual title is '*Aaradhana Karnatateeka*' and the author is Bhrajishnu (Nagarajaih 1992). The date of the text is also uncertain, and is estimated to be between the eighth and tenth century CE. What is beyond dispute, however, is that it preceded the works of Pampa and that it is the first great work of Kannada prose.

Aaradhana Karnatateeka is a collection of tales of varying length, each beginning with a *Gaha* in Prakrit. The tales were originally part of the spiritual training provided to the Jaina believer preparing himself to renounce the world. As such the tales have a distinctive narrative trajectory, taking the main characters through their many lives (*bhavas*) before evolving into liberated beings. These characters are shown to be deeply immersed in the worldly pleasures and passions until they go through an epiphany revealing to them their transitoriness. This epiphanic experience is known as *Nirvega*, and it can be caused by as mundane an experience as the discovery of a grey hair heralding old age. The experience is sudden, unexpected and momentous. With it begins the long process across many lives until all traces of the worldly disappear and total liberation is obtained.

Despite the definite theological purposes with which the tales were written, they provide an intimate portrayal of the society of the period and of the contradictory, unredeemed everyday lives of the human beings who figure in the tales. Though scholars argue that the work is a translation of similar Jaina tales in Sanskrit and Prakrit, their 'Kannadaness' is astonishing. The prose is so close to the speech rhythms of everyday Kannada that the reader feels that he/she is listening to conversations right here on the streets, though the tales were written eleven to twelve centuries ago. They are also incorrigibly 'human', delineating love, passion, hatred and revenge with empathy. For example, in one tale, the king asks for the most attractive (valuable) thing in his kingdom for his pleasure, and discovering that it is his daughter, marries her and has a child by her. The child grows up and asks his mother who his father is, and she tells him 'my father and your father are the same (person)'. Her silence in the tale unmasks the lust, greed and amorality of the kings and rulers of the time. In many of the tales, the king takes away as his right, the beautiful wives of merchants and even of brahmins. Critics have pointed out that the tales describe the struggle for hegemony between Jaina and Vedic religions, though paradoxically, it is a transformed Jaina religion subscribing to the notions of the *Varna* system and the four *Ashramas* of one's life. Though women can also attain liberation (by being born as men in the next *bhava*) according to Jainism, the tales describe how patriarchal norms were accepted and practised without interrogation. In one of the tales, for instance, the husband beats up his wife for feeding someone on the occasion of a festival. Women in both this world and the next are seen as objects of pleasure. The tales confine themselves to the upper classes of the society of kings, merchants and brahmins, though in one of the tales we get the glimpse of an untouchable. The didacticism of the author/translator is limited to individuals who evolve to reach the higher stages of liberation. Otherwise, he provides an unflinching view of the unredeemed world of thieves, criminals and corrupt officers of the king. Hate and revenge cling to the human beings across many lives. A woman kicked on the forehead by her brother-in-law vows to take birth as a fox to bite away his leg, and manages to do so. The tales in *Vaddaradhane* succeed as literary works by opening themselves to the realities of the *Loukika* world which they are constructed to denounce.

This is also true of Pampa's *Aadipurana* which is a retelling of the life of the first Jaina *Thirthankara* Aadideva Vrishabha and his two children, Bharata and Bahubali. Following the conventions of the Jaina narratology, the hagiography portrays the many lives in the process of the evolution of a human being into a *Thirthankara*. The work is a transcreation of the Jaina text *Maha Purana* attributed to Jinasenacharya and Gunabhadra (Basavaraju 2002). As Basavaraju points out, the act of translation here is elevated to the process of 'humanising' what is pedantic and dry in the original text. As the Jaina text and the story of the first *Thirthankara* were already well established in the Jaina canon, Pampa could not take liberties with the narrative framework. But within the constrains, he creates poetry unsurpassed in its sensuous beauty and richness of its verbal texture. For Pampa, *Mārga* and *Desi* were two poetic styles which were not adversarial but complementary. He drew on Sanskrit, Prakrit and Kannada sources with equal authority.

The major philosophical and ethical questions raised by the text are in the sections dealing with the imperial conquests of Bharata and his confrontation with Bahubali (his brother). Though the descriptions of warfare are suffused with fantastic feats and incredible martial ventures narrated in a hyperbolic language, they are about the demonic energies of imperialism. Bharata's conquests involve the subjugation of many communities and societies. The central political experience of the period, namely war and conquest, finds its literary expression in this epic. Probably blending the Jaina critique of worldly victories with his own war-weariness as a subject of a feudatory kingdom, Pampa unravels the hollowness of the fame of the conquerors. Bharata, who wants to inscribe his name on a rock known as Vijayavardha, discovers to his horror that it is already covered with names of past emperors and has no space left for his name to be added. A more intense and greater realisation occurs when Bahubali defeats him in a duel but decides to renounce his victory and share of the kingdom. Bharata says,

> May the goddess of kingdom, who sports with delight,
> like a bee in the lily-grove of soldiers' swords, fascinating all,
> dwell happily on your chest forever. I give you the kingdom given by our father,
> If I covet the woman or the land you love, wouldn't infamy cover me? (Ramachandran and Rai 2015, 114)

Bharata also reflects on desire and greed which 'set brother against brother and sons against the father'. Pampa had seen this happen in all the major royal dynasties of his time. In the passage quoted above, the 'goddess of kingdom' is compared to the bee wandering from flower to flower.

While this is of a piece with the Jaina disillusionment with worldly possessions, critics such as Kuvempu (Shivareddy 2004) and G. H. Nayak (2006) have asked how Pampa, who denounces kingship and martial values in this epic, goes on to valorise them in *Vikramarjuna Vijaya.* Nayak attributes it to a split in Pampa's poetic sensibility which fails to reconcile the contradiction. As discussed earlier, these were the contradictions of the age in which the boundaries between religion and temporal political power were porous. Pre-modern Kannada literature did not see this as a contradiction. It should also be noted that Pampa portrays these fissures even in the martial world he is supposed to be celebrating in *Vikramarjuna Vijaya.* What emerges from both these texts is the sombre awareness of the fragility of power. The famous episode of the dance of Neelanjane in *Aadipurana*, in which the celestial nymph passes away even as she is dancing, foreshadows the disillusionment of Bahubali with the transitoriness of all worldly things.

Most of the Jaina works reinforce the evidence of the inscriptions of the period which testify to the existence of a society based on the *Varna* system, comprising various castes, whose wealth depended on plundering (battles were also a form of plundering) property, land and women as well as on the flourishing trade. Karnataka was a powerful centre of trade including maritime trade with many nations, and inscriptions refer to many large towns and cities, some of which minted their own currency. All the major centres of religious movements were also major trading centres. The merchant class of Shettys, Pattana Shettys (*Shrestis* or merchants) and merchant guilds donated to the local societies, and were part of the local administration. The other powerful class was of brahmins who were gifted *agraharas* and land by all rulers irrespective of their own religious affiliations. A good ruler was one who protected the *Varna* system and patronised brahmins. Poetry was one of the means of establishing the symbolic power of the ruler who was eulogised as the representative of god. The discourse of the divine kingship was necessary in a period when power was always under threat. However, even while participating in the reinforcement of temporal power, poetry also offered its critique. Such a critique is an undercurrent in Pampa's *Vikramarjuna Vijaya.*

The introductory verses of this epic retelling of the *Mahabharata* make certain statements which describe the nature of the work. Pampa was encouraged by his admirers and fellow poets that he alone could 'narrate the vast story of the *Mahabharata* without denting it'. Therefore, he is attempting the impossible, 'swimming the vast ocean of Vyasa's poetry'. He allegorises his patron King Arikesari as the valiant Arjuna. As pointed out earlier, it is a remarkable poetic feat to compare the regional politics of a feudatory ruler with the political narrative of the *Mahabharata*. Sheldon Pollock relates this effort to the rise of the vernacular polities along with that of the vernacular cosmopolis. The epic constructs a dual vision incorporating the regional into a pan-Indian framework. This is supported by Pampa's poetics which sees *Mārga* and *Desi* as complementary. The *Champu* style used by the poet, mixing prose and verse, is said to be of Dravidian origin. Pampa's poetry is a tour de force, with a range which includes the highly stylised, Sanskritised poetic idiom as well as the speech rhythms of the everyday spoken form of Kannada. Pampa epitomises significant episodes from Vyasa's work with an unfailing sense of propriety.

Expectedly, there are long passages and sections centred around Arjuna as well as the conventional eighteen descriptions. Pampa borrows freely from Sanskrit poets but his originality lies in the use of this material to create multi-layered meanings. For example, when Karna is in a rage that he has not been made the commander of the Kaurava army, Bhishma calmly assures him that his turn (*sool*) will also come, the tragic irony being that every great Kaurava army commander is doomed to death. Duryodhana who knows the secret of Karna's birth—that he is the first-born Pandava and Kunti's son—relies on Karna's friendship and loyalty.

Pampa's poetry exemplifies the functions of poetry in a historical period with two dominant power structures—monarchy and religion—interacting in complex ways, usually in collaboration and collusion. It should also be noted that except for folk poetry and performative art forms, other cultural expressions, especially the classical model of poetry practised by Pampa, had a limited audience of courtiers, scholars and some connoisseurs described by Pampa as *Budhajana*, the knowledgeable ones. Inevitably, patronage, either royal or aristocratic, was the only means of circulation through copies made by scribes. Though Pampa expresses his gratitude in advance to those who may recite his poetry or set it to music, not much is known about the number of *gamakis* (reciters) who could take serious poetry to the audience. The other means was to write for religious institutions like Jaina monasteries which could also commission copies of literary works. This unavoidable closeness to the centres of power imposed both ideological and eulogistic restrictions on poetry. It should also be noted that many poets also prepared drafts of inscriptions and considered this a legitimate function of poetry.

In a major revaluation of Pampa, G. H. Nayak has argued that Pampa is forced to reduce himself to a craftsman applying his great talent to a narrow free space. In *Aadipurana* he was retelling a well-known hagiography and in *Vikramarjuna Vijaya* he was allegorising his patron as Arjuna, and in each case had to work in a predefined framework. Nayak concludes that Pampa's poetic expression could not integrate the two different obligations. As we shall see in the discussion of other Jaina and Shaiva texts, we probably need a distinctive framework to understand the functions of poetry in the pre-modern period.

In *Vikramarjuna Vijaya* the question of *kula* (birth, lineage and loosely related to the modern word 'caste') is foregrounded on several occasions. Describing the sexual relationship between Rishi Parashara and Satyavati, the boatwoman from a caste involved in fishing, and the birth of Drona from the sperm ejaculated by Rishi Bharadwaja, Pampa wryly wonders about the strange ways of the ascetics. When Karna is humiliated by not being allowed to participate in the martial competitions because he is a *Sutaputra*, son of a low-caste charioteer, Duryodhana anoints him as ruler of the Vanga region of the kingdom. Though the episode is from the original *Mahabharata*, Pampa's narration is differently nuanced. The codes of the *Varna* system and kshatriya conventions are shown to be unjust. Duryodhana's friendship with Karna is celebrated in a well-known passage by Pampa. Karna, Duryodhana and Duryodhana's wife Bhanumati are portrayed as playing dice in the inner chambers. When Bhanumati, who has wagered her necklace of pearls in the game, loses to Karna, he tries to pull it from her neck. When the necklace breaks and the pearls spill on the ground, it is Duryodhana who picks up the pearls. His generosity and friendship help him keep *kula* out of his relationships. Later, in the council meeting during the war, Karna is not made the commander of the Kaurava army. In his angry outburst Karna says that *kula* is not the caste you are born into; determination and dedication are the indicators of a noble *kula*. However, when Duryodhana ultimately anoints Karna as the commander and visits Shalya to request him to be Karna's charioteer, Shalya's response is couched in caste hatred. He accuses Duryodhana of being like those kings who lack discretion and use their power to make the low-born hold noble positions. Duryodhana has to convince him by assuring that Karna has all the qualities of a noble-born. When Karna visits Bhishma to seek his blessings and also apologises for his rude behaviour earlier, Bhishma wonders whether Karna is highborn. These are among the many references to *kula* in Pampa's work and it can be assumed that the questions of caste and *Varna* were among his major preoccupations. His poetry brings up various discourses on hierarchies based on birth. These discourses do not interrogate caste/*kula* in any radical manner, but argue that noble qualities can be found in the low-born too, thus accepting the premise that noble qualities belong to the noble-born. As discussed earlier, by the tenth century Jainism in Karnataka had made many compromises with the Vedic ideology of the *Varna* system. But the caste question seems to have troubled Pampa so much that in the last sections of the epic Karna and Duryodhana emerge as the central figures of the narrative, and Arjuna (allegorising Pampa's patron) pales into insignificance. In a verse addressed to the reader, Pampa declares that the *Mahabharata* is '*Karna Rasayana*', Karna being the essence of the tragic tale.

Paradoxically, Duryodhana who has usurped the kingdom belonging to the sons of Pandu, now emerges as the good king. Unwilling to negotiate a truce with the Pandavas, and tragically aware of his own end, he affirms his loyalty to friends, elders and family. He also accepts the fact that it is Krishna who is the *Sutradhara* controlling the events. The epic which begins as a eulogistic poem is transformed into a sombre reflection on the tragic potential in all power structures.

In the macabre scene showing Bheema combing Draupadi's hair with the jaws of Dushasana and anointing her with his blood, Bheema rightly says that Draupadi's plait was the seed of the destructive war. The transgression of the moral code in her public humiliation has now found retribution.

In the duel between Duryodhana and Bheema, the former refuses to hit the fallen Bheema with his mace, adhering to the kshatriya code. But on Krishna's instruction Bheema hits Duryodhana on his thighs and wins the duel. This is a transgression justified as legitimate and necessary to end the evil in Duryodhana. But Pampa ensures that in his death Duryodhana emerges as the victim. Pampa's poetry, itself a product of a martial age in which war and violence were celebrated as manly valour, is also a critique of the violence on which kingdoms are founded.

The earlier epic, *Aadipurana*, is encyclopaedic in its structure and attempts to map the development of a civilisation using Jaina myths. One major trajectory of the epic, as discussed above, is to trace the evolution of an ordinary human being into a *Thirthankara*. This spiritual evolution happens across many lives. In each life, the human being liberates himself from his attachment to worldly life. This does not happen through mere ascetic renunciation, but through immersion in the pleasures of life, including carnal pleasures. At some point, the realisation dawns that sensual experience of pleasure and power is self-exhausting. This is the moment to turn away from the worldly. Pampa does not present two dichotomous domains of the physical and the transcendental, but both are seen as essential aspects of life which is frequently compared to the ocean. This also explains how the hagiography of a *Thirthankara* has so much space for *sringara*, the erotic.

Pampa's poetry tries to identify the limits of desire and fulfilment. While there is no puritanic rejection of pleasure, clinging to it beyond a limit is seen as an obstacle to one's evolution. In one of the lives of the protagonist, his well-wishers wonder, 'Why this old man, with sunken and wrinkled cheeks, looking like a wizened old monkey, not realise that it is time to renounce physical pleasures?'. But when the realisation dawns, the path is cleared for the evolution. This narrative plot of many lives and a gradual evolution should not be seen only as a literary device. What Pampa explores are the possibilities for any human being to move through many experiential worlds.

The last section of *Aadipurana* is about the creation of a civilisation with the many structures of control needed to discipline humans. From distribution of land to the appointment of disciplining authorities, every detail is worked out. The fear of disorder and anarchy is used to legitimise the civilisational order. But the order depends ultimately on the king or the ruler who should know the limits he should not cross, though he may have the power to do so. In a suggestive metaphor Pampa says that 'such acts of transgression are a menace to nature'. This was his critique of the excessive use of power he had seen in the politically turbulent age he lived in.

However, the process of ordering and creating a civilisation also involves the *Varna* system and, by extension, the caste system. The order imagined in the epic is a mirror image of the society of the time which was strictly hierarchical. Thus, poetry takes part in establishing the power structure of the age.

Ranna, Pampa and Ponna are considered the three jewels of ancient Kannada poetry. This popular description does not stand critical scrutiny as neither Ranna nor Ponna possesses Pampa's extraordinary ability to integrate aesthetic perfection with a deep and original reflection on the complexities of human existence. Pampa was a learned poet who borrowed from various sources, used literal translations of some of these sources and rewrote the others. What makes his poetry original is the ability to subject this material to a complex exploration of both the contemporary and transcendental concerns. His poetry embodies the deep fissures of an age labelled by Kannada historians as *Kshatra Yuga*, the age of the warrior spirit with its codes and values. While the Jaina world view enabled Pampa to see human history as a small pebble thrown into the ocean of endless time and therefore of little importance, his passionate involvement in love and war, and the attractions of this transitory but fascinating world, also provided a powerful sense of belonging to a world which Jaina theology denounced as worthless. He describes himself as a great lover of women 'from Andhra and Malayala'. Even the Jaina hagiography *Aadipurana* is generally free from the sectarian polemics and satire so prominent in the late Jaina poets such as Nayasena and Brahmashiva. He wrote at a time when Jainism enjoyed a hegemony with the support of royal and feudal dynasties. Pampa does not show the insecurity and touchiness about one's religion which becomes disconcerting in later poets. His statement 'Isn't all humanity one' has been interpreted as iconic of the liberal, tolerant Kannada culture. History, in contrast, speaks of endless sectarian strife with evidence of much violence. Conversions were a matter of public scrutiny, even though there are ample examples of spouses subscribing to different religious faiths. The deeper loyalties in both Pampa and Ranna are to the temporal power of their patrons. This temporal power needs to be reinforced by the cultural power of poetry. Neither poet has any reservations about composing a poetry of power.

Ranna (949–1020 CE) followed Pampa's model in writing a eulogistic *Loukika* epic allegorising his patron King Iriva Bedanga as Bheema in his *Sahasa Bheema Vijayam.* Like Pampa, he self-consciously attempts a retelling of the *Mahabharata*, drawing from Vyasa, Bhatta Narayana and Pampa as well as several other sources. However, unlike Pampa, instead of attempting a synoptic retelling of the entire *Mahabharata* story, Ranna focusses on the *Gadhayuddha* (duel with maces) episode depicting the epic duel between Bheema and Duryodhana. The rest of the story is narrated in what Ranna describes as a 'lion's-eye-view' mode. The style is intensely dramatic and Ranna reveals himself as a great dramatist *manqué*. He transgresses the norms of propriety in his determination to equate his patron king to Bheema. Ironically few readers of this enormously popular poem remember Ranna's patron. The reason is the powerful, devastating denunciation of war which makes the poem one of the most celebrated anti-war works in Kannada literature. Duryodhana emerges as a great tragic figure in a literary tradition which rejected the genre of tragedy until well into the twentieth century. Once again it is the case of an influential work by a Jaina poet, written to eulogise a warrior king, becoming, in the process of writing, a moving denunciation of war and martial valour. This has its roots in the dichotomous existence of the Jaina religion with its central tenet of absolute non-violence flourishing in an age of endless wars and battles and being patronised by royal dynasties and feudal lords. This schism is evident in the poem. Ranna's eulogy to his patron Iriva Bedanga is so self-consciously written by equating him with Bheema that it leads to glaring instances of anachronism and contradictions. At the same time, following Pampa, Ranna makes Duryodhana a counter-hero. Obstinate and unrelenting even in the midst of the devastating ruins of the lost war at Kurukshetra, witness to the horror of losing his son, brothers, friends and teachers, and suffering from a deep sense of guilt, Duryodhana attempts to redeem his self-esteem in a last-ditch battle. C. Veeranna argues that one can locate a Jaina narrative tradition in which the epic heroes valorised by the Vedic–Puranic tradition are subjected to a negative scrutiny and counter-heroes like Duryodhana and Ravana are transformed into noble though tragic characters (Veeranna 1986). He locates Ranna in this tradition. Veeranna also argues that having planned the work as a eulogy to his patron king by allegorising him as Bheema, Ranna had to work within constraints to make Duryodhana a tragic hero. He succeeds mainly by choosing the last episode of the Great War in which the horror and pity of war overtakes questions of individual integrity or failure. The Duryodhana Ranna presents is a wilful self-destructive warrior who adheres to the code of kshatriya nobility, after having transgressed it all too often in the past. Ranna's rendering of Duryodhana's mourning and sorrow is so powerful that it has become indelible in the popular imagination, recited even today by *gamakis* and endlessly performed in the *Yakshagana* and *Talamaddale* popular traditions.

Ranna's other work, *Ajitnathpurana*, is a hagiography in the modular Jaina form. The form is a mixture of the *Champu* style which is said to be of non-Sanskrit origin but by the time of Pampa had become closely associated with a highly Sanskritised epic narrative mode, and the Jaina hagiography which had also become a settled convention. The hagiography traverses a fixed trajectory in narrating the life of the *Thirthankara*—his supernatural birth, life of worldly power and sensual enjoyment, the epiphany that reveals the transitory nature of worldly pleasures, and then the many *bhavas* leading to his emancipation. Such delineation sometimes becomes problematic when the poet also tries to introduce the obligatory eighteen descriptions including those of hunting and visits to the prostitutes' quarters. Ranna vows to avoid this anomaly and succeeds. While the first major portion of the work deals with Ajitnatha, the last part deals with the myths relating to Attimabbe, the great patroness.

The other stated intention of the work is to uphold the Jaina religion as the perfect religion and critiquing other religions as false or illusory (*mithya*). Fortunately, Ranna eschews the ideological virulence of Brahmashiva and other Jaina poets, and his criticism of other sects is tempered. In fact, it is in his retelling of the *Mahabharata* that one finds acerbic comments on the brahmin *Varna* and brahminical practices. The consensus among critics is that *Ajitnathpurana* is bogged down by many instances of pedantry and lapses in taste, which are surprising in a poet of Ranna's calibre. This is true of the other 'jewel' of the age, Ponna.

Ponna also faithfully follows the tradition of composing a *Loukika* work, *Bhuvanaikya Ramabhyudaya*, and the *Āgamika* work, *Shanthipurana*. He was also patronised by a king although he was a Jaina *savana* or monk. His retelling of the story of Rama is one of the many lost texts of the age. *Shanthipurana* is yet another Jaina hagiography with the fixed phases in the evolution of the *Thirthankara*. In Ranna's *Ajitnathpurana*, while the conventional descriptions of the conception, birth, naming ceremony, etc., are dull and imitative, the epiphanies leading to *nirvega* or disenchantment with the temporal world are powerful. In fact, far more powerful is the case of Sagara whose attachment to his children clings to him across many lives. In *Shanthipurana*, the inner struggle to overcome the attachment to the world lacks in power and complexity. Ponna chooses to narrate the life of the *Thirthankara* from his sixth *bhava*. The weight of the poetic conventions is heavy in the descriptions of the city and the brothels. The convoluted narrative with its many strands seems to be constructed in order to conform to the Jaina sources.

The one major instance of deviating from drawing on religious and theological sources is the translation by Nagavarma I of Banabhatta's *Kadambari*. It is a secular work about love and passion, though in the major love story the lovers cannot marry because of the *Varna* system, thus foregrounding social divisions sanctioned by religion. The original work attributed to Banabhatta and his son Bhushanabhatta is an amazing medley of multiple narratives—the most popular one narrated by a parrot—about relationships lasting across many lives and with fantasy rubbing shoulders with reality. Banabhatta is known for his rhetorical style which most of the time overtakes the story itself. Nagavarma locates himself well within the scholarly, rhetorical Sanskrit mode while exhibiting his enormous mastery of the *Desi* linguistic resources. Many critics have commented on the 'timeless' world of the text which shows little connection with the real historical world of either Banabhatta or Nagavarma.

The power of Nagavarma's work lies in its portrayal of the emotions, passions and suffering of the characters who are victims of fate and unrequited love. There is no emancipation through renunciation as in the Jaina literary works. Nagavarma is a superb translator and therefore perhaps it is difficult to infer what his own beliefs were. The work in translation presupposes the existence of a wealthy, leisured class which does not need to look beyond sexual passion and its sublimation in many forms of love.

***

The study of ancient Kannada literature is fraught with the many challenges of interpreting a literary canon which was established along with the composition of the canonical works. The existence and persistence of the literary canon is supported both by the numerous and continuous references to the texts and their authors, and also by the intertextuality of later texts with the earlier canonical ones. For example, though Ranna does not mention Pampa while acknowledging past masters his *Gadhayuddha* is in many respects a rewriting of Pampa's *Vikramarjuna Vijaya*. Pampa's Jaina hagiography *Aadipurana* provides the modular form for later hagiographic works. Many of his passages find an echo in later works. Ancient Kannada poetry also created a literary cultural archive by drawing on Sanskrit and Prakrit sources. Surprisingly, there is little evidence of a creative relationship with Tamil literature. (Elsewhere the possibility of some poets from *Kannadanādu* being part of Tamil Sangam literature has been discussed. But there is little to propose a continuous exchange or engagement with other languages of the south in Old Kannada literature.)

The archive discussed above created possibilities of endless rewriting, translation, adaptation and experimentation, which ensured both continuity and innovation. It can be safely said that there was no radical disjunction during the period. Critics are divided in their assessment of the advantages of a literary canon established so early. Many argue that this meant that writers of great talent had to work within the constraints of established conventions. Originality was restricted to variations on pre-existing themes and motifs. Other critics have argued that the literary canon which introduced the categories of *Mārga* and *Desi* ensured the enrichment of the Kannada literary idiom by suffusing it with both Sanskrit-centric structures and vocabulary and the variegated power of *Desi*. The master genre of *Champu* also led to the development of Kannada prose. There is every reason to believe that the *Vachanakaras* and later poets like Harihara and Raghavanka draw on the energies of Kannada prose even when they are composing poetry.

Looking beyond the linguistic and aesthetic concerns, ancient Kannada literature has to be seen as a product of the dynamic and complex relationship between political power, religion and aesthetic practices which flourished with royal and feudal patronage, and addressed a small class of literary connoisseurs known as *Budha Mandali, Budhajana,* or *Sahrudaya*. As such the experiential worlds it explores are confined to those of the royalty, the courtier class, the feudal aristocracy and the merchant class. The rest of the social world, which was by all historical accounts already very complexly structured, is not even in the margins. There are ample instances evidencing a deeply hierarchical society divided on the lines of *Varna* and caste which seem to be almost unaffected by the non-brahminical, egalitarian ideology of the Jaina religion. The narratives of *Vaddaradhane*, the epics of Pampa and other works provide only a fleeting glimpse of the many social worlds excluded from the literary during the period. These worlds make a powerful entry into Kannada literature with the *Vachanakaras* and later poets like Nayasena and Harihara.

Women figure predominantly in the literature of the period; but with a few exceptions, they are always seen as objects—sexually fetishised objects. None of the hegemonic religions of the time prevent poets from indulging in the *sringara* (erotic) *rasa* in the style associated with Sanskrit texts. Even without the fallacy of imposing the latter-day prudery of codes governing the erotic in poetry, one does not find any justification for the ubiquitous repetitions of the erotic descriptions of the woman's body. However, despite such obsession, some women characters emerge as autonomous ethical, social and sexual beings in ancient Kannada literature.

FOUR

The *Vachanakaras*

Reading the *Vachanakaras* of the twelfth century is like living through an intense overawing experience and then waking up to wonder whether it was true. It was like a conflagration—sudden, unexpected, and overpowering as long as it lasted—and then disappeared as suddenly. As Friar Lawrence says of Romeo and Juliet's love, 'these violent passions have violent ends' (Act II Scene VI). These are metaphors which express a subjective experience and do not usually pass muster in historical scrutiny. In this case however, the *Vachanakara* movement was like an eruption, a disjunction in tradition, a radical movement—some would say too radical—and ahead of its times. Not that its precedents are not clear. The convergence of many things which created the necessary conjuncture is clear. So are the sociocultural structures which legitimised its radical stance. Though the movement at Kalyana, the capital of the Kalachuri king Bijjala, disappeared without much of a trace, its repercussions were long and unpredictable. As Girish Karnad put it in his preface to *Taledanda* (2013), a powerful play on the movement, 'just as the tongue returns to the aching tooth, Kannada consciousness has frequently returned to the "enthusiasm of the age" of the period'. Probably the movement is the most textualised and inter-textualised phenomenon in Karnataka's history. Perhaps because of the huge gaps in the historical narrative about it, the Kannada imagination has been restlessly filling it up with legends, myths and highly anachronistic interpretations (Chenni 2004). P. Lankesh's *Sankranti*, H. S. Shivaprakash's *Mahachaitra*, and numerous poems and novels attempt a revisionist reconstruction of the movement. All movements in Karnataka from the 1970s onwards—the Dalit, protest (*Bandaya*) and feminist movements—have discovered iconic value and fertile cultural memories in the movement.

Although it was a religious movement, it is also being studied as an instantiation of the indigenous tradition of secularism.

1

The consensus is that it was a Bhakti movement, a reformist religious movement which drew on the social and spiritual energies of the myriad classes of artisans, untouchables and women. Its sociocultural dimension cannot be ignored just as the core of its liberationist spiritual quest cannot be overlooked. It was at once a communitarian movement whose objective was both liberation of human beings from the dehumanising hierarchies of the society, and a vigilant relentless struggle to fashion an individual self in the presence of the divine. It was not as homogeneous as the later narratives have tried to portray it. It was many-voiced and dialogic, and even after all these centuries we can clearly hear the individual voices of dissent and interrogation. The *Vachanakaras* came from all possible social locations and also assertively carried their social worlds with them, drawing their images and metaphors from their professions and everyday lives. Basavanna (1131–96), the leader of the movement, was born in a well-connected brahmin family and powerfully articulated his struggle to escape the high-caste identity. He went on to reconstruct his own lineage and caste by declaring that he was a child born to the male servant and maid servant of Dohara Kakkayya and Madar Channayya, who went to the field to make cow dung cakes and instead made love. He even rewrites the horoscope and lineage of Lord Shiva himself!

The *Vachanakaras* identify themselves by their professions. The fiercest 'internal critic' was Chowdayya, the ferryman. Announcing himself and warning the brahmins not to let their shadows fall on him and defile him is Madivala Machaiah, the washerman. There is also Sule Sankavve who was a prostitute. (*Sule* is Kannada for prostitute.) This was possible because of the social theology of the movement which declared that 'labour is heaven', and separated the professions from the stigma and hierarchies they were tied to.

Therefore, the movement was inclusive of all the labouring castes and classes, and those who like Basava came from the 'higher' castes. The movement was driven by two staunch commitments. One was the fierce egalitarianism of all *sharanas* (devotees but here the members of the movement too), irrespective of the *sutakas* (the defilements) which came along with birth in a caste society. These included caste, profession and gender. This was based on an incisive rationalist critique of the illegitimacy of these hierarchies. It also involved a scathing attack on the 'superstitious' rituals and practices usually associated with the so-called folk religions. This of course was highly problematic and shall be discussed in detail later. The other was the intense inner quest involving a merciless self-examination as well as a mystical submission to the individual deity. Historians of the Bhakti movement in India categorise the movement as an example of *nirguna bhakti*, or the devotion to the disembodied supreme reality.

However, the *Vachanas* transform the *nirguna* devotion into the intense passionate love for a personal deity who figures in the 'signatures' (*Ankita*) in the *Vachanas*, such as Kudala Sangama Deva (the lord of the meeting rivers) in Basava, and 'The Lord White as Jasmine' in Akka Mahadevi (c.1130–60). Adopting the *'Lingapati-Sharana Sati'* convention, Basava awaits the coming of his lord like a woman in love. (The convention refers to the male devotee imagining himself as a woman or beloved, and God as the husband and master.) Akka Mahadevi offers a full-bodied erotic love to Chenna Mallikarjuna. The *Vachanakaras* also tease, taunt and provoke their individual deities. It is therefore *nirguna bhakti*, monotheistic but realised as an intense relationship between the devotee and his/her god. This of course is an element in many other streams of the Bhakti movement in India.

What were the social conditions which drew the artisan, labouring and merchant classes to the radical movement? R. N. Nandi (1975) provides a nuanced materialist answer to this question. He draws our attention to the fact that Kalyana was on the major trade route in South India, connecting it by road to several other such places of trade and commerce. Despite the political uncertainties and the several layers of taxes, the economy was robust and the merchant class was dynamic and entrepreneurial. Several historians point out that by the twelfth century the agrarian society was moving towards a mercantile economy. Perhaps it would be better to tone down these statements and say that monarchies and fiefdoms not only showed their loyalty to the priestly class and its ideology of *Varna* and caste, but also to the merchant class which had a transregional network. Large tracts of land and even entire small towns were given away to Pattana Shettys (*Shetty* is *Shresti*, the wealthy merchant) for manufacture (by skilled artisans) and trade. Buddhism and Jainism in earlier periods gave spiritual identity to the merchant class which was otherwise powerful but was denied equality of spiritual status. Similar conditions had existed before the *Vachanakara* movement began. There was great political instability with kingdoms and fiefdoms locked in unending battles with each other. The two erstwhile 'empires' (as named in the historical/literary references), namely the Rashtrakuta and Chalukya empires, had been breaking apart, and the feudal lords of the fiefdoms had been declaring themselves kings. The Kalachuris, who claimed a glorious past lineage, were the *samantas*, or satraps, of the Chalukya kingdom. Bijjala, always playing a clever hand in regional politics, declared his autonomy as a ruler. The regime of the Kalachuris was short-lived and so was Bijjala's. Basava, probably through his influential maternal uncle and his own abilities, became the *bhandari* or treasurer of Bijjala's kingdom. The rest is not history but legends and speculation. Most surprisingly, the inscriptions described by D. R. Nagaraj as public narratives, are almost silent on the movement and its end. Even M. M. Kalburgi's work on the *sharanas* in the inscriptions (1970) provides weak evidences.

On the other hand, the later apotheosis of Basava and the *sharanas* in Harihara's works (twelfth century CE), and the ideologically driven Jaina and Shaiva poetic narratives such as *Basava Puranamu* by Palkuriki Somanatha (translated by Bheemakavi into Kannada) and several Jaina poetic texts, do not provide reliable historical evidence. Owing to this poverty of material, most scholars have resorted to a circularity of method where the social context of the period is constructed from the *Vachanas* themselves, and then the *Vachanas* are examined against this historical context! The only defence is that the *Vachanas* are rich in detail about this worldly life and do provide very specific information about the society of the time.

Apart from the political uncertainties and the permanently insecure social, material context, there are graphic portrayals of the brahminical priestly class indulging in meaningless rituals and expensive (for the kings and princes) sacrifices, in many literary texts. Though we do not know much about the Buddhist influence on the social life earlier, there is ample evidence of royal patronage to Jainism and Vedic Hinduism, which kept changing most of the time. There are any number of instances of the king and his queen consort following different religions. Such changing religious loyalties did not make much impact on the common people because when converted, they were given a secondary status and they generally practised their own rituals. For example, in Janna's *Yashodhara Charite* (thirteenth century) there are at least four systems of religious practice: the worship of Mari, the folk goddess associated with the Shakta traditions, which demands animal/human sacrifice; the Jaina religion which the king patronises and follows; and the queen mother's belief in offering sacrifices to propitiate good fortune. The great poem declares that its ethical purpose is to examine the transition from the old system of beliefs involving sacrifices to the new *naya*, or religion, that is Jainism which considers even *sankalpa himse* (intended violence) a grave sin.

The *Vachanas* also portray such a medley of beliefs and practices. On the one hand there are animistic practices and worship of the winnow, the broomstick and the tree, which the *Vachanakaras* including and especially

Basava, denigrate mercilessly. There are also the *sramana* sects and the Buddhist sects. The Vedic rituals are targeted by the *Vachanakaras*. In a few *Vachanas* Basava suggests that the initiation into Veerashaivism with the wearing of the lingam, makes one a *sharana* even if he were holding a bowl of meat in one hand and toddy in another. Many women *Vachanakaras* raise questions about spouses following different religions. (In a powerful sequence in Karnad's *Taledanda*, Basava is accused of setting up the son against the father because of sectarian loyalties.)

In the midst of such a volatile context, the *Vachanakaras* offered a simple, non-ritualistic, rational belief system as well as practices which were even simpler. The core of the new religion was the belief in the absolute spiritual equality of all human beings. It meant that the community of *sharanas* would not subscribe to *Varna*, caste and gender inequalities. The main support came from the artisans and the untouchable labourers for whom this was real emancipation. Again, from the *Vachanas* themselves, it is clear that the *sharanas* continued to perform their professional tasks. How did this fit into an early-medieval society which had already seen the weakening of royal support to Jainism and the increased patronage of Vedic Hinduism? To borrow from the analysis of the Buddhist *Sangha*, was it only at the *Anubhava Mantapa*, the meeting place of the *sharanas*, and in Basava's *Mahamane* (Basava's residence?), that this egalitarianism was practised? Inscriptions and other evidences do not suggest any structural changes in the caste or class structure. In any case, the movement was too short-lived to accomplish that. It did raise the consciousness of the communities, and created a new ethics and a different sense of social justice. This consciousness has remained an undercurrent in the Kannada tradition.

Therefore, the greatness of the movement lies in its articulation of a powerful vision of radical equality. This vision was articulated by inventing a whole world of verbal communication with no parallels in Kannada literary history.

The movement rejected all forms of power and authority, beginning with the king's authority. Basava's *Vachanas* reveal a troubled relationship with Bijjala, and in fact the very idea of rule by a king. In some *Vachanas* he uses the binary concepts of *Jolawalige* and *Velewalige* which had many connotations. *Jolawalige* was your loyalty to the profession or position you hold, which can be defined as a limited loyalty. In simple words, it is the fixed duties that you perform with diligence and honesty. *Velewalige* is the higher order of loyalty—for example, to truth, to your beliefs—which may sometimes be in conflict with your duties. The suggestion is that if it comes to a choice, one would choose *Velewalige*. The tone of the following *Vachana* on this theme is of rebellion against the notion of loyalty. Ultimately, loyalty is to god and one's conscience:

> I am not a servant working for wages;
> I am a servant wagering my life for the master.
> Listen Koodalasangama deva
> Death is the great festive celebration. (Narayana, P. V. 2018, 74; translated by the author)

We have no knowledge of the choices Basava made when the planned marriage between a brahmin girl and an untouchable boy led to the eruption of terrible violence and retribution. There is no evidence to prove that Basava either committed suicide, or was killed, or attained his final liberation at Kappadi Sangama.

The authority of the priestly class was greatly undermined by the devastating critique of the class in the *Vachanas*. Basava himself is at his satirical best when ridiculing it. He exercises the same skill in satirising the brahmins, and the Buddhist and Jaina monks. The most important element is the rejection of the authority of the Vedas, Puranas and Sastras. From the reading of the *Vachanas* there is no doubt at all that the *Vachanakaras* were uncompromisingly against their authority. The later and ongoing attempts by certain sub-castes of the Lingayats to accommodate the *Vachanakaras* into the traditional Hindu fold are completely misplaced. The issue cannot be reduced to religious politics. The *Vachanas* articulate an epistemology and an ethic in which knowledge derived from the textual authority has no place. On the one hand, the Puranas especially are seen as fraudulently depicting gods as cheating, begging and harassing human beings. Therefore, 'Purana is the chatter of the small-time bullies' (Allama). The entire system of the foundations of religious knowledge, including Shruthi, Smrithi, Shastra and Purana, is dismissed. That leaves the triad of *Guru, Linga* and *Jangama*. *Guru* is the one who initiates and then guides; the *Linga* is the personal deity; and *Jangama* is an extremely problematic concept. Does *Jangama* suggest a class of venerable practitioners of the faith, a revised version of the priestly class? Was the concept itself a later interpolation when the *Vachanas* were being collected and anthologised? The collection and compilation of the *Vachanas* took place during the time of Praudhadevaraya of the Vijayanagara empire, when the Veerashaiva community was trying to negotiate with political power to establish its hegemony. Another similar attempt was made in the fifteenth century with the writing of the *Shunya Sampadane* which were designed as narratives about the *sharanas* at the *Anubhava Mantapa*, with dramatic interface between some of the leading figures and arranging the *Vachanas* to suit the situations thus created. It is not Basava but Allama who ascends the *Shunya Peetha*.[1] In any case, he is the unquestioned intellectual leader who examines the leading figures and succeeds in helping them to discover the truth. The long-drawn-out process of compiling the *Shunya Sampadane* and consolidating the power of the *mathas* (Veerashaiva monasteries) also saw the transformation of the ideals of the *Vachanakara* movement into strategies for mobilising a caste with many sub-castes in it.

Therefore, even if we begin with the formation/consolidation of a caste and then try to move back in time, there will be huge gaps in any narrative which is thus constructed. This takes us back to the question of how was a radical egalitarian religion conceptualised in an early-medieval society with the *Varna* and caste systems intact and the brahminical priestly class remaining practically unaffected by any such movement. This miracle was the form which came to be known as the *Vachana*. It has been translated as 'what is said', 'utterance', 'saying', etc. The name suggests spontaneity (of speech), and refusal to use verse forms and modes of expression established by the Sanskrit-centric *Champu* model. Instead, the *Vachana* is a form of expression which consciously eschews the Sanskritic models and creates a poetics of spontaneous utterance. As H. S. Shivaprakash (2010) points out, it would be naïve to assume that the *Vachanakaras* had no notion of an alternative poetics or that their poetic practice 'just happened'. There are a number of formal features such as repetition, parallelism, use of speech rhythms and intonation, and an extraordinary choice of images and metaphors. The *Vachana* 'The master of the house, is he at home, or isn't he?' (Ramanujan 1973, 72), reveals some of these features. The entire *Vachana* posits a parallel between the condition of the house and the presence or otherwise of the 'master of the house'. The metaphorical meanings of the elaborate parallelism become clear in the second part of the *Vachana*.

---

[1] *Shunya Sampadane* is the title of several works, all structured as narratives interspersed with *Vachanas* which are contextualised as spoken by the *Vachanakaras* participating in the dialogues. The following are the well-known versions of *Shunya Sampadane*: Basavaraju 1969; Bhoosanurmath 1958; Vidyashankar and Siddhalingaiah 1998; Hiremath 1972; and Bhoosanurmath et al. 1965–72.

2

> One major problem impeding efforts to provide a satisfactory historical account of the movement is its genealogy. Who were its ancestors? Where did it begin? What was its relationship to other forms of *Saivism?* (D. R. Nagaraj in Shobhi 2012, xx)

D. R. Nagaraj raises these questions and goes on to say that Kannada scholars who have tried to answer them belong to two categories: the integrationists who see the *Vachanakara* movement as part of the Bhakti movements in India, and though distinctive, integrated with it; and the scholars who seek Kannada-specific contexts to answer the questions.

The Bhakti movement which began in the South, in Tamil Nadu, with the Alwars and the Nayanars in the sixth to seventh centuries, influenced similar movements in Maharashtra and other regions of India until the seventeenth century. By all accounts it was the single most important religious–cultural movement which impacted all sections of society. It was not homogeneous and took different shapes depending on the specific historical and material conditions existing in different regions. Its relationship with political power also varied greatly; it was an ally, opponent, or accomplice, as the conditions demanded.

There are scholars who see the *Vachanakara* movement as originating under the influence of the Bhakti movements in Tamil Nadu. The supporting arguments are that the Bhakti movement had both the Shaivite and Vaishnavite streams; it had a large following among the common people; it attempted to be inclusive, including as its members shudras, women and untouchables; its core element was the intense personal devotion to the individual deity; and most importantly, it believed in the spiritual equality of all devotees irrespective of class, caste and gender. These features are shared by the *Vachanakara* movement. The essential difference was that the Bhakti movements in Tamil Nadu were centred around a temple culture which the *Vachanakaras* resisted most vehemently. As R. Champakalakshmi (2011) has argued, by developing itself around a temple culture, the Bhakti movement unknowingly expanded the power of the temples by rallying the devotees from the lower castes and classes to the temple. Owing to the generous patronage of the royal dynasties who in most cases had built temples, the temples had become wealthy, elitist and powerful. They were also centres of power which could negotiate with the monarchy on equal terms. However, the limitations were due to the extreme rigidity of caste and *Varna* which alienated the common, especially low-caste, people. The Bhakti movement with its egalitarian and liberationist ideology was able to enlist a massive number of followers. Many of the leaders were charismatic spiritual leaders with numerous followers. Some of them were associated with legends in which they had fought for the rights of the underprivileged. Many of these legends themselves make it clear that temple entry for the low-caste remained prohibited. In any case, the temples gained in popularity and wealth. Thus egalitarian Bhakti movements sometimes led to the empowering of the temple culture.

In contrast, the *Vachanakaras* shunned temples. The famous *Vachana* by Basava accomplishes a masterly rejection of the temple only to claim that the devotee's body is the temple: 'My legs are pillars, / the body the shrine' (Ramanujan 1973, 88).

The most radical move was the wearing of the *lingam* on the body, at once abolishing the ascetic disgust at the body as unclean, making the temple '*sthavara*' (or the 'standing'), to perish someday, and the individual body itself a temple to one's deity. This move also cut at the root of the power of the temple. If one remembers the immense gifts of land (*devaswam*) and the wasteful expenditure on the upkeep of the temples, one can understand the revolutionary nature of the act. Temples also encouraged unacceptable practices such as the *devadasi* system.

Therefore, while acknowledging the influence of the Tamil Bhakti movement, it would be difficult to explain the radicalism of the *Vachanakara* movement as originating in it. *Vachanakaras* acknowledge the sixty-three saints of the past as the '*Puratanaru*', the ancient gurus, and refer to their acts of devotion in the *Vachanas*. There is the argument that the Veerashaiva movement was only a more radical version of the existing Shaiva religion. The worship of Shiva goes back to the earliest phases of Indian civilisation. The iconic *lingam* is said to be as old as the Harappa civilisation. However, closer home and closer in time, many Shaiva cults were powerful presences in Karnataka before the Veerashaiva movement. Inscriptions testify to the grants made by kings and feudal lords to the Kalamukha monasteries which were also famous centres of learning. In and around the birth places of Allama and Akka Mahadevi in Shikaripura taluk of Shivamogga district, there are such inscriptions and remains of monasteries and temples. There is also evidence that the ascetic gurus of the sect wielded influence over the rulers. There is no doubt that the *Vachanakaras* had no love lost for the sect, but we do not know if and what roles the sect played in the Veerashaiva movement.

Another historical narrative which has divided the present-day Lingayat community is about the '*panchacharyas*', the five *acharyas* who were said to be the founders of the Veerashaiva religion.[2] Basava was only a latter-day reformer. This has led to two types of monasteries: the Pancha Peethas and the Virakta Mathas. The Pancha Peetha tradition considers the *Jangama* caste as superior and is orthodox in its practices. Their present status does not adequately explain the missing history of the role of these institutions during the *Vachanakara* movement. It is not even imaginable that the radical movement could have originated in such an orthodox tradition. Unfortunately, the early scholarly works of the twentieth century in English on the Veerashaiva movement treat the movement itself as an unproblematic part of the Hindu/Indian tradition (Nandimath 1942).

There are scholars who see the influence of the many non-Vedic sects on the *Vachanakaras*.

The *Natha* tradition which had links across India and particularly in many places in Karnataka could have influenced the deeper mystical element among the *Vachanakaras* (Tarikere 2017). There are also ungrounded speculations whether Allama met Gorakhnath or Matsyendranatha. These legends point towards a network of mystical cults and practices which are alive till today. Apart from drawing attention to the resemblances among the Bhakti and mystical cults, they do not throw much light on the actual history of the origin of the Bhakti movements.

This brings us back to the puzzle that we do not know much about—the origin of the *Vachanakara* movement; nor do we know about its abrupt end. There are reasonable surmises but none of the certainties a historian would prefer. At the same time, the creative energy of the *Vachanas*—compiled and collected much later—is so vast and expansive that it is evidence of a collective churning on several issues relating to caste, religion, gender and power:

> Why do we fight for the pride of caste?
> Not knowing that
> These seven sages
> Reached the salvation through truth. (Swamy 2007, 185)

There are two ways of talking about the irrelevance of caste in the *Vachanas*. One way is demonstrated in this *Vachana* by one of the untouchable

---

[2] There is an ongoing controversy among Veerashaiva lingayats in Karnataka regarding the two sects or divisions. The best that one can say is that the historical evidences presented by the defenders of the sects are fuzzy and unreliable. M. Chidanandamurthy (2000) and Vijayakumar Boratti (2012) have dealt with these issues in detail.

Vachanakaras. This is by referring to the so-called low castes of the saints, poets and heroes of the past. The list continues in many anti-caste arguments—Vyasa was a fisherwoman's son, Valmiki was a hunter, etc. In the Kannada tradition before the *Vachanakaras,* the most powerful critique of caste came from Karna who was denied the opportunity of leading the Kaurava army because of his low caste, being the son of a *suta* (charioteer). We have seen how Pampa, through Karna, fumes against associating the martial values of valour and determination with caste. The early or the 'elderly' *Vachanakaras* also assert the absurdity of caste hierarchies. The other way of denouncing caste is to argue that caste labels are given on the basis of professions, and if all forms of *kayaka* (labour) are equally sacrosanct, these labels should not matter at all.

> One who smelt iron, came to be called a blacksmith.
> He who washed clothes, came to be called a washerman.
> He who laid the warp was called a weaver.
> (translated by the author)

In some *Vachanas* this mode of argument works against itself when certain professions considered demeaning are used to give caste labels. It does not become clear whether the professions themselves are stigmatising. The crucial issue before the *Vachanakara* movement could be stated as follows. The *sharanas* (devotees) were mostly from the artisan class and also from some stigmatised professions. The theory of *kayaka* argued that all forms of labour are equal and all are paths to self-realisation. But outside the community of *sharanas,* how would this equality work in an unequal social world? However, there is no denying that, probably for the first time in Indian history, the untouchable had spoken using a newly forged form of expression.

One of the remarkable *Vachanas* is by a cobbler. He sees Lord Shiva on the tip of the awl he is working with. He says, 'what are you doing here sir? Go to your devotees on the yonder silver mountains where they worship at a temple' (Kalburgi 1993). Other artisan *Vachanakaras* assert vehemently that even a guru or a *Jangama* appearing during the hour of labour is a distraction to be ignored. This runs counter to the assertion that everything should be kept aside to greet a *Jangama.* There are legends embedded in the *Vachanas* in which Shiva tests the devotee by demanding services from his wife. Feminist critics have questioned the 'symbolic' and metaphorical interpretations of these episodes and wondered whether it was a real practice. Even otherwise the exercise of male authority to lend the services of a wife is not an act of devotion (Bannadi 2010). In Harihara's *ragalegalu* (*ragales*, or verse narratives) there are such episodes, and the gift of the wife's services to the *Jangama* is praised as an ultimate act of *bhakti*. When it is revealed that the *Jangama* was Shiva himself who wanted to test the *bhakta*, the crisis is resolved. But this does not mitigate the misuse of male authority. It should also be noted that in Akka Mahadevi, the greatest woman poet of the period, there is not a single *Vachana* glorifying such inhuman trials of the devotee by god or by the *Jangama*. Her poems are replete with images of Chenna Mallikarjuna, her deity, as a playful lover, as her 'true' husband and soul companion. The same is true of Meera's Giridhara Gopala.

One form of resistance to the twin stigmatisation of profession and caste is the sacralisation of the profession, including the tools used in the profession. There is probably no tool or equipment not sanctified by the *Vachanakaras*. Some of the *Vachanakaras* were performing entertainers. Bahurupi Chowdayya feels his job has been usurped by the citizens themselves who are always wearing disguises. In a probably apocryphal tale, Nageya Maritande (literally, one who sells laughter for a livelihood) entertains Shiva himself who appears in disguise as a spectator. Pleased with his performance, Shiva reveals himself and instead of the fee for the entertainment, promises Nageya Maritande a place in Kailasa, the mythical paradise. He bluntly refuses, saying he does not want to be with the lazy ones in Kailasa, who do not earn their living by performing *kayaka*. There is a description in Harihara, which also appears in an extraordinary folk song, in which Shiva dances in joy when he sees the *Vachanakara* saints accepting food in the huts of the untouchable devotees (Kalburgi 2011). Basava describes Shiva as a merchant (Shetty/Harada) who will not let you negotiate the price unless he is convinced. The ferryman Chowdayya says, 'if you are firm of mind, this ferryman will take you to the place without a shore' (Kalburgi 2011). There may not be many other instances of the whole world of work and labour contributing endlessly such metaphors and images to poetry. There may be few parallels to this celebration of work and labour. Such thickness of description itself becomes an assertion of the poetry of work and labour.

The critique of caste in the *Vachanakaras* focuses on the hidden cruelty of ritual sacrifices and ceremonies. In a *Vachana*, Basava addresses a male goat about to be sacrificed and asks it to complain to Shiva about those who want to slaughter it on the pretext of '[mere] words' (the Sastras governing such rituals). In another *Vachana* by Basava, the sheep tied up to be sacrificed soon, to fulfil a vow, keeps jumping to take a bite of the leaves decorating the *pandal*.

> Cry that they kill you for the sake of words
> ...if you cry
> Koodalasangamadeva will do
> what needs to be done. (Swamy 2007, 138)

The brahminical priestly class is constantly ridiculed:

> brother, the ways of these *brahmins*?
> one for themselves, another for the *Sastra*. (Basava in Swamy 2007, 138)

> Like the kingfisher on the bank
> they hold their nose and meditate. (Basava in Swamy 2007, 54)

Basava also refers to stories from the puranas and epics where many great heroes and ascetics were ruined by their trust in brahmins. His anger is roused at the way they mislead common men and women into meaningless rituals and illusion of washing away all sins through sacrifices. Two important Jaina works of the early twelfth century, *Dharmamrutha* and *Samaya Pareekshe*, are far more fiercely critical of brahminical practices than the *Vachanas*. They also come down heavily on the animal sacrifices which accompanied the *yajnas* and *havanas*. Clearly, a powerful critique of the Vedic religious practices had developed over the years as part of the religious strife between Jainism, Shaivism and Vedic brahminism. In some of the *Vachanas* by Basava himself there are attacks on Vaishnavism. What is more significant is the alternative spiritual–ethical religion constructed by the *Vachanakaras*, especially Basava.

'Compassion is the root of religion', says Basava, stating that there is not and cannot be a religion without compassion. As in Buddhism, compassion here is not only for the human but for all living beings (*sakala jeevatmagalige*). This compassion is behind Basava's critique of animal sacrifice. Many of his *Vachanas* describe Vedas and Puranas as the goddess of fate or death (*Māri*) to the goats. Common people are lured into arranging sacrifices under the illusion of attaining a better afterlife.

The collective effort of the *Vachanakaras* was to bring about a major shift in religion, from ritual and sacrifice to the individual search for the ethically good life and the ultimate unity with the divine. Basava prescribes the commandments constituting a personal ethic: 'You shall not steal, You shall not kill, / You shall not lie' (Swamy 2007, 122). In a more traditional register, men are advised not to covet other men's property or desire after their wives. The warning is that all this 'grand show of the world' is impermanent:

> O man,
> The affairs of kings
> The show of wealth
> Are not constant,
> Look
> Kalyana was doomed, devastated. (Basava in Shivaprakash 2010, 63)

However, this needs to be distinguished from the turning away from worldly life preached by other religions. The *Vachanakaras* believe that this world is the 'smithy of the creator' and therefore not to be renounced in disgust, as expressed in the *Vachana* 'Your gift the earth' (Ramanujan 1973, 103) by Basava.

This new orientation was a reaction against the religions which taught that the world was an illusion. It was also a reaction against the brahmins who led a wandering life by renouncing *samsara*. The *Vachanakara* religion is a celebration of the good life. Family life and conjugal happiness are seen as positive values.

> The joy of mating with one's woman
> Eating one's food
> Can any assign it to another. (Basava in Swamy 2007, 128)

The personal ethics advocated by the *Vachanas* is not a set of instructions to be memorised. The temptations of the body and mind are not easy to overcome. What is extraordinary in Basava is the moving, honest record of the struggle to overcome these temptations. He is like a poor beast caught in the swamp bellowing to the lord to help him. He prays to god to make him blind so that 'he won't see this way and that'. This intense, angst-ridden struggle with the conscience makes *bhakti* 'a two-edged saw which cuts when it goes in and cuts when it comes out'. He is the weakest of the weak and feels that his *bhakti* has been a deception, a bag of tricks like the ones known to an acrobat or entertainer. The human soul is like a house. If the dust is not cleared or the front yard is not cleaned up, it is evident that the lord of the house is not here.

This personal ethic is the foundation of the social ethic based on the sacredness of all labour. The social ethic was also against accumulation of property or wealth. Jedara Dasimaiah, the path-breaking *Vachanakara*, speaks about the pride of the wealthy (in Ramanujan 1973). Basava says that those who are 'struck dumb by riches' cannot be made to talk (Ramanujan 1973, 77).

It has been argued that the concept of *dasoha* (literally, feeding the *sharanas*) was introduced so that the excessive wealth accumulated would be spent on the community. There is an interesting legend about Aydakki Marayya who would collect spilled rice grains and sell only enough for livelihood. One day when he collected more grains than necessary, his wife sent him back to return the excess. This was in tune with the protest against monarchy, the feudal system and the greed which drove the merchant class. We do not have detailed historical information of the support the *Vachana* movement received from the merchant class, of the kind we have of the support provided by them to Buddhism. The latter included the building of the *viharas* and *chethavanas* and probably centuries later, the construction of the *stupas* in a grand style (Settar 2007). It is a reasonable surmise that the *Vachanakaras* received support from the traders and the merchants, but the nature of the support is not clear. Much later, during the regime of Praudhadevaraya of the Vijayanagara (fifteenth century), the Lingayats were already a powerful caste comprising both the land-owning communities and the merchant class. However, the utopian ideal for the *Vachanakara* movement was honest labour, avoidance of wealth and the communitarian practice of sharing known as *dasoha*.

To return to the angst of the *sharana*, it is intensely personal and has little reference to the social role one has to play. As pointed out earlier, each *Vachanakara* has his or her own distinctive self, and therefore the path taken by each is different. Akka Mahadevi walked out of home and married life, and declared that the 'husbands of this world' were not for her. Chenna Mallikarjuna was her blemishless husband. She even goes to the extent of naming him the husband inside, and the husband outside as the paramour, and goes on to say that she cannot 'manage them both' (Ramanujan 1973, 127). Hers is the path of sublimating her erotic self into a union with the Lord. This purposiveness also makes her acutely aware of the male gaze which sees her only as a sexualised body. She knows that they look at her rounded breasts and the youthfulness of her body, and think of her only as a female. But she belongs to her lord Chenna Mallikarjuna and appeals to the 'brothers' not to gaze at her. Her love for the lord makes her life a celebration. She asks the birds, bees and flowers if they have seen him. She is the *abhisarika*, the beloved, waiting for her lover. She pleads to all temptations and worldly desires to kindly pause, because she has an urgent letter (*ole*) for the lord. She sees the lord in the form of a young *gorava* (ascetic, or one who might take a vow to become one): 'I saw the lord, white as Jasmine / And woke wide open' (in Ramanujan 1973, 124).

Akka Mahadevi is undoubtedly among the greatest love poets of the world. As poets, only Basava and Akka Mahadevi among the *Vachanakaras* possess the sense of form, the ability to discover the music of poetry (as T. S. Eliot defines it) and the near perfect ability to choose the right image. Their poetry has mastery over various tones with which they 'dramatise' themselves. Akka Mahadevi has no interest at all in the gender stereotypes and ideas of essential 'femininity'. Like Dasimaiah and Basava, she believes in the fluidity of gender. As she warns her lord, if he challenges her she will wear her sari in a *veeragachche* (warrior) style and ride a horse like a warrior queen, and do what all men can (in Swamy 2007, 28). She will ride on the hills and blow the horn (*kombu*) to see her lord.

The philosophical roots of this belief in the fluidity of gender can be found in the primacy of 'becoming' over 'being'. In the intense process of fashioning the self, the *Vachanakaras* treat the static aspect of 'being' as comparable to *sthavara* (the standing, the unchanging, the static). The *sthalas*, or the stages, in the spiritual progress of the self (which are enumerated as six in the Veerashaiva theology), are also supportive of a dynamic conception of the progress of the self. Given this philosophical acceptance of fluidity and change, the *telos* of human life seems to be an endless 'becoming'. The union with the divine may be the end of becoming. It is the *shunya*, the state which Buddhism considered the ultimate liberation, which the *Vachanakaras* translate as '*bayalu*'. A very complex word, *bayalu* can mean the plain, the open field, as against *alaya*, the dwelling place, but the connotative meanings are open to many interpretations. The other word used is '*nirvayalu*', meaning 'to go beyond', or no longer accessible to the senses. For the *sharana*, it indicates a state of oneness with the divine which is beyond articulation and words. The frequently used term is '*shabda mugudanagu*' (that is, a stage when you become innocent of the word itself). That is a spiritual experience which can only be expressed by silence. Or as Allama describes, it is like the silence inside the word itself. (The Kannada word *shabda* means both 'sound' and 'word'.) In the *Shunya Sampadane* there is an interesting debate between Muktayakka and Allama. Muktayakka argues that if the experience of the transcendental is beyond the limits of language, it can be articulated only in silence and not words, and that a mystic who has had the experience should not speak about it.[3]

[3] For a detailed discussion see Nugadoni 2002.

Allama admits the logic of her argument, but takes the view that there is a need to communicate the experience. This is somewhat surprising because Allama's *Vachanas* are centrally about the limits of language and poetic expression. He uses the *bedagu* mode of *Vachanas* far more effectively than the major *Vachanakaras* (Basavaraju 2001, 26–27). The *bedagu* mode is densely metaphorical and uses a code of metaphysical expression. It also uses paradoxes profusely. This was an accepted mode of writing, though it contrasted with the major mode of *Vachana* writing which was transparent, lucid and addressed the listener directly. The *bedagu Vachanas* of Allama are about the frontiers of language. He rejects the established poetic practices of the tradition as the 'chatter of parrots'. He seeks a mode of expression which breaks the conventional bond between word and meaning. He experiments with 'dislocating language into meaning', as Ezra Pound would put it.

> I saw
> Intellect fleeing
> When the heart came
> ...
> The temple fleeing (Allama in Shivaprakash 2010, xxxviii)

The awareness of the two levels of language—the social and the communicative on the one hand, the private and self-circumscribed on the other—is seen in all the *Vachanakaras*. The popular *tatwapadakara* tradition in rural Karnataka is proof that the language of the mystics has not been a barrier to communication.

Basava also sought metaphors to explore the nature of language. His emphasis is on the unity of language and action. The authenticity of the spoken word is substantiated by action. In a special sense, the spoken word is a speech act.

> Speech should be like a string of pearls
> Speech should be like the flash of ruby
> Speech should be like the bar of crystal
> Speech should make the Linga say Yes, Yes.
> If you don't act within the bounds of your words
> How will you win Kudala Sangama's love. (Basava in Swamy 2007, 133)

The spoken word should be self-translucent; but unless it is accompanied by the act, it shall not please the lord. Basava also reflects on the 'steps of words' (*shabda sopana*) built by the predecessors (elders) to help one to reach the truth. Veerashaiva theory also contributed a set of binaries—'*aruhu*' and '*kuruhu*'. *Kuruhu* is the sign which may be verbal or non-verbal.

It is only a sign and there is no need to make a fetish out of it. *Aruhu* is not the signified but knowledge itself. There is a complex relationship between the sign and the knowledge which is reached through the sign but transcends it.

In his *Allama Prabhu Mattu Shaiva Pratibhe* (1999), D. R. Nagaraj offers a radical critique of the *Rasa* theory in the Indian aesthetic philosophical tradition. In order to defend it, he offers a framework to understand the nature of the original philosophical argument/school and the protests against it emerging from within. The latter appear to be so deviant that they seem to abandon the original altogether, but ultimately end up transforming the original and becoming a part of it. He also describes the philosophical debates as veritable battles: '. . . the major position of opposition of Allama in the Indian literary thought and history of poetry is owing to his attitude towards *Rasa* theory' (48–49). Nagaraj sees Allama as a key figure in the medieval interface between the Sanskrit cosmopolis and the vernacular cosmopolis. The most significant event in the medieval period was the attempt made by the vernacular cosmopolis[es] to reformulate themselves by confronting the Sanskrit cosmopolis. He finds two major approaches in a language like Kannada during this confrontation. One is the 'universal *Desi*' in which the *Desi* elements accommodate themselves to the Sanskrit model. The other is the 'regional *Desi*' which leads a rebellion not only against Sanskrit poetics but also against a whole set of social and religious beliefs and practices which go with the Sanskrit cosmopolis. According to Nagaraj, it was Allama who had the philosophical wherewithal to lead this metaphysical rebellion. He ended up developing the most comprehensive critique of the *Rasa* tradition, not merely as an aesthetic tradition, but as a philosophical tradition which had its roots in the Kashmiri mystical Shaiva traditions.

Nagaraj elaborates his thesis in an important essay collected in *Listening to the Loom* (2012):

> Allama is essentially attacking the notion that *Sringara* can be the modality of experiencing the divine. Unlike Bhoja, he cannot accept that *Sringara* can become a vehicle of *Prakasa*, a *Saiva* category for the absolute. Allama is not only quarrelling with Abhinavagupta and the other champions of rasa theory, he is also objecting to poetic practices of his own contemporary, Akka Mahādevi. She was the first poet to perfect the model of *Sringara Bhakti*, and later even male poets used this image, imagining themselves to be female. But Allama refutes such feminization of the self as the mode of memory and desire. (87)

What needs to be noted here is that the Kannada *Vachanakaras* who were thoroughly immersed in the Indian metaphysical traditions had many more quarrels with these traditions. The exclusive emphasis on the *Vachanakara* movement as a collective social protest and a movement of the working class has marginalised this philosophical dimension of the *Vachanas*. Nagaraj attempts to locate the *Vachanakaras* in the larger space of the pan-Indian aesthetic–philosophical debates of the medieval period.

In contrast to Allama, Basava constructs his own poetics of the spoken word as an alternative to the literary poetics of the past. He prays to his 'lord of the meeting rivers' to 'play your thirty-two songs' (Ramanujan 1973, 83). In another well-known *Vachana*, Basava says that he does not know 'time-beats' or 'metre', or 'the count of iambs and dactyl'. He asserts, 'I'll sing as I love' (Ramanujan 1973, 82).

In these *Vachanas* there is a deliberate rejection of formal prosody, rhyme scheme and the counting of syllables and feet. Instead, there is the defence of spontaneity and self-expression. Such poetics of the transparent self should not deceive us into believing that the *Vachanas* are artless poetry. Nor are they gnostic, philosophical prose statements. Some such misconception had led the scribes and copyists to use the format of prose while inscribing the *Vachanas*. F. G. Halakatti and S. S. Basavanal, two of the foremost modern editors of the *Vachanas*, had to 'rediscover' them as poems (Boratti 2012). The analysis of five *Vachanas* by the New Critic M. G. Krishnamurthy, followed by those by H. M. Channaiah (*Jijnase*), unravelled the rich texture of the *Vachanas*. The very understanding of the Kannada poetic tradition remained seriously flawed until the 'discovery' of the *Vachanas*. Their discovery and their dissemination was part of the Lingayat community's struggle to establish its identity in the modern period. This received massive support from the Lingayat monasteries and by the government. The Kannada music industry has also played a major role in the dissemination of the *Vachanas*. It was the progressive writer Aa. Na. Kra. (A. N. Krishna Rao) who not only wrote extensively on the Veerashaiva tradition but also encouraged Mallikarjun Mansur, the legendary Hindustani vocalist, to render the *Vachanas* (Jangamashetty 2016, 95). Kannada films have also contributed to popularising the Veerashaiva saints and their *Vachanas*. These films are part of the Indian film world's preoccupation with the Bhakti traditions. As it happens in literary historiography, the dissemination and reception of literary texts is always bound up with the hegemony of a certain class—in this case, of a dominant caste in Karnataka.

The *Vachanakartis*

The volume containing the *Vachanas* by the women poets of the twelfth century, published by the Government of Karnataka and edited by Veeranna Rajur, has 1104 *Vachanas* by as many as thirty-three women poets. This is probably unprecedented in the history of any sociocultural, literary movement. More significantly, these women poets are from all social locations—from aristocratic oligarchy to the lowest 'untouchable' castes. Most of them are wives of the *sharanas* who chose to follow Basava and others. Though the Alwars and the Nayanars in Tamil Nadu included women poets, there is nothing to match the number and diversity of the women *Vachanakartis*. It was part of the Bhakti traditions in India to believe that 'the soul has no gender' and nothing should prevent women from becoming devotees. This was a strongly held belief among the *Vachanakaras* too. For instance, Jedara Dasimaiah, the 'elder' predecessor of Basava, says that the 'self that hovers' between gender markers 'Is neither man / Nor woman' (Ramanujan 1973, 27).These images are repeated in many *Vachanas*. Basava in an astounding *Vachana* says that 'Sometimes I am man / Sometimes I am woman' (Ramanujan 1973, 87).

The women poets are not passive obedient followers of their husbands' new religion. They are fully individuated and highly gifted with critical intelligence and at times sharp in their critique of empty rituals and practices. Akka Mahadevi is the tallest figure among them and one of the greatest poets in Kannada. There is no clarity in the historical circumstances which made her walk out of her marriage with Koushika who could have been the head of a small fiefdom. Legend has it that she walked out in the nude, reached Kalyana, took active part in the movement, and then travelled to Kadali (near Srisailam in Andhra Pradesh) and united with her lord Chenna Mallikarjuna. There was also Neelambike, the wife of Basava who chose to remain in Kalyana after Basava had left. As mentioned earlier, there is Sankavve who had been a prostitute. Only one of her *Vachanas* has survived. Amuge Rayamma is probably the harshest critic of those who pose as savants and mystics:

> Lust before the eyes, desire before the mind
> And the body filled with pride,
> Would I call them mystics? (in Kalburgi 2016, 854; translated by the author)

The women write in a common register of concepts, metaphors and analogies shared by their male counterparts. Their distinctive voices are heard when they criticise the patriarchy which treats women as objects of lust. Though couched in the traditional language of ethics and morality, the women poets are writing about the unbridled desires of men. Even the ascetics and savants are not free from slavery to Kama, the god of desire. Many of the women are from the artisan and working classes, and employ metaphors taken from their labour. They also adhere to the strict code of *kayaka* which has to be performed without any greed. However, hardly any of them raise questions of the kind Akka Mahadevi does, regarding the male gaze, marriage and companionship. According to the *Shunya Sampadane*, she faces the ordeal of proving her chastity before being admitted to the community of the *sharanas*. The episode is highly controversial and some scholars say it is a later interpolation. Even as an interpolation, it is one of the ugliest instances of a woman's ordeal.

For feminist writings in Kannada, Akka Mahadevi has been the greatest influence. She is seen as a rebel and a radical dissenter. Her presence has also been used to critically examine the attitudes of the *sharanas* towards gender issues. M. S. Ashadevi (2004), for instance, scrutinises the *Vachanas* of Basava and finds him wanting on many counts. She argues that for him, the women's question did not appear to be as central as his other preoccupations such as the caste system, untouchability and false Vedic practices. Apart from reiterating that men and women are equal as members of the *sharana* community and that the human soul is not gendered, Basava does not pay much attention to women's condition in society. When he does talk about women, he regresses into two stereotypes—the woman as '*maya*', the luring illusion, and the woman as the ideal wife. Ashadevi finds it disturbing that Basava is unable to go beyond these stereotypes. It is true that many mystical traditions consider this world to be an illusion and *sansara* as something to be renounced. The *Vachanakaras* also express such a sentiment, though as explained earlier, they do not advocate renunciation. They believe in the ethically good life and in the happiness of married life. Why then do they use this rhetoric of world as an illusion? Why is the woman described as *maya*? This occurs in almost all major male *Vachanakaras*. There are different perspectives which, however, are marginalised. Akka Mahadevi says that just as a skilled snake charmer can handle the snake, one can handle the body too. Allama says,

> They say woman is *maya*;
> Woman is not *maya*
> The desire before the mind is *maya*. (in Swamy 2007, 88)

Instead, what proliferates in the *Vachanas* is the negative image of the woman as untrustworthy, vulnerable to desire and an obstacle to one's spiritual quest. The contradiction between believing that the soul is ungendered and also believing that the woman as a real person is untrustworthy, remains unresolved.

The other stereotype is of the good wife, the ideal *Sati*. The adjective ubiquitously used for the good wife is 'obedient', the one who knows her husband's wishes and acts accordingly. A number of *Vachanas* insist that the good wife should accept the *sharana* religion. The husband being a *sharana* and the wife being a superstitious worshipper of many gods is seen as a disaster. There is no indication if a different religion could be her own choice or if she can exercise her choice. Unfortunately, the women poets do not talk about their struggle in giving up the old faith to accept the new religion.

What is far more jarring is the willingness of the *sharana* to offer his wife to the *Jangama* as a mark of absolute devotion. In a *Vachana*, Basava says that if god were to appear in the form of a *Jangama* and demand the services of his wife and then were to make love to her in his presence, he would not protest. He believes that it is a gift he has made to god as *Jangama*. As M. S. Ashadevi points out, the willingness of the wife is not even considered. To say that it is to god that Basava gifts his wife, and that it is a metaphor for the absolute devotion to god, is a weak defence. Interestingly, Mamata G. Sagar has an essay on Kabir (2007) where her arguments about Kabir's stereotypical images of women are exactly the same as Ashadevi's about Basava. Were the radical mystical traditions unable to transcend the blindness of patriarchy? If so, how are they any different from the more openly patriarchal institutionalised religions? Was their achievement only that they allowed the distinctive voices of the women saints to be heard?

FIVE

Medieval Literature

1

The early medieval society in *Kannadanādu* is characterised by two features—its development as an increasingly mercantile society and sectarian strife. The inscriptions of the time speak of a coalition between the monarchies, the powerful merchant associations, and of land grants and patronage to several religious sects. The numerous references to a large number of taxes in the inscriptions and literary works indicate an efficient bureaucratisation of the administration with the monarchy supporting the local power of the merchant associations. Several main cities and towns flourished on the trade routes to such an extent that some of them, like Lakkundi, possessed their own mint and currency. The agrarian wealthy class and the merchant community shared power over the local society, contributing to its development. Shetty/Setti (*Shreshti*), Pattana Setti/ Shetty and related terms, along with *Nakara*, support the view that there was considerable urbanisation and growth of a mercantile economy. Jaina writers, such as Nayasena and Brahmashiva, not only describe the prosperity of the merchant class but also strongly advocate the values of renunciation of wealth and power. This ambivalence is seen in the portrayal of many merchants as practitioners of the Jaina faith while preaching the impossibility of salvation without absolute renunciation. Critics have argued that the ambivalence itself is a critique of the heartless urban, mercantile world.

Sectarian strife had a long history and it is difficult to surmise just when it became intolerant and even violent. There are also arguments regarding the nature and extent of religious conversions (Devadevan 2016). Did these affect the lives of the majority of ordinary men and women? Were they confined to the elite classes? What actual impact did the conversions of the royal personages have on the power structure? There are references in Harihara and Nayasena to kings and princes supporting sectarian strife and even participating in the destruction of temples and *basadis*. Most of such legends seem to be exaggerated accounts of the consequences of sectarian strife which were real. Many of the Shaiva devotees and heroes of Harihara's tales passionately believe in killing those who oppose and derogate Shaivism. Some of the honorific titles of the rulers of the age describe them as destroyers of 'false faiths/sects'. Probably the entire medieval period witnessed the co-existence of sectarian faith, constantly changing royal patronage of the sects, and a growing mercantile economy, and a powerful and wealthy elite class pursuing worldly pleasures.

What then was the real impact of the *Vachanakara* movement of the twelfth century with its radical egalitarian spiritual world view? Was it only a brief interregnum while the driving historical and economic forces went on uninterrupted creating a society which became more unequal and hierarchical? Recent scholarship has tried to sift through the latter-day reconstructions of the popular historical memories of the *Vachanakara* movement in order to arrive at an objective understanding of what really happened during the period. Surprisingly, the inscriptions of the period are almost silent about the radical movement at Bijjala's Kalyana. References to Basava and other leaders are few and all too brief in the inscriptions. The literary Puranas of the thirteenth century, originally written in Telugu on Basava, can hardly be construed as historical evidence. Historians are therefore left with thousands of *Vachanas* collected and edited from the period of Praudhadevaraya of the Vijayanagara empire (fifteenth century). The details of the social world in the *Vachanas* are so rich, dense and variegated that they cannot be brushed aside as 'literary texts'. What is indubitable is that there was a powerful community of Veerashaiva saints and their followers from all artisan communities and the lower castes as well as from the dominant castes. It is also evident that the spiritual philosophy of the *Vachanakaras* was radically anti-caste and egalitarian. What is uncertain is whether the movement made an actual impact on the hierarchical social structures and the temporal politics of the later period.

It is this enquiry which makes Harihara (twelfth century), the author of *Girija Kalyana* and the *Ragales*, an iconic and important writer. Even with the usual uncertainty about dates, it is clear that he lived and wrote in less than a few generations after the end of the *Vachanakara* movement. It has to be assumed that he knew a great deal about the movement and the popular memories of the leading *Vachanakaras*. His *Ragales* are powerful narratives about Shaiva devotees and saints, many of whom are from the lowest castes and professions derided as 'untouchable'. They are hunters, potters, untouchable forest dwellers, performers and boatmen. They are celebrated as staunch devotees of Shiva and either indifferent or openly hostile to all centres of power, including monarchy. Almost invariably, in Harihara's narratives it is Lord Shiva himself who is overwhelmed by their devotion and is cowed into obedience. In at least two tales, Shiva even acts as a go-between (*kuntini*) for them to fulfil their sexual desires. He also appears in several disguises to put them on trial, or to test their faith, but ultimately liberates them, and often also takes them away to his heavenly abode. The caste radicalism of the *Vachanakaras* is transformed in these tales into a confrontation between orthodox, high-caste practices and the actual lives of these saints; and expectedly the saints triumph over their adversaries. The orthodox practices include religious rituals, modes of worship, food habits and notions of purity and impurity. The triumph of the saints over the orthodoxy takes various forms such as persuasion, conversion, humiliation and, though rarely, violence. The poet is emphatic about the triumph and ends his tales hastily by making Shiva himself declare it. There are also many instances when Shiva brings his consort Parvati to witness the trial and triumph of his devotees. In fact, the fixed and predictable pattern in the *Ragales* is that of trial and triumph with the divine intervention of Shiva himself.

Critics have noted the excesses and improprieties Harihara commits in his haste to celebrate the lives of his saint–heroes (Veeranna 2011). For example, making Shiva himself openly encourage the hero to destroy religious structures of the other sects and justifying the saint's violence, are in contradiction to the declared beliefs of the *Vachanakaras*. It appears as though the roots of Harihara's Bhakti are in the Shaiva sects outside those that are practised by the *Vachanakaras*. This should also explain why Harihara's *Ragales* about Basava, Allama and Akka Mahadevi are among his least successful works. All three make very brief references to the spiritual movement; and even Basava's confrontations with Bijjala, the king, and orthodox brahmins who conspire against him, are 'political' triumphs with little of the spiritual concerns of Basava as reflected in his *Vachanas*.

Harihara's literary contribution lies in perfecting the form *Ragale* which is a loose flowing verse narrative, mixing prose and verse and using the resources of the regional *Desi*, as D. R. Nagaraj terms it (Nagaraj 2014). He invented a distinctive poetic style with strong rhymes, repetitive structures, colloquial expressions, and alternation between the lyrical mode and the dialogic mode. He is a great master of rhetorical skills though vulnerable to verbal excesses and jarring over-emphasis. This style presupposes a comprehensive rejection of the Sanskrit-centric *Champu* mode which he himself uses effectively in his epic *Girija Kalyana*. This work is remarkable for its portrayal of Girija (Parvati) who is a powerful, autonomous determined female figure triumphing over Shiva, the reluctant hermit.

Despite the lapses of taste and propriety in blindly following the classical eighteen descriptions, Harihara demonstrates his extraordinary poetic skills in making the *Champu* mode perform functions which it had not done in the hands of the previous poets.

The *Ragales* are closer in spirit and style to the *Desi* traditions though they were listed as part of the Sanskrit poetic repertory of verse forms. As literary historians point out, very few later poets were able to use the *Ragale* form with the exuberant energy of Harihara. He seems to have made a return to the classical Sanskrit-centric mode impossible for the later poets. Though many of these poets continued to use traditional forms such as *Shatpadi*, Harihara's poetic works proved in many ways a watershed in the tradition.

The social energy released by the *Vachanakara* movement did impact the literary sensibility of the times. Ordinary individuals from the lowest castes and classes appear in Harihara's *Ragales* as spiritual heroes who challenge both temporal and religious authority. This happens for the first time in the Kannada literary tradition. However, as G. S. Shivarudrappa points out, while the presence of these individuals is a radical phenomenon in Kannada poetry, they appear as devotees or *bhaktas*, first and foremost. Their social world, except for some physical details, is largely absent in the narratives (Shivarudrappa 2017). Veeranna is also of similar opinion. Harihara's sole focus is on their *bhakta* selves, and not on the social self, a product of the material conditions they belong to. Though some of the *Ragales* end with Shiva agreeing to take the entire community along with the saint to his heavenly abode, there is no hint of a significant relationship between the saint and the community.

Harihara's poetry also reiterates the *Vachanakara* belief in the sanctity of all professions including the stigmatised 'lowly' professions. Shiva himself literally adores the saint–devotees from the untouchable communities. This is of a piece with the Bhakti tradition of spiritual equality and dignity which does not itself ensure a change in the *Varna* or caste structure. Harihara skirts around the issue of purity and caste by introducing an obligatory ritual of purification before the saint enters the heavenly abode.

Equally important is the presence of strong women characters who adhere to the Shaiva faith in the midst of social pressures. They are shown as willing to bear ostracisation and physical torture to keep their sectarian loyalty intact. But Harihara's *Ragale* on Akka Mahadevi, the greatest woman saint–poet, is disappointing and contradictory. In the *Ragale*, she does not renounce marriage though she imposes certain conditions on Kaushika, her husband. These conditions have to do with her freedom to receive and entertain the *Jangama* priests. Her journey to Kalyana and participation in the *Anubhava Mantapa* are given short shrift.

Harihara's *Ragale* on Basava is said to be a truncated version with many sections missing for unknown reasons. The extant version does depict in some detail Basava's confrontation with Bijjala and orthodox brahmins of his entourage. But these encounters are enveloped in miraculous events and appear to be rhetorical strategies with little significance. This is surprising because Harihara reveals an extensive knowledge of many of the Tamil saints (known as the 'elders') probably from the Tamil works on them. Why then are the three *Ragales* on the leading twelfth-century saints so sketchy? The later *Shunya Sampadane* versions from the fifteenth century treat Allama as a spiritual leader fit to ascend the spiritual seat known as the *Shunya Simhasana.* In Harihara's *Ragale*, Allama's love life with Kamalathe is far more detailed and poetically impressive than his later transformation as a saint. This is sometimes considered as the reason for the rejection of Harihara's work by the orthodox Lingayat community. The other reason being his depiction of the saints as Shiva's *ganas* sent to the earth for either their misdemeanours or for allowing them to enjoy earthly pleasures.

A matter of serious concern is the condonation of violence against the other sects, in many *Ragales*. The violence is directed against the Vedic-brahminical and Jaina sects and takes the form of killings or desecration of temples and Jaina *basadis.* Harihara seems to accept such sectarian intolerance as justified. Similar condonation is extended to the insensitive actions of the saints. In such cases, one wonders how poetic talent of the highest order was employed by Harihara for such narrow sectarian strife. Feminist readings of the *Ragales* have pointed out how they narrate the male saints are willing to permit their wives to 'render services' to the visiting *Jangama* priests, without seeking the women's consent. The women in these *Ragales* are autonomous only as devotees of Shiva, but not as women. Harihara's poetry accommodates patriarchal attitudes towards women, except when they act under the compulsion of devotion to their sect. L. G. Meera also discusses the trope of the woman as an erotic figure in the *Ragales* (Meera 2003).

In an insightful analysis in his book, *Siva's Saints*, Gil Ben-Herut (2018) argues that in the *Ragales*, 'there is no systematized theological framework', nor a 'specific sectarian identity' (13). He believes that these were made specific only in the fifteenth century when the *Vachanas* were compiled. The devotees in Harihara do not follow a specific form of worship either.

It is certainly true that 'the age of compilation and consolidation' of the Lingayat religion witnessed a reconstruction of the tradition of the *Vachanakaras*, and this effort replaced the open-ended fuzziness with rigidity. However, Harihara's *Ragales* do not present as open a stance as Ben-Herut describes. The community of Lingayats seems to have become 'bounded' by Harihara's time, at least in the intolerance towards other faiths.

A similar strain of sectarianism seems to colour the Jaina works of the early medieval period. In the previous chapter, it has been clearly suggested that this was the result of the insecurity owing to the loss of royal patronage to the Jaina religion, and the ascendance of the Vedic-brahminical and Shaiva religions. In addition, the Jaina narrative tradition always had a sectarian and proselytising component. This is largely true of Nayasena's *Dharmamrutha* (1112 CE). This is a work consisting of a number of tales, each designated to deal with one of the virtuous practices or noble values of Jainism. Though written with such a pedagogic purpose, the tales are lively, earthy and written in a poetic idiom described by Nayasena himself as 'new Kannada'. He also opposed the unnecessary mixing of Sanskrit and Kannada. His plain advice is, 'If you can say it in Kannada, do so'. His own poetic style has the rugged strength of the spoken idiom suffused with everyday expressions and proverbs. He is also the master of the 'garland of similes' with similes cascading to describe a single thing. This resonates well with the highly variegated social world he portrays in the tales. It is a Chaucerian world of characters from all professions, with thieves, prostitutes, farmers, merchants, soldiers, etc. There is also delightful wit and humour in the narration and descriptions. Though Nayasena is clear about his propagandist purpose, he does not express sectarian hatred in his satirical tales. As a Jaina monk, he believes staunchly that the Jaina religion is supreme and that other faiths are false and misleading. He directs his satire against the practitioners of other faiths but avoids the virulence of Brahmashiva, the other prominent Jaina poet of the period and author of *Samaya Pareekshe.*

Nayasena's characters are fascinatingly unredeemed and unrepentant until they are converted. They are denizens of a social world in which wealth and power are real. It is not easy for them to transcend this world and its temptations, despite the Jaina religion's promise of an afterlife which is depicted as full of sensuous pleasures. If anything, the promised world of a new cycle of lives and endless pleasure is only a magnified image of what the unredeemed human beings aspire for. Owing to their clinging to earthly passions and pleasures, they also get trapped in deception and crime. The tale of the great thief who transforms himself into a Jaina monk in order to steal a fabulous jewel from a merchant is an example. There are also unruly young men and princes who run riot, carousing with prostitutes and vandalising homes and markets, and even turning into notorious dacoits. But in the Jaina scheme of things, if a person is an *asannabhavya* (the elect), a moment of epiphany will make him renounce the old life. The impulse to renounce comes with the realisation of the transitoriness of every worldly thing. There is also no explanation why an individual is recognised as the elect. It is always a Jaina *rishi* or monk who does the act of recognition and who, in many instances, also becomes the mentor. Often the mentor is a devoted friend who is reborn until he succeeds in converting the individual to the Jaina faith. Interestingly, quite often the mentor happens to be a merchant who is wealthy and successful, and not a renouncer. As critics have pointed out, the elect are always from the elite classes—royalty, courtiers and merchants (Visaji 2008). Despite the egalitarian religious ideology promising liberation to all classes, caste and *Varna* prejudices remain unquestioned in these narratives. If the low-caste saints in Harihara are portrayed as devotees and therefore free from the pollution of caste and class, the lower-class characters in Nayasena bring in a social world of difference. It is understood that they do not qualify for emancipation. Though individuals from the brahmin and vaishya *Varnas* become deluded by the false faith (*mithyadrishti*, i.e., false vision, illusion), they have the chance to convert themselves to the *Samyakjnana* which is Jainism. Literary texts of the period occupy an ambivalent space between egalitarian religious ideologies and an unequal hierarchical social world. They derive their significance by their ability to explore the individual self struggling to obtain salvation in this ambivalent space.

Raghavanka's *Harishchandra Charitra* (c. 1185 CE) has successfully occupied its place in the popular and literary domains since its composition. It was composed probably a few decades after the end of the *Vachanakara* movement and is self-consciously a Shaiva work dedicated to Lord Shiva, specifically to Pampapati, the deity enshrined at Hampi, the locale of the Vijayanagara empire and the geo-poetic cosmos of Raghavanka's imagination. In her introduction to the English translation of the poem, Vanamala Viswanatha (2017) comments on how Raghavanka transforms King Harishchandra, the king of Ayodhya, into a 'Kannada king' and practically a denizen of Hampi. This is in the tradition of Pampa and Ranna who had allegorised their patrons as characters in the *Mahabharata*, thereby laying down a poetic mode in which the local and the regional is elevated to the pan-Indian. A host of critics such as Kuvempu, G. S. Shivarudrappa and others have commented on another transformation which they consider 'a miracle'. The sources of the legend of Harishchandra go back to the Vedas, Puranas and the *Bhagavata*. In most of these sources, Harishchandra is a deceiver who cheats Varuna by not sacrificing his son as promised, and sends someone else in his place. In Raghavanka's work, he becomes the very epitome of truthfulness. This is also the position he occupies in the popular imagination. It appears as though by the time of Raghavanka's work, the transformation of the Harishchandra story had taken place.

Raghavanka, a Shaiva brahmin, did not follow the example of his maternal uncle, the poet Harihara, of writing hagiographies of the Veerashaiva saints. A very popular legend in Kannada narrates that Harihara slapped Raghavanka so angrily for writing a poem celebrating a *Bhavi* and a king, that he knocked off some of the latter's teeth. Raghavanka, however, went on to compose a few hagiographies.

A more important question is regarding the relationship of Raghavanka's poem with the *Vachanakara* movement in the ethos and the normative values it embodies. G. H. Nayak (2006) has argued cogently that in the first six cantos of the poem Harishchandra is portrayed conventionally as a king exhibiting his stupendous wealth and power and indulging in sensual pleasures. He is divided between loyalty to the family traditions (*kulaachara*) as an upper-caste scion of the renowned *Surya Vamsha* and *Ikshwaku* dynasty, and his newly discovered loyalty to truthfulness. This leads to the unreconciled contradictions in the text. As part of the ordeals he goes through, designed by the *rishi* Viswamitra, he is lured and pressurised by two *holatis* (women of the untouchable caste, also known as *anamika* or 'unnamable') who insist on his marrying them. The text forewarns the readers that the two women who have entertained Harishchandra are *maayabale* (or illusionary women figures created by Viswamitra). Raghavanka takes care to repeatedly describe them as 'dark products of evil' whose intention is to make the king break his vow of truth. However, while refusing to accept them, Harishchandra argues that it would be against his *kulaachara* (which also means adhering to the *Varna* and caste norms) to marry untouchable women. He has no answers to the probing question they raise when he also refuses to gift them the royal umbrella. Their question is: if feasting on their shapely forms did not defile him, how would touching them defile him?

> How is it that only our token is defiling?
> How is it that, among the five composite senses,
> One is superior and the other four inferior? (Viswanatha 2017, 329)

In fact, the long debate between the king and the women is one ordeal in which he fails miserably. He is so enraged at their threats to demean him that, '… He seized a whip even as his minister tried to restrain him, and thrashed them both shinning their backs, breaking their teeth, lacerating their mouths, dragging them by the hair, and beating their bodies to a pulp' (Viswanatha 2017, 333). Surely such caste-centric gender violence could not have been possible to imagine, if the radical egalitarian philosophy of the *Vachanakaras* had not already been pushed to the margins.

Traditional Kannada literary criticism has tried verbal acrobatics to defend Raghavanka by reiterating that the two women were not born 'untouchable'. They were creations of Viswamitra. A proper reading of the text confirms that the ethos of which it is a product is the conservative ethos framed by a firm belief in the *Varna* and caste hierarchies. Nor is the episode of the two women an insignificant digression. Caste and untouchability are central to the poem as thematic and problematic. When Harishchandra is forced to sell himself to Virabahuka, the 'untouchable' keeper of the cemetery, who eats beef and drinks toddy from a human skull, his lamentation is about how destiny has made a high-born king live like a *holeya*. In the last episode of the poem when Harishchandra swings the axe to execute his wife Chandramati (who is wrongly accused of killing the young prince), Lord Shiva appears and resolves the ordeals of Harishchandra. Again, when the king repeats that he has been defiled by his living like a *holeya*, the consolation by Lord Shiva, obviously meant to be central to the poem, is: 'A sage who lies is a *Holeya,* a *Holeya* who does not lie is a noble sage' (Viswanatha 2017, 595). This refers to one of the discourses on caste seen in the *Vachanas* too: caste has no relation to birth; it is wrongly attributed to profession; anyone can become a *sharana* by converting to the new faith and by developing noble qualities. This discourse was found palatable by a society which had returned to the *Varna* and caste hierarchies after the brief interregnum of the *Vachanakara* movement. The movement had created consciousness about these unjust hierarchies and Raghavanka's society had to negotiate with it. The poem reinforces the social structures even while bringing in counter-discourses of caste.

Kuvempu interprets the ordeals of Harishchandra as a continuous denuding of the self. From a renowned king, he loses everything he possesses including his caste. Only when he is purified thus, he becomes worthy of Lord Shiva's intervention (Viswanatha 2017). G. H. Nayak disagrees by demonstrating the contradictions which Harishchandra is unable to resolve. At the end of the poem, Harishchandra is reinstated as king, regaining all that he had lost, and in fact with enhanced worldly splendour.

Raghavanka's achievement as a poet was to break away from the *Champu* mode which had very strong affiliations to the pan-Indian Sanskrit poetic conventions. He uses the *Shatpadi* stanza and experiments with the *Desi* in remarkable ways. The poem is a linguistic treasure house, a compendium of all the characteristics of the Kannada speech of the times. Despite lapses into scholastic, ornate writing, Raghavanka creates an energetic and vigorous poetic style. Among the Kannada classics which continue to be rendered in the musical recitation known as *gamaka*, *Harishchandra Charitra* has retained its popularity. It is another example of a poem which exploits the power of the *Desi* in order to reinforce a conservative ideology. Raghavanka was also probably the first great poet to choose a universal theme, i.e., truthfulness, which has no affiliation to any single religious sect or faith.

In the satirical work *Samaya Pareekshe*, Brahmashiva subjects other sects, beliefs and religious practices to scathing scrutiny, employing an instrumentalist rationality. He questions and ridicules the major religious texts such as the Vedas and the *Bhagavad Gita*, and the great epics the *Ramayana* and *Mahabbharata,* with a simple sleight of hand: of treating imaginative, symbolic works as texts for literal reading. The intention is to demonstrate the illogicality and irrationality of many of the beliefs (other than those of the Jaina religion). Expectedly, epic figures and gods become the butt of ridicule. This is similar to the rhetorical strategies used by the Christian missionaries in the colonial period. In fact, in the unending sectarian debates of the times, this strategy was employed by all propagandists. Brahmashiva's *Samaya Pareekshe* (which literally means 'interrogation of religious sects') eschews serious philosophical reflection and settles down to virulent satire and polemics. However, the wit, hyperbole and word play are comparable to that of the polemical satirists of seventeenth- and eighteenth-century England, and to some of the French encyclopaedists.

It appears that the hegemony of religion has to be understood as operating simultaneously at several levels. The works of Pampa and Ranna, although written in a theological framework, are able to offer a complex view of the dialectical relationship between the temporal and transcendental domains. The history of the time is also unobtrusively inscribed into their works such as *Samaya Pareekshe* which reduce religion to a narrow, fixed sect. Janna's *Yashodhara Charite*, composed about a century later, is a complexly structured work which seriously examines both the vulnerability of human passions to destruction and the uncertain power of religion to discipline them. It is also a self-declared assertion of the greatness of the Jaina religion. The framing story is about King Maridatta who has ordered a human sacrifice for the goddess Mari. His deputy Chanda Karma brings two young boys, one of whom blesses the king advising him to follow the right religion. Impressed by the nobility of the boy the king asks him to narrate his story, and what follows is the story of the cycle of many lives of King Yashodhara and Amrutamati, his queen. The more significant framing of the narrative is provided by the images of the natural world suggesting violence and torture. The narrative has to move from the sacrificial violence of the 'popular' religion to the new (*Naya*) religion or the religion of non-violence. Later, the story of Yashodhara, Amrutamati and the queen mother itself emerges as a confrontation between violence (actual and intended) and a religion urging renunciation of all violence. But the text also faithfully records violence of another kind—the violence of sexual passion. Despite Janna's staunch belief in the efficacy of the Jaina religion, the text interrogates the power of religion to control sexuality.

Interestingly, Janna drew on well-known Sanskrit and Prakrit sources, and many passages are said to be literal translations of these sources. The Jaina theological framework about violence is also an age-old one. However, the text obstinately refuses to reduce the human ambivalence and complexity. Amrutamati is lured by the singing of Badaga, a mahout, and resolves to become his lover. His physical ugliness and physical violence do not deter her. Her own explanation is, 'ugliness in the one you love is good'. (The word used here, *pollame*, has the same origin as *holla* and *pole*; *poleya* meaning dirt, filth, badness, etc.) The poet says, 'When fate finds a helping hand in the god of love's spell, wouldn't it slay [humans] and shout in triumph?'. The text oscillates between human intentionality and the spell of sexuality which acts as the destructive weapon of fate as the decisive factor. However, Amrutamati has transgressed the moral code of marital fidelity and religious ethics in committing adultery. Yashodhara, who holds back the sword he had raised to kill the lovers, is forced by the queen mother to participate in a symbolic sacrifice of a cock made of dough. As fate would have it, a '*benthara*' (spirit) hiding in the cock of dough cries when it is slain. In the Jaina theological framework, Yashodhara and his mother are guilty of *sankalpa himse* (i.e., intended violence) and suffer in a cycle of many lives. Amrutamati invites Badaga to live with her in the palace, after poisoning Yashodhara and his mother to death. After her disease-stricken life of suffering, she dies only to be condemned to suffer in hell. After the cycle of births and by accepting the great religion, the mother and son are now born as Abhayamati and Abhayaruchi, reciting their tale to King Maridatta. Expectedly, Maridatta decides to convert himself to the Jaina religion. Probably one of the profoundest explorations of the meaning of violence, Janna's work is a literary master piece.

Many transformations also take place in the literary and philosophical legacies of the *Vachanakaras* from the late fifteenth century. The *Ragales* of Harihara are hagiographies of the *Vachanakaras* and are clearly intended to narrate their lives in the puranic style, drawing on the legends, oral histories and songs that the poet was familiar with. Most of his hagiographic poems begin with one of the companions of Shiva committing a misdemeanour and being ordered by him to be born on the earth and work for his salvation. The authors of the *Shunya Sampadane*, compiled between the fifteenth to sixteenth centuries, are critical of Harihara, without naming him, for even hinting at the possibility of the great souls committing a faux pas. However, Harihara's intention was to treat the *sharanas* such as Basava and Allama as heavenly souls living in the vicinity of Shiva, and describing their sojourn on the earth as designed to carry out a mission. The narratives also end with the return of the great souls to Shiva's abode. This is not merely a narrative technique but a reflection of the process of the apotheosis of the great *Vachanakaras*. Some of the *Vachanakaras* themselves suggest that Allama and Basava were, during their lifetimes, considered godlike. With the dissolution of the radical movement at Kalyana and the scattering of the *Vachanakaras,* the popular imagination began to reconstruct the remembered history in the form of Puranas. The later Basava Puranas by Palkuriki Somanatha and Bheemakavi, take it as literal truth that Basava was god in human form. The process of apotheosis takes place with the compilation of the *Vachanas* and the *Shunya Sampadane* over a century.

Chamarasa's *Prabhulingaleele* (1430 CE) is a textualisation of this process. It also indicates a major shift in the Veerashaiva imagination with Allama Prabhu becoming the indubitable spiritual leader, a mentor to Basava and Siddarama, two of the tallest leaders of the movement. Chamarasa describes an argument between Shiva and Parvati, when Shiva describes Allama as the only one who possesses transcendental knowledge and spirituality. Parvati in her arrogance decides to send the 'darker' part of her own being to take birth on the earth and test Allama with temptation. This preamble leads to the birth of Allama who is progressively seen as an aspect of Shiva himself, and his meeting with Mayadevi sent by Parvati. Chamarasa ties himself in all kinds of knots to prove that Allama is only making an elaborate pretence. (*Leele* means 'play', and metaphors of Allama playacting is emphasised throughout the poem.) This helps Chamarasa in describing the love and passion of Mayadevi and her union with Allama in a conventional style, even while asserting that Allama was 'bodiless' and always eluding Mayadevi. After this somewhat confusing episode and the defeat of Mayadevi, Allama emerges as his true self, a godlike *yogi,* a treasure of knowledge and an authoritative interlocutor and mentor. The rest of the poem has an episodic structure, taking us through episodes of Allama's meeting with several devotees, testing them and showing them the path of salvation. Many of these episodes figure in the *Shunya Sampadane* which turn them into dramatic confrontations providing a context for the 'speaking' of the *Vachanas.* There is little narration and an abundance of philosophical and theological exposition. In fact, in the case of many episodes, the *Shunya Sampadane* are more intense and dramatic in their treatment. The exceptions are Allama's confrontation with Siddarama and Goraksha, the *yogi* of the *Natha* tradition. Siddarama, who is already a legendary leader and *yogi* at Sonnalige, is taunted by Allama as a stone mason building temples and digging ponds. After a fierce duel, he realises that Allama wants him to break out of the worldly bonds and work towards self-realisation. He accompanies Allama to Kalyana where Basava seeks Allama's guidance. Another remarkable episode deals with Allama's recognition of Marula Shankaradeva, a great mystic who lived by eating the leftovers of the *sharanas* and hiding his identity. Some of the passages dealing with spiritual experiences are brilliant with the freshness and power of *Nadugannada* (Middle Kannada which had shed many characteristics of Old Kannada). In a way, Kannada seems to have returned to the transparent idiom of the *Vachanakaras.* It is also evident that there has been a clear departure from the simple ecstasy of *bhakti*; and Allama's discourses make references to yogic practices related to the *Natha* and similar traditions. Though the simple ethic of work and devotion has not been abandoned, the focus is now on mystical and yogic practices. Interestingly, the work is also the first important literary text to name the religion as 'Veerashaiva'. Raghavanka's *Siddarama Charitra*, preceding Chamarasa's work, is also a hagiographic work describing the extraordinary feats of Siddarama who is said to be gifted with the third eye in his forehead by Shiva himself. But it makes no reference to the Veerashaiva sect which came to be known by that name probably during the times of Praudhadevaraya who is credited with its establishment or at least with lending political support to its establishment.

The tradition of the *Shunya Sampadane* is a fascinating record of the concerted effort made in the Lingayat monasteries by groups of *Jangamas* (priests) to compile the *Vachanas* in writing by placing them in loosely structured narratives about the *Vachanakaras*. The narratives describe the contexts in which the *sharanas* meet and debate. There are also dramatic confrontations (such as the trial of Akka Mahadevi's chastity, generally considered a latter-day interpolation) and debates. The purpose is to clarify and authenticate the ethics and beliefs of the religion which is now consolidating itself. Throughout the late medieval period theological works had been composed (some in Sanskrit) which were meant to provide an ideological and theological basis to the eclectic and open-ended thoughts of the *Vachanakaras*. As described in *Prabhulingaleele*, Allama Prabhu has to ascend the *Shunya Simhasana,* the spiritual throne.

There are four major renditions of the *Shunya Sampadane*, compiled over a period of nearly a century. The period also saw the textualisation of the *Vachanas* which were now rendered into writing. Many scholars argue that this process of editing and inscribing the *Vachanas* also involved a great deal of amending and rewriting. This has raised several questions about the authenticity and originality of the *Vachanas* as we know them today. The *Vachanas* had to be 'rediscovered' in the twentieth century, and a great deal of effort went into the preparation of 'authentic' editions. This process has not reached its final stage yet. The rediscovery of the *Vachanas* in the twentieth century also happened in the context of the consolidation of the Lingayat religion during the colonial period. The dominant Lingayat caste was under pressure to 'invent a tradition', in this case the *Vachanakara* tradition, in order to establish its hegemony. There are fascinating studies of this phase by M. Chidanandamurthy and Vijayakumar Boratti. But then that has to do with colonial modernity, to be discussed in a later chapter.

The tradition of compiling the *Shunya Sampadane* continued for over a century. The four major works in the tradition are as follows: (1) compiled by Shivagana Prasadi Mahadevayya (early fifteenth century); (2) compiled by Haligearya (early sixteenth century); (3) compiled by Gummalapurada Siddhalinga Yati (1439); and (4) compiled by Goolur Siddhaveera (sixteenth century). All the four follow the pattern of a loosely constructed narrative built around the encounters of Allama Prabhu with a few leading *sharanas*. The narrative is generally a brief introduction to the context in which the encounter takes place and often explains the motive, such as debating a metaphysical question, questioning and clarifying the beliefs and behaviour of a particular *sharana* or providing a detailed exegesis of a Veerashaiva doctrine or practice. With remarkable dexterity, the *Vachanas* are embedded in a dialogic form in which they become part of a reply or a discussion. This is not always a seamless effort. In Shivagana Prasadi's *Shunya Sampadane,* the *Vachanas* addressed by Basava to pacify an upset Allama (who was welcomed by Basava's deputies while Basava was in the middle of worship) are obviously *Vachanas* originally addressed to his personal deity Kudala Sangama Deva. In the same encounter, many *Vachanas* of Basava, upholding the priority of serving the *Jangama* over the worship of the *linga*, are used to express Basava's repentance for neglecting Allama who had come to visit him. These are less important issues compared to the declared intentions of the compilers of the *Shunya Sampadane*—to offer them as shastric or theological works, providing authenticity to the Veerashaiva beliefs and rituals. It appears as though as part of the institutionalisation of the Veerashaiva religion, the need was felt to construct an authoritative theological text. That the *Shunya Sampadane* did not obtain such hegemonic authority is another matter. There are also aberrations, such as the trial of Akka Mahadevi's renunciation of sexuality (which is proved by the ash in her vagina), which have been dismissed as interpolations. But the fact that all versions of the *Shunya Sampadane* persist with the idea of Akka Mahadevi's trial, in some form or the other, most certainly evidences the presence of a strong patriarchal view of chastity which runs counter to the more open gender notions in the *Vachanas.* There is a decisive effort to install Allama as the spiritual leader of the Veerashaiva religion. There is also a powerful and tragic 'sense of an ending' in the description of the departure of the *sharanas* from Kalyana and their impending departure from this world, having performed the tasks for which they were sent down from Shiva's court.

2

Gadugina Naranappa, popularly known by his pen name Kumara Vyasa, is a great master of verbal brilliance whose powers of sustaining a long and variegated retelling of Vyasa's *Bharata* are enormous and unmatched in the Kannada poetic tradition. In the introductory verses, Kumara Vyasa humbly acknowledges his debt to Vyasa, extols his own work as providing liberation to all those who listen to it, but also says emphatically that he conceived his retelling as *Krishna Katha*, a tale about Krishna who is god and also the puppeteer who pulls the strings of the *Mahabharata* story. This is a decisive shift away from the epic tradition to the *Bhagavata* tradition which is closer in spirit to the Bhakti traditions of the South. Kumara Vyasa's Krishna is a fascinating manipulator, a devoted friend and counsel, but also ruthless in his designs to bring about the fall of the Kauravas. Accused of falsehood, deception and obvious partiality, Krishna is also the supreme lord of the cosmos, whose participation in the bloody dynastic war is ultimately intriguing. Kumara Vyasa's apotheosis of Krishna does not diminish the power of either characterisation or the many narratives woven into the retelling.

Paradoxically, the enormous energies of the *Desi* poetic and narrative traditions are unleashed in this work which openly supports ideological and social structures that are powerfully questioned by these oral traditions. The hierarchical *Varnashrama*, the superiority of brahmins, the valorisation of the kshatriya ruling class, the near total marginalisation of subaltern classes, the sexualisation of the woman's body—these are the strongly entrenched notions which are reinforced in long passages which disrupt the flow of the narrative. Critics such as C. N. Ramachandran and Kirtinath Kurtakoti have argued that Kumara Vyasa manages to be critical of the *kshatra*-ruled social system and reveals the emptiness of its claims to glory (Ramachandran 2014). Lord Krishna himself seems to mourn the end of the *kshatradharma*. However, Kumara Vyasa's efforts to humanise the unequal social system are based on its primary acceptance. Although writing after the *Vachanakara* and Veerashaiva movements, he is decisively in favour of a hierarchical social order which he tries to legitimise in his work through long didactic harangues by Narada and Vidura. This is contradicted by the ironical description of the victorious Pandava heroes occupying the residences of their vanquished enemies, and the same ministers and administrators continuing in the same positions of power after the deadly war and restoration of order.

These contradictions apart, Kumara Vyasa's *Gadugina Bharata* (as it is popularly known) has straddled the popular literary imagination as only the *Vachanas* have done. It is undoubtedly the most popular epic recited even today in many villages. It has also been used for hundreds of years by practitioners of *Yakshagana*, *Talamaddale*, *Bayalata* and many other folk performances. In some regions of Karnataka, the canto *Virata Parva* from the work is recited to induce rains. The tradition of recitation known as *gamaka* has used the work as its central text. Though another retelling, *Jaimini Bharata*, has been equally popular in many regions of Karnataka, Kumara Vyasa's *Bharata* is a vastly superior work.

With the end or paucity of royal patronage and the rejection of such patronage by Veerashaiva poets like Harihara, it was necessary for poetry to find a 'reading public', and it discovered its audience in the social classes which had been introduced into the domain of the literary by the Bhakti movements. Though not many details are known about the modes of recitation and reception, medieval Kannada texts frequently refer to recitation and singing with the accompaniment of music. Harihara's texts and the *Shunya Sampadane* also refer to singing of hymns and *geethe* (which could refer to *Vachanas* too).

Kumara Vyasa's text is definitely a work meant for the ear (*Haadu Gabba)* and profusely employs rhetorical and dramatic strategies. The verse is also replete with interjections, exclamations, forms of colloquial address and hundreds of colloquial expressions from the domain of everyday speech. There are sizeable number of words of Marathi and Persian origin. The work has necessitated full-length glossaries because of its lexical diversity.

What is central to the text is the intense drama of human emotions, and the poet does not miss any opportunity to play on them. There is a powerful earthiness in the language and style which made Kuvempu and other critics describe Naranappa as possessing *gramyapratibhe* (i.e., 'rural' genius, better translated as 'unsophisticated' or 'non-cosmopolitan'). In this, he is a contrast to the classical, Sanskrit-centric *Champu* poets of the past. The epic is written in the *Shatpadi* form (with lines containing six metrical feet), which replaced the *Champu* form. Even avoiding the unsubstantiated claims for its 'demotic' nature, there is no doubt that the verse form was associated with a restructuring of the reading public. Like its predecessors, Kumara Vyasa's epic is also a profound critique of war which must have resonated with people's weariness with the endless battles of crumbling empires after the decline of the Vijayanagara empire. The poet's unqualified devotion to Krishna, at once a great god and alluringly human, must have resonated with the traditions of *saguna bhakti* (devotion to a personalised god both in the Shaiva and Vaishnava sects) of the period. There is also a reconciliation—forced, helpless or otherwise—with a hierarchical society, reflecting the society of the times.

The collusion between the powerful regimes and the Vedic-brahminical priestly class seems to have found devotional cults useful in sublimating the popular disgruntlement with high taxes and social inequality, into a mysticism assuring spiritual equality to all. Throughout the medieval period, there is an unobstructed peregrination of Bhakti cults throughout South India. In the Kannada land, all available historical evidence suggests a strong temple culture and brahminical ritualism that was vehemently opposed by both Veerashaivism and Jainism during one phase. Bhakti poetry ostensibly is critical of the power regimes and caste/*Varna* systems as well as of worldly possessions. Its idiom and metaphors are at times powerfully anti-caste. However, it would be ahistorical to valorise the elements of a radical critique of inequality, which do figure in the poetic compositions of the period, in terms borrowed from latter-day ideologies. This is true of the poetry of the *Dasas* during the fifteenth to seventeenth centuries.

The *Dasas* were wandering poets and bards, devoted to a personal god. Hampi, the capital of Vijayanagara, and Udupi were the two cultural-religious spaces associated with the *Dasa* poets. Purandara Dasa is also the father of the Karnataka musical tradition with his *Kritis* (works) providing its textual basis, like the great *Kritis* of Thyagaraja. He is also a fine poet blending devotional passion with satirical social commentary. He excels at many of the poetic forms such as *Kirtane, Mundige*, etc., popularised by the *Dasas*. He had the courage to declare 'great political regimes, nonsense', and to denounce the caste system. Interestingly, his songs have been effectively used in the theatre (by the late B. V. Karanth), in popular cinema and in the Kannada music industry. This is true of the devotional poets generally, but more so of Purandara Dasa and Kanaka Dasa.

Dasa poetry is a mix of populist didacticism on the themes of the transitoriness of human life, desire to renounce worldly life, the need to perform good deeds, and an intense personal devotion to god. The poetic register uses images and metaphors from everyday life, common expressions and a vocabulary ranging from metaphysical terms to colloquial phrases. These are characteristic of a popular mystical-devotional tradition which runs parallel to mainstream religious traditions. This has a reach and longevity unmatched by any mainstream literary or philosophical tradition. The practitioners of this tradition belong to all sects and religions, and see themselves as members of a rural community. The *Dasa* poets occupy a different cultural space but use a poetic idiom and style similar to such practitioners. In these traditions, the philosophical sophistication goes with the ordinariness of the idiom of expression. Many of the phrases coined by Purandara Dasa are now part of the Kannada language.

Kanaka Dasa, hailing from a shepherd or hunter community (which is a matter of dispute now), has been transformed into an iconic figure in the contemporary discourses on caste and religion in Karnataka. Thimmappa Nayaka by birth, and a military official by profession, Kanaka Dasa gave up his prosperous life to become a wandering devotee dedicating himself to Adikeshava who was worshipped in Kaginele where he lived. An extraordinary legend narrates his visit to the Krishna temple at Udupi where as a low-caste individual he was not allowed into the inner shrine. He stood praying at the back of the temple. The god's idol turned back and a small window-like opening appeared, so that Kanaka Dasa could have a 'sight' of god. The legend has been interpreted variously as a miracle proving Kanaka Dasa's victory over rigid caste prohibitions, and as a tale about the power of *bhakti* to bring god from 'there' to 'here'. It has also been interpreted as an example of the appropriation of a low-caste icon by a powerful high-caste temple culture, to co-opt the devotion of low-caste devotees. Raging controversies have erupted over the legend in debates over the caste system. At the core of the controversies is the ambivalence of Bhakti towards social inequalities which makes the appropriation of Kanaka Dasa as a caste-radical, difficult.

However, Kanaka Dasa is a gifted poet whose longer work *Mohana Tarangini* is cast in the traditional mould and is written in the classical ornate, stylised idiom. It conforms to a modular literary mode to the extent of using the *sringara* or erotic element, including the male gaze on the woman's body. His short narrative *Ramadhanya Charite* is a witty poem about a contest between rice (paddy) and millet. The verbal duel between the two brings up the cultural politics of food, with rice associated with the upper class (but also denigrated as food for the sick!) and millet associated with the lower castes. Rama announces that he would give his judgement on returning from his journey six months later. In six months' time, rice degenerated but millet survived. Though not overtly, the narrative expresses an awareness of the politics of food culture.

His lyrics and songs are works of a high order. A remarkable song on *kula* (caste) admonishes men for fighting over the supremacy of the *kula* into which they are born, asking them if they know the origin of caste. 'All are born of the womb', he says. This and a few other poems reveal his anger at an irrational and unequal social system. This nuance is missing in the other *Dasa* poets. Kanaka Dasa is closer in spirit to a radical Advaita thought which has always attracted poets and mystics opposed to inequality. Therefore, his poetry becomes a site to explore whether Bhakti as a tradition was fully able to mask the anger and frustration at social hierarchies. This is also the case with the great Marathi Bhakti poets. There is also a suppressed anger at the political regimes which at times patronised the Bhakti poets themselves. This explains the iconisation of the devotional poets by several social classes, irrespective of the sects to which they belonged.

SIX

Towards Modernity

1

The last major resistance to British colonialism ended with the death of Tipu in the battle at Srirangapatna in 1799. There is no doubt at all that Tipu was a king of his times: ruling over a vast territory with a diverse historical background, and with the serious problems posed by British imperialism, he had to evolve and implement many policies which have led to the interpretation that he was a bigot and a communal despot. Historical documents are clear about two things. He had an extraordinary insight into the nature of British imperialism. It would be ridiculous to argue that he fought the British as only a part of the tripartite conflict between the British, the Nizam of Hyderabad and the Marathas. He also predicted correctly that British imperialism would go beyond the regional conflicts between Mysore, the Nizam and the Peshwas of Maharashtra. Even before the defeat and death of Tipu, the matriarch of the Mysore dynasty had made overtures to the British claiming that the dynasty was the legitimate ruler of Mysore. As elsewhere in India, the British found this collaborative proposal most advantageous which would help them in controlling both the most important buffer state in South India and also instal a puppet monarchy supervised by a Resident. A perusal of the agreements shows how abject the proposal was. The language and tenor of all correspondence and agreements between the Mysore principality and the British are couched in a language of degrading subjugation. This paradox was to continue throughout the regime of the Mysore principality. The paradox had three elements in it. One was that the great principality remained a supplicant, taxing its peasants and artisans to an unimaginable extent (especially under the administration of Poornaiah, the *dewan*) to pay the British. Famines and extreme rural distress were caused by this system of taxation. The principality also brutally suppressed the peasant and *Paleyagara* rebellions against the British by hanging the rebels at the main entrance (*agasi*) to the villages. As Ranajit Guha (1983) argues, these rebellions were not considered by historians as anti-colonial struggles.

The irony is that with such abject and active collaboration with the British, the Mysore principality developed into a model state, a progressive state, and an example of what colonial modernity could accomplish. As the historian S. Chandrashekhar (2006) argues, the Mysore principality created the powerful myth of it being a modern, progressive state that even today, after over seven decades of independence and sixty-nine years after becoming a linguistic state, people continue to think of the Mysore principality as the best thing that happened after Tipu. Leaving aside the highly communalised historiography of Karnataka today, there are many reasons to interrogate this idealised version of Karnataka's history. The most important questions are the following:

1. Tipu had evolved an efficient administrative system which had regularised the revenue system and had also created a proto-welfare state. How did the Mysore principality improve upon this? In fact, under Poornaiah's *dewanship* the principality was able to meet the exorbitant annual 'fee' to the British for its military expenses to 'protect' Mysore, but the hardships were so extreme that peasants felt that Tipu's regime was better.
2. The most humiliating event was when the British imposed the rule of the residency on grounds that the king of Mysore had failed (Tarikere 2019). The British residency rule is seen as progressive even today. Many buildings, towns, streets and institutions still retain their names after the Residents and officers of the British regime.
3. What in real terms was colonial modernity in Karnataka? How was it different from the way it has been narrated elsewhere in India?
4. The Karnataka unification movement (*Ekikarana* movement), the assertion of Kannada sub-nationalism and the progress of Mysore state as a progressive modern state hold great sway in contemporary discourses. Do these discourses provide an authentic portrayal of the Mysore principality?
5. What was the nature of the conflicting discourses on colonial modernity?

As it should be expected, colonial modernity meant vastly different things to the Kannadigas of the time who were scattered over twenty-nine fragments. Some of these regions had gone through very distinctive historical experiences. Therefore, colonial modernity impacted them differently. For example, the Dharwad region in North Karnataka had been part of the Bombay presidency and was known as the Southern Maratha country. After the termination of the Mysore wars, the Marathas had taken over the region and left behind a Marathi speaking elite who held powerful positions. There were also small principalities like Savanur in the region which had Muslim rulers but Marathi administrators. Marathi was the prestige language and the language of administration. The nearest colleges were in Pune which meant that graduates from the Dharwad region were educated in a Marathi ambience. When the British decided to support vernacular schools, they took it for granted that the vernacular was Marathi. It was the British officers like Walter Elliot and W. A. Russell who wrote to the Bombay government arguing that Kannada was the regional language. Eliot personally funded the running of a Kannada-medium school when the government did not respond to his pleas. Russell, the education officer of the Bombay South region, struggled to bring the Normal School (Teacher Training School, later a college) from Belagavi to Dharwad. He and his assistants had to practically reinvent Kannada fonts to print textbooks for the college in Kannada (Srinivas 1974). The college became the epicentre of the Kannada renaissance and the unification movement.

This was not the case in the Mysore principality where the court actively supported Kannada. Basappa Shastri, who translated Kalidasa and Shakespeare into Kannada, enjoyed the patronage of the principality. In fact, the long years of the rule by the Regent and the pioneering work of the missionaries in the field of education brought such prestige to the English-medium schools that over a thousand citizens signed a petition for another English-medium school. The high school established by the king later grew into the Maharaja College which was the other great centre of Kannada renaissance. Thus, while the Dharwad region experienced colonial modernity as a process of reinstating Kannada, Mysore openly welcomed English as the harbinger of modernity.

Hyderabad Karnataka, which under the Nizam's rule had been pushed to poverty and backwardness by the ruthless feudal class supported by an equally ruthless monarchy, did not have Kannada schools. Urdu was the medium for higher education. Bellari was part of the Madras presidency and Telugu had the status of the 'second first language' for most Kannadigas. The region had been the location of Christian missionary activity which had seen the establishment of the Kannada press very early, and it now went through a fractured experience of modernity.

Coastal Karnataka, which had always been the great centre of pre-modern globalisation and trade, was also the first to have access to colonial modernity. After the fall of Tipu, it was under the rule of the Nayaka dynasty of Ikkeri, until it was annexed by the British. A leading centre of missionary activity, it possessed an excellent educational system. The

Saraswat community which had migrated from Goa to escape the brutal Portuguese regime and fear of conversion, constituted the native elite. The class of officials, lawyers and businessmen were from this community. For them colonial modernity opened up significant debates on tradition and religious practices. Gulavadi Venkata Rao (1844–1913), the author of the first social novel in Kannada, *Indira Bai* (1899), was a Saraswat and led many public debates on prohibitions on sea voyage, widow remarriage and women's education, with the Saraswat *matha* (monastery). The leading writers who experimented with the new genres such as the short story, the novel and the essay, were from this community and region.

There are very few negative images of the colonial regime in the early phase of the Kannada renaissance. In the Mysore region, it was mediated through an enlightened principality and therefore was seen as the vehicle of progress and modernity. In North Karnataka, despite the local rebellions against the British by Chennamma, the queen of Kittur, and Sangolli Rayanna, her chief supporter, the colonial regime was seen as benevolent, owing to many officers who represented the better face of imperialism. This experience of colonialism runs counter to the postcolonial theories with affiliation to the Saidian–Foucauldian model of absolute conquest and absolute power. For many regions in Karnataka, colonial modernity meant the re-discovery of the Kannada tradition, modern scholarly studies of Kannada classics, the inception of Kannada schools, rule of law, and an efficient bureaucracy. The dominant non-brahmin castes in Karnataka welcomed the colonial rule which gave them access to education which was until then the privilege of the brahmins. The associations of these non-brahmin castes, formed during this period, established free hostels to educate their youth so that they could be employed by the colonial government. The *summum bonum* for the emerging educated middle class was the position of an officer who would come home in an impressive procession of peons carrying the *daftars* (office files). In the scramble for such worldly power, the dark underbelly of imperialism was not even a part of the imagination of the middle class.

As elsewhere in India, this colonial modernity was a fragmented and contradictory modernity. In Karnataka, the middle class saw a contest between the traditional brahminical section and the emerging non-brahmin sections from the dominant Lingayat and Vokkaliga communities. With a long history of backwardness and despotic *Paleyagars* (local chieftains), the common people also saw colonial bureaucracy as just and evenhanded. At the same time, the two dominant communities also developed a strong caste-consciousness supported by associations and institutions. In fact, with the existence of a large number of sub-castes in each of the dominant communities, caste consciousness was yet vague and fuzzy. There was confusion regarding which sub-castes could be included in the caste. The smaller sub-castes which were on the margins had little interaction with the major sub-castes. The boundaries of the sub-castes were clear but those of caste were porous and fuzzy. Therefore, paradoxically, modernity was accompanied by an increased caste-consciousness and the consolidation of sub-castes to claim the benefits of colonial administration. The beginnings of Karnataka as a caste society can be seen here. Even with serious disagreements with the postcolonial arguments that the caste system was constructed by colonialism, one could agree that colonialism helped in creating caste-consciousness. This also led to the invention of traditions. The *Vachanas* scattered over the state in the form of palm leaf manuscripts were now collected and published by scholars like F. G. Halakatti and S. S. Basavanal. The support came from the Lingayat community which needed a rich cultural heritage to fight its bitter battles with the brahmins (Boratti 2012). The brahmin elite in the Dharwad region with allegiance to Marathi assumed the leadership in the Karnataka unification movement and also in the Congress-led nationalist movement. As can be seen from the autobiographical writings of Aluru Venkata Rao (1880–1964), the archpriest of the unification movement, and Ra. Ha. Deshpande (1861–1931), the founder of Karnataka Vidya Vardhaka Sangha in Dharwad, these leaders were followers of Bal Gangadhar Tilak and were not free from conservative and revivalist ideologies. But in conceptualising Kannada, and *Karnatakatwa* (the being of Karnataka), they were secular and modern.

Similar contradictions can be seen in the native elite of the Mysore region. B. M. Sri. (Belluru Mylaraiah Srikantaiah, 1884–1946), the father-figure of Kannada renaissance, believed very strongly that in the modern age, Kannada had to revitalise itself not by drawing on Sanskrit but on English. He was a staunch devotee of the Maharaja and composed many poetic tributes for public occasions. He wore with pride the medal honouring him as *Rajasevasakta* (devoted to the service of the king and the colonial regime) and wrote a poem beginning with the Kannada translation of the line 'Rule, Britannia'. Yet, he was the most powerful advocate of the Kannada cause. A great scholar in the Kannada tradition, he wrote a tragedy, *Ashwathaman*, based on episodes from the *Mahabharata*, written in Old and Middle Kannada. For B. M. Sri., Kannada had no political affiliations. He inaugurated modern

Kannada poetry of the *Navodaya* period through his *English Geetegalu*, a collection of translations of English poems (1921, 2013).

The Kannada literary renaissance was inspired by translations of English poetry and adaptations/translations of Shakespeare (Tarakeshwar 2006). In the Mangalore region, Hattiangadi Narayana Rao had also published his translations of English poems by this time. Of all the genres, the novel is both the product and document of colonial modernity in Kannada. It began as a self-conscious imitation of the novel form in English and quickly transformed itself with indigenous and regional elements. Drama had a more complicated history because of the pre-existing professional theatre and the many folk performative art forms. The introduction of drama as a literary genre had to negotiate with these powerful performative traditions which did use literary texts but with a mind-boggling freedom. The literal/literary translations of Shakespeare appeared much later than the adaptations (Tarakeshwar 2006). The Christian missionary scholars collected the *Yakshagana* scripts, whereas the texts of the popular professional theatre (known as 'company theatre') were not. The reason is that so much was added, deleted and rewritten during the rehearsals that the original text remained elusive. *Navodaya* poetry drew the finest talents and was heterogeneous in form.

It is important not to reduce Kannada literature of the colonial period to a mere reflection of the impact of colonialism. Kannada writers saw themselves as inheritors of rich literary, popular and folk traditions, and there are significant continuities despite the new worlds of experience opened up by colonialism. The English poets introduced to them the themes of individuality, the power of emotions and passions, the awareness of nature not as a symbol of the transcendental but as a reality to be experienced with the senses, and the centrality of love and relationships. The national movement introduced ideas of nation, nationalism, the glorious history of the past, and the saints and heroes of the Kannada and Indian traditions. With the awakening of a modern critical sensibility, issues relating to caste and gender were also foregrounded. The social reformist spirit also made writers examine traditional practices. Women writers of the early twentieth century, like Nanjangudu Tirumalamba and Nagaratnamma, wrote about the plight of widows. With the growth of the reading public, the writer had to accept the role of a teacher of the new morality. Huge chunks of the early Kannada novel are authorial interventions, with a direct dialogue with 'dear readers' about morality and ethics. One could argue that institutional religion had lost its ethical authority especially owing to the critique of the retrograde practices associated with it. Modern education had also developed a rationalist critique of religion, undermining blind adherence to its practices. This led to a major shift from collective or institutional authority to the individual conscience and rational behaviour by the individual.

There is also another kind of response in some of the major Kannada novels. This is the profound despair at the ending of an old world which was bound up with values which are no longer there to sustain the new world. This sentiment appears as nostalgia in many of the popular novels. In serious novels, the past provides a criterion with which to evaluate the change in values. In Shivaram Karanth's (1902–97) novels it is the old women, the grandmothers, who have lived honestly according to a set of values, integrity and individual commitment, who emerge as the epitome of norms by which the individual is judged. In *Marali Mannige* (*Return to Earth* 1941, English translation 2002), the two women of the first generation, Sarasoti and Paroti, live a life circumscribed to a few acres of land and the house built by Rama Aital, while the outside world which is going through disturbing changes with the coming of colonial modernity, remains unknown to them. But in their confined world they remain committed to family values and hard relentless physical labour, and to the land. These values remain the ethical core of the novel about three generations.

Modernity is the thematic and problematic of the Kannada novel. Of the two major genres of the novel, the historical romance based on the model of the novels of Bankim Chandra and H. N. Apte, represents a revivalist reconstruction of a 'glorious' past. This was part of the reaction to the colonial denigration of India's history. In reconstructing the past, authors like Galaganatha subscribe to the communal historiography which was based on the narrative of a glorious Hindu past desecrated by the alien Muslim invaders, and the heroism of warriors like Shivaji who attempted to recreate the Hindu empire. Galaganatha was the pen name of Venkatesh Tirako Kulkarni, a Smartha brahmin who spent most of his time in an ashram which was also his publishing house. He edited the popular magazine *Sadbodha Chandrike* which at its peak had over seven thousand subscribers. He was a prolific writer who created a vast readership and during times of financial difficulty toured Karnataka to sell his works which included both translations and original novels. He writes in an unsettled Kannada prose mixing a highly Sanskritised, slightly archaic Kannada with the regional dialect he spoke. His popularity and readership confirm the consensus that the middle class showed towards a communalised historiography. At a time when right-wing organisations were not very active in Karnataka, it was the influence of the conservative politics of Tilak which supported such ideological interpretations of a 'Hindu' history. The celebration of heroism and martial values also generates the stereotypes of the masculine male following the kshatriya code of protecting the chastity of the woman and treating her as the epitome of all traditional Hindu values. The other stereotype is the male construction of the ideal Hindu wife always willing to join her dead husband on the funeral fire, rather than yield to the lechery and lust of the Muslim *mlechas*. The so-called 'Rajput' values of individual valour, chivalry and obedience to the leader are celebrated in the authorial comments. Shivaji is transformed into a mix of Robin Hood, adventurer and strategist. There are also a fair number of sanyasis and mendicants who act as the private army of the Hindu warriors.

Galaganatha evolved a racy narrative style with intrigues, escapes and pursuits, prisons and forts, and extraordinary feats of bravery. His constant switching of codes from the Sanskritised 'H' to the regional dialect 'L' had its appeal to the reader. Galaganatha, in Volume 5 of *Galaganatha Samagra Sahitya*, describes himself as an ordinary rural individual whose only education worth its name was the three-year training at the Dharwad Kannada Training College. He has only a working knowledge of Marathi and Sanskrit, and his Kannada does not go beyond that of a first-language speaker. He does not know the English alphabet. He claims that it is this 'ordinariness' which attracts the common reader to his writings. The books he published while working as a teacher brought him the accolade, 'not bad, Galaganatha writes straight'. He says that it is the ethical and moral issues which are more important to him and therefore he consciously introduces passages dealing with both even in translations. In the profile, he also reveals the secrets of his popularity. He says that he writes only about well-known individuals from the past such as Shivaji, Maharana Pratap Simha, Ashoka, Chandragupta and Madhavacharya (Vidyaranya), one of the founders of the Vijayanagara empire. His novels are popular owing to the readers' familiarity with these historical personages. He argues that his use of language is the most negligible element in his novels. His third secret is that he refuses to be better than his readers. When he writes, he is his reader; when the reader reads his novels the reader is Galaganatha.

Galaganatha further justifies his historical novels by arguing that both India (*Bharata Varsha*) and Karnataka are going through a period of *shawavritti* (phase of extreme decline) which according to savants of the past will be followed by decline (*glani*, the word used by Krishna in the *Bhagavad Gita*). In such a period, the readers should read only those novels which strengthen the *kshatrateja* (the power of the martial) and *dharmateja* (the power of the religious) in them. In his preface to *Eshwari Sutra* (1913), Galaganatha says that owing to the ambitious Aurangazeb in the North and the powerful Badashah of Bijapur, in that period of 'the roaring Muslim tigers', the 'Hindu sheep' were unable even to feed themselves. Then, Shivaji, with the help of the Mavalas, roared and the entire Hindustan trembled. He surprised the Muslim tigers and founded '*swarajya*' (4). Strangely enough, in the very next paragraph, he says that the religious decline was not only in Hinduism but also in the Muslim religion [Islam]. If either Hindus or Muslims had '*dharma*', the other religion would also have come out of the decline. 'Since both the Hindu and Muslim religions are motivated by God [*Ishwara Praneeth*], the awakening in one of them would have brought security to the world. But as both of them had declined due to evil selfishness, Shivaji had to be born' (Galaganatha 1913, 4–5).

This vision of the two god-given religions is not sustained in the novels themselves; nor is the communal historiography dented by the narratives. The historiography takes several shapes, from the mild to the virulent, in Kannada literature of the period. When Karnataka Vidya Vardhaka Sangha, a historic institution, invited writers to send their entries for a prize in fiction, most of the submissions were on the themes popularised by Galaganatha. Masti Venkatesha Iyengar (1891–1986), who began to write short stories in the realistic mode around 1911, wrote a satirical story titled *Rangaswamiya Aviveka* about a young man whose imagination has run wild by reading such historical romances about kshatriya women, that he imagines a married neighbour to be one such woman. Masti's pared-to-the-bone, non-rhetorical prose style was itself a reaction against the Sanskritised verbose style of the historical romances.

The other genre adapted by the Kannada novelists was the realistic novel. This genre went with the avoidance of a revivalist history and a romantically constructed past. The Kannada realistic novel was the expression of regional communities which had developed a distinctive way of life and were now being challenged to negotiate with changes ushered in by modernity. Gulavadi Venkata Rao's (1844–1913) *Indira Bai* is considered the first Kannada social novel. It was published in 1899 and was translated into English by M. E. Couchman and published in 1903, printed at the Basel Mission Press Mangalore. Vanamala Viswanatha and Shivarama Padikkal brought out a fresh translation in 2019. The story is of a scheming and comically villainous couple marrying off their daughter Indira Bai to a young *Amindar* who is riddled with venereal diseases and dies, making her a young widow. Her parents want her to live as a traditional widow and invite a group of singers and preachers home, who try to seduce her. She is rescued by another couple who allow her to read and learn to sew. In the end, she gets married to Bhaskar who is a modern educated young man. Against this narrative, Gulavadi Venkata Rao introduces the major issues relating to the women's question. As pointed out earlier, he belonged to the Saraswat community which had quickly responded to colonial modernity. (The Gazetteer makes a special mention of the intelligence and adaptability of the community.) The literary, educational and cultural work of the missionaries had made a positive impact on the region, and the many schools founded by the missions had created a modern educated native elite of which the educated Saraswats were important members. The Brahma Samaj was established at Mangalore by now, though it was managed by the Billava community which kept the Saraswat young men away (Padikkal 2001).

Narayana Guru (1856–1928), the great spiritual leader from Kerala, had created a new identity for the backward communities. It is beyond the purview of the present work to discuss the great impact Narayana Guru made on the cultural polities of the caste society of that period. Kudmul Ranga Rao (1859–1928), years before Mahatma Gandhi plunged into the Harijan uplift programmes, had created a positive identity for the 'untouchables' by providing them education. It is recorded that Gandhi, during his first visit to Mangalore, did not know about Ranga Rao's work; and during the second visit, he paid a great tribute to Ranga Rao who had by then passed away. This also points to a problem related to the actual practice of subaltern historiography. The work of subaltern historians has constructed an alternative historiography which disagrees with the imperial and nationalist historiographies, but it has been centred around Bengal and North India. Hence, Subaltern Studies created a historical archive in which South India figures rather occasionally in the margins. It has also created the false and misleading impression that nationalism and its critiques originated exclusively in Bengal. The result has been a radical and interesting history of colonialism in North India which is of little significance to the historian of South India.

A novel like *Indira Bai* cannot be analysed by repeated references to Bankim, Aurobindo and the tribals beyond the Vindhya Range. It is a modern novel born out of the complex intellectual debates in coastal

Karnataka. Fortunately, Vivek Rai, in his preface to the recent translation, recognises that *Indira Bai* is an indigenous, or *Desi*, cultural text, rich in detail about the social practices of the Saraswats and other communities around them. Further, the Tulu and Konkani languages form an integral part of the plot and ideology of the text (Rao 2019, ix).

What Gulavadi created was a heteroglossic novel with its intertextuality with Shakespeare's *Macbeth* and the indigenous *Yakshagana* texts. The novel is self-consciously topical, and was therefore correctly recognised by a contemporary reviewer as a 'novel with a purpose'. What is impressive about the work is its self-assured worldliness. The author has an ideological purpose but that does not prevent him from allowing police constables, maids, messengers, neighbours and Indira Bai's peers to speak leisurely and unhurriedly in their own registers and languages. The all-knowing author's humour makes it a readable novel. (It sold over eight hundred copies, a record at that time [see Srinivas 1974].) It looks forward to the radical text on sexuality by Shivaram Karanth, *Sarasammana Samadhi*, published in 1936.

Karanth's slender novel is also 'worldly' and does not hurry over the small details. It is also a novel written in-between genres. Is this affable novel, a mixture of fantasy and realism, a women-centric tract? The devastating irony of the *Samadhi*, the shrine in memory of Sarasamma who committed Sati and is now believed to solve marital discords, is disclosed in the last episode of the novel. Chandrayya, the protagonist, meets Sarasamma's spirit who explains how she was forced to commit Sati after the death of her sick husband. She survives as a spirit or ghost because she died a frustrated woman and is one even now. The novel has extraordinary sketches of women enslaved by the institution of marriage. One, a daughter-in-law, is harassed because she reads newspapers! Another says very plainly that if her husband gets a new woman in her place, she will also find a man in his place.

Kannada literary histories do not record the fact that Karanth was sued for his reformist activities. He wrote to Gandhi about the need to help the Devadasis (literally 'servants of gods', women dedicated to a goddess but exploited as prostitutes) to get married and lead a socially acceptable life. But Gandhi replied saying that these women should lead a life of absolute celibacy. Karanth comments in his autobiography that the reply convinced him that Gandhi had no knowledge of human beings 'who eat salt and spice' (Karanth 1993). The present writer cannot recollect a more pungent comment on Gandhi's confused notions of sexuality and his fetish for celibacy. However, Karanth's first-hand knowledge of women who were forced to become mistresses of wealthy men helped him to write one of the greatest classics of post-independence India, *Mai Managala Suliyalli* (Caught in the Whirlpool of Body and Mind, 1997). The gender issue has been addressed rather superficially in the cosmopolitan anglophile discussions owing to ignorance of the texts in the South Indian Bhashas. Karanth returned to the issue of female sexuality in many later novels such as *Battada Tore* (1953) and *Mookajjiya Kanasugalu* (1968) and *Swapnada Hole* (1966).

Kuvempu's (1904–94) first novel *Kanuru Subbamma Heggadithi* (The Headwoman of Kanuru, 1937) raises radical questions about modernity, education, the horrors of the feudal society, and women. This remarkable novel is about colonial modernity. Hoovaiah, who returns with his cousin Ramaiah to his feudal house at Kanuru, has been described as the first alienated hero in Kannada fiction by U. R. Ananthamurthy and others. At Mysore, he has read Wordsworth and Matthew Arnold somewhat overenthusiastically and is in the habit of entering into meditative trances while discussing them, which makes the servants and the workers believe that he is possessed by a *devva* (ghost or spirit). Even as he is seen pontificating on romantic transcendentalism in the 'upstairs' room, the shudra world of drinking, fornication, exploitation of bonded labourers and the sexual exploitation of women workers, goes on unabated below. Hoovaiah is a failed reformer, exactly like Jagannath of Ananthamurthy's *Bharathipura.* Subbamma, the last wife of Chandregowda, dies trying to abort the pregnancy caused by the *seregara* (the contractor who is from 'below the ghats', that is, the coastal region). It is remarkable that Kannada fiction has a legacy of widows—Indira Bai in Gulavadi's novel (1889); Sarasamma in Karanth's *Sarasammana Samadhi* (1936); Subbamma in Kuvempu's *Kanuru Subbamma Heggadithi* (1937); Phaniyamma in M. K. Indira's novel (1983); Draupadi in H. Nagaveni's *Gandhi Banda* (1999), and many more.

Indira Bai is clear about many things. It does not support the prohibition on widow remarriage. It believes that the new woman, like the heroine, should have access to literacy, knowledge and autonomy. The utopian happy ending established a pattern in which the author ignores the logic of the narrative to imagine a future of gender equality. In Kuvempu's *Kanuru Subbamma Heggadithi*, Seetha, who loves Hoovaiah intensely, is forced to marry Ramaiah, and goes through a phase of hysteria and then a forced sublimation of her love for Hoovaiah. The utopian ending of the novel describes a new world which is based on the Buddhist egalitarian values and the vision of an education based on humanist values. The utopian endings of most novels in Kannada are not examples of a lapse in the aesthetic perfection. In continuation of the argument proposed earlier, the Kannada novelist had to perform the function of a teacher and provide solutions. These questions can be discussed only when we have a poetics of the novel which recognises the sociocultural functions of the novel as a discourse of modernity.

If Gulavadi Venkata Rao's novel inaugurated the Kannada tradition of the novel as a discourse on modernity, the novel *Madiddunno Maharaya* (You Eat What You Make [literally meaning 'you reap what you sow'], 1915) by M. S. Puttanna has been recognised as a classic of the early phase. It is a complex literary text which is, among other things, a critique of the sadism, cruelty and extreme corruption of the local administration which leads to the harassment of the woman protagonist, Seethamma. As most Kannada critics have agreed, the critique has to do with the local institutions of power which have become corrupt, and little to do with the rectitude of the Mysore Maharaja. M. S. Puttanna was a firm believer in the absolute rectitude of the Maharaja, which was unfortunately not followed by the corrupt local officers. The novel is thus a defence of the monarchy and the moral rectitude of the Maharaja. The novel also tries to record the aspirations of the emergent middle classes which were new even in the colonial context.

M. S. Puttanna narrates the story of a poor brahmin family subjected to harassment by the petty local officials and by the gang of thieves who make use of the corrupt and irresponsible bureaucracy. The events take place during the regime of Krishnaraja Wodeyar III in a small village, Sanjawadi. Sadashiva Dikshit and his daughter-in-law Seethamma are consciously presented as the embodiment of traditional values. Critics have also argued that there is an intended parallel between Seethamma and Sita of the *Ramayana*, and that the novel—like the epic—is about the conflict between good and evil. Puttanna, a loyalist of the Mysore principality, has faith in the king as the one who can restore order and justice, despite the failure of the administrative system. The novel is also a veiled plea to the king to acquaint himself with the lives of the ordinary people. While *Indira Bai* places the onus on the individuals to choose the right *dharma* for themselves, *Madiddunno Maharaya* asserts its faith in the moral and political order symbolised by the good king.

The crisis confronted by the colonial society had much to do with the interventions made by the British regime to 'correct' wrong and irrational social practices. The early non-interventionist policy of the colonial regime, beginning with the *Nabobs* like Clive and Hastings, was put under pressure by Christian missionaries and later by Utilitarians. Both believed in taking the benefits of the Western enlightenment and progress to the 'subject people'. There was a realisation that social change had to be supported and even initiated through the passing of laws and by enforcing them. This view received vocal support from some sections of the educated reformist middle class. In Karnataka, the civil society actively debated issues relating to raising the age of consent for marriage to prevent child marriages, education for women and depressed classes, the abolition of Sati and the Devadasi system, and widow remarriage. Some of the *dewans* of Mysore took the initiative to promote reformist laws. There was a considerable reaction not only in the Prajamandali, the council of people's representatives, but in the civil society groups across Karnataka. Apart from the debate on whether these practices had the approval of the Sastras, there was also apprehension that the reforms would lead to the collapse of tradition and *dharma*. Katherine Mayo's *Mother India*, which Gandhi described as 'a drain inspector's report', is in fact an excellent and disturbing record of how social reforms through law were stalled and stonewalled by the people's representatives and leaders of the local society in Tamil Nadu and elsewhere. In Karnataka, the *mathas* (monasteries) of all religions supported the conservatives. What emerges from the civil society debates, petitions and public meetings is that Karnataka was an extremely hierarchical, caste-centric society, deeply patriarchal and opposed to all reform. The novels of Gulavadi, Bolara Babu Rao and other Saraswats represented a small reformist section which exposed the role of institutional religion in reinforcing conservatism. D. V. G. (D. V. Gundappa, 1887–1975) and Masti Venkatesha Iyengar (1891–1986), the leading figures in the modern liberal humanist tradition in Kannada, were deeply conservative in several aspects. How were these contradictions in the modern Kannada world sought to be resolved through literature?

This question can be rephrased as, 'How did the literary become so hegemonic during this period?'. One of the possible answers is that it was accomplished by constructing or reconstructing the notion of literature as a universal, aesthetic space in which human experience of every kind can be expressed and experienced by reducing or minimising its social and political dimensions. This was done by using several resources. First, English literature was received as a repository of universal human experiences and values with its canonical works possessing the capability to reorient the Indian/Kannada tradition to the ordinarily human. The mainstream Indian tradition had been an impersonal tradition oriented towards the transcendental and the philosophical, and had not paid sufficient attention to the quotidian human experiences. The common joys and sorrows which are universal because they emanate from a universal human nature, were better embodied in English literature. However, to receive English literature in this way, the pre-condition was to delink it from its history of imperialism. Shakespeare and Wordsworth could become models of great literature if they could be fitted into an apolitical, ahistorical space called 'literature'. The other resource was Indian aesthetics. The *Navodaya* literary criticism has been described as *Rasa Vimarshe* because of the preponderance of the theory of *rasa* put to modern uses. *Rasa* was interpreted as relating to the process of the *sadharanikarana* of the personal, individual experience. That is the process by which real experience is sufficiently generalised and even aestheticised through literary conventions, *alankaras*, etc., so that it becomes universal. With this, the original individual experience becomes universal and yields itself to literary pleasure among readers from across all humanity. One example often discussed as an instance of this phenomenon is the translation of 'Lead, Kindly Light', originally written by J. H. Newman and translated by B. M. Sri. The translation, which is even today regularly sung as invocation in most programmes in Karnataka, does not have any cues to make the reader realise that it was originally composed by a Christian priest who was also an important participant in the Oxford movement and played an influential role in the debates on science, faith, Protestantism and Catholic tradition, in the Victorian period. In the Indian aesthetic tradition, this would be treated as an example of *sadharanikarana* leading to the experience of *rasa*. It should be remembered that *Navodaya* literary criticism was grounded in Sanskrit poetics and therefore used its resources for the apolitical, ahistorical reception of English literature.

The third factor, discussed earlier, was the near homogeneity of the literary elite of the period. It was predominantly brahminical, traditionalist and conservative. It did not have affiliations with the anti-colonial struggles, though it was respectful towards Gandhi and the Swadeshi movement. It was sensitive to the portrayal of injustice and suffering in literature but stopped well short of relating them to the caste system. But these fault lines led to unexpected eruptions and powerful literary expressions of the misery of individuals in an unequal society.

An example of the eruptions referred to is the public debate between Kuvempu and Masti Venkatesha Iyengar on the writer's freedom to rewrite traditional myths. The occasion was the publication of Kuvempu's play *Shudra Tapaswi* (*The Shudra Sage*, 1944). The play is based on the story of Shambuka, the shudra sage who attempted to perform a great *tapas*, a privilege accorded only to brahmin sages. By coincidence, the child of a brahmin dies and he complains to Lord Rama, the king, that his child's death is the consequence of a shudra doing penance. Rama beheads the shudra *tapaswi* and restores the *Varna* order, and the child is brought back to life. In his preface, Kuvempu asserts that this episode in the *Uttara Kanda* or *Uttara Rama Charita* is certainly an interpolation (Shivareddy 2003, 694–98). Kuvempu himself went on to write *Srimad Ramayana Darshanam* by reinterpreting Valmiki's *Ramayana*, and did not believe that Valmiki could have written such an episode. In his play, the brahmin is described as *'Mata Moodha'* and *'Mati Moodha'* (foolish in creed and in intelligence) by Lord Rama. Kuvempu's Rama is an enlightened king and a great human being who decides to teach the brahmin a lesson. He goes with him to the place where Shambuka is doing his penance and shoots his arrow praying that it should punish the guilty. The arrow salutes the sage and returns to punish the brahmin. Rama clears the cloud of ignorance in the brahmin. Masti reacted to the play with uncharacteristic rudeness, admonishing Puttappa (Kuvempu's Okkaliga name) to avoid the temerity of tampering with myths of the past. He argued that if necessary, the modern writer should create his own new myths. Obviously, Masti was provoked by the attack on the *Varna* system in Kuvempu's play and the portrayal of the brahmin. Kuvempu's reply is a classic of modern Kannada criticism (Shivareddy 2003). He argues that the writer has to rewrite and reinterpret past myths because they are not mere narratives; they are associated with certain attitudes which they reinforce. To critique such attitudes, the writer has to reinterpret the familiar myths precisely because of their familiarity and power of persuasion. The debate in reality was about the claims over the literary past. Kuvempu, the first great shudra writer in Kannada, revisited the myths and legends of the past to use them to critique social asymmetries and to communicate a more humane and egalitarian attitude. For example, in *Beralge Koral* (A Life for a Thumb, 1947), a play about Ekalavya, the shudra disciple of Dronacharya who asks him to gift his right thumb as *guru dakshina*, Kuvempu transforms the character of Ekalavya into a representative of the tribal way of life and its cultural values. He is portrayed as the son of a tribal leader brought up by his tribal mother who is fiercely proud of tribal values. Arjuna is depicted as a selfish, envious representative of the palace culture, who forces his guru Drona to practically incapacitate Ekalavya as an archer, so that his own supremacy remains intact. Drona is a complex figure who regrets his helplessness because of his obligations to the Hastinapura kingdom. He believes that the inexorable law of karma will punish him for the injustice done to Ekalavya. Kuvempu thus makes the play a powerful indictment of the palace culture with its greed and selfishness. The forest in the play is 'an ethical pastoral' in which all living beings coexist with nature. Ekalavya's mother curses Drona and the Pandavas, and declares that for the gift of the thumb he had taken from Ekalavya, Drona would pay with his life. In another play, *Jalagara* (The Sweeper, 1931), Kuvempu makes Shiva declare that he is the world's sweeper and embraces the *Jalagara* who has been shunned by the others.

Kuvempu represents the awakening of a shudra consciousness which was also propelled by the impact of colonisation. The social energy unleashed by the *Vachanakara* movement of the twelfth century with the first collective participation of the artisan class, and the backward and Dalit communities, was gradually absorbed into the caste-society and had remained only as a powerful cultural memory. The non-brahmin movements of Tamil Nadu and Maharashtra did not make a direct impact on Karnataka. There was little to compare with the movement led by Jyotiba Phule or the later Ambedkar movement. Kuvempu himself, hailing from a wealthy Okkaliga family in the Malnad region, learnt about the caste system and the exploitative priestly class from his own experiences. His autobiography *Nenapina Doniyalli* (On the Boat of Memories, 1980) and his two great novels, *Kanuru Subbamma Heggadithi* (1936) and *Malegalalli Madumagalu* (Bride in the Hills, 1967), record these experiences. In Mysore, he stayed at the Ramakrishna Ashrama, and Ramakrishna Paramahansa and Vivekananda were the most powerful influences on him. He found in Vivekananda a powerful intellectual critique of the brahminical priestly class as well as the assertion of the universal values of the Upanishads. These two influences shaped Kuvempu's writings throughout his long career. On the one hand, there was a spiritual vision of the oneness of all living beings and nature. In his poetry, the primordial and grand beauty of the Western Ghats between which his home was nestled, becomes a symbol of the unity of all life. Kuvempu acknowledged that the source of this vision was the Upanishads and the Advaita world view which emerged from them. As Poornachandra Tejaswi points out, for Kuvempu Advaita meant a perception of the endless heterogeneity of the physical world and the great chain of being which held together all living things. In his poems and in the first novel, the vision is experienced in a state of *bhava samadhi*, a heightened emotional state during which the individual mind merges with the transcendental. Words such as '*paravasha*' are frequent in his poetry, describing the temporary loss of the self through the act of merging with the transcendental reality. By the time he wrote his second novel, *Malegalalli Madumagalu,* Kuvempu was trying to understand how such an experience occurs even to the illiterate who may not have the words to express it. He finds an explanatory framework in which Carl Jung's concepts of the collective unconscious, anima and mythopoeia play an important role. He believes that archetypal experiences enter into the collective unconscious and become the heritage of all human beings irrespective of their knowledge or position. Powerful physical sensations and sudden experiences defying logical explanations provoke the collective unconscious and we find the present connecting itself to the primordial or archetypal experience. For instance, on a cold morning when Subbanna Heggade stands near the threshold of the pig pen, some of the physical sensations provoke an archetypal experience of joy which his ancestors must have also experienced. In the novel, Kuvempu describes how some places are so deeply associated with past experiences that unusual states of mind are created among those who go near them. Many such experiences take place on *Hulikallu Nethi*, literally the 'Peak of the Tiger Rock'. Many of the important characters climb the peak during their journeys. Thimmi and Gutti, the runaway servant couple, have to spend a night in the ruins of a *mantapa* on this peak. Gutti goes in search of the other runaway couple, Mukundaiah and Chinnamma, leaving Thimmi alone. Gutti's dog barks as never before, and Thimmi sees a *saradar* (knight, soldier) galloping on his horse, picking up the bride waiting for him and galloping away. This is neither a dream nor a hallucination. A runaway pair of lovers in the unknown past may have been in the *mantapa* and, as a human, Thimmi relives that memory from some far-away past. There is also the extraordinary figure of Gaddadayya, the ascetic with a beard, a stranger to this region, with a collection of books in 'English', but with the supernatural gift of seeing into the future. He also has a telepathic connection with Swami Vivekananda who 'sees' some of the scenes taking place in this nondescript hamlet of the Malnad region. All these fictional strategies are employed to suggest that the events surrounding the future marriage of Chinnamma and Mukundaiah are part of a chain of events leading to the birth of a person who will play a role in the destiny of the culture to which the characters belong. Though the novel begins with the prefatory statement, 'Nothing is important here, nothing is unimportant, No one is important', the multiple narratives of this epic novel have a design behind them, namely the awakening of India's slumbering soul by Vivekananda. Gaddadayya says that, as preparation for that great event, he is here in Malnad to 'awaken the local gods'. The many historical references embedded in the novel support this.

The main events of the novel take place during the colonial period. On the day the local Christian padre is seen walking towards the house of Devayya, Vivekananda is addressing the world religions' meet in Chicago. The first hotel and the first hospital have come up in Thirthalli, the nearest town. A school has also been established where shudra children can also learn. The construction of the church building has started. Reverend Lakehill, the British priest, is later invited for the first conversion of a wealthy Okkaliga from a well-known family. A long section in the chapter openly discusses the issue of conversion. Kuvempu argues that the humiliation and injustice suffered by the shudra and Dalit communities is being used by the missionaries like a trap to catch innocent creatures for conversion. But the more important question is, what are the *mathas* and monasteries doing? Don't they have any concern for the shudras who are leaving the Hindu fold? He blames these religious institutions squarely for their orthodoxy, casteism and practice of untouchability. In the dramatic episode where Mukundaiah uses an empty gun to prevent the conversion of his cousin to Christianity, Reverend Lakehill makes an impassioned speech in which he tells Mukundaiah and others, 'If you do not want our religion we will not force you, but when will you [shudras] stop washing their feet with water and drinking it as holy water?' He also talks about the positive things which have been introduced by the British rule with the help of the missionaries, such as schools. Mukundaiah and his cousin decide that they will send all the children in their families to the school.

For Kuvempu, colonial modernity is double-faced. It can bring about the emancipation of the shudras from the clutches of the brahmin priestly class. Kuvempu himself chose the vehicle of colonial modernity as the medium of expression, to begin with. By the time he entered college he had already published two collections of poems in English, *The Alien Harp* and *The Beginner's Muse.* He had no plans of writing in Kannada. When he showed his English poems to J. H. Cousins, the Irish writer, the latter said dismissively, 'What is all this stuff?', and asked Kuvempu to write in his own language, Kannada. All these events are faithfully recorded in

Kuvempu's autobiography, large chunks of which are in English. It took some self-persuasion to start writing poetry in Kannada. Much later in his life he said, 'But for English I would have been cleaning vessels in some brahmin's house'. Like most shudras of the time, Kuvempu believed that education and English were the doors opened by the colonial masters for emancipation. Later he became a staunch supporter of Kannada as the medium of instruction at all levels. All the four great Kannada writers of the *Navodaya* period had excellent command over the English language and did much of their reading in it. They were not overawed by the great intellectual achievements in English. They were critical of modernity but did not feel threatened by it. They constructed their own versions of modernity freely using both indigenous and Western resources. Kuvempu was modern in his use of rationality to question and condemn the caste system, the *Varna* system and the priestly class. In his revolutionary poem 'Leave the Temple, the Church and Masjid', he advocates reliance only on the voice of the heart and not on Manu's Dharmasastra. He also advises the young to hold up the 'torch of science'.

Kuvempu is able to integrate his Jungian conception of the collective unconscious with his sense of history. It is possible to read *Malegalalli Madumagalu* as a cultural history of the Malnad region. There is a detailed, thick description of the feudal world of Malnad with its property disputes, illicit relationships, gross sexual exploitation of women workers, superstitious practices and scenes of hunting, which constitute the texture of the novel. U. R. Ananthamurthy made an uncharacteristic and naïve remark that Kuvempu's novels are lost in the 'fattened' details (or '*Kobbida*', as in the case of sheep, but also implying 'self-absorption'). In retrospect, it appears that Kuvempu wrote the novel when the *Navya* (literary modernist) school had not yet learnt to read it. The novel was read as rich in anthropological details but lacking in artistic unity. Kannada criticism took time to realise that Kuvempu had written a mythopoeic novel which challenges the normative rules of realism. It was the Dalit writer Devanoora Mahadeva who rediscovered Kuvempu with his own fiction in which the narrative tradition returns to the Dalit epic *Male Madeshwara Kavya*, and to the magic realism of the aural-oral folk traditions (Daniel 2015). Mahadeva has said that he did not have to learn from Latin American magic realism; he just had to return to the oral traditions of Kannada.

It is important to see that Kuvempu felt the need to write *Malegalalli Madumagalu*, which is essentially about sexuality, after he wrote his retelling of the *Ramayana* in *Srimad Ramayana Darshanam*. From every possible point of view, it is remarkable that an iconic, revered poet like Kuvempu should be writing an epic novel about the 'god of desire, ubiquitously present in the bedrooms of the kings and the dilapidated huts of the poor' (trans. Viswanatha 2024). It is a celebration of love and passion continuously trespassing the norms of the society. The elopement of Chinnamma, on the day of her marriage, with Mukundaiah results in the ostracisation of the two families and creates 'a first class scandal' (Ashis Nandy's favourite phrase!). Though there are indications that Kuvempu had written parts of the novel, and published some sections, he wrote the entire work after he had completed *Ramayana Darshanam*. The present writer sees this novel as a tribute to the anarchic energy and creative force of Eros as Freud describes in his last works.

Shivaram Karanth was a writer who wrote in all the known genres of his time, a dancer, singer, musician, photographer, filmmaker, single author of a science encyclopaedia in Kannada, an activist, publisher and ornithologist, among other things. He was also an environmentalist who fought and lost an election in order to stop the Kaiga nuclear plant in Uttara Kannada district. As most critics agree, it is his novels which have made him a household name in Karnataka. In a long career starting with detective thrillers, he wrote forty-odd novels, some of which are classics of modern Kannada fiction. Mention has already been made of the little classic *Sarasammana Samadhi*, probably the first work in Kannada to address the theme of feminine sexuality. Like Kuvempu, Karanth is the chronicler of a region—in his case, the rural coastal Karnataka. His better novels are about the small nondescript hamlets in the region of a time when except for the boats and rafts the only mode of transport was walking. He writes about the brahmin families which sustain themselves through priestly work occasionally, but mainly through hard agricultural labour. Karanth's vast world of fiction is expansive and includes even the cosmopolitan world of art and politics. Unfortunately, his later novels are works lacking in fictional vigour and closer to editorial comments on topical issues. But the great novels of Karanth are innovative and experimental and unmatched in artistic originality. One could make a case for the great damage literary histories can do to the reception of literary texts by noticing how the stereotypical treatment of Karanth as an intellectual rationalist writer, writing 'novels of purpose' which are lacking in aesthetic quality, in Kannada criticism has been an obstacle in the appropriate reading of his works. The *Navya* critics argued that Karanth was indifferent to the issues of form and structure, which explains his sheer inability to achieve artistic unity in his novels. The suggestion is that we read Karanth for the authenticity of the experience despite the artistic experience. Ananthamurthy, who had a troubled relationship with Karanth, wrote a brilliant essay *Karanthara Authentic Prapancha* (The Authentic World of Karanth, 2014). He uses the word 'authentic' in English. The major argument is that the better fiction of Karanth is valuable because of the authenticity of the experience, which also suggests indifference to the aesthetics of the novel. M. G. Krishnamurthy has something similar to say. These New Critics and formalists do not explain just how we understand the authenticity of experience unless it is expressed with original experimentation with the form of fiction. In retrospect, these comments seem totally beside the point.

The major question to be asked is how does Karanth's fiction deal with colonial modernity as well as issues relating to caste and untouchability, the country and the town in Karnataka, marriage, family and sexuality, the disillusionment with the ideals of the nationalist movement and the emergence of a footloose corrupt political and bureaucratic world. There are also the abiding questions about the nature of the self, individual creativity and a deep pessimism about the 'brave new world'. There is also the modernist view of the contradictions in the self. For example, who is the real Manjula of the extraordinary novel *Mai Managala Suliyalli* which narrates Manjula's experimentations with several relationships? The novel is, in a peculiar way, anachronistic. The events belong to the past, but the conceptualisation of feminine sexuality is modern. Even in the less successful novels such as *Bettada Tore* (The Stream That Never Dies, 1953) and *Swapnada Hole* (The River of Dreams, 1966), Karanth explores man–woman relationship from many perspectives. *Mookajjiya Kanasugalu* (Mookajji's Visions, 1968) is, in a way, the culmination of such exploration. Mookajji, confined to the constricted life of a widow, has the extraordinary gift of seeing visions of the passage of humanity through various phases of civilisation. She also has shocking comments to make on the lives of the people known to her. Like Phaniyamma, Mookajji possesses an objective, non-delusional understanding of sexuality. Compared to this kind of understanding in Kuvempu and Karanth, the angst-ridden problems with sexuality in the *Navya* (modernist) phase starting from the late 1950s, are certainly superficial. Wasn't the exploration of sexuality in the *Navya* school reductive and lacking in depth, compared to the later works of the *Navodaya* writers? Why are the major figures representing feminine sexuality in modernist Kannada fiction—such as Kamini in Shantinath Desai's *Mukti*, Chandri in Ananthamurthy's *Samskara*, the low-caste women in the short stories of Yashwanta Chittala—so one dimensional? Jagannatha in *Bharathipura* (1973) can see the woman servant (from a lower caste) as only 'big breasts and large thighs'. The entire *Navya* school was not able to produce a single woman character comparable to the women in the *Navodaya* fiction. It was the fictional writings of Devanoora Mahadeva which introduced the unforgettable Sakavva of *Odalala* and Kusumabale of the eponymous work. The right way to understand Kannada fiction is to read it as a space in which motifs and characters appear and reappear in new avatars in tune with the *yugadharma*, or the spirit of the times. What is required is a re-conceptualisation of literary history as synchronic, with the simultaneous presence of the past and present.

Karanth's novels consistently explore the relationship between the collective and the individual. Characters belonging to the older generation (especially women) attain maturity of mind by adhering to the values they have acquired from the community and society. Among them the most important one is the notion of *runa*, 'obligation' in the ethical sense of the word. These characters possess a deep sense of obligation to others and to the community in general. This is not obligation to a particular individual but the network of obligations one accumulates by being part of a society. This has to be repaid in some form or the other. The idea of obligation is transformed into an individual ethic which guides the actions and choices of the characters. In several novels such as *Chigurida Kanasu* (The Dream that Sprouted), *Marali Mannige* (Back to Earth, 1941) and *Nambidavara Naka Naraka* (The Believers' Heaven, Hell, 1958), this motivates the return to the ancestral land or village. It becomes a bond which is a value in itself.

But the characters belonging to the younger generation are modern individuals who do not find it easy to conform to the given values of the community. They possess a far more complex interiority which makes them interrogate the adequacy of those values themselves. In *Mai Managala Suliyalli*, the lives of the mother and the daughter differ because the values of the community cannot sustain one in a changed world. This brings us to the deep pessimism that Karanth's novels show towards the decline he sees in the modern world. He locates this decline in the corruption which had entered private and public domains during and immediately after the World War. The system of rationing food and other essential goods brought with it black marketing; smuggling of timber created the corrupt bureaucrat and local politician. The power of money made a devastating impact on the small traditional village communities. Added to this was the endemic poverty which destroyed the dreams of the young men who had given up education to participate in the nationalist movement and Gandhi's rural reconstruction programme. Karanth depicts a world of poor teachers, small landholders and small-time businessmen. Many of them returned to the village as Gandhi wanted them to, but they returned to a respectable poverty, and a helpless existence in a money-minded political world. Karanth's major novels of the period such as *Oudaryada Urulalli* (The Noose of Generosity, 1947), *Jaruva Dariyalli* (On the Slippery Path, 1952) and *Mugida Uddha* (The War Ends, 1945) are about the relentless struggle of the ordinary individual. The tragic irony of the last line of the novel *Mugida Uddha*, 'thus the war ended', expresses a deep pessimism because it is not the World War which ends but life which ends without even a whimper.

Karanth's satirical novels about the post-independence society play out the irony of the title of one such novel, *Naavu Kattida Swarga* (The Paradise we Created, 1980). The satire is harsh and negative, generally focussing on political corruption. Unfortunately, they are so heavily ideologically driven that in quality they do not rise above journalistic writing. The better novels of Karanth are constructed across a regional and cultural landscape he is most familiar with. In contrast, the satirical novels seem to be lacking a creative centre. Ananthamurthy came out with the argument that major writers of fiction in Kannada are at their creative best when they are writing about the world they had experienced in their childhood, which happened to be the local rural world. According to him, there is hardly any urban fiction in Kannada. Interestingly, this continues to be true of the Dalit writers who began to write in the 1980s. They also write powerfully about the *keri* (ghetto) of their childhood, and not about the urban spaces where they live. Two writers of the second generation of Dalit writing, Mogalli Ganesh and B. T. Jahnavi are exceptions to this.

Karanth broke the monotony of his satirical novels with some reflective, meditative novels such as *Ala Niraala* and *Sameekshe*, which may be lacking in rich fictional details but impress us with the power of their philosophical exploration.

2

Women's Writing

Women's writing in modern Kannada literature began in the early decades of the twentieth century. As discussed in the preceding section, Kannada fiction since its beginning had foregrounded the women's question and major writers addressed it centrally in their works. Surprisingly, when women writers themselves began to write ('not as objects but as subjects', as a critic has described it) they confronted major problems in the reception of their works. Two episodes in the history of women's writing in Kannada keep reverberating because they epitomise the patriarchy entrenched in the institutions of literature and literary criticism. The first episode is the long and extremely harsh piece of criticism that Masti Venkatesha Iyengar wrote on Nanjangudu Tirumalamba's (1887–1982) works. Tirumalamba, a child widow educated by her father, was an extraordinary individual of her times. She started and managed successfully a publication unit which she named Sati Hitaishini Granthamala, through which she published her novels which had a steady readership and were prescribed as textbooks in various courses of study in Mysore, Madras presidency and Bombay presidency. She was an author and activist who wrote articles and participated in the debates they generated. She wrote plays and also directed some of them for local performances. She belonged to the phase of women's writing named by D. R. Nagaraj as the '*kutumbini* phase' in which the woman is seen in the domestic sphere of marriage, family and children. The domestic world does not lead only to popular fiction (derided as 'kitchen writing') which sentimentally celebrates wifehood and motherhood. It is a site of unfreedom, violence and cruelty in intimate relationships. However, Tirumalamba's fiction is not about the dark world of domesticity. It is about the lives of the widows who, in her novels, 'renounce' all worldly affections, remain chaste and psychologically loyal to the dead husbands, and strictly adhere to the brahminical values. Inevitably, there are encounters with misguided men. The novels are thinly masked appeals to the 'good men' to think of these unfortunate sisters and learn to treat them better. Though this is the general tenor of the novels, Tirumalamba is capable of powerful rhetoric and of creating gritty independent-minded women who raise questions about male supremacy. Between 1911 and 1940 Tirumalamba published twelve novels and several plays. She also composed devotional songs.

Tirumalamba became a widow at the age of thirteen and was encouraged by her father to read and write. As a widow in a large traditional home, most of her time was devoted to cooking and cleaning. Like Lalithambika Antharjanam, she wrote her works at night. Though she did not shave her head, she lived as a traditional brahmin woman always clad in a white *madi* (ritually clean) sari. This was a time when widows were considered inauspicious, and were forced to make themselves practically invisible and survive on spice-less food (served once a day). It was believed that education for women was forbidden by the sastras. Women's education was also seen as a threat because educated women, it was believed, would turn out to be immoral wreckers of families. There was a widely held superstition that education was sure to bring early widowhood. Some of the most powerful and disturbing descriptions of such widowhood have come from Tirumalamba herself. As a young widow and activist-writer, she faced nasty criticism from neighbours and others. Against all odds, she turned her home into an informal school and a hub of activities for children. Critics like Vijaya Dabbe who have studied Tirumalamba's correspondence have commented on her hard work, courtesy and transparency in financial matters. Recent research has found evidence of a couple of novels published by other women before Tirumalamba's novels, but she was the most popular and well-known of the early Kannada women writers.

In 1921–22 Masti Venkatesha Iyengar, considered the father of the Kannada short story, wrote a long critical piece on Sati Hitaishini Granthamala, the publication unit led by Tirumalamba. Much later, he wrote a brief explanation admitting that he should not have been so harsh in his criticism. The flaws and weaknesses in Tirumalamba's novels are obvious to any reader. They are overly didactic with the writer addressing the reader and 'lecturing' (Masti's word). The dialogues are artificial, and the characters are flat and neatly categorised into black and white with no shades of grey. Both the cruel behaviour and the change of heart in the male characters, lack credibility. There are sections in which the author seems to be delivering a public address. Masti uses a sledge-hammer ironical style to expose these flaws. What makes the exercise suspicious is that Masti diligently misses the strengths of her writing—for example, the independence of some of the characters who ruthlessly expose the hypocrisies of the patriarchal society, and the firm assertion of the need to educate women. As pointed out earlier, in Karnataka, women's education faced severe opposition from the conservative groups. The struggle had to go on well into the later decades of the twentieth century. Masti must have noticed the unsettled prose style of early Kannada fiction (as in Galaganatha and Kerura Vasudevacharya) about which not a single comment is made. Nor does he focus only on the flaws in the fictional style. He questions Tirumalamba's insistence on women's education by asking whether uneducated women are ignorant. He questions Tirumalamba's criticism of men, wondering whether there are no good men in the world. These comments seemed to have hurt Tirumalamba greatly though she continued to write until the 1940s, but then she disappeared from the literary world.

The second episode is the rediscovery of Tirumalamba. C. N. Mangala who established Shashwati, the centre for women's studies, had written an article in which she had assumed that Tirumalamba was no more. When she came to know that Tirumalamba was in Chennai, she went in search of her. At the address given to her, she found an old woman who told her that Tirumalamba had 'gone away'. (The last phrase can also mean 'died' in Kannada.) However, Mangala discovered that the old woman was Tirumalamba herself. The episode was symbolic, because texts by many women writers of the past had disappeared, and had to be rediscovered by women academics such as Vijaya Dabbe and B. N. Sumitrabai. What emerges from such diligent research is that many women writers in the early phase were active journalists, founders of associations and institutions, and publishers and polemicists. Some of them were first-rate short story writers such as Kodagina Gowramma, Saraswatibai Rajwade, Shyamala Belgaumkar and Vasanthi Padukone. What did modernity mean to them? How did they formulate their own discourses of modernity?

There is no doubt that the debates on women's education, widow remarriage and professions for women were galvanised by the efforts of the colonial regime and the reformist section of the educated middle class. The British policy of education for all, and the efforts of the Christian missionaries as well as many British women themselves, encouraged girl children to join schools. In Karnataka it was the initiative taken by the Maharani of Mysore and some of her officers which helped the establishment of schools for women. The Bengal renaissance and Bangla novels influenced such debates among the educated class. Some of the reformists were in correspondence with Ishwar Chandra Vidyasagar. B. Venkatacharya was inspired by Vidyasagar to learn the Bangla language and he went on to translate nearly seventy works directly from Bangla. Many magazines and journals were also platforms for public debates on women's issues. Most women writers considered education as the gift of modernity. Tirumalamba argues that an educated woman can be a better wife and mother. Motherhood and wifehood were considered the supreme achievements for women. Tirumalamba, who wrote so powerfully about the plight of the widows, was opposed to widow remarriage and advocated celibacy and self-sacrifice for widows. There is a long discussion in her novel *Nabha* where Nabha argues that widow remarriage is against the values of *Bharata Varsha*. On the other hand, in another novel, *Vidyullata*, the heroine holds men responsible for the immoral behaviour of some women. Therefore, modernity had to be disciplined by the ancient Indian values. The autonomy of women beyond the domestic sphere was strictly out of bounds. There is an awareness of the unfreedom of women in a male-dominated society, but choices outside matrimony are not even imagined. It is difficult to believe that Karanth's *Sarasammana Samadhi* was published just fifteen years after the publication of Tirumalamba's novels. It was during these decades that major educational institutions and industries were established in Karnataka. There was considerable gap between the modernity of the state and the modernity experienced by women. This contradictory relationship between material progress (understood as modernity) and cultural conservatism (especially about women) has persisted in Karnataka society.

Tirumalamba expressed in her writing a small fragment of the women's experience of the period. Her adherence to the traditional image of the woman as *kutumbini*, as the epitome of all traditional values of 'Hindu' culture, prevented her from fully understanding the emerging formulations of womanhood. As Vijaya Dabbe says (1989), her critique of patriarchy was reformist without interrogating the foundational relationship between patriarchy and the 'womanly' values of chastity, and loyalty to the husband and family. In novels such as *Nandini*, Tirumalamba courageously exposes the hypocrisy of the *matha* (monastery) which resolves to impose a heavy fine on those who question tradition. Conservative readers were shocked that the widowed young daughter of a reputed Iyengar brahmin could satirise a religious institution. The paradox was that Tirumalamba in her novels reinforced the gender stereotypes which were the mainstay of religious tradition.

R. Kalyanamma (1891–1965), writer journalist and activist, also wrote on the same issues as Tirumalamba. She also tried to perpetuate the image of the Indian woman as a Rajput woman, a mix of courage and chastity. However, she participated in the contemporary debates on women's questions as a powerful voice speaking for gender equality. She wrote:

> Woman was not created to lie in man's power like a creature without intelligence, to pleasure him and to be his ornament. Woman has been created to secure the welfare of her own and the society. (quoted in Sumitrabai 2009)
>
> Though women and men are different in some aspects, they possess equal knowledge, intelligence, etc. Therefore enhancement of knowledge is of the highest utility to women as it is for men. (Ibid.)
>
> The present system of education has only earning money as its purpose and it is of no use in social service and the welfare of the family. (Ibid.)

B. N. Sumitrabai (2009) comments that when Kalyanamma wrote this in the second decade of the twentieth century, it was still considered a crime for women to walk on the streets alone. The Indian renaissance as well as the politics of the time, including Gandhian politics, supported the image of the Hindu wife as the preserver of the ancient values of motherhood, wifehood and the ideas of the *grihini*. Rabindranath Tagore, whose fiction explored the new Indian woman's experience with radical insights, would also regress to the adoration of the Indian woman as '*grihini*' and '*grihalakshmi*'. The Kannada women writers and their readers had no other idiom to conceptualise women. It should also be remembered that the readers were brought up on a steady diet of Bankim's novels and Marathi historical romances. Within such a shared cultural milieu, women writers of fiction examined the contradictions of a traditional society with irony and passion. The short stories of Kodagina Gowramma (1912–39) and Saraswatibai Rajwade (1913–94) are remarkable texts in the history of Indian feminism (Srivalli 2015). They reject the view that sexuality is a sin and condemn the hypocrisy of *brahmacharya*. H. V. Savitramma (1913–95) who translated Tagore's works into Kannada went on to write a powerful feminist retelling of the *Ramayana* story (Dabbe 1989).

One of the significant factors ignored in the literary histories is the extraordinary circulation of major discursive texts from one Bhasha to another, from one region to another, during this period. For example, in the Kannada novel *Indira Bai*, discussed earlier, one of the works Indira Bai reads is Pandita Ramabai's *Stri Dharma Niti*. This book was translated into Kannada and its publication was sponsored by the Mysore principality as part of the series H. H. Maharani Girls School Series (Dodamani 2014). The translation was published in 1919. Therefore, the Kannada reading public were familiar with the Tilak-led conservative school as well as with Ramabai. U. Maheshwari has also reproduced in her book the debates in the leading magazines of the period. When read together, the Kannada novels by women seem to be only an extension of these public debates. There seem to be very few studies of the astonishing peregrination and circulation of texts across India during this period. It should be mentioned that many members of the *Geleyara Gumpu* (friends' group), created by D. R. Bendre, went to Shantiniketan and met with Tagore. Halasangi, a small village from where another member of the group and poet Madhura Chenna (pen name of Halasangi Channamallappa) hailed, was recognised as an important centre for the study of Aurobindo's philosophy (Dodamani 2014). Shyamala Belgaumkar, in a later period, was a delegate to the AIWA meeting at Delhi, and was probably the first woman editor of a magazine to run a special section where readers could seek remedies for sexual problems. All these are excluded from literary historiography. The exclusive emphasis on the poetry of the *Navodaya* period (overlapping the same early decades) has excluded a whole world of debate in the civil society on the seminal issues of the time.

There are also interesting similarities among Indian Bhasha literatures in their responses to modernity. Tanika Sarkar (2003) has analysed the highly negative images of modern, educated women in the popular culture and popular performative arts in Bengal during the colonial period. These images of the imitative, Anglophone 'deracine', modern women also figure in the popular fiction of the period in Karnataka. (Though the distinction between serious literature and popular literature was a later phenomenon.)

Literary historiography has also ignored the cultural and ideological role of translation in the colonial period in Karnataka. B. Venkatacharya corresponded with Ishwar Chandra Vidyasagar, learnt Bangla in six months, and by 1877 had translated Vidyasagar's *Bhranti Bilas.* Thereafter, he went on to translate Bankim Chandra. Ananthamurthy and many others have recorded that in book shops, Kannada readers would ask for a 'Venkatacharya novel' without mentioning Bankim Chandra. The translations were immensely popular and influential. Venkatacharya was clear about the purpose of his translations of women-centric novels: his purpose was pedagogical, to educate readers on the true nature of Indian womanhood and to protect them from the obnoxious European notions of womanhood. Modern Kannada literature was articulating the male-centric traditional images of women, acquired through these translations.

3

The event inaugurating *Navodaya* poetry is said to be the publication of *English Geetegalu* by B. M. Sri. in 1926. M. V. Seetharamiah's foreword informs us that probably the manuscript of the work was ready by 1915–16 and that some of the translations were published in 1919, 1921 and 1924. The first edition was brought out by the Karnataka Sangha of Central College, one of the epicentres of the Kannada renaissance (Rajendra 1983). It is also clear that before B. M. Sri., Hattiangadi Narayana Rao had brought out a collection of translations of English poems. M. Govinda Pai (1883–1963) of Kasaragodu, a renowned poet and researcher, had also contributed to the birth of modern Kannada poetry by taking a vow that he would write poetry without maintaining *aadiprasa* (initial rhyme). This meant breaking away from the fundamental prosodic norm of Kannada poetry—the rhyming of every first syllable in any continuous verse form. None of these innovators were suggesting anything as radical as free verse. In fact, they all use conventional stanza forms and a regular rhyme scheme (terminal rhyme). But the act of breaking the conventional *aadiprasa* was seen as revolutionary.

B. M. Sri. had unequivocally declared (1921) that in the modern age Kannada should draw on the resources of English and not on Sanskrit. His views are part of a larger cultural politics. He felt that Kannada had been shackled by the scholarly conventions of Sanskrit. This was reflected in the predominance of verse forms of Sanskrit origin which did not suit the speech rhythms of Kannada and its natural flow. There had been *Desi* prosodic forms in the past but they were relegated to a lower position as forms of folk poetry. B. M. Sri. wanted to integrate these forms with the stanzaic forms of English poetry (Ibid.).

This prosodic innovation would unleash the creative energies of the modern age. As discussed earlier, English poetry also provided a repertoire of universal experiences and emotions common to human nature, such as love, war, nature and suffering. Though he did not see the need to theorise it, B. M. Sri. decided that the lexical choice in modern poetry should be the *achcha* (pure, kernel) Kannada words familiar to the educated Kannada speakers. Somewhat unselfconsciously, in his famous speech, he had said that we needed a Kannada which even women and shudras could understand (Ibid.). If one remembers the unsettled, cumbersome prose of the early novels of the period, one can understand the significance of B. M. Sri.'s plea for a standard literary dialect of Kannada.

There has been a great deal of discussion about B. M. Sri.'s choice of English poems, the consensus being that they do not represent the best of the English poetic tradition. Most of them were widely anthologised poems familiar from the texts used in the educational system. B. M. Sri. knew this and had explained that his criterion for choice was their familiarity. In a way, he de-contextualised and de-historicised the poems, treating them as dealing with universal human experience. The choice does not reflect the ideological and intellectual concerns of a literary movement such as British Romanticism. The poems are too varied and do not cohere into a representative group. These poems, some of them ordinary, had a great impact on Kannada poetry because they were 'secular' and 'this-worldly'. They were not poems preoccupied with the transcendental or even the spiritual. In the classicist, impersonal tradition, such 'worldly' poems about everyday experiences brought about a paradigm shift. (It is nobody's argument that either Sanskrit or Kannada poetry of the past did not possess these elements. But the dominant, hegemonic constructions of the two traditions prioritised the philosophical and transcendental.) As shall be discussed later, *Navodaya* poetry itself aimed at 'transforming the everyday into the transcendental', but the medium and vehicle would be everyday experience. As Bendre said in a fine poem, 'A flowering tamarind tree is enough' for the poet's mind.

The translations by B. M. Sri. are stunning in their originality and innovation. He takes considerable liberties with the originals and avoids the culturally unfamiliar elements, and does not believe in faithful translations which retain the foreignness of the original. He is clear about the functions of the translations—they are not meant to add to the knowledge of the reader; they are meant to galvanise a new kind of poetry in Kannada. In the introductory poem, *Kanike* (Gift), English and Kannada are described as two beloved women who share his love. He desires to see the one 'clad in the other's beauty', and the other 'dressed in the clothes of the one'. In an independent poem elsewhere, B. M. Sri. describes English/Britannia as the 'foster mother'. *English Geetegalu* includes a beautiful translation of the song 'Rule Britannia' which gave rise to a discussion on B. M. Sri.'s divided loyalties. As indicated earlier, the postcolonial perspective on English as the 'mask of conquest' was not part of the intellectual context of the *Navodaya* period. As the translations demonstrate, though on a lower scale, Kannada poets freely misread the English tradition and reinvented it to make it perform contemporary cultural tasks in Kannada. The postcolonial terms such as 'imitation' and 'influence' are not applicable in this creative process of the native/local tradition reformulating itself by pragmatically using another tradition. Postcolonial theories seem to attribute greater power to the imperial language and literary tradition than they exercised in the historical context (Chenni 2009).

Given the historical diversity of the 'local' cultures in Karnataka, it is not surprising that *Navodaya* poetry developed different trajectories at different epicentres of Kannada renaissance. At Mysore, B. M. Sri. himself was part of the institutionalised, academic trajectory of *Navodaya* writing. This was the product of a distinctive elite loyal to the Mysore principality, classicist in its Sanskrit-centric scholarship and with little direct experience of the linguistic pluralism of the kind which existed in North Karnataka. The Mysore tradition was also urban and did not have an intimate relationship with oral and folk traditions. The scholar–poets were well-informed about these traditions but did not introduce them into their poetic practice. B. M. Sri., Pu. Ti. Na. (P. T. Narasimhachar, 1908–98) and later K. S. Narasimhaswamy (1915–2003) and Gopalakrishna Adiga (1918–92) wrote in the standard literary dialect and show little influence of the oral traditions. Interestingly, a great deal of effort to collect folk literature and to research them was carried out at the University of Mysore, later in the 1950s and 60s; but this did not have an impact on Kannada poetry until the beginning of the Dalit and *Bandaya* literary movements of the 80s. In contrast, D. R. Bendre (1896–1981) and his *Geleyara Gumpu* belonged to a very different part of the cultural landscape where the urban-rural divide did not exist on the same scale and a 'separatist' idea of the folk made little sense.

The same was true of performative arts such as *Doddata*, *Bayalata* and *Krishna Parijata*. These forms themselves were heteroglossic and were products of multiple traditions. Even among the canonical works of Kannada poetry, it was Kumara Vyasa's (Gadugina Naranappa) retelling of the *Mahabharata*, Lakshmeesha's *Jaimini Bharata* and Ratnakaravarni's *Bharatesha Vaibhava* which were popular. These works are embedded in the oral traditions and use the *Shatpadi* and *Sangatya* metres which are also of folk origin. The geographical proximity to Maharashtra also meant familiarity with the Bhakti traditions of the region, as well as the oral literature associated with the popular cults. It was this hybrid and multilingual tradition which provided the creative sources for the *Navodaya* poetry of North Karnataka. In his preface to his famous collection of poems, *Gari* (1932), Bendre clearly states his understanding of *Navodaya*. Interestingly, there is no mention of English literature in the preface. He says that Kannada renaissance should aim at mirroring universal experiences and the spirit of the age in and through Kannada. He makes the significant statement that this can happen only when Kannada is empowered by scholars and writers to produce all forms of knowledge in it. Thirdly, he says that the Kannada dialect of the 'north of the Tungabhadra river' should also became the language of mainstream poetry. He also says that scholars should collect folk literature. His own poetic practice was very different from the kind B. M. Sri.'s translations promoted. It was poetry meant for recitation and singing. His 'performances' of reading/singing his own poems were mesmerising and quickly entered the repertory of the audience. Yet his poems drew also on the scholarly, Sanskrit-centric and sastric traditions. He did not have to make a conscious effort like W. B. Yeats to reconstruct a Celtic tradition of myths. Bendre was part of a living tradition. He could therefore present himself as the bard of the people, singing in a language of myths, cults and cultural memories which his audience were familiar with.

Also, his poems are complex and have, at times, an intricate symbolist structure. There is endless wordplay and use of puns, only a part of which is communicated in a recitation. There are also reverberations of literary memories from the entire tradition. He uses the Vedic metre as confidently as the folk ballad. In this context it is necessary to keep aside the many personae which Bendre donned and attempt to historicise his work in the context of the construction of modernity which was central to *Navodaya*.

Chandrashekhar Kambar argues (in Shivarudrappa 1975) that Bendre is not a folk poet singing the experiences of an organic community. He is, like all modern poets, a latecomer when the pre-modern organic community has already been split by the advent of colonial modernity. The community no longer possesses the cultural unity to facilitate a spontaneous expression. The poet has to be necessarily self-conscious and complex. He may be immersed thoroughly in the traditional poetic models and practices, but he has to mould them to explore new experiences.

Like all Kannada poets of the time, Bendre saw his poetry as a participant in the unification of Kannada. His poetry was to be the recreation of all possible emotions, feelings, experiences and gestures of the Kannada people. The poetic cosmos was to be the counterpart of the *Kannadanādu* now becoming a political and historical reality; therefore his poetry had to be as diverse as the imagined community itself. He had to begin with Sadhankeri, the outskirts of Dharwad where he lived, and his poetry would transform it into the universe itself. The reconstruction of the *Kannadanādu* demanded everything from the poet.

In a remarkable poem *Kanasinolagondu Kanasu* (A Vision in a Dream), Bendre encounters the figure of Mother Kannada in a dream and asks her what she would demand from him. She replies, 'If you are man enough, will you sacrifice yourself?' In another poem, the Mother loudly laments her 'good-for-nothing thirty-three crore children'. The very register of the unification movement was replete with images of the mother—that is, language as mother and the land as mother. Bendre subverts the image by comparing her to *Chandi* and *Chamundi*—mother in her darker aspect, demanding sacrifice. For Bendre, the idea of Kannada goes far beyond the agenda of constituting a linguistic state. In his vision, Kannada should expand to include the world itself.

There is no doubt that Bendre's major concerns are philosophical. He has repeatedly explored the relationship between the ordinary and the transcendental. But for him the exploration does not involve the rejection of the real sensuous world. One of his finest poems, *Belagu* (Dawn), describes the beauty of the dawn as seen near Attikolla in Dharwad in metaphors of stunning originality. There are few parallels to his recreation of the rich sensuous world in this poem. However, in the last stanza he says that it is not merely a dawn but the embodiment of the *shanti rasa.* His meditations on the mysteries of the earth take him to metaphysical densities.

However, Bendre has also written the most enduring and intense descriptions of the contemporary world. He describes the farmer as the 'eldest born of mother earth', but poverty and deprivation have made him a walking corpse. His lungs seem to be blackened with soot. In another poem, *Tuttina Cheela* (The Food Sac), he uses dark irony to show the contrast between 'the belly of stored wealth so full and struggling to ease itself', and the stomachs of the poor like 'empty bags without food'. The world is like the 'intoxicated devotees of the money goddess who wore around her neck, the chain made of the bones of pregnant women and sockets of the eyes of dead children'. He blames gods for taking ten avatars but not the *Annavatar* ('god as food'). There are such dark and disturbing images of poverty in many of his poems. One such poem, titled *Narabali* (Human Sacrifice), so angered the British that Bendre was jailed and then kept under surveillance. This made it difficult for him to find a steady job. He also wrote a 'poem of those without work', a remarkably Brechtian poem. The distinctive quality of his dark wit pervades the two absurd plays he wrote many decades before the term 'absurd' was even heard of. *Sayo Aata*, the 'Game of Dying', surpasses *The Threepenny Opera* in its motley characters—the thief, his wife, the corrupt guard, the lunatic king and his prime minister. Bendre was deeply suspicious of power and employed hyperbole to ridicule it. He writes that 'the gods are said not to blink their eyes (they are *animesha*) but their ever-open eyes are unable to see poverty. This is the problem with those who are drunk on *Amrutha* and burp [in pleasure]' (Bendre 1932, 57–60). He also satirised religion and the sastras which are indifferent to the plight of child widows and abandoned widows.

Bendre was also the first modern poet in Kannada to write about the destruction of the earth by human greed and aggression. He describes the arrogant kings of the past who tried to subjugate the earth for their pleasure and glory as 'mother fuckers'. But the mother earth in the poem is capable of devouring them 'in fistfuls'. In another poem, mother earth in her gentle but sad aspect, says to man, 'Son, I am not a thing that you can beat [at your pleasure]: I am the living womb'.

At a time when the new poetry of the age was becoming alienated from common readers, Bendre created a poetry of extraordinary depth which reached out to all: 'The palace, the hut and the street', as he put it.

Kuvempu (K. V. Puttappa, 1904–94) declared his poetic manifesto in the poem *Gobbara* (Manure). He questions why, according to the conventions of poetics, it is inappropriate to write on manure. He writes this in his distinctive poetic style with a mix of *Nadugannada* (middle Kannada) and the earthy spoken Kannada. Being the first important shudra writer, he raises questions about the exclusion of a whole domain of experience, of the peasants, as unworthy to be the subject of poetry. The poem also becomes an evaluation of mainstream poetry with its long history of being about palaces, kings and queens. It was only during the *Vachanakara* movement that the artisan class and the lower castes entered the domain of the literary. For about eight centuries until the *Navodaya* period, their social worlds remained unrepresented. Kuvempu wrote another poem titled *Karisidda*, the name itself suggesting the inferior status of the person. At a time when Kannada novels had outlandish Bangla names for all characters, Kuvempu subverts the meaningless convention by using the name Karisidda. His novels were the first literary works in Kannada to feature Dalit characters in flesh and blood. Kuvempu employs two very different poetic registers. One is closer to the 'educated' speech and avoids obsolete expressions. The other is where he uses a Sanskritised diction and writes on philosophical themes centred around his vision of the unity of all life. These are meditative poems exploring the merging of the individual soul with nature. M. H. Abrams' phrase about English, Romanticism, 'natural supernaturalism', is an appropriate description of Kuvempu's poetry. However, as Shankar Mokashi Punekar (2012) points out, Kannada *Navodaya* poetry, sometimes called *Ramya* (Romantic) poetry, had indigenous philosophical sources such as Advaita, the philosophy of Ramakrishna Paramahansa. For the English Romantics, poetry was the means to bridge the Cartesian subject-object split, while the Kannada *Navodaya* poets draw on Indian philosophical sources which believe in the oneness of the subject and object. Both Bendre and Kuvempu see nature as the embodiment of the divine.

The other poetic mode used by Kuvempu is that of 'poetry as speech'. It is an open-ended form directly addressing the reader with very little effort to achieve an aesthetic structure—the style of most of the poems in the collection *Kogile Mattu Soviet Russia* (1944). The title poem 'The Cuckoo and Soviet Russia' is an extraordinary satire on the system of surveillance and espionage of the iron-curtain era. In another poem, Kuvempu mocks the political regime by asserting that Kannada has a permanent cabinet of ministers with the poet Pampa as the chief minister. His poem celebrating the multi-religious pluralistic traditions of Karnataka as 'a garden of peace where all communities live together' has been adopted as the state anthem of Karnataka. Another poem eulogising the farmer as *Negila Yogi* (Yogi with the Plough) has been adopted as the *Raitageethe* or the song of the farmers. Unfortunately, not many have seriously studied how poetry emerged as a public discourse during the *Navodaya* period. Like the songs of Tagore, the songs of the *Navodaya* poets penetrated deep into the public domain and became part of the aesthetic experience of the ordinary men and women who had little to do with the 'literary'.

G. H. Nayak has argued that Kuvempu attempted to create a democratic literary culture in which the traditional aesthetic conceptions would not prevent a poet from writing about the suffering and dignity of the common people. The very landscape of the Malnad region, until then known only as the region of wild animals and dreadful diseases, emerges in his poetry and fiction as a distinctive 'culture land' (term used by Sheldon Pollock in a different context). Though Kuvempu himself thought of *Ramayana Darshanam*, his epic retelling, as his greatest work, it is his poems, essays, plays and the two great novels which earned him the title *Yugada Kavi*, the poet of the age.

4

The many facets of modernity were also the central concern of Masti Venkatesha Iyengar (1891–1986) who began writing short stories around 1911. He was a poet, playwright, novelist, essayist, and editor of the long-running magazine *Jeevana*. His early short stories with Rangaswamy (Rangappa) as the protagonist are about the absurd anomalies caused by a hasty and superficial modernity adopted by the educated young men of the time. Rangaswamy's indiscretions in trying to impose his modern ways on the traditional society lead to hilarious situations. The narrator is a liberal, tolerant elder who narrates these incidents with great enjoyment. Rangaswamy's insistence that there should be a long 'courtship' and that his wife should write letters to him, etc., lead to unexpected consequences. The most significant aspect of the stories is the consciousness represented by the narrator. He is confident that 'tradition' is large enough to absorb the new tangled modernity. There is the understanding that colonial modernity has brought 'individuality' which is suspicious of tradition. This has the potential to create conflicts and probably threaten the traditional institution of marriage, unless modernity is accommodated. The stories do not consider the confrontation of tradition and modernity as a serious conflict. But if a false notion of modernity leads to the transgression of social morality, it cannot be condoned. In some of the stories of the period Masti deals with the trespassing of marital and sexual normative rules by indiscreet young men. Masti's writings reveal a distinctive life-view integrating a liberal humanist tradition with an expansive conservatism. The later short stories of Masti deal more openly with extra-marital relationships and even incest.

There is a group of stories in which the narrators are English—Emily, Farquhar and Courtney. These are individuals with interest in and respect for Indian and local traditions. They are also aware that scholars and collectors like them are taking away the remnants of a historical legacy. In one of the stories, they visit a small village in search of the paintings of a painter who had left behind unfinished paintings. The old man of the house narrates how the beautiful painting of Krishna was left unfinished when the painter was killed trying to defend the village. When the English visitors express their desire to take the painting away, the old man says that there is a belief that one of the children born into the family would someday complete the painting. For Emily the entire episode seems symbolic of the encounter between the two cultures, owing to colonialism. She argues that like the unfinished painting, Indian culture is awaiting the birth of someone who would have the talent and vision to complete it. By wanting to take away the painting the English are disrupting a tradition which will someday discover its own resources. This theme reappears in *Rangenahalliya Rama* in which an English officer and scholar decodes a popular song which indicates where the original temple of Lord Rama was hidden to protect it from a marauding army. The stories in this group assert the greatness of the native culture by creating sympathetic English characters who admire the hidden resources of the colonised culture and society. D. R. Nagaraj takes a very negative view of these stories as poorly written propaganda of native culture. He also criticises Masti for his non-conflictual interpretation of the encounter of two cultures under the rubric of a powerful imperial power.

It is in the novels *Chikka Veera Rajendra* and *Channabasava Nayaka* that Masti unravels the dark face of imperialism. In *Chikka Veera Rajendra*, the last of the Kodagu kings causes the downfall of the ruling dynasty by his unbridled sexuality and the extreme sadistic violence of his personality. But in the opening passage Masti makes it clear that the imperial regime wanted the important geopolitical region of Kodagu and was eagerly awaiting the downfall of the king through his own misdeeds. The reports of the English officers on this issue are brilliantly used by Masti to examine how the imperial narrative of protecting the natives from cruel rulers was being created. The council of the elders of Kodagu is caught in a dilemma whether it should allow the English to intervene. A powerful section of the novel deals with the indigenous system of checks and balances within the community itself, and with how it had been in the past able to exercise control over the excessive power of the king. With the coming of the British such indigenous systems also become irrelevant. The juggernaut of imperialism moves on, ending local cultures. From his early stories about the indiscretions of modernity, to a profound understanding of the laws of imperialism, Masti's writings map a whole area of exploration.

***

Colonial modernity energised the Kannada renaissance, and it also helps us to understand the fragmented nature of literary and intellectual traditions generated by the renaissance. In many important ways, the renaissance was not a disruption or a disjuncture. Major Kannada writers went on to draw from the indigenous cultural and religious resources, and had near absolute faith in the capability of such resources to negotiate with colonial modernity. It is not surprising that Vivekananda and Aurobindo were the intellectual leaders chosen by the major Kannada writers of the period. The idea that the technological superiority and political power of the imperial West could not make a dent on the supremacy of Indian spiritual traditions, influenced the writers. Such frameworks, from one perspective, prevented a radical understanding of colonialism itself. From another perspective, despite all the major writers being familiar with the Western literary and philosophical traditions, they did not become Eurocentric in their effort to face up to colonialism. However, the expression of the cultural-literary aspiration of the subalternised groups, which had made a small beginning, had to wait for some more decades to come to the forefront. The hegemony of the educated middle class remained firm, despite the diversity of the innovation and experimentation in the literature of the period.

SEVEN

Literary Modernism: The *Navya* Phase

1

The inaugural moment of the literary modernist movement in Kannada (*Navya*) is generally considered to be the publication of *Chande Maddale*, a collection of poems by Gopalakrishna Adiga (1918–92). What is interesting is that the two terms in the title, *Chande* and *Maddale*, refer to two percussion musical instruments used in the performative art named *Chande-Maddale*. Gopalakrishna Adiga, who had served a long apprenticeship with *Navodaya* poetry, declared his view of the Kannada poetry to come, along with a negative critique of *Navodaya* poetry. This act of literary patricide caused passionate and ideological debates in the Kannada literary context. In retrospect it appears as though colonial modernity did not cause as much a disruption as did the *Navya* movement. In turn, this led to a major split in the reading public. The supporters of the *Navodaya* school of poetry argued that *Navya* literature was the product of a small clique of Anglophile imitators of the West. *Navya* poets and critics had serious disagreements with the vague and amorphous idealism and spiritualism of *Navodaya* poetry. G. H. Nayak summarises the *Navya* critique of this poetry:

> Though the works in the *Navodaya* tradition were the fruits of a unique and rare synthesis, it appears as though a situation arose in which it was not possible for the creative spirit of the writers of this tradition to fully respond to the experiences of life from a specific centre and source of their personality. . . . That is why the *Navodaya* writers seem to use their creative spirit sometimes in the individualist mode, sometimes in a societal mode and at other times in a mixed mode. (Nayak 1989, 23–24)

The unique synthesis Nayak mentions is the complex blend of the individualism which colonial modernity and the influence of English literature had created and the societal orientation created by nationalism. Shankar Mokashi Punekar argues that nationalism worked as a 'barrage' or a filter which prevented the devastating flood of Western modernity (in Harish 2012, 151–53). Major writers of the colonial period drew their creative energy from indigenous cultural and intellectual resources. But this synthesis did not hold in the post-independence period. The disillusionment of the Nehru era, the failure of the idealism of the freedom struggle and the decline of democratic institutions created a spirit of critical realism. Adiga, the leader of the *Navya* movement, constructed a complex, multipronged critique of *Navodaya* poetry. It had declined into a sentimental rhetoric and an amorphous idealism. The best of *Navodaya* poetry centred around the spiritualisation of the ordinary experience and a vision of the transcendental. In the hands of the lesser poets it had become a posture and a dishonest jugglery with words. In a satirical poem, *Hale Maneya Mandi* (People of the Old House), Adiga describes the poet indulging in a 'badminton play' with words. He describes him as 'a soul wearing cloth made without the spool of thread': He also uses the metaphor of 'lovemaking of an old couple' for the spiritual poetry with no tension in it (Adiga 1999–2000, 268–70). Adiga's critique focuses on the lack of creative tension masked by an impressive but empty rhetoric. The failure is both aesthetic and ethical. The poetry does not become an event in language, an enactment of the experience in words, images and symbols, held together by a sense of structure. The ethical failure is a collective one in which the word and the act became separated. There was no substantial basis any longer for the idealism which was now a dishonest gesture. The iconic figure of this decline is Nehru who is described as an eternal young hero who refuses to leave the stage even when the curtain has come down (Adiga 1999–2000, 283–84). His politics is compared to 'sailing on two boats, one foot in each and pining for the third way'. This is a reference to the state socialism and the mixed economy as well as to the alternative Third World politics Nehru spoke of. Interestingly, Girish Karnad (1971) also suggests that his play *Tughlaq* had to do with the disillusionment of the Nehru era.[1] In several satirical poems, Adiga describes the decline of democratic politics into demagoguery and mindless sloganeering. It is evident that he was rebelling against his own idealism derived from the long apprenticeship to *Navodaya* poetry. But as U. R. Ananthamurthy argued, Adiga's personal, individual concerns were also the cultural concerns of the period (in the Preface to *Bhoomigeetha*, in Adiga 1999–2000, 581–602). Adiga's rebellion was also against a metaphysical tradition which was abstract and impersonal and treated the real world as secondary to a transcendental order of reality. This tradition did not insist on the authenticity of individual experience. In a seminal essay, 'The Smell of the Soil', Adiga reflects on the metaphor 'smell of the soil' which he finds missing in many of the Indian aesthetic and philosophical traditions as well as in *Navodaya* poetry. The metaphor

[1] Karnad Girish, *Tughlaq*. Introduction to the English translation. OUP, 1971. In the introduction, U. R. Ananthamurthy quotes Karnad's interview in *Enact*.

refers to the concrete individual experience which involves confrontation with the unresolvable contradictions of human existence:

> The soil is dirt, rubbish, manure, worms and the rotting foul-smelling product of the bodies; it is also the budding leaf, blossoming flower; the sourness of the raw fruit. . . . A rejection of the duality inherent in life leads to smug sermonising in life and rhetoric in poetry, and to a marked preference for the sound and not the meaning of the words. (translated and quoted in Chenni 2009)

The deliberate choice of the smell of the soil as metaphor indicates the intensity of Adiga's revolt against a certain kind of poetic practice based on a philosophical tradition which did not acknowledge the dualities of real existence. In his view, *Navya* poetics valorised the concrete recreation of experience in all its complexity in words, so that the poem becomes an act, an event in language. He coined the Kannada equivalent for Eliot's 'objective correlative' and made it central to *Navya* criticism.

Kirtinath Kurtakoti (2015, 38–40) wrote a long response to Adiga's arguments, expressing the view that literary modernism came to Kannada as the 'personal necessity' of Adiga and others, and not as a response to a changed social context as Adiga claimed. He says that the English Romantic tradition had exhausted its energy and therefore the modernist poets needed a radical breaking away from it. Adiga's comments that *Navodaya* poetry was lost in the fog of Vedanta was not true. There was nothing comparable to the post-war (First World War) trauma in the Indian context to justify the talk about disillusionment. Kurtakoti was wrong because literary modernism, expressing a deep sense of disillusionment and alienation, was not confined to the Kannada context. From the 1960s, most of the Bhasha traditions went through a phase of literary modernism. There was a shared sentiment of the failure of the pre-independence idealism. There is no denying the fact that the models for the new writing came from the Anglo-American high modernism of Ezra Pound, T. S. Eliot and later W. H. Auden. Adiga acknowledges the influence of this movement on his poetry. It should also be mentioned that this was the decade when European existentialism made a big impact on the Kannada writers. Girish Karnad (1980) records in his autobiography how his initiation into modernism took place through August Strindberg's plays and then through Jean Anouilh and Albert Camus. U. R. Ananthamurthy introduced Sartre and existentialism through his essays in *Prajne Mattu Parisara* (1971). Shantinath Desai (1929–98), the author of the first modernist novel in Kannada, *Mukti* (1961), was a self-declared existentialist. That the post-war European existentialism should be a major influence on Kannada writing in the 1960s is an interesting phenomenon.

Two 'little journals' played an important role in publishing modernist poetry and criticism, and also in keeping many debates alive. Adiga edited *Sakshi* and Chandrashekhar Patil and others edited *Sankramana*, two of the most influential journals of the period. The Coffee Club at Mysore, presided over by Adiga; Manohara Grantha Mala at Dharwad; and the book houses in Gandhibazar in Bengaluru were the *addas* of the *Navya* school. There were accusations of *Navya* being the product of a small clique, consisting basically of professors of English, disdainful of the Kannada tradition of the past. There were also charges of conscious or unconscious plagiarism of Western literary modernism. What was new was the critical spirit which cared little for established reputations and revered icons. It was Adiga, Ramachandra Sharma and Chandrashekhar Patil who created a new literary environment in which the writers were not seen as visionaries and gurus. There were debates, controversies and also acrimonious quarrels but the spirit of enquiry was kept alive.

Compared with the *Navodaya* movement which was part of the Indian renaissance and therefore addressed issues of seminal historical importance, the canvas of the *Navya* movement was a much diminished one. Though the term alienation was used rather glibly during the *Navya* movement, there was a real sense of the loss of connection with tradition. Most of the *Navya* writers did not have an intimate knowledge of the Kannada tradition of the past. Ananthamurthy declared that the contemporary Kannada writer needed to know only Camus, Kafka, Sartre and the twelfth-century *Vachanakaras*, to be creative (2014). Religion and spirituality seemed irrelevant and false. The young writer saw them as part of a 'bad faith'. *Navya* was essentially a literary revolt against middle-class morality and hypocrisy. There was also the need to confront the real nature of sexuality. In the novel *Mukti* (Liberation, 1961), the education of the hero Girish takes place first through his failure to accept Kamini's sexuality and later through the liberating sexual experience with Dolly in Mumbai. In Ananthamurthy's *Samskara* Praneshacharya's realisation of the inadequacy of the brahminical values comes through the unexpected sexual union with Chandri. In Yashwanta Chittala's (1928–2014) short stories such as *Havu* and *Sere*, sexuality is both the central theme and the metaphor. In his novel *Mooru Darigalu* (1964), the scandal of Nirmala's supposed intimacy with a man shatters the local society. Ramachandra Sharma's (1925–2005) famous poem *Yelu Suttina Kote* (The Seven-Walled Fort) is about the discovery of the sexual self. The predominance of sexuality as the major theme in *Navya* literature drew sharp and shocked responses. Adiga's poem *Prarthane* was accused of being pornographic and attempts were made to censor it. One of Adiga's finest poems, *Prarthane* uses sexual metaphors for explaining the serious theme of the extremes of introversion and extroversion, of solipsism and promiscuous worldliness. Like Auden's poem 'Sir, No Man's Enemy', the poem is an ironical prayer to God to provide a sense of balance between the contradictions of the human personality. Critics have also commented on how sexual experience is used in relation to the authenticity of individual experience. The problem is that individual experience is defined in a reductionist manner, as the experience of a small section of the post-independence generation finding itself in an emotional crisis. As Ananthamurthy repeatedly pointed out, *Navya* Kannada fiction was about the experience of young writers leaving their small regional roots and arriving in the city. As in P. Lankesh's (1935–2000) novel *Biruku* (The Split, 1967), the city is a Kafkaesque place where the bewildered protagonist encounters strange experiences. He is an alienated individual with a split consciousness. While it is true that this was the experience of a generation in post-independence India, *Navya* claimed it to be a universal existential phenomenon. The individual experience became unconnected with the collective experience.

Yashwanta Chittala is a master craftsman; and his short stories, carefully sculpted, deal with sexuality as well as the passions of revenge, aggression and cruelty, which seem to lurk just below the façade of the civilised self. In stories such as *Aata* (Game) and *Savu* (Death), Chittala explores the uncanny and the unanticipated in human life. His major novel *Shikari* (The Hunt/The Hunted) is about the trials of Nagappa, an innocent individual trapped in the hunting game that the invisible powers of the multinational corporate world play. The unexpected turns and twists in the plot make it a gripping detective story, but the themes are serious. Nagappa is stripped to the bare bones of life and is made to confront the truth about himself, which he had suppressed. The stories of Chittala take place either in Hanehalli, a village, or in a Bombay (Mumbai) chawl, or in corporate offices. But the disturbing aspects of human nature depicted in the narratives remain the same. In a later novel, *Purushottama*, the underbelly of Bombay with its criminal underworld and the realty business mafia, is at the centre. Human grit and determination is tested to the extreme in the novel, and the first rays of light are seen only at the end of the narrative. Chittala's fictional world is close to the world as Freud imagines it in *Civilization and Its Discontents*—an endless battle between the life force and the death instinct hiding behind the sophisticated cosmopolitan life. There is always the mysterious and the unexpected traumatising ordinary human beings.

B. C. Ramachandra Sharma (1925–2005), the most articulate figure of *Navya* literature before Adiga, wrote a highly experimental, symbolist poetry on diasporic experience, the contemporary West as well as on myths and legends from the past. Unlike Adiga, who attempted to recover an Indian past and tradition in his later poetry, Sharma remained an unrepentant modernist. Some of his finest poems are on the act of writing poetry.

P. Lankesh (1935–2000) explores the hypocrisy, self-deception and evil in human beings, and unravels the motives behind human behaviour. His characteristic work is the play *Teregalu* (Waves) in which three unknown outsiders walk into a middle-class home and turn the visit into a terrifying trial. In his later novel, *Mussanjeya Katha Prasanga* (Listening to Tales at Twilight), Lankesh returns to the village milieu of his childhood to portray a hilarious and absurd world of love and politics.

Gopalakrishna Adiga revisits the theme of tradition and modernity in his poetry. In *Aagaboti* (Steamship) he uses the stranded unmoving steamship as a metaphor for stagnant tradition. Once upon a time the ship used to make voyages to the seven seas and unknown islands and continents with the spirit of intellectual adventure and creativity. But for many centuries the pilot and the navigators chose to keep it still, believing that there was nothing more to explore. 'But of late, the typhoon from the West hit the ship, splintering its boards. Some jumped into the sea and swam ashore'. The stagnant tradition has been rocked by the devastating impact of the West and its modernity. The resolution at the end of the poem is to rebuild the ship, using the surviving boards, and start on a fresh voyage. The possibility hinted here of regathering the resources of the indigenous culture is developed in poems such as *Bhootha* (The Past, Ghost and Unconscious). In this poem, the unpropitiated ancestors haunt the present like ghosts. An un-reclaimed past can also turn the present into a ghost. What went wrong was that 'we trusted the priests and became *Pashimabuddhi*'. The pun on the word can also mean 'possessed by the West'. The rest of the poem enacts the process of digging for gold, finding the ore, smelting it into gold and making 'one's own deities' with it. This is the process of exploring the past and remaking it to suit the needs of the present. In another poem, *Shri Ramanavamiya Divasa*, Lord Rama is imagined as the 'greatest of men' (*Purushottama*) who was also the creation of Valmiki who meditated until anthills grew around him. In Rama, the dualities of action and contemplation were integrated. But 'does darkness have only ten heads?' The battle between good and evil enacted in the epic has to be re-enacted, again and again.

Adiga's preoccupation with the past, imagined in traditional myths and puranic legends, provoked a backlash from the post-*Navya* writers—that his was a poetry of conservative brahminical sensibility despite his aesthetics of modernity. How was his search for a brahminical past different from the Western-Orientalist reconstruction of the Indian past? Wasn't he repeating the conservative response to modernity which was also revivalist in its conception of the past?

In his satirical political poems, Adiga's condemnation of ideologically driven mass politics sounds almost undemocratic. Even a sensitive reader and critic like P. Lankesh commented harshly on these elements in Adiga's poetry.

U. R. Ananthamurthy's (1932–2014) major preoccupations figure in *Bharathipura* (1973) which received a mixed response from Kannada critics. The protagonist Jagannatha has returned from the UK to his ancestral home, with a mix of Lohiaite-Marxist notions about the stagnation of his hometown as owing to the grip of Lord Manjunatheshwara, the local deity worshiped in the famous temple. He feels that every form of creativity is at a standstill because no one wants to be responsible for anything. He decides that he will make the wheel of history move again by making the Dalits enter the temple. The novel is replete with semi-allegorical characters representing various perspectives on Indian society—such as the Westernised Mr Puranik (Nirad Chaudhary), Adiga the priest (conservative brahmin), Sripathi Rao (the failed Gandhian) and a young Ambedkarite politician. The plan of temple entry is subverted, ending in the reinforcement of the miraculous power of Lord Manjunatha. *Avasthe* (State of Being, 1978) is a political novel based on the life of Gopala Gowda, a charismatic socialist leader in Shivamogga district. Despite the interesting analysis of contemporary Karnataka politics, the novel does not succeed in integrating the personal quest of Krishnappa, the politician–hero, with the real political world.

Ananthamurthy's short stories are his greatest achievements, with a complex verbal texture, the blend of realism and symbolism and the ambitious purpose of the writer to address the fundamental aspects of existence such as sexuality, the mind-body conflict, and the contradictions of the real and the transcendental. The story *Suryana Kudure* (The Stallion of the Sun) works around two childhood friends, Ananthu and Hade

Venkata, meeting after many years. Ananthu is the successful Westernised, modern individual, while Venkata has been a failure, hated by his son, disliked by his family and ridiculed by the community. For Ananthu, he is the symbol of the backwardness and stagnation of tradition with its indifference to the everyday world. But Venkata is a mystic masseur who can show stars with his magical massage. He is the one who stands beyond conflicts and one who cannot be colonised by modernity. The story becomes a philosophical exploration of two world views and two types of personalities that cultures can create. Venkata cannot be a part of the rational world of progress and power. Ananthamurthy's skill in moving deftly between two contraries is in evidence in this story. The theme is an extension of his reflective prose writings collected in *Poorvapara* (which also means *Poorva*, the East, and *Apara,* the West). Several of his essays including 'Why not Worship in the Nude?' are about the Indian writer's tryst with modernity and tradition. From the radical modernity of *Samskara* he moved towards positioning himself as a critical insider and expressed his disillusionment with modernity, but always acknowledging his debts to it.

2

Navya literature in Kannada moved along a distinctive trajectory. The initial phase illustrated by Adiga and Ramachandra Sharma, and taken further by Ananthamurthy, Lankesh, T. G. Raghava, Girish Karnad and many others, was followed by its transformation under the impact of other literary movements such as Dalit and *Bandaya*, as well as by the people's movements during as 1970s and 80s. D. R. Nagaraj used the nomenclature *Moola Navya* (original *Navya*) and *Parivartita Navya* (transformed *Navya*) for the two phases. The Dalit and *Bandaya* movements raised radical questions about Kannada literature in general and *Navya* in particular. The questions were about the concepts of tradition and mainstream, about the exclusion of shudra and Dalit communities from the literary, the use of language and the New Critical categories of irony, complexity and structure, which were the major terms in Kannada *Navya* criticism too. These movements were anti-brahminical and targeted Adiga and *Navya* as expressions of a brahminical sensibility, in fact the entire literary establishment as brahminical. The public event which gave a new shape to the cultural battle was the statement by Basavalingappa, a Dalit minister in Devaraj Urs's cabinet, that from the perspective of the Dalits' position, Kannada literature was mere *'Boosa',* that is, 'cattle feed' or 'fodder'. This was construed as an insult to the glorious Kannada tradition and language, and violent demonstrations were held against Basavalingappa. The Dalit poet Siddalingaiah was physically attacked, and so was P. Lankesh for supporting him. Ironically, the incident proved to the letter Basavalingappa's statement. It proved that Kannada, as literature, language and culture, was exclusionist, upper-caste elitist and violently intolerant of criticism from subalternist perspectives. Though Basavalingappa was forced to resign, it was a watershed, with the Dalit Sangharsha Samiti and similar organisations asserting the cultural rights of the Dalits.[2] With the emergence of Dalit literature, questioning the hegemony of the upper-caste elite in Kannada literature became the starting point for many debates. The *Bandaya* (protest) literature movement began in the 1990s and became a common platform for many left-leaning movements. The movement straddled across literature, culture and politics, and transformed the nature of the literary as never before. It did away with the universalist frameworks in which literature had been conceptualised, and made the issues of caste, class and gender the reference points for any discussion of Kannada literature. Though it did not produce great works of literature, it made an impact on the major *Navya* writers. Shantinath Desai wrote *Beeja* (The Seed, 1983)—a novel in which the protagonist returns to his feudal home from Bombay and gradually gets involved in the intricacies of the life there. Mention has already been made of P. Lankesh's novel *Mussanjeya Katha Prasanga*. Yashwanta Chittala wrote stories such as *Kateyadalu Hudugi* (The Girl Who Became a Story) on entirely new themes. This is a pattern often seen in the literary historiography of Kannada. A new literary movement does not completely replace an existing one. But the practitioners of the earlier movement transform themselves, accommodating many elements of the new movement. Even at the height of the *Navya* movement, talented poets like K. S. Narasimhaswamy (1925–2003), G. S. Shivarudrappa (1926–2013) and Chennaveera Kanavi (1928–2022), who were of the *Navodaya* tradition, continued to write though learning much from the *Navya* movement. In fact, a new term, *Samanvaya Kavya*, was introduced to describe poetry which integrated *Navodaya* and *Navya* orientations. Similarly, in its second phase, *Navya* expanded itself by integrating elements from Dalit and *Bandaya* movements. K. S. Nissar Ahmed (1936–2020), B. R. Lakshman Rao and others, who began as *Navya* poets, shifted to writing lyrics (*Bhavageete*) and contributed songs to the Kannada music industry.

---

[2] For a succinct analysis of the *Boosa* episode, see the introduction to Satyanarayana K. and Susie Tharu (2003). *Steel Nibs Are Sprouting*, Harper Collins. pp. 1--10.

The most significant of the young *Navya* writers to make a complete break with it was Poornachandra Tejaswi (1938–2007). His early novels, *Nigudha Manushyaru* (Mysterious Men) and *Swaroopa*, are written in the *Navya* mould, the second one with close resemblances in tone and narrative style to Albert Camus' *The Fall.* He took the decision to leave Mysore for a place near Mudigere in the Western Ghats to become a farmer. He also gave up the option of becoming an academic. In his preface to *Abachoorina Post Office* (The Post Office of Abachur), a collection of short stories, Tejaswi declared that he would no longer have anything to do with the *Navya* mode of writing. The preface is titled 'Toward a New Horizon'. He says,

> It is time now to leave the *Navya* tradition altogether, and explore in a new direction. . . . In the last fifteen-twenty years the *Navya* writers have pursued dishonesty in the name of honesty. The leadership politics in the name of criticism and reducing the freedom to experience and the power of expression in the name of expanding them—these are the bane of the writers of this tradition. (Tejaswi 1973)

He says that in ego-centred writers like Ananthamurthy, the artist's consciousness itself becomes the centre of the work and the artist the hero. The modular symbolist style and techniques have become stale and incapable of expressing anything original. The system of education and the literary establishment have conspired to keep a large majority away from literature and have made it the property of the upper castes. He argues that the brahminical leadership has prevented the social movements from becoming radical.

Tejaswi made an astonishing departure from the *Navya* movement and went on to write stories and novels which used the genres of popular literature (the adventure tale, the detective story, the thriller, etc.), and created a vast readership. He also wrote travelogues, essays, books on the environment and condensed versions of historical works. The themes he dealt with focused on contemporary India—such as the caste system, the decline of politics, the criminal underworld, etc. His interests being philosophical, he uses the popular genres to explore serious issues. His writings on the environment have made a deep impact on the environmental awareness and movements in Karnataka. His narratives and essays are full of ordinary individuals who are from the artisan and other 'lowly' professions. But they are gifted with a superior knowledge of the world of nature. In the novel *Carvalho*, though the scientist Carvalho leads a team in search of the flying lizard, according to the writer, Mandanna and Kariyappa are the real naturalists. The hegemony of modern science has devalued their knowledge and they are treated as buffoons in the world outside the forest. Tejaswi was an enthusiastic supporter of science but was keenly aware of its role in the new colonialism. Modern education and the caste system had destroyed the indigenous knowledge systems known to the marginalised individuals.

Literary movements have the power to create an adversarial relationship between two traditions, thereby making one forget the plurality of the literary practices and texts outside of the two contending traditions. The period between 1960 and 1980 also exhibited this characteristic.

Shivaram Karanth's (1902–97) indifference to the discussion of the novelistic form and structure has often been discussed by many critics. For him, the novel was one of the many forms of expression he experimented with. He valorised only two qualities in the novel as a genre. One is its amenability to narrativise the vast experience he gathered, and the other is the possibilities it presented for reflecting on that experience. Most of his novels are in the form of a loosely structured narration in which the incidents are rarely dramatic or exciting, accompanied by a serious reflection on the behaviour of the characters. There have been comments on how his focus is not on the 'interiority' of the characters but their socially visible actions. This has much to do with his belief that our understanding and judgment of individuals should be based on their action. Human beings are social and ethical actors and become objects of our scrutiny through their actions. The reflections in these novels are rarely by the omniscient author himself. It is either the narrator or the central consciousness who reflects on the actions. One of the more successful fictional strategies used by him is narrating an accidental visit to a place or meeting up with a person which draws him deeper into the effort to understand that person. In *Bettada Jeeva* (The Spirit of the Hill, 1943), the narrator loses his way and ends up at the house of a couple who are cocooned in the midst of a thick forest surrounded by hills. This chance meeting with Shankarayya unfolds the heroic story of an individual who has tamed nature and lives there like the spirit of the hill. It is as though the extreme ordinariness of the landscape and the lives of the people hide unexpected heroism and suffering. The author's interest is in the code of values and behaviour which people like Shankarayya and his wife gather from their life's struggle.

In *Alida Mele* (After the End) the narrator Shivaram has the task of putting together the bits and pieces of the life of his friend Yashawantha Rao who is dead. It is an act of constructing an absent person's self from the traces left by him in the memories of others, and in letters, notes and drawings.

The unspoken question in the novel is: Isn't this what we constantly do when we think we know a person? Is there a self that is complete and integrated—beyond the traces? As Shivaram visits Yashawantha's wife and associates, and decodes the puzzle of names and signs in the notes, he begins to understand the ambivalences and contradictions associated with the absent person. Shivaram's admiration for Yashawantha Rao goes through several qualifications. In the process, he also reflects on the unexpected consequences of human actions.

Mookajjiya Kanasugalu (Mookajji's Visions, 1968), which won him the Jnanpith Award, is probably Karanth's most experimental novel. Mookajji, now a wizened old woman, narrates her visions to her interlocutor and grandson, Subbaraya. Some objects send her into a trance and she begins to speak of what happened probably in the early phases of the human civilisation. She does this through myths, legends and songs about the local deities. In fact, the visions are mythopoeic reconstructions of anthropological myths. The myths are fertility myths and associated with human sexuality which Mookajji sees as the energy that drives civilisations. She sees the mother goddess Hinduganamma as a symbolic figure created by the human imagination of this sexuality. Subbaraya is a modern-day rationalist who excavates relics of the past. But Mookajji, an old woman whose life has been confined to the small village, is a prophetess who can see the past and future of humankind.

It is not a coincidence that the greatest novelists in Kannada, Kuvempu and Karanth, should write during the *Navya* period, two novels which celebrate sexuality as the driving force of civilisation and society. With the two novels, Kannada fiction liberated itself from the prison house of realism. Still retaining their roots in the regional narrative mode, the two novels break the mould of realism. Nor is this only a question of fictional technique. The two writers were also evaluating the validity of reason and rationality, the two ambivalent gifts of modernity.

What then is distinctive about the *Navya* sensibility? The *Navodaya* writers see the actions and choices of human beings, even when they are deviant or rebellious, as shaped by the collective life. Not that they are uncritical about the collective life of the community. In fact, modernity presupposes the writer's critical distance from the community. In Kuvempu's *Kanuru Subbamma Heggadithi*, Hoovaiah is a Mysore-educated alienated modern individual. He sees the Okkaliga community and his own feudal family as caught in the mire of superstition and backwardness. Kuvempu, in a direct authorial comment, describes this as '*Kusamskriti*' and '*Asamskriti*', lacking in culture and/or possessing a retrograde culture. So the community has to be reformed and civilised. But the novel also makes it clear that his actions which disturb the society and also bring about tragedies, had to happen in the community. In Shivaram Karanth's novels, the younger Rama Aital in *Marali Mannige* (Return to Earth), Krishna in *Swapnada Hole* (River of Dreams), and Shankar in *Chigurida Kanasu* (The Dream that Sprouted), are representatives of a modern generation who have to return to the community.

In contrast, in the fiction of Shantinath Desai and P. Lankesh there is no such sense of community. The actions and choices of the characters are individual in an extreme sense. They have their relevance only in the personal quest of the individuals. In Yashwanta Chittala, though the characters are obsessed with their past and family legacies (in Hanehalli), their present is in Mumbai. Nagappa in *Shikari* and Purushottama in *Purushottama* are condemned to confront the traumatic, suppressed past. But the resolution does not involve the community of their childhood. They have to negotiate with the metropolis and its real-estate mafia and multinational corporations.

Ananthamurthy described himself as a critical insider, probably to explain how he differs from other *Navya* writers in being burdened with a sense of community. Desai, Lankesh and Poornachandra Tejaswi do not carry the baggage of tradition and community. For Lankesh and Tejaswi, the preoccupation is with the contemporary social and political world. Praneshacharya in *Samskara* has no existence outside the *agrahara*, the brahmin ghetto. His resolve at the end of the novel is to return to the community, confess his recent deeds and then reconstruct his life. Leaving the community is not even a possibility for him. In Tejaswi's *Chidambara Rahasya* (Ultimate Mystery) there is Kesaruru (mud town), allegorical of contemporary India. It is a town as beautiful as Switzerland but destroyed by caste, corruption and selfish politics. The major philosophical theme of the novel is the nature of human actions—do they emerge from individual nature or are they shaped by the sociopolitical context? The novel seems to affirm that human beings can transcend the material conditions (in this case, the Indian society in decline) only through powerful ethical choices and actions. Even this does not succeed because at the end of the novel, self-destructive politics and reckless destruction of the environment causes the apocalypse—Kesaruru burns to ashes. Tejaswi has created in his fiction the most powerful satirical images of contemporary India—the bureaucracy in *Tabarana Kathe* (The Story of Tabara), the underworld in *Jugari Cross*, and the absurd local politics in *Mayaloka* can hardly be matched in the satirical power of their depiction. Though portrayed with tolerant humour, the village Kamballi in P. Lankesh's novel is no less self-destructive. But the two writers do not see the town and the village as symbolic of a collective or community. There are no ethical or cultural resources for the individual to draw upon. The writers can think only of individual choices which save some people in this morass. It is with the Dalit writers that the sense of community returns to Kannada writing.

In his essay on Chandrashekhar Kambar (b. 1937), D. R. Nagaraj uses a framework which categorises modernist (*Navya*) Kannada writers. In a talk delivered at 'Neenasam' Heggodu, he elaborates on this framework. The framework has to do with the responses to tradition or past in the *Navya* writer. As discussed earlier, major Kannada *Navya* writers like Tejaswi, Lankesh and Shantinath Desai reject the past and tradition. They take the existentialist view that human beings have the freedom of choice and they are responsible for their choices and actions. They are sceptical about traditional values. On the other hand, there are writers like Gopalakrishna Adiga who negotiate with the past but they conceptualise it as the Indian tradition. For Adiga it is the Vedic past. Chandrashekhar Kambar follows the inward-looking *Desi* tradition. Nagaraj comments:

> In ancient Kannada poetics there are two modes of creativity, *Marga* and *Desi*. The former is characterised by its capacity and desire to interact with the larger cosmopolis, and in the Indian case that's Sanskrit. *Marga* remains the creative adaptation of the powerful model that operates from outside. *Desi* is the inward-looking imagination, basically at the level of forms. (Nagaraj 2012)

He goes on to describe Kambar as a critical *Desivadi*. Kambar's explanation is far simpler. He was born in a village, Ghodageri in Belagavi district, in a shudra community, and grew up in the folk world of gods, demons, fairies, legends and myths. In a poem he describes how his mother's storytelling would bring Lord Shiva himself down to their hut. Therefore, he says he is '*Desi*', a 'folk person', simply because he could not be anything else.

Kambar began writing when *Navya* poetry was in its heyday. His first long poem, *Helatenakela* (Listen, I'll Tell You, 1964), was in the form of a folk ballad using the folk narrative style and folk metre. All his major concerns are embodied in this poem. The story is about Sivapura, an imaginary village where everything in Kambar's prolific writing has taken place. The first part of the poem describes the organic rural world guarded by the local goddess Parambi Karevva and the wisdom of Kariyajja, the village elder. The *Gowda* (village headman) and *Gowdthi* (his wife) are veritable gods to the villagers. The idyllic, pastoral world is disturbed by the coming of modernity. The tree sheltering the goddess is cut down to construct a school, and Kariyajja dies. A demon kills the *Gowda* and takes on his guise. Out of its unnatural relationship with *Gowdthi* Balagonda is born. Kambar extended the theme in the play *Rishyashrunga* in which the old world is destroyed by the demon and Balagonda, like Hamlet, is unable to set it right.

The total immersion in a folk world of creative imagination, the nostalgia for a lost world, ambivalence about modernity, and the celebration of sexuality and fertility characterise the works of Kambar. Kambar is clear that the premodern folk world is no longer a historical reality, and folk literature cannot be created in a modern urban world. The poet can at best use the rich repertory of the narrative styles and forms, the metres and the language, to express a modernist sensibility. Kambar also locates the beginning of modern poetry in the disruption (*vighatane*) of the community. His poetry and plays offer a complex blend of folk forms and a modern sensibility. His relationship with tradition is not as unproblematic as he sometimes argues. He is harshly critical of the myth of organic Indian traditions of the past. His poem *Gangamai*—about a stagnant village pond described in images of disgust—is meant to symbolise this tradition. It is full of rotting filth and is not life-giving any longer. In two poems addressed to Mao Zedong, Kambar satirises how Mother India can transform even radical revolutionary politics into a ritual. Mao himself is described ironically as the great leader who 'destroyed human beings for the sake of humanity'. In another poem, *Ramayanavu Godutayiyu* (The *Ramayana* and Godutayi), Godutayi who pretends to be a religious, prudish woman, is found to be hiding a condom inside the volume of the *Ramayana* she carries with her all the time. In his plays, the feudal rural world is depicted as not only exploitative but also impotent. In the plays *Jokumaraswamy* and *Jaisidanayaka*, the feudal lord boasting of his sexual prowess is in fact impotent. The young rebels from the labouring peasant class are the fertility gods.

Therefore, with all his regret over the loss of an old world, Kambar is far more critical of both tradition and the feudal past than many of the progressive writers. He is modernist in his exploration of the themes of the fragmented self, the ambivalent nature of sexuality, alienation and solipsism. One of his powerful plays is *Narcissus* which is about the destructive absorption in the individual self. He does not see the cultural resources of the past as providing solutions to these conflicts. He discovers alternatives in creativity. For Kambar, creativity is basically artistic or poetic creativity. In the highly experimental works beginning with *Chakori,* he explains the unity of creativity and imagination, in contrast to reason or rationality which can become destructive. Like the Yeatsian contrarieties of the lunar and the solar, in *Chakori* and *Shikhara Surya* Kambar creates the two characters Chandamutta and Suryamutta, and also those who are *Chandrana Okkalu,* followers or devotees of the moon, as well as *Suryana Okkalu,* followers of the sun. In *Shikhara Surya,* the conflict is between the followers of the mother who want to protect the earth and Shikhara Surya, the hero who wants to transform all earth into gold. It appears as though Kambar uses all the traditional resources of myths, legends, magic and alchemy to explore the foundational forces which are central to human life. In his recent collection of poems, *Yellide Sivapura*? (*Where is Sivapura*), there is the autumnal feeling that Sivapura, the village of his imagination, has changed beyond recognition. He even wonders whether it existed outside his imagination at all.

The range of Kambar's poetry in both form and experience is astonishingly wide. H. S. Shivaprakash argues that Kambar avoided the entrapment of the influence of the West as well as subservience to the *Mārga* and *Vedic* traditions. Instead, he has constructed a rich repertory of myths and cultural forms of expression from the subaltern traditions. Only Devanoora Mahadeva, who uses the Dalit cultural traditions equally powerfully, can be compared with Kambar in this aspect.

K. S. Narasimhaswamy (1915–2003) began as a poet of the *Navodaya* School and achieved great popularity with *Mysore Mallige,* a collection of poems celebrating marital love in a distinctly middle-class background which is untouched by conflicts, modernity or changes. It is a nostalgically reconstructed social world, rural and suburban, which was the background of popular Kannada fiction as well as the rural-pastoral model adopted in popular Kannada films. He then went on to write reflective poems without altogether giving up the lyrical-aesthetic mode. With the advent of *Navya* poetry, Narasimhaswamy's poetry began to be seen as an example of the weaknesses of *Navodaya* poetry. However, he responded creatively to the challenges posed by the *Navya* movement by evolving a distinctive new style supple enough to deal with the philosophical, existential issues introduced by the movement. In poems such as *Gadiyaradangadiya Eduru* (In Front of the Clock Shop) and *Kumkuma Bhoomi* (Vermillion Earth), he traverses the areas of experience introduced by Adiga but with a humanist vision of his own. His preoccupation is with the relationship between the self and the world, and the everyday world and the transcendental experience. The poems are remarkable for the ease with which they handle complex metaphysical explorations while avoiding the opaqueness of modernist poetry.

Soon after the ebbing out of high modernism (led by Ezra Pound and T. S. Eliot), many critics were already predicting a return to the 'English tradition', treating high modernism as an avant-garde intervention. There were certainly no major poets writing in the style of Eliot and Pound. There were very different voices, but not in the avant-garde mode. Something similar seems to have happened in the Kannada context too. Adiga himself abandoned the dense, symbolist style of *Bhoomigeetha* and experimented with a more relaxed style in *Koopa Manduka*. The younger poets, like Chandrashekhar Patil (1939–2022) and K. V. Tirumalesh (1940–2023), moved away from the *Navya* of the early modernist phase with such changes in idiom and style, and the poetry of K. S. Narasimhaswamy began to receive greater critical attention. Soon, with the inception of the Dalit and *Bandaya* movements, it was no longer possible to speak of one dominant mode of poetry. The long surviving paradigm of literary historiography—that is, one based on major poets and major trends—is finally a matter of the past. The present attempts (in 2025) to resurrect some of the major writers as continuing influences is hardly convincing.

3

Mention has already been made of the famous *Boosa* episode which transformed the Dalit movement in Karnataka. The Dalita Lekhaka Kalavidara Balaga (Daleka), the first association of Dalit writers and artists, was formed in 1974 and it was later expanded into Dalit Sangharsha Samiti (DSS). The *Boosa* incident took place on 19 November 1973. It was a lecture by B. Basavalingappa, a minister in Devaraj Urs's cabinet, delivered at Dr Babasaheb Ambedkar School of Thought in Mysore. Probably we will never know the exact words used by him because they have been 'rewritten' by so many. Among other things, he is said to have commented, 'There is a lot of *Boosa* in Kannada literature'. *Boosa* means 'cattle feed' or 'fodder' and also has the association of 'worthless' in Kannada. He had also spoken about the need to learn English. The furore and the violence which followed the reports of the speech were unprecedented. It was clearly an attempt to present the episode as sacrilege committed against the sacrosanct institution of Kannada literature by a Dalit. It was also an upper-caste strategy of using Kannada and Kannada culture to browbeat oppositional movements by Dalits and the backward classes. Though Basavalingappa was forced to resign, the result was the consolidation of the DSS as a literary and cultural movement, one of the most significant phenomena in post-independence India.

It began as an assertion of the rights and dignity of the Dalits and quickly expanded into a movement for land rights, protection of landless labourers and protection of women from sexual exploitation. It was led by B. Krishnappa (1938–97), and Devanoora Mahadeva (b. 1948) and Siddalingaiah (1954–2021), two of the finest Dalit writers in Kannada. The DSS had its branches in every town and village and developed into a powerful pressure group in Karnataka. Hundreds of artists, writers and activists contributed to its growth. It was a cultural movement in the true sense with hundreds of 'songs of struggle' feeding its energy. Events and incidents of the time were narrativised in the songs and street plays, thus creating a vibrant public culture. Siddalingaiah, Devanoora Mahadeva and K. B. Siddaiah (1954–2019) of the first generation were followed by Mogalli Ganesh, Du. Saraswathi, B. T. Jahnavi and many others. In the literary domain, the Dalit movement radically interrogated tradition, literary practice and conventions, and above all the invisibility of the Dalit communities in Kannada literature. Their absence was total and they did not figure even on the margins. Dalit critics questioned the representation of Dalit characters even in the writings of Kuvempu and Shivaram Karanth. B. Krishnappa analysed how the fictional world of Kuvempu's novels is the shudra Okkaliga social world with Dalit characters featured as mere shadows. His complaint was similar to Chinua Achebe's charges against Joseph Conrad's representation of the Africans. Karanth's Dalit protagonist Choma in *Chomana Dudi* (1933) was seen as passive and totally dependent on the generosity of the upper-caste landlord. The fact that Jagannatha, the brahmin revolutionary in *Bharathipura* who wants to lead the temple entry of Dalits, describes them as '*Avu*' '*Ivu*'—'these' and 'those'—words used in Kannada for animals, drew flack. Young Dalit women, like Belli, are always available (as in *Samskara*) to liberate young brahmins from sexual prudery. B. Krishnappa led a movement for the dignity of Dalit women with the protest against nude worship at Chandragutti. (U. R. Ananthamurthy had talked about nude worship as a mystical surrender, to an audience in a US university in English, in order to enlighten them about the non-rational mystical rituals in India.) This is just a short list of the debates which raged with the inception of the Dalit literary movement. Ram Manohar Lohia, Karl Marx and Dr B. R. Ambedkar were the ideologues whose works were found most relevant by the movement. Interestingly, the other people's movements of the 1970s and 80s also drew their inspiration from these ideologues.

Siddalingaiah resurrected the song as a form of poetry and public communication, a long time after the *Navodaya* poetry had ebbed out. For him, it is not a vehicle of self-expression. His is the voice of the Dalit community speaking of 'we' and 'us'. Anupama Rao's thesis about the category 'Dalit' being made into an inclusive term for the oppressed and bringing together hundreds of Dalit sub-castes into one community marked by suffering and humiliation as well as by protest, best explains the impact of Kannada Dalit literature (Rao 2009). For the first time, the category 'Dalit' gave a unitary identity to the many Dalit sub-castes. This was the original achievement of Dr B. R. Ambedkar who constructed the identity of the depressed classes.

In Siddalingaiah's songs, the Dalit community speaks of the feudal oppression in villages and the urban poverty of the migrant labourers, in stark images: 'our bones decorate the door of the *Gowda's* house'; 'we are the ones who carry the huge slabs to build their houses' (Siddalingaiah 1975). This is not the voice of a pathetic victim. It is the new voice which says, 'Beat them, kick them, these bastards' (Siddalingaiah 1975). It is also the voice of the Dalit poet who sees his people like 'a thousand rivers joining the ocean of struggle'. Most DSS programmes would begin with the song 'Who got freedom in 1947? Not us but the Tatas and Birlas'. The old Dalit self, of the victim and sufferer, is now replaced by the new self of the angry, rebellious Dalit. The significance of Dalit writing lies in its creation of this new self. This self has no bonds with the history of humiliation and the tradition of oppression and absence. It has to be made now, in the present, through acts of rebellion. As Albert Camus said, 'I rebel, therefore we exist'.

D. R. Nagaraj wrote an enthusiastic review of Siddalingaiah's autobiography *Ooru, Keri* (1997), originally written as one volume. Nagaraj analyses how the comic genius of Siddalingaiah transcends suffering through its laughter. The laughter is also an act of rebellion against being trapped in images of perpetual victimisation. Except occasionally in *Uchalya*, this does not happen in most Dalit autobiographies. Siddalingaiah's description of writing poetry sitting in the cemetery of Srirampura in Bengaluru, or seeing his own televised interview sitting in a bar, are among the episodes in the autobiography. His hilarious tales of the local gods and goddesses are about a robust egalitarian culture, practically unknown to the mainstream.

The whole body of fiction written by Devanoora Mahadeva runs into just about 150 printed pages, which has amazed him more than anyone else. Some of his early stories, such as *Ondu Dahanada Kathe* (The Story of a Cremation), were written in the shadow of the *Navya* mode of writing. They are very much like the angry-young-men stories of that mode. However, with *Amasa* and *Dambaru Bandudu* ('Tar Arrives') Mahadeva went to the oral traditions of Dalit culture and evolved a narrative style which has a distinctive flow of its own. The language hewn with the rhythms of Dalit Kannada speech, spoken around Nanjanagudu, lifts itself naturally to a poetic level and is rich with images and metaphors. In *Dambaru Bandudu*, the feudal politics of the village chief and his cronies is opposed by a group of youngsters who try to expose them. But a little child lured by liquid tar gets trapped in it. *Mudal Seemeli Kole Gile* is about the starvation of a Dalit labourer's family and his sheer helplessness in the face of feudal exploitation. The ironic title, 'Of Murder in the Eastern Region', highlights the labourer's inability to protest or even talk about his hunger.

Odalala (Deep Within), the novelette, is a classic of modern Kannada. The story of Sakavva and her sons living in a dilapidated hut is transformed into a myth about survival. One of the sons brings home stolen groundnuts, and the family sits around a small fire eating them and throwing the shells into the fire to erase all evidence of the theft. U. R. Ananthamurthy compares the scene to a ritual sacrifice (*yajna*) for sheer survival. The slender text is replete with unforgettable images and scenes such as the one showing a girl child of the family drawing peacocks on the tattered wall. In another, Sakavva tells her grandson that when Yama, the god of death, came to take her away, she sent him back saying she had yet to look after her grandson. In his eyes Sakavva becomes a fairy flying in the sky. Thus, the story about starvation is also a celebration of the possibilities of Dalit life. Sakavva, tough and querulous, is among the best remembered women characters in Kannada fiction.

Kusumabale is a heteroglossic work with multiple narratives, one of them told by a cot. At the heart of the many stories is the transgressive relationship between Channa the Dalit and Kusumabale, the daughter of the village headman. There is a similar tale about Kempi, the daughter of Torara Tooramma. The novel begins with the lamps of the village meeting late in the night to share stories and gossip of this kind. The seemingly rambling narrative picks up many threads and also introduces epiphanies of Dalit life. Probably for the first time in Kannada, we have a full-fledged manifestation of a Dalit life world created with a rich mythopoeic texture. There is also an episode showing a protest and procession by the DSS led by B. Krishnappa, narrated in a low mimetic comic style.

K. B. Siddaiah also goes beyond the stereotyping of Dalit experiences by reclaiming and reinterpreting myths. His long poems, *Bakala* (Bakala, the Sage) and *Gallebani* (The Trough), present a complex world of myths, legends and cultural memories. Instead of questioning or debunking myths of mainstream culture, Siddaiah explores the long cultural history of Dalits. With such poetic practices, Dalit writing in Kannada has fostered our awareness of the co-existence and encounter of many cultural worlds in the real history of India.

Sometimes, Dalit writing is considered 'caste-centric' in the negative sense, as though that is its limitation. Critics also observe that the experience of caste becomes stereotypical in the Dalit writings which do not address the more complex issues of modernity and (now) globalisation. The charge of the experience of caste being stereotypical is also because it occurs in the rural, feudal society which itself is described as unchanging. Several factors need to be considered in this discussion. Firstly, contrary to the expectation that the feudal social structures with the headman (*Gowda*) from the dominant caste (either Okkaliga or Lingayat) who is also the local *zamindar*, would disappear with the processes of modernity, the social structures remain intact. In fact, with the arrival of modernity, the chief takes on the additional role of the political representative. Untouchability is still practised in many villages. There are cases regularly being reported of ostracisation and severe caste discrimination—Dalits not being allowed to enter hotels, barbers refusing to attend to Dalits, Dalits being prevented from participating in local festivals, and many such incidents regularly take place (like the well-known incident at Hangaranahalli where Dalits had contributed to the construction of a community centre but were prevented from using it). The ostracisation is so severe that many Dalit communities are forced to leave their villages. The political hegemony still belongs to the dominant castes and therefore no one is punished for caste discrimination. Instead, government officers are deputed to hold peace meetings and 'persuade' the upper castes. Therefore, it is the political-social structures which continue to be stereotypical, not their depiction by the Dalit writers. M. S. Shekhar (2010) says in a poem: 'I fear to think of my native village'. This is a subversion of the idyllic image of the native village of the childhood. One of the reasons why it evokes fear and not nostalgia is the memories associated with it. One such memory is of an upper-caste boy addressing the poet's father in humiliating terms. Neither constitutional equality nor modernity has penetrated deep into the rural society.

EIGHT

Drama and Theatre

Shankar Mokashi Punekar (1928–2004), eminent writer and critic, raised some fundamental questions about the historiography of Kannada theatre which were also questions about the impact of modernity on indigenous cultural forms. The first question is regarding the decline of commercial professional theatre popularly known as *Company Nataka* in Kannada. Professional theatre was itself a product of modernity. Indigenous theatre in Karnataka has a rich and varied history. Mention has already been made earlier of references in literary texts and works on poetics such as *Kavirajamarga* to folk performative arts. Though the details are meagre, there is evidence that these flourished in all regions of Karnataka. In North Karnataka, *Srikrishna Parijata, Doddata* and *Bayalata* were popular, while *Yakshagana* and *Talamaddale* were the prominent forms on the coastal belt and the interior regions (Ranganath 2011). K. V. Subbanna estimated that there are fourteen such forms of folk theatre and that at least seventy per cent of the population participated in the theatrical activities (quoted in Akshara 2018). He also estimates that forms like *Yakshagana* and *Talamaddale* have a continuous history of about four hundred years. These indigenous forms were cultural practices embedded in the material conditions of the regions where they developed. They were performed during the period of four to five months that are free from rains and when the agricultural community was relatively free. Everything, from the materials for constructing the theatre to the performers, was drawn from local resources. At some point, performing troupes must have started travelling to places. Such troupes—named after the villages and towns they come from—are recognised by people even today. Though the performances were not tied to religious rituals, a tradition emerged in which people took vows to sponsor them at temples. (This is known as *Harake*, a vow made to god.) K. V. Akshara, eminent theatre personality and writer, informs that a famous troupe, Mandarti Mela, has been booked up to 2027 for such *Harake* sponsored performances! (2018).

Yakshagana performances are based on mythological and puranic episodes and they are a blend of songs, dance and narration. Though there are 'texts' of these performances, generally there is near total autonomy for the *Bhagavata* and the actors to create contingent and contextual meanings in every performance. Many centuries before Derrida, these performative traditions deconstructed the notions of the text, meaning and interpretation, though not theoretically but creatively. Every performance creates its own interpretations, with the original storyline and characters providing an amorphous boundary for the sake of intelligibility. In *Talamaddale*, a shortened version of *Yakshagana*, the central element is the *artha*, interpretation emerging from a dialogue. These performances can be described as a form of theatrical bricolage. They are also products of the enormous cultural capital in the rural/regional societies. The audience possesses the cultural capital to understand and respond to the interpretations which are based on philosophical debates of a high order. Not that these performances are cerebral. They are vigorous, energetic and colourful. From costume to dance steps, they employ a grammar of performance with two major styles known as the *tenka tittu* (the southern style) and the *badaga tittu* (the northern style). The grammar is a set of theatrical practices, conventions and codes known to both the performers and the audience.

The same is true of *Srikrishna Parijata* performances. The name is derived from the story of the Parijata flower which causes a dispute between Krishna's two wives, Rukmini and Satyabhame. This episode is the core around which every performance weaves endless variation and interpretation. As in the case of all popular cultural forms, there is a repertory of related episodes, stereotypical stock characters, and prosodic and verse forms, which are available to the performers.

It is against this background of a living theatre that one has to understand the emergence of modern drama. In the middle decades of the nineteenth century the Mysore principality patronised theatrical activities at its court. Basappa Shastri brought out his Kannada translation of Kalidasa's *Abhijnana Shankuntalam* in 1880. This was performed by the palace troupe in 1881. The king also invited a Parsi theatre troupe and Marathi troupes. Though it is disputed, there is evidence that *Yakshagana* performances inspired Marathi theatre which then went on to literally conquer North Karnataka and some other regions as the most popular theatrical form. There was considerable exchange and intertextuality between Kannada and Marathi theatre for a very long time. A few years before the palace troupe performed *Shakuntalam*, Shanthakavi (1856–1921) founded the Kritapura Company at Gadag. Balacharya Sakkari (known as Shanthakavi) was an extraordinary cultural figure. He called himself the messiah of Kannada and started the theatre troupe to challenge the hegemony of the Marathi plays. He wrote several plays and directed them. In a few decades, theatre troupes and companies began to emerge from several places in North Karnataka and in Bellari. These were professional theatre troupes which travelled throughout Karnataka, camping in many places, sometime for months together. They would perform in a tent made of bamboo poles and jute cloth. They had charismatic and popular actors who drew large crowds. The plays were categorised as mythological and social. Mythological plays were based on episodes from the epics and puranas, and socials on contemporary issues. Owing to a hybridised notion of stage realism, backdrops, sceneries and stage property began to be introduced (Akshara 2018). Songs were the major vehicles of communication, with each play comprising sixty to seventy songs. These songs were an inalienable part of Kannada popular culture. Interestingly, many adaptations of Shakespearean plays were also part of the theatrical repertory. Legendary actors, such as A. V. Varadachar, Bellari Raghava and Gubbi Veeranna, were part of the star cast. The professional companies in their heydays were large, supporting over a hundred members. The legendary Gubbi Company used to hire a special train to travel. Though each company was distinctive, most of them went through a similar trajectory—of modest beginnings, rapid prosperity and rise in popularity, and then decline and disbanding. Roughly the period spanning from the last quarter of the nineteenth century to the 1940s, was the golden period of professional companies.

There were several shortcomings in the professional theatre which became the subject of a public debate, which was published in the journals of the period, especially in the 1920s and 30s. K. V. Akshara suggests that the debates were on the excessive use of songs and music, loosely structured plots, risqué comic dialogues and vulgarity, and the question whether women should play female roles in this theatre. The participants in these debates were from the educated middle class and included some theatre personalities. Shankar Mokashi Punekar sees these debates as the locus of a critique of popular culture by the educated native elite. For the elite, professional theatre was almost absurd in its lack of artistic quality and a product of low taste. It pandered to the uneducated desire for cheap entertainment. The Victorian prudery which had become the code of morality for the educated Indian middle class was behind this negative perception. Expectedly, two of the contemporary 'national' issues shaped the tenor of this critique. One was the status of women and their freedom. The debates in the Kannada journals, while acknowledging the legitimacy of women's freedom, also expressed apprehensions about the vulgarity and amorality of the professional theatre as threats to the chastity of the Arya/Hindu woman. It should be noted that despite such civil society debates, for a long time, women actors were mostly women from low castes and professions. The professional theatre became the 'fall guy' for the proponents of middle-class morality.

Meanwhile a new phenomenon, the amateur theatre (*Havyasi Nataka* in Kannada), had made its appearance. This referred to small non-professional groups which would come together to produce serious plays for the urban proscenium stage. These groups were not travelling troupes and had no connection with the rural makeshift theatre. The amateur groups performed on occasions such as annual day celebrations at colleges and schools, for which Shankar Mokashi Punekar names the amateur theatre as the 'school and college day theatre'. Two major playwrights, T. P. Kailasam (1884–1946) and Sriranga (1904–84) emerged as the leading figures of this urban-centric theatre. Both of them were heavily influenced by Bernard Shaw (both had been to England) and introduced the social, realistic drama, addressing the problems of the contemporary society. The plays were prose plays sans songs and music, relying on witty dialogue written in 'modern educated' Kannada. Kailasam wrote in '*Kanglish*', a mixture of Kannada and English, typical of the educated middle class, and Sriranga often used the North Karnataka dialogue, and both of them wrote for the educated middle class. Both of them ridiculed *company drama* in their plays. Kailasam's *Nam Company* (1920) is a hilarious satire on professional theatre.

Mokashi Punekar argues that such satire and ridicule was instrumental in keeping the middle-class audience away from professional theatre. The new hegemonic notions of good taste and avoidance of vulgarity, coupled with the idea of theatre as a serious medium, made them shun popular theatre. Mokashi Punekar does not consider the other reasons, such as overambitious, expensive productions and financial mismanagement, as responsible for the decline of professional theatre. He argues that the popularity of the new medium, cinema, was not the cause either, because Marathi and Bengali theatres flourished despite the popularity of cinema (2012, 506–27).

Hence, modernity produced the professional theatre which was very distinct in its organisation and performance from folk theatre, although it drew its material and styles from folk theatre. But modernity also created the urban-centric amateur theatre which disowned the legacy of both folk and professional theatres. The result was a cleavage between popular culture and 'serious' culture, which modernity created. K. V. Subbanna also sees a breach in the relationship between community and theatre, which was irreversible. He takes the example of *Sangya-Balya*, a popular play authored by a certain Pattar Master and based on a real incident of adultery and murder (in Akshara 2018, 160–66). While the play is written in the style and conventions of *Srikrishna Parijata*, the major incidents and the structure of feeling are modern. As Akshara says, 'The play abounds in similar instances of the encounter between the old and modern values. All the characters refer to traditional values and try to live up to them. At the same time, however, they also go on opening themselves to the unfettered joys and pleasures of the new ideals' (2018, 157). The play introduces the bureaucracy and the court of law as institutions of colonial modernity. At the end of the play, the brothers who had killed Sangya surrender themselves to the court of law. The adultery and murder are presented as transgressive acts taking place in a rural world transiting to modernity. Interestingly, the family of the brothers brought an injunction against the performance of the play under the Dramatic Performance Act or DPA (1876), which officially survives even today though the play has been performed thousands of times!

Iggappa Heggade Vivaha Prahasana (The Farce of Iggappa Heggade's Wedding), written by Karki Venkataramana Shastri Suri in 1887, is considered the first modern social play in Kannada. The author, a Havyaka brahmin settled in Bombay, was also a journalist who was persecuted for his writings. The play is a *prahasana* (a comedy which ends with the resolution of the problems it presents). The theme revolves around the problems relating to the arrangement of marriages in the Havyaka community and the machinations over property. This was probably the first play which had no traces of the traditional theatre in it. It also uses the minority Havyaka dialect.

The amateur theatre supported by the plays of Kailasam and Sriranga came to be recognised as 'mainstream' Kannada drama, and both folk theatre and professional theatre were relegated to a minor status. Among other things, this is indicative of how modern literary historiography is itself grounded on criteria produced by colonial modernity. A whole variegated world of indigenous theatre with the majority of the people participating in it makes way for a minority theatre with an urban audience. Some of the processes of modernity being irreversible, the amateur theatre and drama continued to be designated as 'modern' Kannada drama and theatre.

Meanwhile, professional theatre declined and struggled for survival. Though two or three companies still continue to perform, there is no possibility of a revival. The material conditions which produced it are no longer there. Folk theatre, in the form of *Yakshagana* and *Talamaddale,* is flourishing. In fact, it has been receiving support from urban centres too. Connoisseurs are critical of many of the changes taking place in the style and content, but the form would not have survived without its adaptability to change.

Professional Kannada theatre responded to the nationalist politics of the time with vigour. Majority of the playwrights (some of them were also proprietors of the companies they started) had contacts with Maharashtra, especially Pune. North Karnataka was part of the Bombay Presidency (officially known as Southern Bombay Presidency), and had a long historical legacy of a bilingual elite for whom Marathi was the prestige language. In the absence of educational institutions, members of the elite went to Pune for higher education. Almost invariably, they came under the influence of Bal Gangadhar Tilak and the popular Marathi playwrights like Ram Ganesh Gadkari. This was the time when the Marathi playwrights were writing about nationalist politics and issues of social reform, especially about widow remarriage, education for women, abolition of child marriage, etc. Playwrights such as Garuda Sadashivaraya, Kandgal Hanumantharao were in Pune at some point of their career. Gandhian politics had also made its impact on rural Karnataka.

Both Marathi and Kannada writers used the popular genre of the puranic drama for dealing with nationalism. With the liberty provided by the professional theatre of shifting time-frames, from the puranic past to the political present, they made puranic episodes allegories of the anticolonial struggle. Keechaka and Kamsa, popular villains from the *Mahabharata*, were turned into symbols of the colonial regime. In *Akshayambara* (The Everlasting Apparel, 1935), Krishna who protects Draupadi from disrobement in the royal council (*sabha*) with the miracle of the 'unending sari', appears on the stage and gifts her with cloth made of *khadi*, and tells her that *khadi* is both protector of honour and weapon against poverty. It is reported that the audience would respond to the scene by shouting 'Long live Mother India', 'Long live Gandhi'. In another play, Draupadi addresses the audience saying, 'When I, a woman, can protect my honour, what about you'. The audience did not find it inappropriate that puranic characters discussed contemporary nationalist politics. This was true of the other popular genre, namely the pseudo-historical play about legendary heroes. These figures were transformed into icons of anticolonial struggle and became part of the political consciousness of the Kannada people.

Echama Nayaka, Rani Chennamma of Kittur and Rudramma were the historical figures reconstructed in the nationalist discourse. The colonial government was aware of the political role of professional theatre and passed the Dramatic Performance Act. Censorship of scripts and licensing of performances were used as its strategy of containment. For instance, two brothers who had financed the company staging the play on Kittur Rani Chennamma had to leave North Karnataka with the denial of licence. Kandgal Hanumantharao, very early in his career, was taken to a police station for writing a nationalist play.[1] It must also be mentioned that communalised popular history, 'othering' Muslim kings and heroes, was made to collaborate with nationalist politics. In many of these plays, Muslim regimes were allegorised as colonial regimes and anticolonial struggle was formulated as a Hindu struggle for restoration of honour. H. N. Apte's novel on the fall of Vijayanagara, translated into Kannada by Galaganatha, reinforced the notion of the Vijayanagara empire as a Hindu empire. The killing of Aliya Ramaraya in the final battle was depicted as revenge plotted by his Muslim mistress Meharjan whom he had abandoned. Many Kannada plays used such pseudo-historical material to construct the popular narrative of the fall of the Hindu/Kannada Empire.

The third genre recruited for nationalist politics was the social-reformist play. Both the reformist and nationalist themes of untouchability, women's education, widow remarriage, *khadi*, and anticolonial struggle were the subjects of this genre. The model was taken from Marathi drama and theatre. In *Akshayambara*, Krishna visits the home of an untouchable and preaches against the practice of untouchability. Garuda Sadashivaraya, legendary actor and playwright, devoted his plays to the cause of nationalism and social reform. The loosely structured, heterogeneous form of the professional theatre had space for didactic speeches, songs with a nationalist spirit and even long debates. The very defects and weaknesses of professional theatre—analysed by the educated elite—made it a powerful vehicle for nationalist political discourses. Ironically, T. P. Kailasam and Sriranga, who attacked professional theatre and ridiculed it, began by writing on the same themes involving a critique of society. They did so by introducing the Shaw–Ibsen model of the social play meant for the proscenium stage of the amateur theatre. Interestingly, the later plays of Sriranga continue to deal with politics, but express disillusionment with the corruption and moral decline in politics.

---

[1] For a description of the incident, see *Company Natak Arthath Vritti Rangabhumi by* Prakash Garuda (2015).

What is visible in this period is the field of popular culture with porous boundaries allowing an unimpeded flow of themes, genres, expressive forms and discourses from all cultural texts. It would be difficult to distinguish the journalism of the period from the debates in professional theatre. The historical romance which had travelled from Bankim in Bangla to H. N. Apte in Marathi and was 'translated' (in every sense of the term) by writers like Galaganatha, provided material for professional drama. Costumes and stage design borrowed from Parsi theatre travelled to the small towns of Karnataka. Nationalist political discourses found a free passage in books on Kannada nationalism, *Navodaya* poetry and professional drama. The endless intertextuality across languages during this period deserves scholarly attention.

Therefore, it would be wrong to speak of a disjuncture as Kannada theatre moved away from professional to amateur theatre. There were continuities in themes and the participation in public discourses. The major shift was in the theatre and the audience. Amateur theatre did not travel mainly because the actors were not professionals and would come together only for the production and performance. It was only much later that some of the amateur groups turned semi-professional and began to perform in several places. The audience was the urban, educated middle class. Though amateur theatre broke away from the hybrid stage design and properties, its proscenium stage was constrained by the notions of realism and naturalism. For example, it is only with the play *Kattale Belaku* (Darkness, Light, 1959) that Sriranga begins to experiment with the possibilities of the theatrical space. He begins to use the frontstage and backstage for different time-frames of the dramatic action. He introduces the *Sutradhara*, the playwright and choric characters who provide commentary on the dramatic action. In *Kattale Belaku*, the reluctant playwright keeps arguing that there is no dramatic material in real life, while the backstage provides a drama involving adultery, deception and crime. The policeman who is seeking proof and corroboration for his enquiry begins to find it in the drama proper. The characteristic mainstay of Sriranga's plays, the racy, witty and at times verbose dialogues, continue unchanged in the second, experimental, phase of his drama. In *Rangabharatha* (1965), the choric commentary is provided by characters who belong to the present time-frame (though named after characters from the *Mahabharata*), while the main dramatic action takes place in the epic time-frame. In *Sanjeevini* (1968) he employs the dual frame of 'outer drama' and 'inner drama', mainly to emphasise the continuities between the past and the present, especially in the human passions. There is also a sombre vision of the 'eternal' nature of the power structure which leaves human beings frustrated and fragmented. Interestingly, in this phase, Sriranga explores mythological and puranic material which was the source for professional theatre. But the material is used for an anti-romantic intellectual exploration of human nature. *Sanjeevini* deals with the Yayathi-Puru-Sharmistha-Devayani tale used by Girish Karnad later for his first play. Sriranga's play is superior in its complexity and philosophical depth. Devayani, first cheated by Kacha who wanted the secret of immortality, and then by Yayati, the king who enters into a sexual relationship with her companion Sharmistha, emerges as the major figure of this paly. The core of the play is the complex relationship between sexuality, power and the exploitative nature of intimate human relationships.

Kelu Janamejaya (Listen, Janamejaya, 1960), which was seen as a path-breaking play in the Indian context, once again employs a bifurcated theatrical space. The 'outer' drama involves the *Sutradhara* and the 'Leader', while the 'inner' drama involves the four major characters who unravel the degenerate contemporary society. In his autobiography, *Sahitiya Atma Jijnase* (part of which was translated into English by his daughter and renowned novelist Shashi Deshpande), Sriranga admits that his plays have always been intellectual plays.[2] His intellectuality functions as a two-edged sword in the plays. While it brings seriousness of purpose and analytical depth, it also dwindles into cerebral debate working against the dramatic power of the plays. It is, for example, surprising that a competent translator of the *Natyashastra* and an authority on Kalidasa should expend so much energy on plays about the difference between the truth of life and the truth of its presentation on the stage. The professional theatre which Sriranga ridiculed did not find this a philosophical problem. It always knew—and its audience knew—that theatre is not life.

Sriranga also gave powerful expression to the issue of sexual politics in his mythological plays. In *Rangabharatha*, Draupadi tells Duryodhana, 'I will tell you who I am. I am the manliness all the men in your kingdom lost'. His later plays also deal with submerged and darker aspects of sexual relationships within and outside marriage. He also attempts to grapple with broad civilisational themes of the conflict between instinctive forces and civilisational constraints. His was a long journey from the early, provocative

[2] Sriranga's *Sahitiya Atma Jijnase* was partly translated by Shashi Deshpande (2006) as *Opening Scene: Early Memoirs of a Dramatist and a Play*. Some of Sriranga's plays are available in English translation.

social drama such as *Harijanwara* (1930) to the dark reflective plays of the later years. He had founded the Amateur Association at Dharwad and directed his own plays for some time. *Harijanwara*, a play about caste prejudices, untouchability and politics, created a furore and drew the wrath of the upper-caste society. Incidentally, he spoke to Nehru about the unification of Karnataka at a time when Nehru would go into a rage at even a mention of linguistic states.

Girish Karnad (1938–2019) has repeatedly linked the existential angst portrayed in his play *Yayati* (1961) with his own turbulent emotional state as he was preparing to leave for England on a Rhodes fellowship. The desire to escape from the narrow, superficial middle-class life, the ambition of becoming a celebrated poet in English, suppressed sexuality—all these converged into a critique of and rebellion against the traditional norms. The play also explores the depths of the inner self of the characters, even though the story and the characters are from the *Mahabharata*. It has all the recognisable elements of a mythological play of the professional theatre, but the agonising exploration of the human psyche through all the major characters owes itself to the modernist plays of Jean Anouilh and Luigi Pirandello. Karnad also speaks about the influence of French existentialism, of Sartre and Camus, on him and his generation. In my view, there were two strands in Karnad's sensibility which remained practically unchanged during his entire career as a dramatist. One is the vision of the ghosts inhabiting and writhing in the nooks and corners of the mental cosmos which he explores and unravels in play after play. The atheistic existentialism of Sartre with its notions of 'bad faith', being condemned to be free, and the responsibility of choice, remained major preoccupations for Karnad. His less successful plays, such as *Anjumallige* (1977), *Hittina Hunja* (*Bali, the Sacrifice*, 1980) and *Broken Images* (2006) are examples of this confrontation with the deep ambiguities of human existence. The power of his better plays also comes from the relentless manner in which the suppressed motives, hidden passions and the practised deceptions are brought to light in unexpected and dramatic revelations. The relationship between Tughlaq and his stepmother is tantalisingly ambivalent. Did Tughlaq have his father and brother killed for seizing power to realise his ideals? Or is this a post-facto legitimisation of a deed done out of sheer lust for power? When the king in *Bali, the Sacrifice* wants to copulate with the queen in the presence of the mahout or when he discusses the erogenous parts of her body with him, we see a glimpse of the perverted sexuality, compared to which the queen's adultery does not seem to be a sin at all.

In *Taledanda* (literally, 'death by beheading', 1990), a play which operates mostly on the public and political level, both Jagannatha and Sovideya are motivated by the psychological knots in their personalities which they do not fully understand.

The other strand in Karnad's sensibility was his preoccupation with history and the attempt to connect the individual self with a history reconstructed through the lens of modernity. What is often missing in the criticism of *Tughlaq* (1964) is the understanding that Tughlaq is a prisoner of the history of his times. He is the ruler of a vast empire where the majority of his subjects are Hindu. His conflictual relationship with religion is not entirely a result of his personal struggles. As we see in the episode involving Sheikh Imam-ud-din, the conflict between religion and state was a real and troublesome issue for the medieval society. His 'secular' actions are seen as pro-Hindu and anti-Islamic by many of his subjects and even courtiers. Similarly, Basava in *Taledanda* is Bijjala's treasurer and the leader of a large community of artisan-devotees who are crucial to the prosperity of the kingdom. In fact, Karnad shows Basava as 'a saint living in the slum of politics'. In the play, Bijjala, who is in a way a historian and interpreter of his own kingdom and society, understands this. He has a more realistic knowledge of the complexities of society, though he admires the utopian idealism of Basava. The point is that without giving up his modernist, existentialist world view, Karnad sees the individual self of his major protagonists as a product of history. The sadistic cruelty of *Tughlaq* is therefore a reflection of the violence of the contemporary society. Karnad uses the 'inner' and 'outer' division of the stage to great effect to reinforce the linkages between the individual private self and the world out there. In the last meeting of Tughlaq and Aziz the two worlds confront each other and Aziz turns out to be an inverted mirror image of Tughlaq. Every act of Tughlaq is turned on its head by Aziz in a villainous parody for personal greed. The play suggests that whatever the motives of Tughlaq, conscious and unconscious, his actions could be perversely used by someone like Aziz. Therefore, what is acted out on the stage is not the personal or private drama of Tughlaq's fragmented self. The drama lies in the confrontation of the individual self with the realities of history.

When this does not happen Karnad's plays appear flawed and weak. *Tipu Sultan Kanda Kanasu* (The Dreams of Tipu Sultan, 1997), despite some powerful scenes and episodes and a sound but self-conscious perspective on history and historiography, does not succeed in dramatising the individual self's confrontation with history. The historical 'public' scenes (most of them taken from archival records) seem to be merely stringed up together chronologically, whereas the powerful 'private' scenes do not achieve much beyond giving some glimpses of the 'real' Tipu. Similarly, in *Crossing to Talikota* (*Rakshasa Tangadagi* in the original Kannada, 2018) there is a one-dimensional sequence of actions, all originating from Aliya Ramaraya's paranoid and megalomaniac personality. So much so that the other characters are marginalised. While keeping out the communalised historical interpretations of the end of the Vijayanagara empire ('Muslim *Nawabs* destroyed a Hindu empire', etc.), Karnad reduces history to merely the consequence of a powerful but self-destructive individual's actions. This is not to question the authenticity of the historical details in the play. It is about an uncharacteristic absence of the attempt to relate the individual self to history.

Taledanda emerges as a great play because of the mastery with which diverse strands of history are woven into the very texture of the dramatic action without obtruding on its flow. The spectators/readers are affected by a powerful sense of the inevitability of the tragic end right from the first mention of the inter-caste wedding. When the parents of the bride and groom seek Basava's blessings (read consent) for the wedding, his eyes fill up with tears but he holds back his blessings. From this point onwards the multiple conflicts in the play lead us to the inevitable denouement. But practically every episode brings up an important strand of history and society into the play. For example, when Bijjala tries to explain his admiration for Basava and the *sharanas*, he mentions how his ancestors performed every ritual and sacrifice, in their quest to be included in the higher *Varna*, but every child in Kalyana knows that 'Kalachuri', the name of the dynasty, reveals the barber caste to which it originally belonged. However, Basava and the *sharanas* did not see his caste in him. They also made Kalyana prosperous by the work ethic (*kayaka*) they cultivated. Similarly, the priest Damodara Bhatta and Manchanya Kramita also explain why people did not support the revolutionary wedding. It was the fear among the upper castes that the wedding would breach all hierarchies and the lower castes ('untouchables' mainly) would overrun the society. The play demonstrates that a socio-religious creed which begins with the premise of the annihilation of caste will surely be pursued by its built-in logic of a final violent confrontation with tradition. In the play, Bijjala is an outstanding character, gifted with a clear and pragmatic understanding of history and politics. The *sharanas* are impatient with Basava and even suspect him of supporting Bijjala who is against the inter-caste wedding. They also think that Basava's feeling that time is not yet ripe for the wedding of a kind that has not happened in two thousand years, is merely a tactic to postpone it. As it always happens in Karnad's plays, *Taledanda* forces us to look at reality as though in a kaleidoscope. There are so many diverse perspectives and the truth remains elusive. Nor is this a postmodernist stance undermining the possibility of any ethical choice since truth itself is uncertain and contingent. The play is an elegy on the 'brilliance and the enthusiasm of an epoch to which the Kannada consciousness returns again and again, like the tongue returning to an aching tooth' (Karnad's words in the preface to the original Kannada play). The movement of the *sharanas* may have ended in failure, but the play affirms the greatness of the values they fought for.

An interesting feature of the three major Kannada plays on Basava and the *sharanas* is the powerful role played by Bijjala in them. In P. Lankesh's *Sankranti* (1971) and in H. S. Shivaprakash's *Mahachaitra* (1986), Bijjala is the pragmatic, politically mature counterfoil to the idealistic Basava. The little historical material available does not indicate that Bijjala was an extraordinary individual. A couple of *Vachanas* by Basava certainly hint at a complex relationship between Basava and Bijjala. The former seems to have considered his service to Bijjala as '*Jolawalige*' and not '*Velewalige*'—'*Jolawalige*' is service done as a profession, for a living, whereas '*Velewalige*' is dedication as service. In *Taledanda*, with the departure of Basava, Bijjala feels orphaned and loses his will to fight. In the play, Basava's departure is abrupt and his saying to Bijjala that he is going in search of god is not very convincing.

The Fire and the Rain (*Agni Mattu Male* in Kannada, 1998) returns to myths and emphatically eschews any historical connections. Karnad also seems to be returning to his existentialist exploration of the self with renewed vigour if one were to go by the sheer intensity of the passions of envy, hatred, lust and lust for power which seem to buffet the major characters. In some places the passions seem to be savage and primitive, in complete contrast to the Vedic religious ambience of the sacrifice. However, the play rises far above a display of brutal passions in its serious exploration of the power of knowledge. It also emerges as a profound critique of knowledge divorced from humanity. Though designed as a play about a mythical past, it can also be read as a veiled dystopic vision of the human world destroying itself in search of a sterile knowledge without ethics. Though one may find the attempt to project the tribals and players as counterfoil to the sterile brahminical world a little contrived and weak, the play succeeds in revealing the destructive power of both passion and knowledge.

Chandrashekhar Kambar (b. 1937) has reconstructed a tradition in which the playwright enjoys the unique privilege accorded only to the *Sutradhara* and the clown. This is the privilege of moving uninhibitedly between the many worlds which constitute Indian folk theatre. It is a theatre in which temporal and spatial dislocations are not only permissible but not even seen as dislocations. The past is not revered as so sacrosanct as to be unchangeable. Traditions of narration, performance, myth-making and constructing the verbal text can all be played with and modulated at will. Nor is the contemporary privileged as new, unprecedented or as a complete departure from the past. Many times it turns out that the contemporary is, in fact, one of the many elements constituting the past. The Indian folk theatre has consistently rejected the hegemony of time and linear history, just as it has rejected the authority of the written text.

That is why the introduction of the Brechtian model of 'total theatre' was not an 'invention' for a playwright like Kambar. The folk theatre which he had inherited has always been 'total', until the elite, urban amateur theatre disrupted the traditions of both folk theatre and professional theatre, only to hoist on the stage an anaemic version of the realistic-social drama of the West. More dangerously, it translated theatre from its truly social/public site of a ritual into the confinement of an aesthetic performance.

Kambar is not an unselfconscious practitioner of folk theatre. Nor does it make much sense to project him as a non-modernist writer with a seamless, organic relationship with the folk traditions he uses in his plays. The truth is that the moment of the beginning of his creative career is a moment of rupture, of the unambiguous realisation that the organic world of Shivapura—the feudal, rural world wherein everything has taken place for Kambar in a career spanning more than forty years—has been fissured irrevocably by the potent historical force of colonialism.

His first major narrative poem *Helathena Kela* (Listen, I Will Tell You, 1964), enacts this moment of disruption. The prelapsarian world of Shivapura is reconstructed in the early sections of the poem, somewhat nostalgically, as a pastoral-rural utopia, possessing fertility and plenitude. It is god's own country where Lord Shiva's dwelling place, Kailasa, blooms in every little flower; where men speak not in ordinary words but in proverbs of ageless wisdom; where private morality and public ethic are governed not by organised religion but by Kariyajja, the village elder symbolising the traditional mores, and by Parambi Kariyawa, the local deity who dwells in the ancient banyan tree marking the village boundary. Interestingly, and also intriguingly, Kambar's Shivapura is unaffected by organised religion—it is in fact absent. Shivapura's traditional world is made of folk cults of worship (especially the phallic worship of fertility), of the feudal social codes which equate female sexuality with the earth's fertility, and of a rich subaltern imagination which evades the limitations of the 'great tradition'. The last one, the subaltern imagination, rejects the separation between 'this-worldly' and 'other-worldly' ('*Iha*' and '*Para*') categories, just as it refuses to acknowledge the barriers between the real and the imagined. Shivapura is a place where demons, elves and fairies can wander. However, the alluring richness of the imagination should not blind us to the fact that there also seems to be a lack of comprehensiveness in the vision which does not see organised religion as a real presence and as a site of conflict and confrontation. Equally problematic in Kambar's works is the unchanging, curiously ahistorical, feudal world in which the village headman (*Gowda*) or the *zamindar* (Desai) are timeless figures of absolute power. These figures of feudal power contribute to reducing the anti-feudal struggles to mere contests for superior male virility, as in *Jaisidanayaka* (1975), *Jokumaraswamy* (1972) and *Kadukudure* (1979). I intend to discuss this problematic area a little later.

Some of the major plays of Kambar are a part of this creative effort to understand the historical process of change. The richness and plenitude of the images and metaphors which Kambar uses to depict the world of Shivapura may deceive us into believing that he looks back to its pre-modern, pre-colonial world with nostalgia, and constructs a utopian organic society which could never have been a historical reality. This is not true for two reasons. One, the feudal world is presented as unequal and oppressive, masquerading as virile and all powerful, while in reality it suffers from impotence and insecurity. In Kambar's vision, feudal authority is a sham, a pretence. In *Jokumaraswamy,* the Gowda who claims his right to violate every virgin in the village, is a joke among the prostitutes for his impotence. It is Basanna, the counterpart of Jokumaraswamy, the phallic god, who has satiated the women who sought him out. It is he who becomes the Gowdthi's lover and impregnates her. In *Kadukudure* (Wild Horse), the Gowdthi's aggressive authority, wiles and cunning cannot put a leash on either her three daughters' sexuality or on the hero's love for freedom. The much vaunted and feared gun, symbolising her authority, misfires, allowing the rebellious lovers to escape on the wild stallion. In a more recent play, *Mahamayi,* the figure of oppressive authority—the foster mother Mahamayi (her name can mean 'the great mother' as well as Mother Fate)—is, for a change, female; and she is also imagined as intolerant of love, sexuality and freedom.

Kambar has commented on the influences on his own writing:

> I am aware of the deep influence of modernism on many of the finest contemporary Kannada writers. In a way, a small part of my own writing reflects such influence. But now when I think of it from some distance, I feel that perhaps the frameworks of modernism were not a necessary means in the process of my establishing a relationship with my environment. Eliot and his alienation, existentialism, consciousness of the absurd, the European attempt to retrieve the primitive, the attempts of the kind made by Arnold and Pound to search for and identify the characteristics of culture; the modern European feeling of alienation from Sartre to the hippies – I accept the potential validity of all these without a second word. But I have my own reservations about making them my own ways. Aren't the questions we have among ourselves about the human condition far more fundamental and therefore more universal than the perspective of the greatest Europeans? (Kambar 2009, 9)

A major part of Kambar's oeuvre comprises the 'urban' plays written in the urban dialect of Bengaluru, with characters belonging to the middle class and to the political class. It is remarkable that Kambar has written powerful plays in this mode for the urban, realistic theatre. Despite his conviction that the mythopoeic mode is the authentic one for the Indian playwright, Kambar has proved his mastery over this other mode too. Whether it is in the mythopoeic mode or where the action takes place in an anonymous city, his plays explore the dualities of human existence—frustration and fulfilment, oppression and liberation, faith and betrayal, mastery and slavery, fertility and barrenness, the self and the other. In his brilliant introduction to the play *Rishyashringa* (1965), Kirtinath Kurtakoti describes Shivapura as a place that has lost its moral bearings. The traditional mores governing social and sexual behaviour have collapsed. Ramagonda is, for the expectant people of Shivapura, Rishyashringa, a version of the fertility/vegetation god. In a powerful but ultimately problematic equation, Kambar projects both the land and the woman as awaiting the healing touch of fertility. The equation helps Kambar to introduce a metaphorical intensity unequalled in Kannada drama. The struggle for mastery over land takes the added dimension of the assertion of sexual power. It is problematic because it leads to the repeated imaging of the woman as predominantly a sexual being, pining for male virility to quench her desire. Whatever little agency and individuality that is allowed to the woman is only due to her defiance of the social mores governing sexual behaviour. In fact, for both men and women in Kambar's plays, sexuality is the wild horse untamed by parental, societal or religious authority, waiting just outside the boundaries of the domestic and societal spheres to carry human beings away to the unknown worlds of magical fulfilment or devastating frustration. But in Kambar's plays, it is the woman who is more vulnerable and in danger of becoming only a vehicle of sexuality. Interestingly, it is the marginalised women like Kamali in this play, who either belong to the lower castes or are village concubines, who seem to possess some individuality.

Jokumaraswamy (1972) initiated a new, creative phase in Kannada theatre. The production of the play under the direction of the late B. V. Karanth is by consensus the most significant event in modern Kannada theatre. Here was a play for 'total theatre'. It had great songs set to music by Karanth, ritual worship of the phallic fertility god, humour, uninhibited treatment of sexuality, and conflict and tragedy, albeit muted. Kannada theatre seemed to have undergone a major scene shift, from the realistic proscenium 'prosy' stage to the colours, movement, music and rhythms of a mythopoeic folk theatre. It was also a very intriguing play because the aesthetic power of the play seemed almost independent, with a life of its own, while its thematic content was disturbing and its Brechtian ironies uncomfortably sharp. The Gowda, feudal lord and village chieftain, is a comic villain with his gun, farcical band of ragtag followers and empty boast of excessive virility. But his power in the feudal village is real. Through years of usury, he has taken away the land belonging to the others, and he also shamelessly declares his right to violate every virgin. In reality, he is impotent and leaves the Gowdthi, his wife, lonely and languishing. The loyal wife that she is, she abjectly begs the village concubine Shari to let her perform the worship of the phallic fertility god, Jokumaraswamy. In a rite reminiscent of the most ancient fertility cults, the snake gourd worshipped as Jokumaraswamy has to be cut and later fed to the male companion (the husband in case of all 'respectable' women). In a devastating twist of irony, it is Basanna, the young rebel and rogue and the Gowda's opponent, who persuades the Gowdthi to perform the fertility rite with him. There is also the social protest against usury and bondage. Basanna not only defies Gowda's authority openly but also announces that things have changed, and that the new principle, of 'the tiller of the land is the owner of the land', has brought an end to the Gowda's feudal regime. The motif is repeated in *Jaisidanayaka*. It would of course be inappropriate to treat Kambar's mythopoeic plays as political plays and thereby interrogate the maturity of the ideology presented through Basanna and Jaisidanayaka. At the same time, it is also clear that Kambar consciously presents a conflict between the oppressive old feudal order which has already become obsolete but is hanging on to power through usurpation and deceit, and the new, as yet utopian, social order where the tiller of the land is also its master.

In a later play *Nayee Kathe* (1980) this becomes the central theme. The obedient dog (*Nayee Maga*, the faithful servant) subverts the master's authority by refusing to be a dog any longer. Kambar's imagination shows its preoccupation with the 'dogginess' of human beings which makes them victims and tools of exploitation. Somanna in *Nayee Kathe* is yet another feudal lord who sees himself as a 'hunter of women'. He has been successful in his exploits mainly due to his servant, the *Nayee Maga* (literally 'son of dog'), who has been his human shield. Nayee Maga has reduced himself to his image in the master's gaze. He is abject, shows automatic obedience and has never realised that he has an identity of his own. In some of the most powerful scenes in *Jaisidanayaka*, Desai, the feudal lord, proves his point that in every human being, even in the poet-dreamer Omkari, there is a hidden self which would rather wear the headgear of a Desai and reduce everybody else to slavery. Servitude is also a state of mind, a surrender of oneself to the master's gaze. In *Harakeya Kuri* (The Sacrificial Sheep, 1983), the middle-class couple becomes victim of the politicians' manoeuvrings because of their willingness to surrender to the powerful. Without denying the reality of social and political power and of the mechanisms of oppression, Kambar probes into the psychological states which force human beings to abjectly surrender to the powerful. The master and the dog are also two states of the soul. This provides one explanation for the ironical reversals in the play *Jaisidanayaka* which turn the rebel and liberator Sidanayaka into an oppressor worse than Desai.

In the farcical play *Tukrana Kanasu* (Tukra's Dream, 1989), Kambar returns to the theme of the dream of justice and a humane social order. But here, instead of the idealist hero we have Tukra, a liminal figure, forever being bullied, beaten up and insulted. All this because he 'sees' things from his perspective and speaks out, making the rich and powerful uncomfortable. He also has his dreams of a just society. He is a bungler annoying people with his inappropriate talk. He has the audacity to say in public that the village Patel is his illegitimate son. He discovers a bigger arena for his irrepressible spirit in the troubled times of the Gandhian freedom movement. Of course, he remains a true picaro at heart, using Gandhian satyagraha for his own needs. Though it is hard to separate fact from fancy in his imaginative recounting of his adventures, it is clear that for a brief period the situation allows him to enjoy some dignity in the eyes of his peers. But his anarchic plans of looting the Patel's property misfires. His companions make away with the loot and he wakes up only to be arrested by the police. He is forced to put his sign (a zero) on a document admitting to crimes he had not even dreamed of committing. In the play, Tukra has his moment before the end, making a moving speech about his dreams and his failures. Tukra's picaresque vitality does not altogether suppress the tragedy of a liminal individual who is punished for his dreams.

Harakeya Kuri is a brilliant political play by Kambar. It is an urban play written in the educated Kannada spoken in Bengaluru. In style and idiom it is vastly different from his mythopoeic plays. Written for the proscenium theatre employing stage realism, the play sustains its oppressive intensity through the twists and turns of the plot. It is set in the typical middle-class household of the couple Prakash and Saroja who lead nondescript lives with their middle-class aspirations. They are unaware that their house is being used by Rudrappa, the politician, as his unofficial office where he hatches his clever plots including the murder of a well-known actor-turned-politician. The cruel world of politics impinges upon the 'innocent' middle-class domestic world when Siddalingu, the assassin used by Rudrappa, accidentally seeks shelter in the couple's house. Thereafter the couple is caught in a nightmarish series of incidents which reveal their inadequacy, vulnerability and, as they realise towards the end, their culpability too. It is Siddalingu who in his second visit confronts the couple with their suppressed desires and hypocrisy which make them easy preys for wily politicians. They cannot take a 'holier-than-thou' attitude because their own lives are made of lies and deception. The intense scene between the three characters functions as a catharsis, and at the end of it, they make a pledge to stand together to defeat Rudrappa in his plans to become chief minister. But he has already made his moves, and his hired assassins shoot down Siddalingu before the curtains come down. The play is a remarkable achievement and Kambar is able to unravel the symbiotic relationship between the innocent domestic world and the cruel murderous world of politics. The play ends with the shattering realisation that if innocence cannot save us, nor can newly discovered bravery. The atmosphere of the play communicates powerfully the frightening erosion of private lives by the vicious political world.

In the play *Sirisampige* (1991), Shivanaga, the young prince, has been refusing to get married saying that he has not found the perfect woman. His mother, the Queen Mother, is worried because fortunetellers have predicted that delaying the marriage will be dangerous. One night, in a trance-like state in sleep, he sees the statue of a nymph with a lamp in her hand coming to life and enchanting him with her dance before leaving him desolate. She seems to be the perfect woman he has been looking for.

He also realises that she seemed to have come out from his body, like an emanation. He forces his mother and the palace councillors to cleave his body into two equal parts and bury them separately in flowers. He hopes that from one half of his body the nymph with the lamp will emerge. But to everybody's dismay, while Sivanaga emerges from one half, a king cobra emerges from the other and slithers away. Disappointed and still reluctant Shivanaga marries Sirisampige. He does not consummate the marriage. In his nocturnal wanderings he sees his own image in a pond and believes that it is either god or his own true self. As the clown ironically points out, it is his corpse rising up from the pond.

At a later stage in the play, Shivanaga admits to his wife Sirisampige that it was indeed his corpse which he saw in the pond. While he is lost in his pursuit of fulfilment in self-love, Sirisampige realises that she is a 'half-widow'. When the cobra pursues her, she yields to him. Her defense is that Shivanaga has not consummated the marriage, thus leaving her pining for love. The painful realisation comes to Shivanaga also that he is incomplete and that separating his body from the soul was a grievous fault. He now declares that the body does not sin unlike the soul, which does.

Kambar's play *Mahamayi* (1999) is of a piece with his epic novel in verse *Chakori,* in its style and the Yeatsian resolve to directly address the dualities of existence, even at the risk of reducing the characters to allegorical figures. The Mahamayi (great mother) is Shetavi Taayi, the goddess of death. She is ironically the mother of Sanjiva Shiva who is a *vaidya* (healer) who can save only those whom the death goddess does not want to kill. She has threatened him often that if he were to try to save someone against her will, he would lose his gifts of healing. Tantalisingly for him, it is the princess who has been marked out by his mother, while he wants to save her even at the risk of losing everything including his mother. The situation is extraordinary, pitching the lovers against the demon mother. In this mythopoeic play, Kambar examines the paradoxical relationship between life and death, illness and cure and creativity and destruction. The play ends with Sanjiva Shiva saving the princess but losing the gift of healing. Even without the intensity of, say *Jokumaraswamy,* this play dramatises the incorrigible dualities of human existence. In this play, Kambar seems to have moved on from his ironical analysis of the contradictions in human beings to the larger forces of Eros and Thanatos, ruling human destiny.

The unique genius of Kambar made it possible for Kannada drama to negotiate with the conflicts of a modern sensibility by employing non-modern theatrical traditions. In comparison with intellectual decolonisation, the effort to achieve decolonisation through the symbolic forms of culture (including drama) is far more challenging.

Three European movements influenced Kannada drama during the 1970s and after. These were existentialism, the angry-young-man drama, and the theatre of the absurd. These influences which shaped a generation of Indian theatre made their impact through translations from other Bhashas and by performances of these plays. Badal Sarkar's *Evam Indrajit* saw many performances across Karnataka by amateur theatre groups. Mohan Rakesh's *Ashad ka Ek Din* in an excellent translation by Siddalinga Pattanashetty was very well received. There were also translations and discussions of Ionesco, Strindberg and Camus in the literary journals of the period. The theatre of the absurd led to the short-lived movement of *Asangatha Nataka* (*Asangatha* is Kannada for absurd) with Chandrakanth Kusnoor and Chandrashekhar Patil being the leading practitioners.

P. Lankesh's (1935–2000) plays mark an important shift in Kannada theatre. His early plays are a blend of existentialist drama and the angry-young-man theatre. In *Nanna Tangigondu Gandu Kodi* (Find a Bridegroom for My Sister, 1963), the hero Jagannath rebels against the hypocrisy and dishonesty of his father who is a respected and influential individual in society. Jagannath has discovered the moral corruption under the mask of respectability in his father. He persuades his sister to join him in his rebellion. But in the last part of the play she realises that Jagannath's rebellion was also an attempt to exercise power over her and was a product of the contradictions in his own personality. As in his fiction, Lankesh unravels the ambivalences in human action even while using the protagonist to satirise the hypocrisies of the middle class.

T. Prasannana Grahasthashrama (T. Prasanna's Householdership, 1964) is a powerful satire on the institution of marriage. Prasanna, the protagonist, has discovered that his wife is in an adulterous relationship with her doctor. In the shocking climax of the play he brings them together in his home. The wife realises that she has been used by both her husband and lover for their own purposes. The ambivalences in intimate relationships are unmasked in the play. In *Kranthi Bantu Kranthi* (There Comes the Revolution, 1965), Bhagavan, an academic intellectual, gives shelter to a Naxalite, who was his former student, for a night, against the vehement protests by his wife. An accidental encounter during the night between the Naxalite and a thief leads to a powerful exposure of Bhagavan's pretentious radicalism. It is revealed that he is 'both the establishment and the protest against it'.

Lankesh's *Teregalu* (Waves, 1964) is closer in spirit to the theatre of menace and cruelty, than to absurd drama. Three unknown men enter the house of the protagonist and begin to question him. Soon, it turns into both a trial and ordeal through which the protagonist's pretensions to middle-class respectability are dissected. It is a Kafkaesque play in which the trial and judgement are equally absurd. From this phase of intense, existentialist probing into the essential ambivalence of human existence, Lankesh went on to write two plays which examine the contradictions of society and history. *Sankranti* (1971) is about the inter-caste marriage which is supposed to have provoked the violent suppression of the *Vachanakara* movement of the twelfth century led by Basava. The focus of the play is not on the public events alone but also on the individuals who participate in it. Usha, a lively unconventional brahmin young woman, is attracted to Rudra, a handsome Dalit who has recently joined the movement of the *sharanas*. He is struggling to 'Sanskritise' himself by giving up the lifestyle of the community he belongs to. Usha who is attracted to him because he belongs to a life world unknown to her and wants to know it through Rudra, provokes him to make love to her. This episode leads to a virtual caste war and the brahmins complain to Bijjala, the king, who summons Basava to be part of the trial of Rudra. In a stunning reversal, Usha answers Bijjala's question—'Was it an act of love or rape'?—by saying it was rape. Her argument is that she loved Rudra who embodies for her the Dalit manhood, but through his conversion by the *sharana* movement, Rudra has become another person. Therefore, the man who made love to her was not the man she had loved. Apart from the confrontation between Bijjala and Basava, which involves a complex evaluation of the movement, the people's involvement and its contractions, the play foregrounds the issue of conversion to a new religion. One of the major preoccupations of the new religion of Basava was the equality of all human beings and the abrogation of caste. But didn't it also involve a rejection of the values and life-style that one had grown up with? Lankesh presents a critique of the new religion which dismissed the folk and animistic beliefs and rituals of the lower castes as superstitious. He explores the turmoil the individuals are forced to go through in times of radical change.

His last play *Gunamukha* (1993) is about Nader Shah during his invasion of India. Himself a cruel, lusty marauder, Nader Shah is shocked by the dishonesty and perfidy of the Indians which provokes him into more violent acts. However, he is ill and forced to take the help of Alavi Khan, a hakim and spiritual practitioner. Alavi Khan attempts to persuade Nader Shah that his illness is a result of continual corruption of mind and body. Shah who resents Alavi Khan's method of healing begins to understand himself. Thus, the play is about corruption and healing, using history as backdrop.

G. B. Joshi (1904–93), who wrote under the penname Jadabharatha, was also the founder of Manohara Grantha Mala, a publishing house which introduced several major writers including Girish Karnad. He was an exceptionally gifted playwright whose plays continue to be performed by many theatre groups. His most popular play is *Kadadida Neeru* (Troubled Waters, 1963), a tragedy about the failure of idealism in the real world. The play narrates the ruination of the family of Shivappa, a Gandhian, with the rise of the new rural political class. Gandhian ideals of service to the community are irrelevant to the new politics of money, sex and violence. Shivappa finds himself abandoned by the village community when he faces a financial crisis and an assault on his daughter. He is unable to defend himself, which forces his son to kill the local politician. Shivappa ends up compromising against his conscience. The play, with its authentic rural ambience and the rich texture of North Karnataka dialect, is profoundly melancholic about the transition of the rural society into an unethical political world.

Sattavara Neralu (The Shadow of the Dead, 1974) offers a brilliant analysis of the decline of a monastery (*matha*) owing to the greed and weak morals of people who cannot sustain the religious institution which was a symbol of faith for ordinary people. The play takes us deep into the machinations used to keep the monastery as a seat of power even when it has been hollowed out from the inside. It raises profound questions about religious faith, belief in institutions and morality. B. V. Karanth's production of the play, with a chorus singing the compositions of the *Dasas* (devotional poets), is considered one of the most memorable in the history of Kannada theatre.

Chandrashekhar Patil's (1939–2022) plays, written in the style of absurd drama, are short and poetic works exploring serious themes with his typical humour. *Appa* (Father, 1969), inspired by a *Vachana* by Basava, is about the agony of the son of a woman who has earned her living by selling her body to many men and who cannot tell her child who his father is. We see the son first as an innocent child trying to understand the innuendos of the elders taunting him about the absent father. Later we see him as an angry young man painfully trying to accept the fact that he is a bastard child of a mother who loves him so intensely. The play transforms his condition into the universal condition of human existence, thrown into an absurd world.

Tinger Buddanna (1971) is an allegory based on a folk tale as well as on the myth of Bhasmasura who in trying to destroy everything destroys himself. The play works at the metaphorical level all through. An old couple dig up a huge onion out of which emerges a child whom they begin to treat as their own. The mother is overprotective about the son who now goes to school. He feels humiliated when everyone including butterflies, squirrels and classmates make fun of him. The mother teaches him a mantra repeating which he can destroy anyone who taunts him. After taking his revenge on everyone, the son uses the mantra against the parents and, in the end, against himself. The lyrical power of the play effectively unravels the destructive and self-destructive forces in human personality. It also becomes an allegory of the modern individual's self-destructive tendencies. *Kunta Kunta Kuruvatti* (Hop, Hop, Lame Guy, 1970) reads almost like an adaptation of *Waiting for Godot* and explores the absurd world of human desires.

Absurd drama was short-lived though the plays themselves were popular, especially as they do not demand complicated stage arrangements. All the absurd plays were short plays and no full-fledged play emerged from the absurd school of drama. It should also be noted that major plays in Kannada have a complex relationship with literary movements. While they respond to the changes in sensibility ushered in by the movements and also share their preoccupations, the major plays do not adhere to the expectations formulated by the movements. They are innovative and experimental in their search for an adequate theatrical form.

NINE

Women's Writing

In an earlier section we have seen how Kannada women writers of the first phase responded to the women's question as it was formulated during that period, under the impact of the educational and social reform initiatives. The major women writers were from the educated upper-caste middle class and saw their writing and activism as a venture carried out under male tutelage and within the consensual matrix of conservative, traditional frameworks. Within this constricted space, they were able to articulate their pleas for a more compassionate and liberal response from men. It does not need much effort to demonstrate that they neither intended nor accomplished a radical interrogation of the existing patriarchal norms. In the specific context of Karnataka, and with little contact with the few attempts made in other states by women to question patriarchal discourses, women writers necessarily adopted the model of appealing to the good sense and compassion of their male counterparts. This did not prevent them from developing arguments with the potential to question the tradition. A review of the women's journals of the period by B. N. Sumitrabai is illuminating (2009, 146–82). She analyses the journals *Saraswati* and *Sodari*, edited by R. Kalyanamma for over twenty years against all odds. It is remarkable that Kalyanamma created in her journals a democratic space for discussing contemporary issues. She also made it a platform for hundreds of women to write and articulate their views. Therefore, comments on the conservatism of the early women writers need to be qualified with the knowledge of their engagement with the national and international events of the time. Though the surviving copies of the journals of the time show ample evidence of the participation of women in these discussions, the literary establishment seems to have ignored them altogether. The convenient division of the social milieu into 'male' and 'female' spheres was evident in the literary domain too. Despite the active interest Bendre took in the writings of Belagere Janakamma (1912–66) and Kodagina Gowramma (1912–39), there was little attempt to acknowledge the significance of women's writing.

It was in the post-independence period that the changes in society transformed women's consciousness in relation to gender. There was a complex legacy of women's participation in the nationalist movement in the Gandhian social praxis. There was also an awareness of the women's movements across the world. As mentioned earlier, women writers from Karnataka were members of various all-India women's associations. There are hundreds of brief references to the women in Karnataka who were actively involved in the nationalist movement but detailed information is scarce. The progressive writers' movement (*Pragatisheela* movement) also addressed women as social issues invariably involved them. It introduced the hitherto prohibited images of women as actresses in professional theatre and as prostitutes. These images of women as victims of sexual exploitation, especially when embedded in a provocative naturalistic style, were not acceptable to the reading public. Aa. Na. Kra. (A. N. Krishna Rao), a popular novelist, was targeted for his open descriptions of the lives of prostitutes and was castigated as a writer of pornography. Though he defended himself with a long essay on literature and pornography (1983), his critics were right in pointing out that his sanctimonious criticism of the societal sanction for prostitution was used to introduce titillating descriptions which contradicted his moral stance. Unfortunately, an opportunity to develop a critique of the ambivalence of the society towards prostitution was lost in the controversy and the literary establishment was able to impose a 'censorship by consensus' on any discussion of sexuality.[1]

It is clear that the literary critical establishment was efficient in gatekeeping, using the middle-class code of normativity to prohibit the exploration of many genuine issues relating to women. It was only in the 1960s and 70s that women writers were able to freely articulate their critique of the patriarchal norms. In Karnataka these were the decades of many people's movements which generally supported an anti-establishment stance. *Navya* writing, as discussed earlier, was critical of middle-class morality and tradition to the extent of ignoring it altogether. It foregrounded sexuality as the site for interrogating the hypocrisy of middle-class notions of sexuality. Authenticity of individual experience was valorised. This encouraged women writers to explore more boldly their own experiences by breaking the stereotypes of the homemaker, self-sacrificing loyal wife and mother. *Mullugalu* (Thorns, 1990), the first collection of short stories by Veena Shanteshwar, received critical attention and acclaim despite shocking many male readers. The short stories took an ironical and scathing view of the duplicity of men. Written with controlled fury,

---

[1] Krishna Rao, A. N. (Aa. Na. Kra.) (1983). *Sahitya Mattu Kama Prachodane*; for a discussion of the essay, see Amur 1983.

the stories deal with unfaithfulness, lack of courage and honesty among men who abandon relationships when they are transgressive. There is also the attempt by women to rebel against their imprisonment in domesticity and traditional values. There is also, though not very openly articulated, a discovery of their own sexuality.

However, despite their power to shock and disturb, the stories are not radical in asserting the autonomy of women. Women are depicted as still bonded to the memory of the men who have betrayed them. Many of them make compromising choices to remain within the institution of marriage, and remain dependent on the men. H. S. Raghavendra Rao describes the major theme of Veena's stories as a 'post-mortem of marriage' (2009, 143–54). But not many of her stories suggest an alternative. Her strength lies in the clarity and power with which she dismantles the patriarchal structures in intimate relationships. Her stories unravel the sexual politics in love and marriage. They also question the cultural roles imposed on women by showing how unnatural they are.

Veena's writings set up the tone for many women writers who began to interrogate the real nature of family and the domestic world. In Vaidehi's (Janaki Srinivasa Murthy, b. 1945) short stories, there are two distinctive ways of examining this 'woman's world'. In the middle-class regional society that she deals with, it is not just wives but also the maids and women servants who bear the brunt of domesticity. They are usually portrayed as young women who have the pluck to assert themselves though unable to find the freedom they desire. Their dreams and desires are rudely shattered by exploitative situations in which they are trapped. In one of her poems, a servant girl who makes dung cakes sees the moon and dreams of the moon descending like the hero of a fairy tale to take her to his world. But she sees him turning into a dung cake and crumbling. She takes a piece, burns it to ashes and smears a bit of it on her forehead, as a sign of turning into an ascetic. Vaidehi sees the domestic world as a site of violence and suffering. In her remarkable story *Ammachchi Yemba Nenapu* (Remembering Ammachchi) the narrator, a young girl and an admirer of the strong-willed and rebellious Ammachchi, narrates Ammachchi's story. She is the daughter of a widow. She is harassed by Yenkappaiah whom her mother had trusted as a saviour. Yenkappaiah is a crude beast and is determined to curb Ammachchi's desire for freedom. The freedom she desires is of wearing a fashionably cut blouse, and of going for a walk on her own. Yenkappaiah exercises his authority in the name of protecting the honour of the young woman. The horror of this kind of patriarchy is revealed when he rapes Ammachchi in her own home to 'teach her a lesson'. And she is married off to him (2006, 73–84). The social world Vaidehi deals with is the small provincial traditional world. But in this nondescript world where freedom and rebellion by women are unheard of, there is such invisible violence and cruelty that the critique of the domestic holocaust of women leaves the readers disturbed. At the same time, many of the women characters are guerrilla fighters who find their own ways to hit back. The example is the story *Vanimayi,* who is another victim like Ammachchi, harassed by Narasimha, another version of Yenkappaiah. Vanimayi is bedridden, probably in her last days. Narasimha keeps ridiculing her, even scratching her feet to show that her body is losing sensation. In the climactic scene, Vanimayi gestures him to come close and kicks him in the face (2006, 185–99).

Vaidehi's stories reveal the verbal violence constantly unleashed by men on women. They speak in the culturally approved language which reduces women to unthinking idiots and dependent servants. Many male readers have labelled women's writings as 'kitchen literature' because they believe it is confined to cooking and gossip. Vaidehi shows how this 'kitchen world' is the site of violent sexual politics. She also subverts this hierarchy of the 'kitchen' and the world outside, by saying that there is no need for women to internalise the male attitudes to domesticity. She says that men deserve pity and sympathy because they are forever excluded from experiences meant for women alone. In a witty poem she tells them that they may know the *Rasa* theory of Indian poetics, but they will never understand the mystery of making *Rasam.* In another poem, she warns men not to peep into the 'vanity bags' of women, because they contain traces of experiences totally forbidden to men. She does not agree with the feminist denigration of motherhood; she believes in the power of bonding and relationships which men cannot experience to the full.

In the story *Chandale,* a young girl, Beena, declares, 'I wish I could become a prostitute', to the shocked middle-class narrator. Though the narrator Rami admits that she does not know whether it is right or wrong to feel so, she at once begins to suspect that Beena may seduce her own son (Vaidehi 2006, 63–72). In *Antaralada Baduku* (The Inner Life) two sisters who are forced to live in their aunt's house by their parents, find the aunt strange and even mentally abnormal. She uses their presence to avoid sleeping with her husband. There is only one line in the entire story which reveals the reason for her strange behaviour. When the narrator returns after a brief absence, she notices how haggard the aunt looks, 'she looked like a tired prostitute' (Vaidehi 2006, 214–21). Vaidehi's stories are replete with such moments of unmasking the hidden realities of ordinary women's lives.

Gulabi Talkies is an unusual narrative of the coming of modernity to a little town. Gulabi, a woman who had run away to Bombay and made money through sex work, funds Gulabi Talkies, a film-tent theatre. Lillibai, the local midwife, now begins to double as the gatekeeper of the women's section and makes money by not insisting on tickets to let people in. For the first time, the women of the town begin to go out to the talkies and demand money from their men. The author/narrator tells us how such small waves launched by Gulabi Talkies and Lillibai created subtle changes which impacted the future of small towns like the one in the story (2006, 1–14). In another story, the young Kamalavathi's dreams of freedom are crushed when she begins to work in a garment factory. Though her grandmother thinks that 'proper medicine has been given for her arrogance', the story tells us about the young girl's desires crushed by poverty ('Puttammatte and Her Granddaughter', Vaidehi 2006, 139–62). Vaidehi subverts the notion of the 'domestic' and of women writing as 'kitchen writing'.

Pratibha Nandakumar (b. 1955) is equally scathing about the domestic world of the urban middle-class woman. In the poem *Naavu Hudigiyare Heege* (We Girls are Like This), the narrator tells her friend how the middle-class life of a woman is all about the suppression and burial of dreams and dwindling into a homemaker with two children and her own body sagging. She writes ironically about the woman's daily circus to balance the needs of the family (2007, 5). 'I have no home of my own / But can't leave this home': Pratibha sees the domestic world as a prison but also understands the inability of the woman to walk out of it. In another poem, she compares marital life to a never-ending saw which moves but does not cut. Her poems include many images of the claustrophobic family life. ('The room is too small to hold two persons' anger.') There are also ironical portrayals of herself flaunting a facile modern pose without freedom. When the husband slaps her for not ironing his shirt properly, her grandmother tells her, 'Take off your jeans and thrust them into the oven'.

However, the brilliant poetry of Pratibha is not limited to the post-mortem of middle-class family life. Her poetry is also an honest record of the needs of her mind and body. She creates, for herself, the image of the modern woman who acknowledges her sexuality and asserts her freedom to seek fulfilment. In a poem she wonders why all the *pativratas* (loyal wives, chaste women) in the myths and puranas are always hounded by lusty men. She provides a list of the horrible punishments prescribed for the non-*pativritas* in the Dharmic works. She wants to defy these proscriptions and invite the lusty men (2007, 80). If Akka Mahadevi, the saint–poet of the twelfth century, walked alone, saying that there are streams to quench her thirst and fruit-bearing trees for hunger, she, the modern woman, can find bars to quench her thirst and restaurants to feed her. There are such allusions and instances of intertextuality in Pratibha's poetry, evidencing her engagement with tradition, though only to subvert it.

In fact, revisiting the women figures of the myths and puranas is a dominant theme in modern Kannada poetry by women. The revisiting has a double purpose – to critique the patriarchal past and to recast the women figures of the past from a feminist perspective. Sukanya Maruti writes the soliloquy of Draupadi, married to the five Pandava brothers but dreaming of Karna who unknown to her is the eldest of the Pandavas (2007, 84). According to the poet, when Lord Ram touched Ahalya who had turned into stone by her husband's curse, 'Yes, the stone exploded, but little else happened'. Akka Mahadevi is seen as the prototype of the liberated woman who walked out in the nude, rejecting her husband, but also as the victim of a demeaning trial by the male *Vachanakaras* about her chastity. The famous line 'But Raghava is not at fault' is repeated ironically by Pratibha and many other women poets who see Sita as the victim of the cruel patriarchy. This recasting of women figures from the past is a rejection of the attempt by the first-generation women poets who celebrated the 'Arya' women of the past as role models. These figures are now seen as legitimising the oppressive norms of patriarchy. Instead, Pratibha addresses a poem to Bipasha Basu, the celebrity model and actress, advising her how to wear a saree. Kannada women poets are scathing in their comments on the contemporary evils of communalism which they rightly see as a male affair. Lines from one of Pratibha's poems say it all: 'In my funeral procession / Sing sufi gazals.'

Lalita Siddabasavaiah, an eminent poet, deconstructed the Ayyappa myth and the Sabarimala controversy a decade before it actually took place, in her poem *Irumadi*. When the lady doctor informs the speaker that she has reached menopause, she declares, 'At least now I can give my *darshana* to that adolescent boy-god Ayyappa'. She addresses him by assuring him, 'Look, dear boy, don't be so scared of women. A handsome young Malayali like you has no business to sit here in the dark temple, soot ridden, like a smoked pot. Come out, liberate yourself, get on a boat and go in search of your mother' (2009, 33–34). K. Sharifa requests god to take his next birth as a woman. Banu Mushtaq, the short story writer, ends one of her stories with the same prayer (for which she was harassed). With irony, wit and sarcasm, women poets have carnivalised the myths created by men of chaste women, and loyal and long-suffering wives. This was necessary because the reinforcement of such gender stereotypes still continues with the support of these myths.

Lalita Siddabasavaiah rewrites the Shiva-Parvathi myth by making Parvathi take the initiative (2009, 29–32). Parvathi, the daughter of Parwatharaja, ensconced in her palace, is so attracted by Shiva, the ascetic mendicant, that she follows him all the way to Kailasa. There, embracing him, 'she feeds him', thus reconstructing the idea of *Ardhanarishwara* (Shiva as half woman, Parvathi being a part of his body). Vaidehi wrote a poem titled 'The Play of Bathing Shiva' in which the feet of Shiva, who wanders across the three worlds, are gently massaged with oil and bathed. There are intense images of fulfilment, of love and passion. There is no rejection of love, despite the patriarchy. As a character in Veena Shanteshwar's story says, 'I am not willing to reject everything as romantic fantasy. Even if it is fraught with pain, is all that intensity nothing?' Feminism in Kannada writing is so complexly nuanced and distinctive. Fitting it into a model ignores the variety and richness of the texture of the writing.

Women's writing in Kannada in its second phase was part of the churning that took place in Karnataka from the decade of the 1970s. A number of initiatives also played an important role: the founding of Shashwati, a research centre for women's studies, by C. N. Mangala at NMKRV College, the institutional awards to recognise women writers, and the establishment of the Lekhakiyara Sangha, were among these initiatives. Equally important was the publication of women's journals like *Namma Manasa*. Probably the most influential role was played by *Lankesh Patrike*, a popular tabloid edited by P. Lankesh. At its peak, it had a circulation of 1,50,000 and was considered the voice of modern-day Karnataka. The tabloid encouraged women reporters and also published the major women writers. Vaidehi, Banu Mushtaq, Sara Abubakar and many more became household names with their writings for the tabloid. This did not happen by allocating a small corner of the publication to women's writing. The tabloid fought for a just, equal and secular society, and represented women as natural and equal partners in that struggle. When Sara Abubakar was attacked by communalists, *Lankesh Patrike* supported her. It defended Banu Mushtaq when she was accused of blasphemy. *Namma Manasa*, a little journal managed by women, provided a national gender perspective with its articles and reviews. Women's groups were active in most cities in Karnataka. The project of retrieving the 'lost texts' of the early phase also created a sense of continuity for women's writing. Women began to make significant interventions in the public debates and controversies (on the 'beauty contest' at Bengaluru, for example). Women from different social and caste locations began to write. As in the case of Western feminism, women academics played a major role in interrogating the literary canon. There were also debates over texts prescribed in the educational system. For example, girl students enrolled for the Pre-University (PUC) course protested against the inclusion of a poem by Sanchi Honnamma because it affirmed that only a son could guarantee parents a place in heaven.[2] These multiple factors in the domain of culture not only influenced women's writing, but women's writing itself shaped the discourses of the period. It attempted to deconstruct the idea of literature as universal and gender-neutral. It also drew attention to the contradictions and ambivalences in the canonical authors of the tradition. This was done more vigorously in the *Bandaya* movement which took a strong anti-brahminical view of the literary tradition. Films like *Samskara* (1970) and *Phaniyamma* (1983) were discussed from a woman-centric point of view. Popular fiction by women and men and popular Kannada films were analysed with regard to their representation of women. Women's writing was part of the intellectual ferment of the period.

The divide between 'serious' literature and 'popular' literature has also affected women's writing in Kannada. The divide itself was not very sharp in the *Navodaya* or *Pragatisheela* period. Kuvempu, Karanth, Bendre and Masti, the great *Navodaya* writers, had a large readership and were visible figures in literary culture. There were lesser contemporary writers but they were not categorised as 'popular' writers. Ta. Ra. Su. (T. R. Subba Rao, 1920–84) and Aa. Na. Kra., the leaders of the *Pragatisheela* movement, were very popular novelists and with them we have the new image of the professional writer in Kannada. They created the genre of the popular novel which was the social-domestic novel, with the familiar urban or rural background, familiar characters and themes related to family values or the

[2] Sanchi Honnamma is a well-known woman poet of the seventeenth century. She wrote *Hadibadeya Dharma* (The *Dharma* of the Chaste Woman) from which some verses were prescribed for a pre-university Kannada textbook. The verses say that only a son can ensure a good afterlife for the parents. Girl students protested and a public debate took place in the columns of *Praja Vani*, a leading Kannada newspaper.

values of an ideal community, which the novels themselves created. The novels had a strong sub-structure of sentimentality and rarely explored any experience in depth. During their life time they were not labelled as 'popular' writers as distinguished from the 'serious' writers. The categorisation came with *Navya* criticism which was strongly influenced by F. R. Leavis and a somewhat vague notion of urban popular culture. U. R. Ananthamurthy wrote an influential essay (*Janapriya Kale*) which contained his response to the popular film *Naagarahaavu* based on the novels by Ta. Ra. Su. and also to the novels of S. L. Bhyrappa. He takes a Leavisite view of popular fiction as melodramatic, sentimental and not requiring serious reflection by the reader. He employs Leavis's terms 'experience' and 'seriousness' in his analysis. By the time the essay was published there had already been similar criticism of the *Pragatisheela* writers.

This discussion of popular fiction took place at a time when Karnataka was witnessing the phenomenon of circulating libraries whose subscribers were mainly women and preferred to read the popular novels by women. It was a typically middle-class phenomenon with neighbourhood circulating libraries also offering Kannada popular magazines which had women as readers. The most popular section of these weekly or fortnightly magazines was the serial novel. Women writers contributed to this section until the magazines went for detective fiction and thrillers for serialisation.

These popular novels by women writers constituted a genre by themselves. These were domestic novels with a distinctive middle-class urban background. The themes were woman-centric in the sense that they dealt with the quotidian problems of the middle-class woman within the framework of the family. The gender stereotypes of the selfless loyal wife, sister and mother were the model for the women characters. There were also the negative models of the arrogant independent modern woman who wrecked families. Another significant element was the 'psychology of women' first introduced by Triveni (Anasuya Shankar, 1928–63). Triveni's novels continue to be popular even today. She portrays the marginalisation of women in a patriarchal society, though stopping well short of offering a radical analysis.[3] In *Sharapanjara* (1962), for instance, Kaveri is haunted by the suppressed memory of a forced sexual union which leads to hysteria. She recovers with psychiatric treatment and returns home only to find her husband in an adulterous relationship, and to her

[3] For a detailed analysis of Triveni and popular literature see Niranjana Seemanthini's essay published in *New Quest*, 14, March–April 1989, pp. 77–85. The essay has been included in Kannada translation in Niranjana and Niranjana 1994.

own stigmatisation by the society as a 'mad woman'. In M. K. Indira's (1917–94) *Gejje Pooje* (1966), the protagonist who is born to a Devadasi and hopes to become a free woman through education and a love marriage, is abandoned by the man she loves and is forced into becoming a concubine. She ends her life out of despair. In many of her novels Triveni relates the hysteria of the women characters to the injustice done to them, but portrays them as not strong enough to seek liberation. Triveni's blend of familiar middle-class life and women's psychological suffering was transformed into a popular form of fiction by the women writers. The celebrated popular film director Puttanna Kanagal chose three of Triveni's novels for his films. Incidentally, some of the most successful popular Kannada films of the 1970s and 80s were based on popular novels by women.

However, it was the popular novels by women which created the negative notion of 'kitchen literature' referred to earlier. The success of the popular domestic-social novel depended on its complete conformity with the traditional values. Though the women characters did have their moments of rebellion and autonomy, these were in the end accommodated into the frame of the family which depended on her conformity. In keeping with the preoccupations of the popular films, these novels also contained the element of romance. The feminine desire was always centred on the search for an ideal male partner. No serious studies have been done on the popular Kannada novel by women and the aspirations of an expanding urban middle class (of the kind we find in Nancy Armstrong's *Desire and Domestic Fiction*).

The 'serious' woman writers in Kannada had to negotiate with a well-established reading culture. There was the challenge that any writing which questioned gender stereotypes and represented women as rebels would be dubbed as 'feminist' or 'modernist'. The new writing by women was received well by the *Navya* critics and by the small readership that *Navya* writing had created. Since then, its reception has been improving but is still not a match for the popular writing by women. The situation is further complicated by the expansion of entertainment TV channels which telecast 'serials' (soaps) round the clock. Once again, the audience for these serials are almost entirely women. Therefore, the soaps are superficially woman-centric; but the sentimental, melodramatic and sensational mode of presentation and the gross misogynist representations they perpetuate have created a cultural malaise. This cannot be dismissed as an elitist apprehension about popular culture. There is a culture industry, in the original sense of the term, and its products have a reach cutting across class, caste and location. The post-culture industry critical theorisation on popular culture in the West has little relevance for the sociocultural context here. The functions performed by popular culture as theorised by cultural studies are in fact being performed by the mainstream critique of the hegemonic culture, articulation of sub-cultures and oppositional cultural groups, subalternist politics, etc. Kannada urban popular culture has become an effective vehicle for the mainstream culture.

As a consequence, the legacy of the women's struggles from the reformist phase of the colonial period is under threat from the popular culture industry. Recent women's writing has had to confront this paradoxical situation. The rise of the right-wing cultural politics has found powerful support from the popular culture industry, since it depends heavily on gender stereotypes. The evidence of this is found in the series of attacks on 'modern' women—such as the attack on women visiting pubs in Mangaluru. The discourse of 'Hindu women versus modern women' is making it difficult to hold any discussion on genuine women-centric issues.

The relevance of recent women's writing in Kannada has to be understood in this context. H. S. Nagaveni, for instance, in *Gandhi Banda*, presents a thick description of the micro-history of the Dakshina Kannada region during the age of Gandhi. The novel deals with an explosive subject—the marriage of Draupadi, the widowed daughter of the brahmin landlord Hebbar, with a young Muslim, Adrama. As mentioned earlier, it is a many-layered complex text, involving the struggle for hegemony between the brahmins and the powerful *Banta* caste. It also involves the popular mythopoeic reception of Gandhi by the lower castes and untouchable communities. It is also about the nationalist movement led in the region by Karnad Sadashiva Rao (who appears in the novel). After the death of Adrama, the twice-widowed Draupadi is invited by Gandhi to come on the stage during his second visit, and he requests the women to decorate her with all the signs of a *muttaide* (a woman with a living husband, but also an auspicious woman). This highly utopian scene is a symbolic representation of the changed aspirations of the local society. Nagaveni's short stories collected in *Meeyuva Ata* present the heterogeneous identities of women across a variegated social spectrum. Together, the stories describe a society that is traditional and patriarchal but also possessing the resources to respect individuals beyond their religion and caste. In her non-fictional writings, Nagaveni records her childhood experiences of a society which accommodated difference and was far more humane. Some of the extraordinary essays narrate how the *beedi* industry, by allowing women to work near their homes, brought them some independence (as wage earners) and autonomy. She records in detail the changes which became visible in their body language; they had self-confidence and were proud of being productive. Woven into this narrative is also the story of Kudla transforming itself into Mangalore. Unfortunately, the communal ideologies which developed to curb the upward mobility of the Muslims (who had work contracts with *beedi* factories), also meant the loss of the autonomy temporarily enjoyed by women. Communal politics was also used to set up an adversarial relationship between the Muslim fishermen and the *mogaveeras*. Girish Kasaravalli's film *Gulabi Talkies* (2008), loosely based on Vaidehi's short story, presents a lucid interpretation of the communalisation of the region. Gulabi is for the first time addressed by her original Muslim name by the zealots of Hindutwa. Nagaveni writes insightfully about Dakshina Kannada, the epicentre of global trade in the past, and a multilingual and multi-religious society which is now turned into a hotbed of communal politics. The novel *Gandhi Banda* participates in these historical discourses. Nagaveni does not suggest merely that there were historical-material circumstances which created certain discourses which the novel form could employ. She presents a complex of material conditions and discourses which produce and reproduce each other. The novel leaves ample space to question the very manner in which it imagines itself.

Gandhi Banda is also optimistic about the future. Soorakkai, who is derided as Shikhandi, a transvestite, and neglected by her activist husband, at last discovers the happiness of companionship. Draupadi, twice-widowed, discovers the happiness of motherhood.

Du. Saraswathi, poet, writer, scholar and activist, has written short one-act plays meant for single-actor performances—by women actors—which have been successfully staged by Saraswathi herself. These scripts are based on a subalternist reinterpretation of the *Ramayana* and other canonical texts. The narrator–performer retells the text in her distinctive, earthy and unselfconsciously women-centric perspective. The result is a radical, subversive reinterpretation of the *Ramayana*. Sannathimmi, the narrator, presents her reinterpretation in her dialect with absolutely no reverence for the Sanskritic conventions of the epic. Her tone is intimate and persuasive. Saraswathi's one-act plays pre-suppose an important shift. There have been women-centric reinterpretations of the *Ramayana* from H. Savitramma to S. L. Bhyrappa, but in Saraswathi's work there is no felt need to engage with the mainstream interpretations. A subaltern woman uses the freedom of folk traditions to re-narrativise the mainstream puranas and myths. Saraswathi also addresses the bias in feminist retellings towards an upper-caste women's perspective.

It would not be out of place to compare Vaidehi's *Shakuntaleyondige Ondu Aparahna* (An Afternoon with Shakuntala) with the works of Du. Saraswathi. In the short story, Shakuntala is the narrator, and her version is different from that of Kalidasa. She says that she was a girl entering into early womanhood and therefore it was she who desired Dushyanta. She deconstructs Kalidasa's fictional narrative of an innocent young girl living in an Ashrama, foster daughter of Kanva the great rishi, being seduced by a much-married king, Dushyanta. She claims responsibility for her actions. The narrative is subversive, and the brilliant insight is that the story of an innocent girl's seduction by a powerful king deprives her of her autonomy and reduces her to a naïve victim. In the story, Shakuntala rejects her victimhood and asserts her agency by saying that she desired Dushyanta. The many aspects of the intertextuality in the story cannot be dealt with here. With all the complexity, Vaidehi still writes as a dissident within a hegemonic cultural narrative. In contrast, Sannathimmi in Saraswathi's narrative is under no such obligations. She speaks from a perspective which is not overweighed by the dominant culture. What emerges from this is the fact that there have been many narratives, many stories, jostling with each other in the Kannada tradition. If we can evade the notion of *one story* (say the colonial narrative) and admit the co-existence of many narratives, we can make better sense of the distinctive narrative of women-centric writing in Kannada.

TEN

Post-*Navya* Kannada Literature

1

In the chapter on Kannada modernist writing, we have already mentioned the internal transformation of *Navya* writing by referring to D. R. Nagaraj's categorisation of the 'original *Navya*' and 'transformed *Navya*'. The internal transformation was in response to the realisation that 'original *Navya*' with its exclusive emphasis on individual experience, on the self as alienated and solipsistically absorbed in itself, had exhausted itself. There was also frustration with the aesthetics of complex structure, irony and ambiguity, and self-conscious employment of symbolism. The later poems of Adiga almost abandon this aesthetics in favour of a more loosely structured, open-ended dialogic poetic form. Apart from satirical and polemical poems he wrote in the later phase, Adiga also wrote poems like *Chinthamaniyalli Kanda Mukha*, *Aagaboti* and *Bandaya,* which enter into a dialogue with the intended reader. The impact of these fine poems was marred by the many rhetorical, loud polemical poems Adiga wrote defending conservative right-wing opinions. Though few and far between, his sensitive and contemplative poems demonstrate his move towards a mode of poetry which was far more accessible to the readers.

Many of Adiga's protégés and younger admirers began to disown his influence and criticise his conservative views. P. Lankesh and Chandrashekhar Patil openly rebelled against him. In a poem Lankesh wondered how a shudra like him could understand Adiga's 'brahminical poetry'. The rebellion was an expression of the need felt by the younger writers to break new ground and invent a new poetic idiom.

K. V. Tirumalesh (1940–2023), who did not identify himself with any literary movement, found his authentic voice by writing about the ordinariness of everyday living. Unlike the protagonists of Adiga's poetry, like the one in *Bhoomigeetha*, Tirumalesh's poetry projects ordinary individuals like Pentaiah whose one attempt to wear a neatly washed and ironed dress is defeated. He employs irony and satire against the ambitious and complex individuals featured in *Navya* poetry. The major change in his poetic career took place with the collection *Maha Prasthana* in which he revisits epic myths and legends (Tirumalesh 2011). Some of the ambitious poems in the collection attempt to negotiate with the past through the lens of modernity. He succeeds in inventing a poetic medium which integrates verse and poetry and also shows an amazing fertility in creating innovative metaphors and images. In later collections, Tirumalesh introduces the concrete specificities of a town and a city, and peoples his poetry with their contemporary denizens. He is a prolific writer who has experimented with various styles and modes. He even described a collection of poems as a sketchbook. His insistence has been on the essentially fragmentary, incomplete nature of human experience. He refuses to impose an aesthetic unity on them. His recent work, *Akshaya Kavya* (literally 'inexhaustible poetry'), invites the reader to enter and exit the text at any point. The reader is thus prevented from imposing his/her own sense of unity and order on the poem (Tirumalesh 2015).

Two important poets, G. S. Shivarudrappa (1926–2013) and Chennaveera Kanavi (1928–2022), came to be called *Samanvaya* poets, poets who integrated in their practice the modes of *Navodaya* and *Navya* poetry. As pointed out in the previous chapter, K. S. Narasimhaswamy and to some extent Pu. Ti. Na. (P. T. Narasimhachar) had done this successfully. Kanavi is a contemplative poet who celebrates the endless creativity of life, though he is aware of the destruction of the traditional way of life. In a remarkable poem, *Ugadi*, the traditional new year is personified as a village elder whom no one recognises. The disturbing images of the modern city appear in his poetry but he believes in the potential of life and nature to revitalise themselves, and celebrates change and movement through a supple poetic register. He is a master of the sonnet form and some of his finest poems are classics in this form (Kanavi 1975).

G. S. Shivarudrappa reclaimed the *Navodaya* lyric along with its song-like quality. His serious and at times philosophical poems have been rendered as popular songs in the style which came to be called *Sugama Sangeetha* (literally 'felicitous music' but refers to the revolution ushered in by singers like C. S. Ashwath, Mysore Narayana Swamy and Shivamogga Subbanna, who rendered fine Kannada lyrics into songs and thereby created a new style of popular music in Karnataka). His poems eschew dense symbolism and verbal complexity but address themselves to contemporary issues. He was much disturbed by the communal politics and violence he witnessed in his last years (Shivarudrappa 2020).

Su. Ram. Ekkundi (1923–95) was also a poet who drew on the resources of *Navodaya* poetry but employed them in his unique attempt to synthesise Marxism with the *Madhva* philosophy. However, it is his poems about the coastal life and his portraits of the fisher folk which continue to be read now (Ekkundi 2006).

Gangadhara Chittala (1923–87), who also began as a progressive poet and a committed M. N. Royist, went on to write some of the finest poems in Kannada (Chittala 2004). He employs a controlled rhetorical style, enlivened by powerful images and symbols to contemplate the elemental experiences of life—sexuality, death, disease and renewal. His long poem *Kamasutra* is probably the finest Kannada poem celebrating sexuality. His poems about existential angst and primordial fears are able to negotiate such areas of experience even while employing an open-ended poetic style. In their appreciative readings of his poetry, two modernist critics, Ananthamurthy and Shantinath Desai, try to explain how Chittala was able to accomplish all this without employing the modernist mode of writing (Desai 1987).

H. S. Venkateshamurthy (b. 1944) is a prolific poet who published his first collection in 1968. From the beginning, his poems were distinguished by his felicity with language and his skilful use of the traditional elements of poetry including prosodic forms and formal features. He fashioned for his poetry an urbane poetic idiom, not straying away too far from the literary and spoken variations of language. In retrospect, he appears to have been closer to the *Navodaya* mode of poetry than the modernist poetry of Adiga. His early poems, especially short narrative poems, were about the mysterious and the unanticipated. His poem about Sindbad the Sailor ends abruptly just when he is about to describe what he saw. He manages to create anticipation in the reader only to leave him/her right on the edge of the unimagined experience (Venkateshamurthy 2021). He developed as a poet who immersed himself in the epics and puranas and with the classical Sanskrit and Kannada traditions. In recent years, Venkateshamurthy has been retelling (partially) and reflecting on these cultural memories in a unique form he has named as '*Kathanthara*'. His poems on Rama and Krishna are neither radically revisionist nor revivalist. He attempts a poetic vision in which the traditionally revered divine characters and events become part of the ordinary. In a remarkable poem he portrays Rama as a *samsari*, a householder, who has to lay down his weapon, the great bow, to be with his family. His attempt is to create a counter-narrative in which the epic figures are not allowed to be appropriated for the wrong kind of politics. Sanity and balance are to be sought in the ordinary and routine lives and not in the rare transcendental epiphanies. He has therefore paid poetic tributes to the great Kannada poets through brief poetic portraits.

His recent long near-epic poem *Buddhacharana* on the Buddha is a narrative, philosophical poem.

H. S. Shivaprakash (b. 1954) is the most prominent among poets who began to write in the 1980s. In his very first collection he had constructed a poetic lineage for himself and a distinctive area of experience as the subject to be explored. This had few parallels in the modernist tradition. He created for himself an archive of non-Vedic, subaltern metaphysical and spiritual traditions. The predominant constituents of the archive were the twelfth-century *Vachanakaras*. The other important constituents were the spiritual gurus known as *anubhavis* who, in his view, spoke about the cruelties of the feudal world, the hierarchical religious institutions and traditions which had lost the cultural memories of the struggles for radical equality, and the threat of a colonial modern machine civilisation which was impinging upon rural societies. For Shivaprakash, this was an act of rediscovery because the writings of the spiritual poets were couched in the traditional metaphysical idiom though they also used the rough and earthy spoken language. Shivaprakash was decolonising his sensibility, thereby also attempting to free Kannada poetry from imitations of modernist Anglo-American poetry (Shivaprakash 2010). The subject matter he discovered for his poetry was history—more precisely, a subalternist history. He wrote about the Buddha, Basava, Kalyana, Shishunala Sharif and other such cultural figures, in order to diagnose the crisis of the present. There was no recourse to nostalgia or valorisation of the past. With such promising beginnings, Shivaprakash has made a long poetic journey with his recent collected poems running into over 900 pages. The heterogeneity in his work is incredible and vast. Baghdad, Caliban, Latin America, corporate capital and Gorakhnath crowd his poetry. The styles vary from lullabies to philosophical lyrics. He exhibits an amazing inwardness with many Indian languages and poetic-philosophical traditions of the world.

Shivaprakash's preoccupation is with healing the wounds of history, especially of imperialism, by rediscovering the living energy of the subaltern traditions. He is not a nativist, however. He contemplates modernity as a fact of history and of our everyday lives, needing our attention for curing its distortions. In his prose poem, 'The Soliloquy of Caliban', Caliban confesses that he is now turning into a native Prospero, apotheosising the market and globalisation. He appeals to the Rudras to keep vigil, and prays to the goddess of primeval energy to revitalise us. He confronts history head on, and accepts his burden of the past as a modern individual. He discovers the spiritual and material power to transform the world in the subalternised classes. Shivaprakash's poetry is a two-pronged struggle to defeat the hegemonies within the society and to overcome the distortions caused first by colonialism and now by its new avatar, globalisation. He has also written scores of powerful poems which are unencumbered by a historical consciousness and address the simple perennial themes of love and compassion.

2

Kannada fiction, since its inception, has always been a variegated territory, where several genres and fictional modes coexisted. As analysed in an earlier chapter, both the historical romance and the social realist novel flourished at the same time during the early phase of the last quarter of the nineteenth century. The realistic novel of the *Navodaya* period was at its creative best when the progressive novel began a new trend. The period of the modernist fiction (from the late 1960s to 80s) also saw the publication of great novels such as *Gramayana* (1955) by Rao Bahaddur and *Gangavva Gangamayi* (1956) by Shankar Mokashi Punekar, which have little to do with modernist fiction. The finest novels published in the late 1990s were realistic, regional novels like the ones published in the late 1930s and 40s. It would therefore be of little help to rely on the familiar categorisation.

Mention has already been made of Poornachandra Tejaswi (1938–2007), whose first two novels were in the modernist mode, abandoning *Navya* altogether and reinventing himself as a short story writer and novelist. He employed the sub-genres of the popular novel such as the detective novel, novel of adventure, science fiction and crime thriller, to write powerful novels about the contemporary society. *Carvalho* is an adventurous tale about the search for a flying lizard. An oddly assorted group led by the scientist Carvalho journeys deep into the forest in search of the flying lizard which is the missing link in the story of evolution. Far from the hierarchical social world of class, caste and politics, the group of men go through a near-mystical experience when they catch a fleeting glimpse of the flying lizard. The major novels of Tejaswi have already been mentioned in an earlier chapter. Undoubtedly, Tejaswi transformed Kannada fiction from the modernist mould. He writes lively narratives spiced with mystery and unexpected happenings, creates eccentric but significant characters, and uses a fair amount of thrill and suspense to deal with serious issues of communalism, corrupt politics, environmental destruction and the threatened extinction of the highly skilled marginalised communities. For him, the idiotic-looking Mandanna is a born naturalist of a high calibre.

Engta the snake charmer is a treasure of indigenous knowledge. Tejaswi writes with a deep sense of the irrationality and absurdity of the social world which contrasts with the mysterious sense of order in the natural world. His short story *Tabarana Kathe* (Tabara's Tale), made into a classic film by Girish Kasaravalli, is probably the most powerful satire on Indian bureaucracy in any language. Tejaswi remained sceptical about the capability of this absurd modern Indian society to survive. In the present author's view, it is Tejaswi who took fiction to the common reader and expanded its social horizons. He never subscribed to any ideology or movement. Tejaswi continues to be the most popular writer in Kannada whose non-fictional works have also been phenomenally successful. His novels have demonstrated the possibilities of portraying contemporary social and political realities and at the same time exploring philosophical concerns of the highest kind (Tejaswi 2014).

It has often been said that the post-*Navya* period is marked by the absence of literary and political movements. The *Bandaya* movement which began in the 1980s was probably the last of the movements with an ideological coherence. It attempted to fashion a new aesthetics and a consensual view of literature as resistance. It shared many of the concerns and preoccupations of the *Pragatisheela* (progressive) movement of the 1940s. The *Bandaya* movement was the product of many factors which go back in time. The Samajavadi Yuvajana Sabha (Socialist Youth Forum) acted as an incubation centre shaping talented activists, such as Tejaswi, Kadidal Shamanna and Ravivarma Kumar. This allied itself at least indirectly with the socialist movements especially in the Malnad region of Karnataka. The Kagodu Tenant Farmers' Movement of the 1950s had been supported by the socialists, and Ram Manohar Lohia led the movement in its last phase. The movement did not meet with immediate success but later motivated Devaraj Urs, the chief minister, to introduce the Land Reforms Act (1961) which can be described as the most significant sociopolitical move in modern Karnataka. It provided a strong political voice to the backward classes who had been tenant farmers. Urs also cobbled together a cabinet in which there were OBC leaders, and thus challenged the two dominant castes which had enjoyed political hegemony in Karnataka. These events created an anti-hegemonic political and social consciousness which resulted in the anti-brahminical resistance by writers who established the *Barahagarara Okkuta*. *Bandaya* was an offshoot of these events which took place in the 1970s and 80s. The first *Bandaya* conference was held at Bengaluru in 1979. The manifesto of the movement described it as a movement by all progressive writers, artists and thinkers against all forms of domination and exploitation. It made a call for literature committed to the ideology of resistance. It rejected *Navya* literature as the product of a small coterie of middle-class writers led by brahmin writers who were alienated from the larger society. *Navya* had created a solipsistic, individualist literature which prioritised personal angst and sexuality by ignoring issues of social relevance. The *Navya* aesthetics of symbolic structure and dense metaphorical style had led to a literature of obscurity and elitism. The *Bandaya* writer has to be an activist–writer involving himself/herself in social movements against caste, class and gender inequality. The entire tradition of Kannada literature should now be subjected to scrutiny for its failure to represent the experiences of the shudras and Dalits. The writer could ally himself/herself only to the few past attempts in the Kannada tradition to speak for the subalternised classes. For example, the *Vachanakaras* and shudra writers like Kuvempu. As Devanoora Mahadeva said, 'Ours is the difficult task of making a rock sprout'. Though the more sober members of the movement cautioned against it, there was an attempt to treat certain subjects as taboo for serious protest literature. The manifesto declared that 'poetry should become a sword: a friend of the people responding to their pain'. (The motto was coined by the late D. R. Nagaraj.) A large number of writers joined the movement, conferences and seminars were held across Karnataka, and anthologies of the new writings were published. The movement succeeded in claiming that literature shall now onwards be the expression of the downtrodden and the oppressed. Its success lay in unleashing the creative and imaginative energies of the social classes which had hitherto kept away from the literary domain. Poetry returned to the phatic and communicative mode of the *Navodaya* period. Songs were composed to accompany protests and demonstrations.

It is interesting that every significant literary movement in Kannada has moulded poetry as an act of orality and public discourse. Poetry is reconceptualised as '*haadu gabba*', poetry for the ear and not the eye. In the *Navodaya* movement, poetry-as-song was used to arouse the Kannada sub-nationalist sentiments and to appeal to the Kannada pride. In fact, one of the early poets, Shanthakavi, went around like a singer of *keerthanas* (devotional songs) with ankle bells and a *tala*, singing songs about the Kannadiga's lost pride. Bendre recited his poems to large audiences before they were published. The Dalit movement led by the D.S.S. created a huge repertoire of songs which were sung in chorus at all protest meets. This happened as well with the *Bandaya* movement. These songs should be studied as part of the new orality and of subaltern political praxis.

The *Bandaya* movement led to the production of fiction and poetry about all forms of social inequality, the oppressive caste-system, and evil social customs and practices. There was as such little difference between the themes and styles of *Bandaya* literature and Dalit literature. For some time, the movement itself was known as the *Dalit-Bandaya* movement. But then Dalit writers felt that the exploitation and humiliation associated with Dalit lives were not the same as those of the other classes and that only writers born as Dalits could write authentically about Dalit experience. This led to an inconclusive debate, settled by Baraguru Ramachandrappa (b. 1946), founder-leader of the *Bandaya* movement, by saying that 'while every Dalit writer is a *Bandaya* writer every *Bandaya* writer is not a Dalit'. The *Bandaya* movement was more inclusive and open to left-leaning politics, while the Dalit literary movement moved closer to Ambedkarite caste-centric ideologies.

Despite the manifesto and the vocal declarations, the *Bandaya* movement did not produce significant literary works. Most Kannada writers responded positively to its aspirations and many major writers began to address themes which had overt social dimensions. (See the sections on Chittala in the chapter on literary modernism.) However, this was a development in their already well-established writing careers. Others like Bolwar Mahammad Kunhi, who were members of *Bandaya*, wrote their best works by exploring experiences of their communities. Powerful short stories by *Bandaya* writers seemed to replicate what had been done by the progressive writers. The *Bandaya* movement played a major role in organising resistance movements in Karnataka. It provided a healthy counter to the excesses of *Navya* writing. It also created ethical pressure on writers to introspect about the social relevance of their writings. However, it would be difficult to single out significant works as products of and embodying the aspirations of the *Bandaya* movement. It produced talented poets such as Sarju Katkar and Satheesh Kulkarni and a host of young writers. Baraguru Ramachandrappa and Chandrashekhar Patil, the two leaders of the movement, were well-known writers.

Baraguru explains the aspirations of the *Bandaya* movement by saying (in Patil 1993) that the ultimate aim of the movement was to bring together all left-leaning (*vāma pantheeya*) writers under one banner and organisation. He underlines the need for an organisation to fight against the hegemony of conservative forces in the field of culture. He also argues with examples that the essential quality of the Kannada tradition is resistance against centres of authority, and *Bandaya* was an effort to reclaim that legacy and revitalise its energies in the contemporary social context. He denounces M. S. Golwalkar's advocacy of a Hindu *Rashtra* against socialism. Taking a more nuanced view of the Kannada tradition, Rahamat Tarikere argues that resistance becomes inevitable when the established values become deadened. He finds elements of authentic rebellion in the poems of Siddalingaiah and the short stories of Devanoora Mahadeva, both Dalit writers. He refers to Govindaiah, C. Veeranna, Ramjan Darga and D. Vijaya as practitioners of *Bandaya* poetry (in Patil 1993).

It has been the present author's view that in the Kannada context the literary-cultural movements did not in themselves produce important literary texts but opened up new areas of experience, sharpened the ideological perspectives and introduced experimentation with form, which were absorbed by the major authors who transformed their writing practices. There is a definite attitudinal change in the writers under the impact of the *Bandaya* movement. Literary movements have fertilised new writing without causing a radical rupture with the tradition.

With the ebbing of the *Bandaya* movement several talented writers with no declared allegiance to any movement have produced major works. The short stories and the novel *Gandhi Banda* by H. Nagaveni have been discussed in the chapter on women's writing. *Gandhi Banda* is a fictional embodiment of the resistance of shudra and Dalit communities to the brahminical hegemony through the iconic presence of Gandhi. The novel is about Gandhi only as a symbol invented by the oppressed communities to express their resistance to inequality. Written in the tradition of realism, the novel has attained the status of a modern classic.

Bolwar Mahammad Kunhi (b. 1951) has authored four novels of which *Swatantryada Ota* (Freedom Run, 2012), an epic novel about partition and the freedom movement, is extraordinary. The multiple narratives of the novel converge and end in Muthupadi, Bolwar's own utopian small town of communal harmony and co-existence. It is the story of a Pakistani youth who crosses over to India during the Partition to help two Hindu sisters and is unable to return to his hometown. A series of events bring him to Muthupadi where he settles down as its denizen. A work of amazing narrative power, the novel is an assertion (albeit an emotional one) of the communitarian values of harmony. Crowded with characters and incidents, it reads like an oral history of the freedom movement.

His earlier novel *Jehad* (2010) is about the trauma and conflicts associated with interfaith marriages. The novel also asserts the importance of personal honesty and courage in the midst of the irrationalities of a polarised society. Bolwar's more recent novels, *Odiri* (2015) and *Umma* (2018), are about the Holy Prophet and his wife respectively. *Odiri* is described by the author as a historical novel but is a moving tale about the Prophet, faithfully recording his struggles. Bolwar has written some of the finest stories in Kannada which blend the myths, legends, beliefs and lifestyles of the Muslim community without any self-consciousness.

Abdul Rashid (b. 1965) and Banu Mushtaq (b. 1948) are among the talented practitioners of the short story in Kannada. Rashid demonstrates his uncanny ability to transform the ordinary into the magical through his distinctive blend of humour and fantasy. Mushtaq is sharply critical of the social and religious patriarchies which constantly oppress women. One of her short stories ends with the prayer, 'Oh Allah, the next time be born as a woman'.

Sara Abubakar (1936–2023) entered the literary scene with her writings first appearing in *Lankesh Patrike*, the popular tabloid edited by P. Lankesh. In a deceptively transparent style, she writes about the struggles of the Muslim girl child to educate herself, and the trauma of *talaq* and abandonment.

Srikrishna Alanahalli (1947–89), whose poetry with its raw sensuality and visceral imagery broke new ground, was also a leading short story writer and novelist. His slender novel *Kadu* (The Jungle), made into a remarkable film by Girish Karnad, is about the violent feudal world dominated by two powerful castes, the Okkaligas and the Lingayats, as seen through the eyes of a little boy, Kitti. The novel has women characters who are victims of the competitive hyper-masculinity of the men of the two caste groups. Srikrishna evokes the rural world with authentic details only to show its tragic self-destruction. His novel *Parasangada Gende Thimma* (Gende Thimma the Performer, 1978) is about the disruption of the traditional rural life with the entry of modernity. The author employs the image of a superficial urban modernity as a disruptive force. The innocent Gende Thimma, a singer, teller of tales and an itinerant merchant, is destroyed by his wife's adultery and by the disruption he has unwittingly caused by selling 'modern' items such as cosmetics and women's innerwear. Srikrishna handles this stereotypical theme of urban modernity with sensitivity.

Bhujangayyana Dashavataragalu (The Ten Avatars of Bhujangayya, 1985) is a major novel which raises disturbing questions about the relationship between the individual and the community. Bhujangayya in his many avatars tries to help his village community only to be brutally targeted by vicissitudes of the tragic kind. The sufferings of the protagonist raise questions about the vulnerability of the good intentions of an individual in a self-centred cruel society. The death of Srikrishna Alanahalli in his early forties cut short a promising career.

An extraordinary phenomenon in post-*Navya* Kannada fiction has been the rise of the regional novel, a genre prominently used in the 1930s and 40s. Kuvempu and Karanth were the great exemplars of this genre. Rao Bahaddur's *Gramayana* was probably the greatest novel in this genre, next only to Kuvempu's *Malegalalli Madumagalu*. The interesting phenomenon refers to a spate of novels which reconstruct the past and present of a region with thick description and details which would be the envy of any social anthropologist. However, these are not ethnological in intention but use the vast canvas of a region and a community to explore certain fundamental social and philosophical issues. Shrinivas Vaidya's (1936–2023) *Halla Banthu Halla* (2008, translated as *A Handful of Sesame* by Maithreyi Karnoor), is an epic novel about the history of a village near Naragunda in North Karnataka. It begins with the aftermath of the Mutiny in 1857 which forces Kamalacharya Panth, a young man from North India, to visit the place. Unable to return, he marries into a traditional Madhva brahmin family and becomes a naturalised citizen of the rural society. The novel traces the story of generations of the family and records all the political and natural vicissitudes of the British rule, and the plague. With stunning objectivity and critical distance, the author examines the received values of caste purity and hierarchy, patriarchy and transgressive women, and then, towards the end, the devastating impact of modernisation. He creates several unforgettable characters to demonstrate how humanly impossible it is to demarcate the boundary between dharmic rules and exigencies of human existence. Vaidya also examines the fragility of ethical norms in the presence of the primordial drives, sexuality and aggression.

Swapna Saraswatha (2011) by Gopalakrishna Pai is another novel of epic proportions and vision, and narrates the story of the migration of the Saraswat community from the Konkan region of Goa to Karnataka, to escape the persecution by the Portuguese. Employing multiple narratives and narrators, the author reconstructs the remembered history of a community. There is no trace of nostalgia or valorisation of the past. There is the intensity of individual lives, of guilt and unredeemed failures, which prevent the novel from becoming a mere historical chronicle. The myths and legends shared by the community come alive to connect the past with the present.

Mallikarjun Hiremath's (b. 1946) novel *Havana* (2001) deals with the life in a Banjara community, in a *tanda* (a Banjara settlement). An idealistic school teacher—who is the point of view in the first part of the novel—becomes a participant–narrator when he tries to improve the local school and also to advise the community leaders. In the second half, there are multiple narrations about the struggles of the community to survive the onslaught of unscrupulous contractors, and politicians who want to exploit the land which the Banjara community has acquired after a long struggle. As in Achebe's *Things Fall Apart*, here also the fissures within the community, and the lure of urban modernity, make the community vulnerable. The novel thus becomes an analysis of the forces which are capable of destroying a local community with its rich memories of its past. Hiremath's recent novel *Havali* (2021) is about the persecution by the Razakars, supported by the Nizam of Hyderabad who resisted accession into the Indian Union and allowed the Razakars to harass villages. The region narrated in the novel is Gadag and Dambal in North Karnataka.

It is interesting that many young writers of the present generation are revisiting the memories of their childhood world as well as those of their region and community. Suresh Nagalamadike argues that this is a response to the feeling of alienation in the young writers who have relocated themselves to Bengaluru, the 'IT hub' and the 'happening' place of globalisation (Nagalamadike 2018). They are now members of a 'lonely crowd', feeling uprooted. Interestingly, the major theme of early *Navya* writing was also a similar response to the culture shock felt by the younger generation of those times when they left their villages for Bengaluru. Suresh also points out how the poetry of the younger writers is replete with negative images of the city and of the threats to the rural world they have left behind. Uma Rao, Vasudhendra and Nagaraja Vastare have written about the urban world in a different tone. Their portrayal of the 'gated' communities accepts urbanisation as an irreversible fact of contemporary life, but they also see it as fraught with conflicts and contradictions. Ananthamurthy's statement that Kannada fiction is always about the 'lost' rural world of childhood and rarely about the adult life in urban locations, is now being proved wrong by a small group of writers. Vivek Shanbhag and Vasudhendra are two major writers who have been exploring the globalised urban world in their fiction.

In many ways, Vivek Shanbhag is an heir to Yashwanta Chittala who also wrote about Uttara Kannada (about Hanehalli specifically) but went on to write powerful disturbing novels about Mumbai, the corporate world and the real-estate mafia. Shanbhag has also written powerfully about the small rural world of his childhood. A major section of his novel *Ooru Bhanga* (2015) deals with the failed attempts of an school teacher to realise his idealistic dreams in a village society. The novel *Ondu Badi Kadalu* (2007) is reminiscent of Chittala's fiction and is about the unnoticed tragedies in the lives of women in a provincial place. Shanbhag's short stories about corporate companies (such as *Huli Savari*) introduced a new dimension to Kannada fiction. Despite the anti-globalisation farmers' movement started by M. D. Nanjundaswamy way back in the early 1990s, there were few writers who had first-hand experience of working in multinational companies and could provide a glimpse of how the new global system worked. Shanbhag provided a brief glimpse of it in his short stories.

Vasudhendra, who can write intensely about middle-class families from small towns, has written a great deal of non-fiction about the world of multinational companies. In the story *Kempu Gini* (Red Parrot), he had written about the devastation which mining can bring about, both to the environment and to the traditional ways of life. But in the later stories he takes us into workplaces in the 'gated communities'. In a disturbing story (*Kshame Illada Oorondalli* [In an Unforgiving City], 2008), the trivial incident of a girl child accidentally urinating in the swimming pool leads to much havoc and even death, thanks to the destructive power of mobile phones, laptops and communication technology. The internet community within the gated community is shown to be as oppressive and heartless as any traditional community, though far more equipped to hurt while remaining invisible.

Vastare takes a more celebratory view of the cosmopolitan world though he is also keenly aware of its vulnerability.

S. R. Vijayashankara, a leading contemporary Kannada critic, estimates that there are at least a thousand writers writing in Kannada at present, though many of them may only post their poems and writings on social media and may not publish them in print. It is difficult for any literary historian to even survey the writing.

3

Dalit writing—represented in its early phase by Siddalingaiah, Devanoora Mahadeva and Govindaiah—has been steadily growing and transforming itself in the context of vastly changed social realities. On the one hand, after the ebbing away of anti-caste movements, Karnataka has regressed into a caste society. Violence, social boycott, and harassment of Dalit women and children has increased. There is a paradoxical split in the cultural being of Karnataka which is frantically trying to continue to be the 'Silicon Valley of India' and one of the favoured destinations of global financial investment, while simultaneously regressing into a communalised caste-centric society. The Dalit writer is thus forced to encounter the opposing forces of regressive casteism and global capitalism.

The poet N. K. Hanumantayya (1974–2010), who tragically ended his life early, wrote intensely about his Dalit parents, especially his mother who went through untold suffering. The helplessness and the humiliations haunt him without relief. But the rebel in him makes him declare that, 'Having eaten the cow (beef), he has become like the cow'. This is a poor translation of the memorable line packed with cultural associations of the images of the cow. There are echoes of the cow's image in the famous folk poem 'The Song of the Cow' in which the self-sacrificing, truthful cow wins over the tiger which kills itself out of remorse (Hanumantayya 2016). Mogalli Ganesh, a brilliant Dalit poet, short story writer and critic, had created controversy by his reading of 'The Song of the Cow' as embodying cultural aggression aimed at demonising the tiger. All these cultural and literary memories provide the sub-text to Hanumantayya's poem.

The assertion of Dalit culture, and the confrontation with mainstream, upper-caste culture, takes many forms in the major poems of Subbu Holeyar. L. Hanumanthaiah is another major poet who negotiates with the heterogeneous experiences that a modern Dalit individual encounters. His poetry deals with the many lives a Dalit lives in contemporary society. Du. Saraswathi is an extraordinarily gifted poet, researcher, actor and dramatist. Her pathbreaking autobiography was followed by a collection of short stories (*Bachchisu,* 2016), and another collection of exquisite poems (*Jeeva Sampige,* 2016). She has spent years fighting for the rights of *safai karmacharis*, sanitation workers, and has the distinction of training them for dramatic performances.

Mudnakudu Chinnaswamy (b. 1954) is a highly accomplished poet who discovered his own distinctive voice and poetic personality at a time when the Siddalingaiah mode of angry denunciative poetry was the model for Dalit poets. He adopts a controlled, urbane style to communicate the pain and suffering of Dalit communities. Critics have described his allegiance to the tradition of Dalit poetry and then to the *Dalit-Bandaya* movement. His poetry is not confined to Dalit experience; he has written witty love poems and poems celebrating the many charms of the natural world. Some of his poems rendered as songs have achieved extraordinary popularity. He has an admirable mastery over the many poetic forms he uses and the ability to use the nuances of the spoken language. His images are the strength of his poetry. In one of his poems the human body is described as housing a masjid, a church and a temple. The skeleton itself is like the cross on which Jesus was crucified. In a cryptic stanza in another poem, Chinnaswamy says that when he goes to a temple he does not keep his footwear outside because he himself has to remain outside. His poetry is immersed in the memories of myths and past history, though he uses them sparingly.

Aravind Malagatti (b. 1956) is known for his novel *Karya* and his autobiography *Government Brahmana*. *Karya* (The Death Ceremony, 1988) is a short, dense and intensely written narrative constructed around a death ritual but drawing in details of the Dalit community. His autobiography (1994) is a path-breaking work and significantly different from the Marathi Dalit autobiographies which were a major influence on Kannada Dalit literature. It moves from the early memories of his Dalit family and the feudal world, to his education, coming of age and a failed relationship. In a sombre and controlled manner, the work analyses the way in which caste prejudices monitor the lives of individuals. He is also a prolific poet who wrote a large number of songs in the early phase of his poetic career. Thereafter he evolved into a major poet who wrote about modernity, globalisation and issues relating to nationalism. Like Mudnakudu Chinnaswamy, Malagatti's poetic world is diverse and variegated.

Mogalli Ganesh's short stories mark the maturity and complexity of the second generation of Dalit writing in Kannada. Like the earlier writers, he also writes about the Dalit *keri* (ghetto or colony), its misery and humiliations. However, Ganesh writes honestly and objectively about the male dominance and cruelty in the Dalit families. As he moves away from the ghetto to the city in pursuit of education and research, he realises his own alienation from the Dalit world of his childhood. There is also the guilt that for him, as a writer, the Dalit experience has become material for stories. In an interesting episode in a story (*Kali*, 1998), the writer's family and friends accuse him of treating them as characters in the stories he writes. Mogalli Ganesh is an innovative writer whose short stories have explored realism, magic realism and the mythopoeic narrative style.

K. B. Siddaiah (1954–2019) was unique among Dalit writers in Kannada. Though he had composed some of the most memorable songs for the D.S.S. protest meets, demonstrating his ability to employ poetry as a public discourse, he went on to write long mythopoeic poems drawing on the

Dalit myths and spiritual traditions. Among the long poems, *Bakala* and *Gallebani* are seminal poetic works. They create a counter-world of Dalit imagination in which the creation myths brush shoulders with the iconic spiritual figures of the subaltern traditions. The form of poetry he employs is new to the Kannada tradition and makes the poetry opaque in places. However, the poetry carries Dalit creative expression into unexplored scenes of mythopoeic narration. Siddaiah's achievement has been to reconstruct the inexhaustible imaginative energy of Dalit culture and life, and employ it to create a self-sufficient counter-world.

4

Amaresh Nugadoni is a leading short story writer who broke new ground with his extraordinary ability to explore the dark depths of humiliation and exploitation in a feudal society he describes without resorting to the simple binaries of the oppressor and the victim. In the feudal system portrayed in a majority of his stories there exists a strange, unequal but symbiotic relationship between the two. The oppressor is the village Gowda or a wealthy landlord, but his bonded labourer (usually from the untouchable Madiga caste) is inseparable from him. The latter serves the master without any question, is his companion, at times advisor and above all, someone without whom the Gowda's home cannot manage itself. This does not prevent the Gowda from literally dragging the labourer's daughter to his bed, or having liaisons with women of the Madiga caste. There is no attempt here to resurrect the 'organic bonds' of a feudal society between the master and the slave. The stories employ a stark realism to underline the cruelty of the social system. In one of Nugadoni's finest stories (*Tamandhada Kedu*, 2016) the slave carries the master on his shoulders across a shallow river, a haunting metaphor for how the master literally rides on the servant. But there are moments of crisis and rebellion showing how the system is unable to sustain itself. It is threatened by the younger generation, the children of the servants, who are now studying in cities and are desired by the Gowda's daughter. The author is keenly aware of how the seemingly unchanging and eternal feudal world is falling apart and has nothing to defend itself with, except violence and cruelty. The opportunities for rebellion are meagre. But the moral power is with the servant and there are no answers to questions that he raises. In the story referred to earlier, the servant comes to know about the plans made by the Gowda's sister to have his son murdered (to prevent the son's relationship with the Gowda's daughter). On the way back, again carrying the Gowda on his shoulder to cross the river, he seems to falter and walks into the river with the master 'riding him'. In another story, there is an encounter between an aging lonely Gowda and a young Naxal who is the son of one of his servants. The Gowda is persuaded to give away his land to his former servants as compensation for having exploited them. But when he calls his old servants, they say categorically that they do not want the land but a *noukari* (job) in the city. Ironically, the Gowda is the only one who is attached to the land. In the story *Neeru Tandavaru* (Those Who Brought Water), the young Dalit leaders are planning a violent protest against the upper castes who have blocked their access to water in the past. However, (though a little unconvincingly) the elders of the community decide to take water to their adversaries. In the story *Savari*, the untouchable gravedigger has always trusted his dreams which foretell the deaths about to take place. He has dreamt this time that the senior Gowda is dead and he goes to his house to take instructions to dig the grave. But the Gowda's son is a politician who wants a business deal to be concluded on the same day, and hides the fact of his father's death. The gravedigger persists, only to be beaten almost to death. When the deal is concluded, Gowda's death is announced but the gravedigger himself is dead. The raw power of the story contrasts the indifference and selfishness of the upper-caste Gowda's family with the honesty of the gravedigger.

Nugadoni employs an impressive range of narrative styles. In the short story *Daivakke Modalu Sharananembevu* (To God, We Pray First) the narrative shifts from the realistic to the mythopoeic and to the satirical. It is about a couple who are the ordained singers of the myths surrounding a little island village in which they live. However, they are (especially the husband is) lured into becoming the anthropological 'native informants' and folk narrators, for money. But a university professor 'steals' the stories and songs and builds his research on them. The couple is shunned and ostracised for having sold themselves and alienated themselves from the community. Their moral decline and repentance are powerfully portrayed. The story weaves together episodes which raise questions about indigenous knowledge, amoral academic world, the breakdown of a community and the advent of modernity. Nugadoni's stories constitute a fictional world rich in detail, complex with many perspectives, and imbued strongly with the sense of the inhuman inequality of a caste society. The region of Hyderabad Karnataka (especially around Raichur) has found a narrator and a chronicler in Nugadoni.

Jayanth Kaikini (b. 1955) is among the finest short story writers in the Kannada tradition. Like Yashwanta Chittala, his stories are about two social worlds. One is the regional small-town social world of Uttara Kannada and the other Mumbai. As in Anton Chekhov, his stories are about 'non-happenings' in a world which is ordinary and banal. The non-incidents which form the core of his stories are unanticipated and contingent. But they reveal as though in snapshots depths of human emotions and relationships. The son who hates his father for neglecting his family for his teaching profession discovers that his father is now quietly dedicating himself to helping people who are neither his friends nor relations. He also begins to understand the mystery of life in which people unknown to each other show compassion and care. Two unsuccessful men for no ostensible reason decide to help a young pregnant girl who has no one to take care of her. Another young man is initially puzzled but then understands why his mother should take away his clothes for an unknown young man hospitalised after being badly wounded. These are not acts of heroism or extraordinary sacrifice. They just happen and the author, like the readers, wonders at the hidden sources of goodness and compassion in ordinary human beings. In another story, on a night of heavy rains and flooding of streets in Mumbai, a taxi driver and two passengers are forced to spend hours together, facing the fury of the rain. The taxi driver emerges as the friendly Mumbaikar who has the grit, patience and humour to lend a helping hand to individuals who are strangers to each other. Kaikini's stories are about the nameless, orphaned and rootless ordinary men and women who have learnt to survive in Mumbai. 'No Presents Please' is an extraordinary story in which a young woman brought up in an orphanage is getting married to a man called 'Popat 'by people but who does not know his real name or family. She has a name given by the orphanage where she grew up. When they decide to have their wedding invitation printed, Popat is devastated because he discovers that he has no name. In another story, to help the marriage negotiations of an unknown customer's family, the young man who keeps a studio lends his dead father's photograph to be shown as someone's father. In the heartless Maximum City of Mumbai Jayanth discovers ordinary men and women who are incorrigibly human and resourceful. His stories, seemingly about evanescent and ephemeral things, are in fact profound meditations on the mysteries of existence. Despite his penchant for the good and the benevolent in life, Jayanth is also capable of portraying the mean cruelties of lower-middle-class families and the 'banality of evil'. His prose is a supple and unendingly creative medium through which he explores many experiences which seem to challenge the possibilities of language itself.

Kum. Vee. (Kumbar Veerabhadrappa) (b. 1953) is a prolific short story writer and a novelist who has also written about the feudal world in the border regions of Andhra and Karnataka. He was recognised as a major voice of the *Bandaya* movement as most of his stories are disturbing narratives about the untouchables and the bonded labourers in a feudal society. Many of his tales take place in and around 'Vagili', his dystopian Malgudi. Many of his stories employ an extreme naturalistic style, dealing with the shocking details of those condemned to live like animals. The horrors of a society which condemns human beings to such an unredeemed struggle to survive are revealed in his stories. The protagonists of his stories are gravediggers, bonded labourers, those who skin carcasses, and generally the oppressed who are eternally hungry. But Kum. Vee.'s fictional world is vast and varied. He writes with a distinctive blend of sarcasm, exaggeration and even verbal excess, about the absurd lives of individuals in an unequal society. No other Kannada writer has created such a huge rogues' gallery in fiction. His novels work on a large canvas and employ innovative narrative styles. His novel *Aramane* (2007) reconstructs the colonial world of the administration of Thomas Monro who is portrayed as an enlightened westerner who works tirelessly to help the marginalised in the traditional Indian society. The novel tries to understand why illiterate parents in Andhra and Karnataka villages even today name their children 'Mundrappa' in memory of Munro. Munro had to deal with scores of feudal lords who claimed to be kings and princes hailing from ancestral royal families. Kum. Vee. is at his sarcastic best in his portrayal of these absurd characters. The novel uses a pastiche of realism, myth, fantasy and poetry in its reconstruction of the colonial past.

Besagarahalli Ramanna was an accomplished short story writer who began writing when the *Navya* short story was making way for the *Bandaya* stories of resistance that unmasked caste- and class-centred exploitation. His early stories are about the large and well-to-do farmer families. While celebrating the rural world of labour, fertility and close family ties, Ramanna also showed how the affluent men of such families sexually exploited the poor women of the lower castes and treated their bonded labourers as property. Ramanna went on to write stories about this world from the perspective of the marginalised. He also wrote about the small-time politics and corruption which had taken over the rural society in independent India. His Kafkaesque stories about bureaucracy are among his most powerful. In his most memorable story (*Gandhi*) a poor sick boy named Mohandas Karamchand Gandhi is shunted from a health centre to a hospital and dies. His father, who has sold his last patch of land to pay the hospital expenses, reaches late, only to find Gandhi dead. Ramanna wrote some of the fiercest denunciations of the bureaucratic state masquerading as a democratic institution. In one of his stories (*Bettada Melondu Maneya Madi* [Having Built a House on the Mountain]) a former bonded labourer walks to the police station to surrender, carrying in his hands the severed head of his feudal master. Ramanna's stories are dark and sombre studies in the decline of democratic institutions. A heartless bureaucracy and corrupt politics have nothing to offer to those who live on the margins of the republic. Ramanna's satirical stories are treated as major achievements of the *Bandaya* literary movement.

Among writers who began writing in the heydays of the *Navya* school, S. Diwakar created for himself a supple narrative style, moving from the realistic mode to fantasy in order to portray the cruelty, violence and the alienation of the individual. His best-known short story is titled *Krourya* (Cruelty). He writes not only about the systemic cruelty of the bureaucratised state and society, but also about the cruelty lurking in personal and familial relationships. In a style reminiscent of Kafka and the existentialist writers, Diwakar writes about the angst of living in an absurd world. In a brilliant short story (*Komuvadi* [The Communal Person]),[1] the narrator goes in search of a communal individual and fails to find such a person. At the end of the story, the narrator's wife jokingly suggests that it could be him and he is shattered looking at his own image in the mirror. Diwakar is also a fine poet and essayist.

Both T. G. Raghava and Raghavendra Khasnis wrote during the *Navya* period. Raghava's short stories, like those of Ananthamurthy, are able to use the regional middle-class world as the location of the experience of existentialist angst. His short story *Shraddha* is intense and painful, and unmasks the oppressiveness of the family as an institution (see Nayak 2018).

Raghavendra Khasnis is an exceptionally gifted writer who reconstructs traumatic experiences by using the uncanny and the unexpected suddenly impinging on the everyday 'normal' world. He also powerfully employs Kafkaesque fantasy. His characters are unredeemed, fragmented and tortured individuals. Sadly, Khasnis was not a prolific writer, though he left behind some of the most disturbing short stories in Kannada. His short story *Tabbaligalu* (The Orphans) is a classic of modern Kannada literature.

---

[1] *Komuvadi* is unpublished. It was shared with the present author by the writer.

K. Sadashiva, a brilliant writer who died early, wrote about the pain of past memories, the torture of failed relationships, in a style which eschewed the dense symbolic mode of the *Navya* school. He could also write with compassion and understanding about the small everyday world. His story *Nalliyalli Neeru Banthu* (Water in the Tap) moves from the ugliness and claustrophobia of ordinary life to the realisation of its power to sustain the lives of those who cannot transcend the limitations of their everyday existence. Adiga says, in a tributary poem on Sadashiva, that 'he did not write stories; he offered slices of personal pain as stories'.

5

One of the oft-repeated statements about contemporary Kannada writing is about the absence of a recognisable literary-cultural movement after the *Bandaya* movement of the 1980s. There is also a mix of nostalgia and regret about the 'great decades' of the 1970s and 80s. Representatives of the farmers' movement and the Dalit movement continue to reminisce about the social energies unleashed by the movements in those decades. As discussed earlier, the period saw a confluence of many movements which straddled over many domains such as the political, the social and the literary. Remarkably, many of the leaders were either writers or were deeply interested in literature. The community of intellectuals and activists being small, there was coordination and joint action in many of the major protests of the period. This was helped by the little magazines of the time, with *Lankesh Patrike* enjoying phenomenal popularity from its inception in 1980. One could speak of an urban public sphere which had its impact on Karnataka politics. It was the Devaraj Urs regime which brought about major changes in Karnataka politics. For almost the first time, young leaders from the shudra and backward communities figured in the cabinet. Basavalingappa, a Dalit minister, provided leadership to the Dalit communities, while the Land Reform Act resulted in the political consolidation of Other Backward Communities (OBCs). The farmers and Dalit groups made significant interventions. However, in retrospect, apart from the distribution of land to former tenant farmers, it is doubtful if these decades made any major structural changes in Karnataka society. However, there was a 'rising of consciousness' among the hitherto marginalised castes and communities. For the first time, they enjoyed political power, though within the framework of Congress politics. With the end of the Urs regime, the two dominant castes regained their political hegemony and began to co-opt the Dalit and backward castes for their patented politics.

The impact of the re-hegemonisation by the dominant castes and the co-optation of the backward classes was such that it broke the back of the people's movements. The Dalit and farmer organisations splintered, owing to differences among the leaders, and, more importantly, the capability of the political class to co-opt the leaders and also to implement programmes which used the rhetoric borrowed from the people's movements. From the 1990s, Karnataka saw the emergence of globalisation and communal right-wing politics. There are certainly pockets of resistance, but the protests have been sporadic.

The processes of modernisation (which had begun earlier) and the wave of urbanisation, and the growth of Bengaluru as the IT capital, led to a new social dynamism. The second generation of Dalit and backward youth had different aspirations. There were also conflicts and tensions as the priorities of the society were changing quickly. These began to find expression on social media. Suddenly, writing was no longer an elite activity controlled by the literary establishment which until then had included the literary journals, popular magazines, printing and publishing houses and the book market. Now it was literally 'free' expression supported by the media groups. Young creative writers were no longer from the teaching profession. Increasingly, readers were from diverse backgrounds and locations. Active theatre groups, poetry circles and informal associations encouraged this new writing. At the time of writing this chapter, there has not yet been a complete transition to the digital media, but the sale of books is certainly moving away from the traditional bookshops. Information about new books is quickly shared and obtaining books is easier. One can look forward to a very different kind of reading culture in Kannada in the coming decades. The last two decades (2000 to 2020) have seen the debut of many young and talented writers.

In these decades, women's writing emerged as the major literary expression in Kannada. Pratibha Nandakumar, Lalita Siddabasavaiah, Vaidehi and Savita Nagabhushan continue to write. H. S. Anupama, a prolific writer who has experimented with several genres, has published *Sabarmati*, a long reflective poem which combines myths and legends about the river with the deep memories of Gandhi and Kasturba, as well as with the horrendous genocide in Gujarat. Her *Nanu Kastur* is a fictional autobiography of Kasturba Gandhi. Ja. Na. Tejashree is an important poet whose poetry explores in depth experiences of the natural world, of the intimate physical experience of love, and also of the social world. Her poetry possesses a rich texture of imagery and metaphors closer to the idiom of the previous *Navya* generation. Her poems are a search for the woman's autonomous world.

H. L. Pushpa revisits myths as they have been narrated and interpreted in the Kannada literary tradition, and excavates them for her analysis of patriarchy and resistance by women. Sa. Usha is a leading poet who examines the stereotypes about institutions such as the family and notions of motherhood. Recent poetry by women in Kannada is many-voiced and deals with experiences of women from many locations. Sukanya Maruti, Mamta Sagar, Muktayakka and Tarini Shubhadayini are among the many women poets who have made women's writing in Kannada fascinatingly diverse, offering a self-assured, autonomous vision of the contemporary world.

In his brief critical survey of contemporary Kannada literature, Rahamat Tarikere (2006) argues that its major preoccupation is resistance to the many ways in which globalisation has been destroying the roots of local cultures. He describes this resistance as filled with anxiety, anger and the desire to protect the vanishing ways of life. The anxiety and frustration is a response to the way in which large sections of the society have adapted themselves to globalisation. The ever-enlarging middle class, the diaspora and the urbanising youth see globalisation as the opening up of opportunities. The consumerist way of life is seen as 'modern' and cosmopolitan. The challenge for the writer is to find an idiom in which to question the consent given by the majority to the processes of globalisation. At the same time, a superficial nostalgic 'return to the roots' is an inadequate response. The young writers, most of them from the lower castes and under-privileged communities, have introduced hitherto unexplored social experiences into Kannada writing. However, Tarikere feels that they have not succeeded yet in innovating the necessary means of expression. The well-known critic T. P. Ashok, on the other hand, is enthusiastic about a host of young writers like Ashok Hegde, Guruprasad Kaginele and Kavya Kadame, who have experimented with new narrative modes in order to deal with the complex experiences of contemporary society (Ashoka 2021). In his excellent analysis of recent writers, Suresh Nagalamadike (2018) has shown how the writings of Vinaya Vakkunda, Ramesh Aroli, Roopa Hassan and others have provided creative expression to the new ethos of a society which has few resemblances with what was portrayed in Kannada literature until a few decades ago.

ELEVEN
Literary Criticism

This chapter does not offer a chronological history of literary criticism in Kannada. The field of literary criticism and theory in Kannada is vast, variegated and diverse; and, therefore, it would be unrealistic to attempt such a study in the space of a chapter. Instead the author intends to look briefly at the three major phases—call them three paradigms, if you will—in Kannada criticism, focusing on their major preoccupations and theoretical formulations and their engagement with the larger changes in the sociocultural domains of the various periods. The traditional, academically accepted nomenclature of the three phases—namely, *Navodaya*, *Navya* and *Navyottara*—shall be used, despite reservations about their adequacy.

The *Navodaya* phase refers to the period of the Kannada renaissance referred to throughout this volume, approximately from the last quarter of the nineteenth century to the fourth decade of the twentieth. This period converged with the movement for the unification of Karnataka, the nationalist movement and the *Ramya* or Romantic movement in Kannada. The period should be analysed as part of the Indian renaissance and encounter with colonial modernity. During this phase, like many other literary traditions, Kannada literary tradition broke away from the stagnation and lack of creativity of the previous period, revitalised itself through the influence of English literature, experimented with new prosodic forms and genres, created a fairly well-defined readership for itself, and also went through academic institutionalisation. In some of the previous chapters repeated references have been made to the impact on Kannada and Karnataka made by the missionaries, Western scholars and administrators, the introduction of print technology, the circulation of journals and magazines, and the strengthening of the educational system.

The major preoccupations of the *Navodaya* phase can be described as the construction of a Kannada literary tradition of the past based on the recovery of old texts and their reproduction under the norms of textual scholarship, the reformulation of the notion of the literary and search for sources for the rejuvenation of Kannada writing. The two aspects of the literary critical efforts prioritised in the period were textual scholarship and the outlining of a Kannada literary historiography. The major texts of the tradition were scattered among private collections and in religious institutions such as *mathas* and *basadis* in the form of palmyra manuscripts and copies made by scribes. These had to be collected and carefully scrutinised for authenticity; variants had to be noted and sifted; detailed references had to be appended and the biographies of the authors had to be reconstructed on the basis of the undependable and sketchy material available. Though textual scholarship of this kind is now treated as separate from literary criticism, intellectual energies of the highest order were invested by Kannada scholars and writers in such work, and this needs to be treated as literary criticism. For example, *Pampa Bharata Deepike* by D. L. Narasimhachar (1971) is designed as a close critical exegesis of the epic by Pampa, but in fact is a serious work of criticism. His introductions and prefaces, collected in one volume, are also of the same order. The work done by Fa. Gu. Halakatti (1926) and S. S. Basavanal (1968) in preparing modern editions of the *Vachanas* are also brilliant contributions to criticism. This can be said about the rigorous scholarly–critical work involved in the preparation of the major texts of the Kannada tradition throughout the *Navodaya* phase. The initial momentum came from the work done by the Christian missionaries and administrators who introduced the norms of modern textual scholarship.

The availability of the major texts led to their close readings and interpretations, thus laying the foundations of literary criticism. Undoubtedly, this model of criticism was at times overenthusiastic and uncritical with every rediscovered work being hailed as a 'gem' or a 'diamond'. But to derogate the whole of this criticism as *rasa vimarshe*, impressionistic criticism or sentimental eulogy, is unjustified. There is very little in the post-1960 New Criticism in Kannada which declared its allegiance to close reading, practical criticism and formalist exegesis, to match the readings of the canonical texts by the *Navodaya* writers and scholars. Kuvempu's readings of the epics (*Sarovarada Siriganndiyalli*, *Draupadiya Srimudi*) are examples of critical analysis of a high order (Shivareddy 2003). Though couched in his somewhat cryptic and esoteric prose, Bendre's writings on Lakshmeesha and others are insightful. A. R. Krishnashastri, Ti. Nam. Shri (T. N. Srikantaiah) and T. S. Venkannaiah are among the *Navodaya* scholars who wrote with clarity and inwardness on the works of the past. In fact, what characterises the critics of this phase is their extraordinary inwardness with the ancient Kannada, Sanskrit and, in some cases, Prakrit traditions. Their readings also led them to raise seminal questions about the relationship between Kannada and Sanskrit, the creative problems faced by the Kannada writers bound by the hegemonic Sanskrit aesthetics and practice, and also problems relating to *dharma* and culture. For example, commenting on the restraints under which Pampa wrote his two epics—that is, the constraint of retelling *Vyasa Bharata* and the *Aadipurana*, because not too many liberties could be taken with the original sources—Ti. Nam. Shri. says that Pampa was 'like a wrestler entering the ring with both arms tied'. Kuvempu comments on the verbosity and excesses in Kumara Vyasa as compared to the admirable economy of Pampa. D. L. N. demonstrates the intertextuality in the Kannada *Champu* works with his amazing knowledge of many literary traditions. Therefore, the *Navya* charge against *Navodaya* criticism that it did not address literary texts, needs to be re-examined. Though not exactly in the jargon of New Criticism, *Navodaya* critics did read the literary texts closely. Masti Venkatesha Iyengar's preface to Bendre's collection of poems, *Nadaleele,* offers an extraordinary reading of a line from the famous poem *Belagu* (Dawn), relating the metaphor in it to the integrated vision of the poet in which the tree and the birdsong blend. One reason for the unwillingness to demonstrate close readings could have been the notion of the '*sahrudaya*' reader, the ideal reader, which the New Critics like Cleanth Brooks and F. R. Leavis assume. The small reading public of the times comprised competent poetry readers who knew most of the traditional texts by heart and were familiar with prosody, stanza forms, and use of tropes and poetic devices.

Modernist criticism used the term *rasa vimarshe* in a negative sense, almost equating it with the false kind of reader response based on unsubstantiated enthusiastic over-reading. Much later, Gopalakrishna Adiga complained that critics confused criticism with emotional response and evaluation with easy appreciation. One has to remember the context of *Navodaya* criticism. The overarching preoccupation was the unification of the *Kannadanādu* which was mainly a culturalist notion with the literary tradition playing a major role in it. Therefore, there was indeed an enthusiastic response to the rediscovered texts of the past and to the new literature taking its birth. As discussed in other chapters, recitation and reading of poetry and long lectures were the major modes of literary communication; and the written, printed forms were secondary in the period. Naturally this communication depended on an immediate spontaneous response by large audiences. Criticism was expected to appreciate the new literature in the making. The reading public was almost homogeneous, and writers and critics were from the upper-caste, middle-class background. Modernist critics complained that this made criticism an affair 'of gentlemanly civilised exchange of mutual appreciation'. However, from the autobiographies and personal essays of the time, it does not appear to be so. Of course it took some time for the emergence of literary criticism as we understand it today. Many of the reviews by A. R. Krishnashastri and others are fine examples of criticism.

What were the philosophical concerns of *Navodaya* criticism? In the first place, these concerns were discussed as part of poetics or aesthetics (*meemamse*) and not literary criticism. Most of the literary critical terms were taken from Sanskrit poetics, though Kuvempu and others coined neologisms when necessary. In a complex argument, Kuvempu states that literature is not *anukrithi* (imitation or mimesis) but *anusrishti* (recreation). He warns that a literary text should not be reduced to a one-to-one imitation of reality, thus making fidelity a critical value. Literature is a parallel recreation within the formal and aesthetic norms. Therefore, criticism should not judge a work of literature on the criterion of mere verisimilitude. Masti Venkatesha Iyengar begins his discussion of Valmiki's *Ramayana* by stating unambiguously that the epic is *kavya* (imaginative, non-discursive literature) and not *dharma*. He even states that when a literary text like the *Ramayana* achieves great popularity, religion appropriates it and attempts to convert it to a *dharmic* text. He clearly says that this is a loss and a diminution of literature. Other critics use the term *pratisrishti* (counter-creation), thus affirming the unique ontological status of literature. Not all of them adhere to the simplistic taxonomy of the nine *rasas*. They emphasise *dhwani*, the suggestive power of literature which demands a different cognitive effort to understand this. These arguments are not new to Sanskrit aesthetics. But the *Navodaya* critics employ these arguments to uphold the unique status of literature.

The other major philosophical issue was the nature of the experience of literature. The *rasa* school of poetics had compared it, in fact at times equated it with, the experience of oneness with the transcendental. *Navodaya* Kannada criticism abounds in terms such as *aloukika* (otherworldly), *abhoutika* (non-material) and *anubhava* (spiritual/mystical) to describe the experience of literature. Kuvempu describes the experience of *bhooma* (the sublime) in such terms. A large component of *Navodaya* criticism dealt with such issues of poetics which were a little too general and non-specific. On the other hand, as Mokashi Punekar (2012) and Rahamat Tarikere (2011) have argued, real Kannada poetics is not to be found in the works on poetics. It is to be found in the comments in the literary texts themselves and in the actual poetic practices. From this perspective,

Navodaya criticism was about the secular social impact of literature. Bendre and Kuvempu declare that poetry should be a clarion call for the cause of Kannada. It should speak to and for the common man (*Sri Samanya*). It has the duty to awaken the sluggish souls of the Kannadigas. No *Navodaya* poet believes that poetry has no social function. Bendre said that there is no literature unrelated to society.

Navodaya criticism was conscious of the unique conjuncture in which contemporary literature was being created. It was a moment of 'rebirth' and 'reawakening' which involved breaking the shackles of the past and tradition. Kuvempu uses the terms '*nutana*' and '*hosa*' (new) for his own poetry. One of the prolonged debates around the time was on freeing poetry (versification) from the initial rhyme (*aadiprasa*). The latter referred to the repetition of the same sound at the beginning of every line of a stanza or poetic unit. The debate was carried on with all seriousness; and Govind Pai described his decision to abandon it as a revolutionary act! This is only one example of the struggle to reject the deadwood of tradition and 'to make it new'. Far bolder was the decisive argument of B. M. Sri., that it was now time for Kannada literature to draw its resources from English and not any longer from Sanskrit. The following extracts from his speeches and writings make this amply clear: 'In the past our poetry drew sustenance from Sanskrit language and literature. Now is the time to let it grow by nourishing itself on English language and literature' (Shrikanthaiah 1985). 'Instead of blindly following the worn-out path of tradition, let our poets devote themselves to the study of how poets of other nations have vastly enriched the materials of poetry. The universal experiences . . . of simple joys and sorrows of human life such as war, love, death, patriotism . . . have been their poetic material' (ibid). B. M. Sri rightly believed that it is the simple joys and sorrows which were missing in the traditional poetry which was about the extraordinary and the transcendental. Indirectly, he was critiquing the impersonal, mystical and religious poetic tradition which had ignored the lives of the common people. His translations from English poetry, in *English Geetegalu*, introduced this personal world of emotions, joys and sorrows. It should be noted that B. M. Sri. is echoing the points made by Wordsworth who was a major influence on *Navodaya* poetry, especially on Kuvempu. Under his influence, Kannada poets eschewed the poetic conventions used for describing nature and began to write about the real, sensuous world they were living in, such as Kuvempu's Malnad region. Agreeing with Wordsworth's idea that poetry should be about ordinary men and women, it was a small step for Kuvempu to dissociate himself from the poetry about nobles, courtiers, princes and kings and to write about the Dalits of his village. It has been difficult for later critics to understand that this was a major paradigm shift in Kannada literature towards a secular humanist philosophy.

It has to be admitted that *Navodaya* criticism could not keep in step with the enormous creativity of *Navodaya* literature. Innovations in form and themes, experimentation with genres like the lyric, the short story and the novel, the personal essay, translations—so many diverse movements were taking place simultaneously. There was also the pressure of integrating the traditional poetics with Western poetics and to indigenise the Western influence. The actual writing practices were heterogeneous and theorising all this was not an easy task. There were also the many epicentres of the unification movement, and this led to literary sub-cultures mainly based in Mysore, Dharwad and Mangalore (Mangaluru). There were major differences among these sub-cultures regarding the poetics of the *Navodaya* phase. No single critic could address such diversities of the period. There were, for example, disagreements on the desirable poetic idiom. While B. M. Sri. and the old Mysore school sought to establish a standard literary dialect close to the urban educated speech of the region, Bendre and his followers wanted to explore the *desi* dialects and the folk literary forms. Though B. M. Sri. described folk literature as the 'mother root' of all literature, his own practice, unlike Bendre's, owes little to the folk traditions. The regional novel in Kannada was written, as mentioned in another chapter, in the many genres of the novel—such as the historical romance, the domestic novel, and the social-realist novel. This also led to debates over the question of realism in fiction.

The modernist debate on the poetic idiom had much to do with the opposition to the school of *Navodaya* poetry. By the early 1950s, the latter had run out of steam and its idiom had dwindled into a patented effete medium in which a vague idealism and amorphous spiritualism were finding dull expression. It had also developed a loose and abstract 'social' rhetoric used to adopt empty postures about social responsibility and nationalism. Such otherworldly postures couched in a tired over-worn idiom angered the post-independence poets. The poetry itself was found to be lacking in authentic personal experience. G. H. Nayak summarises its shortcomings as follows: 'Though the works in the *Navodaya* tradition were the fruits of [such] a unique and rare synthesis, it appears as though a situation arose in which it was not possible for the creative spirit of the writers of this tradition to fully respond to the experiences of life from a specific centre and source of their personality' (Nayak 1989, 33–34). *Navodaya* literature had begun by emphasising the importance of individual experience but it also believed that this experience is universal human experience. Nayak argues that the writers lost the ability to respond to experience from a 'specific centre of their personality'. What was vaguely described as universal was not authenticated by individual experience. Instead, the known and familiar attitudes and responses of tradition were repeated in cliches. Gopalakrishna Adiga attributes this to the rhetorical idealism of the nationalist movement which had lost touch with reality. The despair and disillusionment in the post-independence era showed up the hollowness of the rhetoric. Using a powerful metaphor, Adiga (1977) argued that it was lacking in the 'smell of the soil' ('*mannina vasane*'). He advocated a realistic and complex response to experience with all its contradictions and dualities.

Adiga created a poetics out of this insistence on authentic individual experience. The only way of achieving authenticity in poetry was by recreating experience in the language and form of poetry, by 'making it happen' in language. Adiga, who acknowledged his debt to Eliot and Auden, made use of Eliot's notion of the objective correlative to emphasise the importance of concrete and objective recreation of experience in poetry. The opposition to rhetoric in social life has a parallel in the rejection of verbal excess in poetry. While Eliot used his critical apparatus to argue for the merging of the individual talent with tradition, Adiga employs much of the same apparatus to emphasise individual experience. Like Eliot, he also believed that the complexity of the modern world necessitated complexity in poetry. Use of concrete imagery, symbolism, a non-linear poetic structure, a poetic language marked by irony, paradox and ambiguity, had to be the constituents of the new poetry. The prudery and moral hypocrisy of the past tradition had to be abandoned in order to deal with the existential realities. In Adiga's poetry man was the unnatural progeny of mother earth and could not integrate body and soul. He was condemned to an ambivalent existence. The modern world was a *Gondalapura* (city of chaos) ruled by the demon of chaos. Ideologies and institutions had become the enemies of his autonomy.

However, *Navya* criticism had to negotiate with a highly experimental, innovative writing in the major writers like Ramachandra Sharma, U. R. Ananthamurthy, Yashwanta Chittala and Shantinath Desai. There was also the search for a new poetic idiom which could take in the 'impurities' of the real world. Images and symbols were drawn from everyday urban life. Sexuality was confronted head-on and as G. H. Nayak said, sexuality was employed as the touchstone of the validity of one's beliefs. Middle-class morality and religious traditions were brought under sharp scrutiny. Even though the locale was the familiar regional world, modernist fiction portrayed alienated human beings who led a fragmented life in it. There was protest and resistance against a society which impinged on the autonomy of the individual.

Navya Kannada criticism, on the one hand, took up the defense of the new, complex and, at times, opaque, writing. Essays appeared in the little magazines like *Sakshi* and *Sankramana* explaining the symbolist structure of the new fiction. Close reading and exegesis were the favoured tools for critical analysis; debates were held on the efficacy of modernist writing. Adiga's long editorials in *Sakshi* and the prolific critical writings by Shantinath Desai in *Sankramana* offered a strong defense of the new writing. In the initial stages, Chandrashekhar Patil, P. Lankesh, T. G. Raghava and Sumatheendra Nadig were staunch supporters of *Navya* writing. U. R. Ananthamurthy's introduction to Adiga's major collection, *Bhoomigeetha* (Earth Song), is a classic of *Navya* criticism. His sensitive readings of the poems set up high standards for *Navya* criticism. This was followed by equally brilliant readings and interpretations by Shantinath Desai, M. G. Krishnamurthy, H. M. Channaiah and others.

However, as critics have pointed out, *Navya* criticism was not rigidly formalist. It addressed itself to cultural and social issues. Ananthamurthy argued that Adiga's poetry was relevant because his concerns were those of contemporary culture. He justified this statement by discussing Adiga's critique of an impersonal culture with abstract metaphysical concerns. Like many poets of the 1960s, Adiga was preoccupied with the Westernising tendencies which had alienated his generration from tradition. In his search for tradition in major poems like *Bhootha* and *Shri Ramanavamiya Divasa*, Adiga seemed to support the *Arsha* ancient tradition, using quite profusely the myths and images relating to the Vedic tradition. This led to a revolt against him by the younger generation of modernist poets. (See the chapter on literary modernism for a detailed discussion of this.) With this controversy, *Navya* criticism shifted from a formalist framework to a culturalist framework.

Critics have raised two major concerns against *Navya*. One was that *Navya*'s emphasis on individual experience had gradually led to a highly subjective orientation and even to solipsism. The *Navya* writer was projecting his or her personal experiences, ignoring the sociocultural issues of contemporary society. With the growth of the people's movements of the 1980s, *Navya* writing began to be seen as the literature of a small coterie alienated from societal turmoils. Adiga and Ananthamurthy were identified as 'brahmin' writers and were kept out of the *Barahagarara Okkuta*.

Before returning to the polemics of the period it would be useful to look at the deeper concerns of *Navya* criticism. In its critique of *Navodaya* literature, it raises serious questions about the spiritual element in it. The *Navodaya* writer believed in the ultimate significance of the transcendental reality and subjugated the everyday material reality to it. Under the influence of Aurobindo, *Navodaya* poetry turned to the transcendental by ignoring the everyday reality. The debate on Bendre's later poetry took place in this context. While *Navya* critics considered the two novels by Kuvempu as classics, they had little to say about his epic and his poetry. Both Ananthamurthy and M. G. Krishnamurthy also felt that his novels were rich in detail but they lacked a centre that provided coherence to the various parts of the novels. Later, post-*Navya* critics have seen this as a case of blindness and inability to imagine a mythopoeic narrative structure which has a different kind of unity.

Ananthamurthy wrote profoundly about the complex fate of the Indian writer caught between tradition and modernity. His own position was that of a 'critical insider' to tradition. This was his response to the debate on identity and tradition, which occupied the central stage in Indian literature for a decade. In the Kannada context of the period, there was a cultural resistance against the Vedic-brahminical traditions; and Ananthamurthy was seen with scepticism by the Dalit and *Bandaya* writers and critics. His essay *English Brahmana, Kannada Shudra* provoked a great deal of debate, though he was only tangentially looking at 'brahmin' and 'shudra' as sociological categories.

In his seminal work, *Bharatiya Samskriti Mattu Lekhaka* (Indian Culture and the Writer), M. G. Krishnamurthy (1970) wrote brilliantly on the *Vachanas*, Kuvempu, Karanth and Ananthamurthy. A thoroughgoing formalist, he engaged with the complex relationship between Indian culture and the writer. He saw the writer as vulnerable to the abstractions circulated in culture, which made Indian writing weak. He saw the relationship as essentially complex and conflictual.

Shantinath Desai declared himself an existentialist and a modernist. He argued that *Navodaya* literature had exhausted its possibilities and saw *Navya* as a liberating mode of writing. He emphasised the relevance of individual experience. However, in his interpretations of literary texts,

Desai seemed closer to Lionel Trilling rather than to Eliot or Leavis. His enthusiastic and brilliant discussions of *Samskara* (both the novel and the film), the *Navya* short story, the poetry of Gangadhar Chittala and Adiga, and the short stories of Veena Shanteshwar, went a long way in establishing *Navya* literature.

Giraddi Govindaraj has written prolifically on *Navya* literature. His excellent study of the Kannada short story demonstrates how and why the genre became the major medium of expression for the *Navya* writers. His essays on *Samskara*, Karnad's plays and discussion of S. L. Bhyrappa's novels, are fine examples of objective literary analysis. Discussing the modernity advocated by Gokak as essentially a new technique of writing, Giraddi disagrees with him. He argues that the *Navya* form of writing is inalienably related to a changed sensibility and world view. He does not agree that the *Navya* techniques can be employed to communicate any sensibility (Govindaraj 2012).

Kirtinath Kurtakoti, considered one of the greatest Kannada critics, initially argued that Kannada *Navya* writing began as a 'personal necessity' of writers like Adiga, and that the Kannada writer had witnessed nothing resembling the devastation caused by the World War and the many dislocations caused by the processes of modernity which had led to the inception of literary modernism in Europe and England. In the Kannada context, it was essentially the search by a group of writers to imitate (although creatively) European modernity. Like Shankar Mokashi Punekar, Kurtakoti did not believe that there was a disjuncture in the Kannada tradition with the coming of *Navya*. An erudite scholar immersed in the Kannada tradition, his *Sahitya Mattu Yugadhrama* was a path-breaking work initiating serious literary criticism in Kannada (Kurtakoti 1962).

In contrast to Kurtakoti's arguments, Ananthamurthy writes that writers of the earlier generation, such as Shivaram Karanth, wrote novels which examined whether the inner world of the characters conformed to or deviated from the outside world. In a way, Karanth did not interrogate the beliefs and values of his characters. He examined how honestly they lived according to their beliefs. Ananthamurthy says that the *Navya* writer poses the question whether the individual is authentic to himself or herself, to his or her own self.

Interestingly, the finest interpretations of the *Vachanas* have come from *Navya* critics like M. G. Krishnamurthy, H. M. Channaiah, B. Damodar Rao and Giraddi Govindaraj. Similarly, the most insightful discussions of Bendre's poetry were also by the *Navya* critics, though none can match the depth of Kurtakoti's readings of Bendre. G. S. Amur, probably the most prolific of the New Critics, wrote *Bhuvanada Bhagya*, a comprehensive study of Bendre's poetry. In retrospect, the much debated rejection of the past and tradition by *Navya* criticism was unfounded. Though most of the *Navya* critics wrote little about ancient Kannada literature, G. H. Nayak's interpretation of Pampa, Ranna and Raghavanka remain unsurpassed.

Ki. Rum. Nagaraj was a living legend and a myth in his own life time, probably the only literary critic to be treated so. His major writings were collected in the volume *Tereda Pathya* only after his death, because of his unwillingness to publish them. One of the reasons was that he was a great believer in orality and through thousands of talks, lectures and discussions, achieved the impossible—making serious literary criticism of a high order a part of the modern oral tradition. An original thinker, Nagaraj did not confine himself to any theoretical model of criticism, though he was one of the few who was thoroughly familiar with contemporary literary theories of the West. His deep inwardness with the entire Kannada tradition and intellectual engagement with both Indian and Western aesthetics enabled his insightful interpretations of ancient and contemporary texts. His early path-breaking essay on Pampa interpreted the two epics by him as authentic and complex expressions of a regional sensibility defining itself against the pan-Indian Sanskrit modular aesthetic norms. He also argued that Pampa's attempt to allegorise his patron Arikesari as Arjuna was one of the earliest attempts to place regional politics on the Indian political map. This interpretation was part of his project to analyse major Kannada texts as resistant texts that challenged aesthetic and political hegemonies. He was deeply interested in the counter-worlds represented in folk literature and folk performative expressive forms. His talk on the folk epic *Manteswamy Kavya* demonstrates how the undercurrent of resistance and subversion in the oral tradition opposed what was propagated in the colonial texts (Nagaraj 2012).

Like D. R. Nagaraj, Ki. Rum. Nagaraj also read the *Kavirajamarga* as a text of cultural politics. His argument that the author of the *Kavirajamarga* was preparing the theoretical ground for making Kannada the vehicle of all knowledge, deserves wider scholarly attention. Ki. Rum. laid the foundations of a sophisticated theoretically rigorous form of Kannada nativism. He did this by pursuing a two-pronged critical project. On the one hand he offered an interdisciplinary description of how the Kannada tradition had resisted the pan-Indian Sanskrit frameworks in aesthetics, prosody and choice of subject for literary creation. His nativistic thinking was free from the false reconstruction of a 'pure Kannada past'. For Ki. Rum. it had always been a pluralistic, many-voiced tradition. Kannada had great powers of assimilation and had developed strategies to integrate diverse and heterogeneous literary, philosophical traditions. Much later, U. R. Ananthamurthy referred to this assimilative power as '*Jeernagni*', the fire-like power to devour and digest. Therefore, though modern Kannada opened itself to Western influence and to colonial modernity in the modern period, it was not overwhelmed or inundated by these forces. Ki. Rum. showed how Shishunala Sharif, a saint and composer of philosophical songs who lived in a village near Hubli during the colonial period, wrote about the cotton ginning factory in Hubli. Sharif also prophesised the harm that the colonial regime would bring, using the metaphor of the locust. Similarly, Ki. Rum. read the medieval Kannada texts by contextualising them. His essays on Kumara Vyasa and the *Vachanakaras* have initiated new interpretations of the early- and late-medieval Kannada literature. Ki. Rum. was an insightful commentator on U. R. Ananthamurthy, Lankesh and Gopalakrishna Adiga. His original ideas transformed Kannada literary criticism.

K. V. Narayana is one of the finest contemporary critics in Kannada. The range of his scholarship is impressive. He has written on language and linguistics, including a monograph on Chomskyan linguistics, on stylistics, on Sanskrit aesthetics (a book on rereading *Dhvanyaloka*), and on drama and theatre. He is an authority on ancient Kannada literature and on most of the significant texts of the modern period. His writings are marked by exemplary faultless scholarship, close reading of texts, theoretical rigour and a consistent intellectual enquiry. His essay *Kannadigalu Saku* (No More Mirrors Now) is a major contribution to postcolonial literary theory in which he argues for liberation from subservience to Euro-centric theories. He questions Kannada criticism which engaged itself in reading Kannada texts under the lens of Western theories. He advocated an intellectually rigorous reconstruction of indigenous models of interpretation which would avoid the pitfalls of ahistorical, apolitical valorisation of all indigenous texts. Just as it was wrong to construct Kannada grammar on the rules of the Sanskrit language, it was a fallacy to follow Euro-centric theories in criticism. Narayana's major collection is titled *Beru. Kanda. Chiguru.* (Root, Stem and Sprout, 2017) which is also his metaphor for continuities in a literary tradition. His writings have been collected in multiple volumes and contain his forays into several knowledge domains. His analysis of Kannada in the modern half-century is authoritative. It is a linguistic–cultural study on the status of Kannada in the age of globalisation, as a medium of instruction, as state language and as a language of knowledge. The work also looks at the changes in the morphology of the language (Narayana 1997).

It would be difficult to speak of a critical framework employed by Narayana, because he has written on a large number of texts and he rarely enunciates the critical framework he intends to employ in his analysis. He seems to rely on what every text demands from its imagined ideal reader. However, on the basis of a close reading, he formulates questions and observations which have implications beyond the text. For example, in his essay on *Mārga* and *Desi*, Narayana insists on considering them as two modes of writing and then examines the literary-cultural connotations they have acquired in literary history. In most of his writings, he questions the received opinions on interpretations of texts and on conceptual terms employed in criticism. His essay on Sham. Ba. Joshi, the eminent researcher, was among the first to draw attention to the philosophical assumptions behind Joshi's analysis of cultural symbols and myths. Narayana did not feel the need to declare his allegiance to *Navya* criticism though he was very much a part of the debates on it.

D. R. Nagaraj, who passed away at the age of forty-three, is undoubtedly the most influential critic in Kannada. A well-received volume of translations of his writings, *Listening to the Loom: Essays on Literature, Politics and Violence* (2012), edited by Prithvi Datta Chandra Shobhi, has brought D. R. international critical attention. His writings are distinguished by intellectual brilliance and his ability to bring a number of theoretical approaches to his analysis. His intellectual enthusiasm varied throughout his career, from a broad Marxist perspective, to the Frankfurt school of critical theory and then to a postcolonial, sophisticated *Desi* stance. He remained unswerving in his belief that the knowledge provided by literature was in no way inferior to what other discourses and disciplines provided. He was fond of saying that 'all knowledge is narrative'. In his last great work, *Allama Prabhu Mattu Shaiva Pratibhe*, after a closely argued, dense and intellectually challenging analysis of the *Vachanas* of Allama in the context of Indian philosophical traditions, Nagaraj offers close readings of the *Vachanas* as literary texts. He also started a major project with Akshara Prakashana, Heggodu, to bring out a series of works relating to the subaltern or counter-philosophical-cultural traditions. One of the texts published in the series was *Daru Prathima Na Poojive.* His scholarly introductions to the works elaborated on the significance of the project. It was an ambitious project aiming to go beyond the binaries created by colonialism. It was also a way of acknowledging the plurality of traditions. Nagaraj's book on Allama begins with a vigorous critique of S. N. Dasgupta whose comments on Basava and the *Vachanakaras* were based on wrong sources. Thereafter, D. R. brings to his analysis several Bhakti, mystical and yogic traditions to explicate the philosophy of Allama.

D. R.'s *The Flaming Feet* has been recognised as a major contribution to the analysis of Dalit movements and ideologies. D. R. was also responsible to some extent for dismantling the long-held notion of an adversarial relationship between Gandhi and Ambedkar. Reference has already been made to D. R.'s conceptualisation of subnationality in another chapter. He was critical about the anxiety-ridden linguistic subnationalism which tried to define itself by constructing a linguistic Other. He drew attention to a different subnationalist philosophy which saw Karnataka as a linguistic and cultural plurality. D. R.'s readings of Bendre's poetry and the *Vachanas* remain unsurpassed in their brilliance.

H. S. Raghavendra Rao, C. N. Ramachandran, T. P. Ashok, G. Rajashekhar and many others deserve to be considered as leading Indian critics whose engagement with Indian literature and culture is of a high order.

***

The next paradigm shift in Kannada literary criticism came after the high noon of *Navya* criticism. This owed to two factors. One was the internal critique and interrogation by some of the leading erstwhile practitioners of the *Navya* school. As mentioned earlier, P. Lankesh and Chandrashekhar Patil had already turned away from the excesses of formalist criticism and had ridiculed the absurdity of practical criticism as a mechanical tool of analysis. Both of them had rebelled against Adiga's deep-seated cultural conservatism. As pointed out elsewhere, theirs was a protest against the hegemony of the brahminical element in the literary establishment. Lankesh evolved his own model of criticism which was deeply sceptical about theory. He believed in what he described as 'honest' criticism based on one's reading and addressed to the common reader. The numerous book reviews he wrote for his weekly tabloid *Lankesh Patrike* were a mix of sensitive reading and authoritative judgement. Lankesh argued that the only worthwhile function of the critic was to tell the reader whether he or she would benefit from reading the book under discussion. He was a modernist who did not consider the past traditions relevant. He believed that a meaningful text should make a difference to the existing secular democratic society.

We find a stronger theoretical critique in Poornachandra Tejaswi. In the collection of critical essays *Vimarsheya Vimarshe* (2009) he attacks the arguments presented by Ananthamurthy in his essay *Bharatiya Samskriti Mattu Lekhaka*. Tejaswi argues that Indian culture as described by Ananthamurthy is in fact brahminical culture. G. H. Nayak had also argued that Ananthamurthy projects the brahminical context (*sandharbha*) as the Indian context. Tejaswi describes *Navya* literature, in fact the mainstream literary tradition itself, as the expression of a small class which in a caste society has no access to the experiences of the other social sections. It therefore projects its own limited experiences as those of Indian society. However, he also argues that the evolution of the Kannada literary tradition has been in the form of a gradual manifestation of the shudra sensibility. (He uses the expression *gamyavaguvudu* which means 'to become visible' or 'manifest'.) He sees Kuvempu as the first great shudra writer who gave expression to the experiential world of the shudras. This trajectory of the evolution of the Kannada tradition should be kept in mind in the interpretation of texts.

Tejaswi's preface to *Abachoorina Post Office* has been discussed in an earlier chapter. In his piece, Tejaswi describes *Navya* literature as 'subjective', centred around the individual consciousness of the author. He proposes that the new writing to come should bear witness to the happenings in society objectively. This was also the perspective in several discussions which used the terms *vyasti* and *samasti* (the subjective individual and the collective) in evaluating *Navya* literature.

The major shift in post-*Navya* criticism was towards theorising and describing alternative, subaltern literary and cultural traditions. As pointed our earlier, D. R. Nagaraj's intellectual project was to examine such traditions in the Indian context. Rahamat Tarikere's extensive field work and research has been on such traditions in Karnataka. His work *Karnatakada Sufigalu* (1998) analyses the *sankara saamskriti*, the (hybrid, mixed, plural) cultural and religious traditions in North Karnataka and Kalyan Karnataka. There was not only inter-faith dialogue in these regions, there was the 'third-way' in which there were beliefs and practices that were a mixture of Sufism and subaltern forms of Hinduism, specifically the Shaivite sects. Dargahs and saints' tombs bear mixed names; and some of the legends clearly describe certain saints as belonging to two religions. This Sufism is very different from the Sufism in the royal-supported *Khanaquas*, with Sufi saints holding authority over kings. The *sankara* religion is a subaltern religion whose followers were peasants and artisans. It had little to do with the elite forms of the two religions. Tarikere moved away from the metaphor of *sankara* to the metaphor of the third-way because he discovered that the subaltern traditions which mingled went on to form a new entity.

Tarikere's analysis of the Shakta traditions, the Muharram rituals and songs, and the *Guru* tradition in Karnataka, are based on extensive field work and dialogues with the ordinary people who follow these traditions in the contemporary world. Many of them are *tatwapadakaras*, composers of a spiritual, philosophical poetry in the oral tradition. Though hardly literate, they are capable of participating in philosophical discourses. Tarikere's emphasis is on the living contemporary traditions, and not on an imagined past. Taken together, his scholarly work effectively deconstructs the entrenched notions of mainstream and little traditions, Vedic and non-Vedic traditions. In short, what his work urges is a radically new historiography and social analysis. Brahminisation, Sanskritisation, dominant religions—these concepts need to be placed under erasure. What we in fact see is a mindboggling plurality and hybridity. Some of the oldest belief systems such as Shakta still survive and flourish in Karnataka.

Tarikere began as a *Bandaya* critic supporting the idea of a counter-culture (*prati samskruti*). His later works have demonstrated the need to go beyond binaries in order to understand the real nature of the dialogue among many cultures and traditions. He has also written brilliantly on *Navya* and post-*Navya* literature.

Nataraj Budal believes that the roots of the Karnataka culture go back to the Buddhist origins. His interest is also in the non-Vedic, non-hierarchical cultural traditions founded on notions of equality and co-existence. In his book on *Kannada Kavya Meemamse*, Budal argues that Kannada aesthetics is distinctive and non-imitative of Sanskrit aesthetics. He has written on Saranapada and Allama to examine the existence of a distinctive metaphysics and ontology which has survived in the subaltern traditions.

Thus, the dual engagement of recent Kannada criticism has been with the impact of the processes of globalisation on culture and literature on the one hand, and with the living subaltern cultural traditions on the other.

TWELVE

Popular Kannada Literature

In a preceding chapter, we have discussed the evidence of a continuous tradition of folk creative expressions, which was generally categorised as non-elite or unsophisticated. Despite such elite derision, a remarkable number of folk poems, long poetic narratives, folk epics and other performative forms were produced throughout known history. The present chapter focuses on popular literature in Kannada in the modern period. Information is somewhat scarce on the early colonial period when Western missionaries had just introduced printing technology, first in the coastal region and then in Bellary, Dharwad and Bengaluru. Hermann Mögling published the first Kannada newspaper, *Mangalore Samachara*, which covered local events, administration and other sundry news. From Srinivas Havanur's (1974) research on the missionary work, it does not appear that they paid a lot of attention to popular culture, as was done by the newspapers and magazines published from Calcutta and Bombay. It is only from the later short stories and novels that we know a little about the *Yakshagana* and *Talamaddale* performances sponsored by wealthy individuals and families. From the works collected and published in print form by the missionaries and administrators, it is clear that many of the canonical works of Kannada literature such as *Basava Purana, Jaimini Bharata* and *Gadugina Bharata* were popular through the modes of public recital (*gamaka*) and reading out to small groups in the houses of the landlords. The folk dramatic forms such as *Doddata*, *Bayalata* and *Yakshagana* were forms which combined entertainment, debate and knowledge of traditions.

Colonial education, missionary work and print culture changed much of this. Canonical literary works which had entered the popular domain were now reverted to the literary domain as printed texts, though they continued to be in the oral–folk domain also for a long time. With little linear continuity but with breaks and re-beginnings, print culture made a distinctive advance in Kannada. It did not cause a rupture but reinforced the existing traditions. Colonial education and employment created a small urban public sphere which began to patronise the new literary writings. There was also growth in the number of periodicals and magazines published from Belagavi, Dharwad and Bengaluru. From all available accounts, the readership for them was varied and uncertain. Every issue of the magazines carried appeals to defaulting subscribers and to possible new subscribers. Circulation depended on the postal department and this led to unending problems and confusions. The impression one gathers is that the patronage through subscription was sporadic and undependable. The literary journals published by institutions, like the Karnataka Vidya Vardhaka Sangha, Dharwad ('*Vagbhushana*'), had longevity and a steady readership, and played a seminal role in circulating and also encouraging new writings in Kannada. There were also significant shifts in the readers' tastes: for example, from the moral fables from *Aesop* and the *Panchatantra* to historical romances and realistic narratives. 'Secularisation' would perhaps be too strong a word to characterise this shift. From the details available about the themes of the short stories and novels submitted for the literary competitions organised by the Karnataka Vidya Vardhaka Sangha, it appears that historical romances, adventure stories and fictional works on historical figures were most popular. This was related to the rise of national consciousness which in turn drew on an idealised reconstruction of history.

However, at this point of time, there was no bifurcation into 'serious' and 'popular'. The *Navodaya* movement, a product of the negotiation with the English literary tradition and colonial modernity, had been by then already leading to the production of significant writing in many genres. The fine translations of English poetry into Kannada by Hattiangadi Narayana Rao and B. M. Sri. as well as short stories of Govinda Pai and Panje Mangesh Rao, had also been published. Academic institutions, Kannada associations and scholarly journals had started publishing these works. Most of B. M. Sri.'s translations and Bendre's poems were published in such journals years before they were collected in book form. *Navodaya* poetry was essentially poetry for singing and recitation, and some of the best-known poems reached a large audience through recitations at the literary conferences and meets. Bendre's recitation of the poem *Hakki Harutide Nodidira* (Look, How the Bird Flies) became a legend in itself. Kuvempu records in his autobiography the instantaneous admiration his poems received at poet's meets and literary gatherings. Many of the *Navodaya* poems continue to be sung today. Therefore, at least in the case of poetry, the distinction between 'serious' and 'popular' made no sense in the Kannada context. The enthusiasm and the spirit of the unification movement welcomed all Kannada literary works in a celebratory mood.

Probably the one outstanding example of the 'popular' making an impact was the publication of Galaganatha's novels which were serialised in the popular magazine *Sadbhodha Chandrike* which he edited and published. As already discussed in an earlier chapter, Galaganatha wrote in the model established by H. N. Apte, the Marathi writer of historical romances. As he himself admits, many of his novels are free translations and part-adaptations of the original novels by Apte. The historical works are examples of the pseudo-historical romances introduced by Bankim Chandra in Bengali. They are part of the effort to reconstruct a glorious Indian past through melodramatic narratives about the martial heroes of the past. The historical content is thin and lacking in authenticity.

Galaganatha drew with abandon on such sources, giving free vent to his imagination. He developed a style moving between the rhetorical Sanskritic register and the everyday spoken Kannada of North Karnataka. The overlong narratives are punctuated with chapter-long addresses to the reader, mourning the present decadence of India. His women characters are invariably *kshatra mahila*, or women from the warrior communities, sacrificing their lives to protect their chastity from the Muslim marauders. There are frequent authorial comments extolling the virtues of the Hindu women and the bravery of the warriors. All these are of a piece with the revivalist, emotional-nationalist sentiments of the period. The narratives are spiced with political and palace intrigues, unexpected turn of events and heroic feats.

In an extraordinary and elaborate autobiographical statement, Galaganatha speaks with candour about his writings. He describes himself as a villager, educated in small villages until he began to train at the Teacher Training College at Dharwad. He confesses that he has only a sketchy knowledge of Sanskrit, is unable to write the English alphabet and uses a Kannada which is only of utilitarian quality. He does not take any credit for the enormous popularity of his novels. He has only employed the formula of writing about well-known heroes of the past who are familiar to the readers. He uses historical episodes which are already a part of the readers' imagination. He says that he imaginatively puts himself in the position of his reader and addresses himself to this reader, Galaganatha. He is the author, publisher and book seller, all rolled into one.

With the publication of the first social novel in Kannada in 1899, the tradition of seriously engaged realistic novels started. The novel, *Indira Bai* written by Gulavadi Venkata Rao, seems to have attained instant popularity and the first edition sold out quickly. (However, Srinivas Havanur hints that since the author was with the police department, the department facilitated the sale of books.) However, the satirical novel with a frontal attack on the *matha* (monastery) and boldly celebrating widow remarriage, stirred up a controversy. So the novel was in circulation and drew immediate responses, though it would be difficult to make a conjecture about the number of readers it reached. *Indira Bai* was followed by *Vagdevi* (1905) by Bolara Babu Rao and *Indira* (1908) by Kerura Vasudevacharya. *Vagdevi* was a powerful satire against the pontiff of a *matha* and the corruption and sexual exploitation in and around the religious system. Kerura Vasudevacharya was a popular writer, essayist and dramatist, and editor of a popular magazine. *Indira* is a romantic novel which expresses an ambivalent attitude to modernity. While presenting romantic love between modern individuals, the novel satirises women social reformers and widows looking out for men to get married again. Sufficient details are not available to categorise Vasudevacharya as a popular writer. His free adaptations from Shakespeare and Oliver Goldsmith for the stage were certainly very popular.

From the late 1920s, fiction writing in Kannada gathered momentum; and the great realist novelists Shivaram Karanth and Kuvempu wrote their major novels in the 1930s and 40s. Karanth began by using the most popular subgenre of the novel—the novel of crime and detection—but abandoned it quickly in favour of the realistic social novel. Though he chose to make a living by writing, Karanth did not consider himself a popular writer. For him the novel was a medium for a deep philosophical enquiry into human experience. It would also be unjustified to categorise Kannada fiction of the time as popular or/and serious. The readership was small and did not make a distinction between serious and popular writing. The rise of the novel in England had witnessed the emergence of popular subgenres of fiction such as crime fiction, Gothic fiction and the city novel. At the same time, serious fiction was also serialised in the popular magazines of the time. Nothing comparable to this was witnessed in the Kannada context. The historical romance introduced by Galaganatha continued to be popular but the predominant form was realistic fiction.

The progressive literature movement of the 1940s and 50s had declared its intention to fight against the elitism in the literary establishment and vowed to write for the common reader. The two major writers who joined the movement for a while, Aa. Na. Kra. (A. N. Krishna Rao, 1908–71) and Ta. Ra. Su. (Ta. Ra. Subba Rao, 1920–84), were popular novelists who made a living by writing, and wrote prolifically and enjoyed immense popularity. Aa. Na. Kra. courted controversy by writing about sex workers in a style which was criticised for being titillating and bordering on obscenity. He also wrote social and domestic fiction which reached a wide readership. Unfortunately, the allegations of obscenity created a public rift in the progressive literary movement and also tarnished the image of the progressive movement itself. Writers like Niranjana dissociated themselves from Aa. Na. Kra.'s position. Both Aa. Na. Kra. and Ta. Ra. Su., despite their early radical posturing, turned out to be conservative in their attitudes. There is no doubt that both of them had a wide 'cult-readership' and were staunch supporters of Kannada. Aa. Na. Kra. was an erudite scholar who wrote on fine arts and encouraged practitioners of Hindustani and Karnataka music to render Kannada poems and compositions. His novels cover a vast range of characters and experiences though the form is generally the domestic, social-realist fiction. He developed a racy style almost wholly based on dialogues, eschewing long descriptions. His characters are not complex and are easily identifiable with the middle-class individuals of his times. There is usually a sub-structure of sentimentality and idealism in the narratives. His successful novels, like *Sandhya Raga*, make a direct emotional appeal to the readers.

Ta. Ra. Su. was a talented writer who experimented with different narrative modes. Some of his short stories are modernist in their innovative form. However, his popular novels employ two major genres, the historical novel and the domestic-social novel. His celebrated novel *Chandavalliya Thota* (The Chandavalli Farm) is a powerful and moving story of a family. Many of his novels were made into popular films. He was passionately devoted to the history of Chitradurga with its famous fort. He wrote *Durgasthamana*, a vast and complex novel about the great *Nayaka* who fought against Hyder Ali. He also wrote novels about the royal dynasties and heroes of Karnataka's past. His novel *Hamsa Geethe* was made into an iconic modernist film by G. V. Iyer. It appears as though Ta. Ra. Su. saw the two genres as two modes of expression for different and separate worlds of experience: namely, the domestic-social world of the urban middle class or the rural society, and the imagined world of Karnataka's history. While the social novels are written in a vigorous, attractive modern Kannada idiom, the historical novels employ the patented rhetorical, artificial register. (Among writers of historical novels, it is only Masti who makes historical characters speak in plain modern Kannada.) The valorisation of the martial values and heroism in the historical novels is a contrast to the everyday ethics of the family and the community in the social novels. Ta. Ra. Su. was patronised by a large enthusiastic readership which admired both types of novels. One of the most popular Kannada films *Naagarahaavu*

(The Cobra, 1972) was based on a trilogy he wrote (though he expressed his disappointment with the film).

Another writer of the progressive group, Basavaraj Kattimani (1919–89) was also a popular novelist who wrote about the rural society in the Belagavi region. He chose to be a professional writer; and titled his autobiography *A Novelist's Life.* He wrote forty novels, ten short story collections, and a vast quantity of discursive prose. A left-leaning writer, he was also partially sympathetic to the Gandhian freedom struggle. His major novels are about rural poverty and feudal exploitation. His novels *Swatantradedege* (Towards Freedom) and *Madi Madidavaru* (The Martyrs) locate the freedom struggle in rural Karnataka and offer a critique of the Congress-led freedom movement which is portrayed as elitist and driven by bourgeois interests. The real martyrs are the young idealist men and women who have left the comfort of an urban middle-class life and are now with the ordinary village folk. Fearless heroes and martyrs emerge from among the illiterate. The feudal land-owning class and Congress politicians side with the British because their class interests are threatened by the rising consciousness among the rural peasant and artisan classes. In a way, Kattimani effectively deconstructs the vague idealism and sentimental nationalism of the historical romances and the usual novels about the freedom movement. The stark naturalism of his fictional depiction of rural poverty, debt-ridden farmers, famines and pandemics, raises questions about the ultimate purpose of the freedom struggle which has left the unequal rural society unchanged. At the same time, there is no denying the emotional appeal of the freedom struggle. But for his controlled unadorned narrative style, the novels would have been not very different from those of Aa. Na. Kra. and Ta. Ra. Su.

Kattimani stirred up many controversies by his scathing satirical novels about depraved godmen and pontiffs of *mathas* who are shown to be womanisers and corrupt. His *Jarathari Jagadguru*, purportedly based on a real-life character, created a virtual storm and led to threats on the author. This was followed by several other satirical works on the pretensions of religious men. However, the better novels of Kattimani deal with the themes of untouchability, the caste system and women's suffering under patriarchy. Among his contemporaries, Kattimani had a thorough inwardness with the rural society as well as with the factory workers and trade unionists, which he demonstrates in *Jwalamukhiya Mele* (On a Volcano). He eschewed the weaknesses of Aa. Na. Kra., even while writing about the problems of prostitution.

Triveni (Anasuya Shankar, 1928–63), whose novels in the 1950s and 60s attracted a huge readership, was a talented writer who wrote twenty-one novels and several collections of short stories in a span of thirteen years, before she passed away at the age of thirty-five. Neglected by the literary-critical establishment as a popular woman writer, her writings have been receiving critical attention in recent years. A graduate in psychology who had some acquaintance with practising psychologists, she wrote powerful novels on the psychological problems faced by middle-class urban women. As C. N. Ramachandran (1999) argues, Triveni is able to depict powerfully the victimisation of women in a patriarchal system, though she does not subscribe to a radical feminist perspective. She ultimately seems to support the middle-class Hindu notions of the woman as the backbone of the family, of the family as an enduring institution, and valorises women who sacrifice their individual desires to support the family. But within this traditional framework of the domestic novel, Triveni is able to unravel the marginalisation of women, the cruelty and humiliation forced upon them and the severe threat to their mental health. The sensitive portrayal of mental distress and the critique of the social structures save her novels from becoming case histories. As C. N. Ramachandran says, Triveni threw open for the readers (especially women readers) the troubled inner world of middle-class women which was at once familiar and unexplored (Ramachandran 1999). The psychological novels also offer solutions through psychiatric intervention. The scores of women characters created by Triveni held a great appeal to the readers. A close reading of the novels discloses a sharp understanding of the female perspective on mental illness. In the better novels in this genre, such as *Bekkina Kannu* (Cat Eyes, 1954) and *Sharapanjara*, the focus is on human tragedies in a gender-unequal society.

Triveni wrote many novels on the experience of unfreedom, and the inability to resist (and the pressure to compromise with) familial and traditional values among middle-class young women. The desire for love and romance was to be suppressed, or young women may succumb to seduction by selfish men or face sexual exploitation. Most young women in the novels end up accepting the routine, dull life of a middle-class homemaker. The phenomenal popularity of Triveni depended on her ability to adhere to the ordinariness of her women characters who are deprived of freedom, choice and autonomy. Triveni's was undoubtedly a strong voice on women-centric issues. She created a large readership for other women writers who went on to flourish for nearly two decades.

Kakolu Saroja Rao, Vani, Aryamba Pattabhi (Triveni's sister) and Saisuthe were the forerunners among these.

D. R. Nagaraj describes the early phase of women's writing in Kannada as the '*Kutumbini*' phase which conceptualises the woman as inalienable from the Hindu family and as symbolising the traditional values of loyalty, willingness to sacrifice her individuality and as one who considers motherhood as the ultimate fruition and fulfilment of her existence (Nagaraj 1994). This is closely related to the cultural nationalism of the pre-independence period, as discussed by Tanika Sarkar (2003). However, women's writing does not express an uncritical acceptance of the traditional roles. Colonial modernity, education (though accessible only to a minority of women) and the impact of social reforms had made women conscious of the unjust treatment of women. The suffering of child widows, for example, was a theme which the women writers explored. Sympathy and understanding was sought from men without in any way questioning the normative structure of the Hindu family. The fear of the loss of *sheela*, chastity or sexual purity, was decisive for the women characters in their individual choices. There was also the fear of transgressive modernity which was seen as encouraging sexual immorality and false Westernisation among women. What is surprising is that many of these basic preoccupations seem to continue in Triveni and her contemporaries. Triveni's novels raise powerful questions about women's dependence on male authority and the imprisonment of women in the domestic chores and responsibilities which curtail their personal quest for happiness and freedom. In the novel *Hoovu-Hannu* (Flowers and Fruits), the protagonist, a widow, is forced to take to prostitution in order to save her daughter from the same fate. She disappears from her daughter's life, supporting her secretly. Unable to bear the hatred her daughter has towards her lost mother and towards her as a woman of no character, she decides to disappear again. As Seemanthini Niranjana points out, Triveni's novels do not offer the single woman anything other than suicide or madness if she does not agree to totally efface herself and turn herself into a nonexistent non-autonomous entity. Triveni is sharp and forthright in her analysis of how middle-class brahmin women are dwarfed and subjugated to a quotidian life and cannot even visualise a way out. Marriage, even widow remarriage as in *Hannele Chiguridaga* (When the Ripened Leaf Sprouts), is the only way out (Niranjana 1994).

P. Radhika argues that popular fiction by women in Kannada created a space for the expression and exploration of the subjectivity of the middle-class woman within frameworks which are far from radical (Radhika 2006).

There is no doubt at all that popular fiction allowed a large number of women readers to identify themselves with the women protagonists who seemed to live out by proxy their own struggles in middle-class families that are caught between tradition and a limited kind of modernity. Without considering this affective power of fiction, it is not possible to make sense of its popularity. The tragedies and the deep fears of loss and alienation experienced by the women protagonists held a powerful appeal to women readers. This is supported by the fact that popular films based on Triveni's novels and those by other women writers, where male characters were marginal figures, achieved a cult following. As Seemanthini Niranjana points out, in Triveni's novels, the notion of morality is clear and unambiguous, with prostitution and loose living at one extreme and motherhood and happy conjugality at the other, with no shades of gray in between. Such an uncomplicated notion of morality reinforces the received beliefs in conservative families and is very reassuring to the reader. There is the satisfaction of emotionally participating in the turmoils of the protagonist only to be reassured in the end, of the validity of the normative middle-class morality. This writing does not resonate with the changes occurring in the consciousness of women outside this comfort zone of the middle class during the 1960s and 70s. The modernist movement and the later Dalit-*Bandaya* movement saw the emergence of women writers who began to speak differently about resistance and rebellion.

Unfortunately, some of the distinctive voices of women writers did not receive the critical attention they deserved in the attempt to conceptualise women's writing as one homogeneous category. Anupama Niranjana's (1934–91) novels, which revisit the historical and puranic past, powerfully deconstruct the misogyny of traditional value systems. Her novel *Madhavi*, about a married woman who is 'rented out' to many men so that the husband can pay his *guru dakshina*, is devastating in its critique of revered past customs. H. Savithramma's *Rama, Ravana, Sita* remains unsurpassed as a retelling of the *Ramayana* from women's perspective. Despite the ambiguities pointed out by Sumitrabai, M. K. Indira's (1917–94) novel *Phaniyamma* unravels the hypocrisies of a local culture about sexuality and its fear of feminine sexuality (Sumitrabai 1994).

The phenomenal success and popularity of Triveni has made her writings an exemplary case in any discussion on popular fiction in Kannada. While she created a huge readership for her novels, the Kannada literary-critical establishment was tardy in according critical attention to her writings. Initially she was relegated to the ghetto of 'popular women's writing', and to the genre of 'popular domestic fiction'. Even a discerning critic like Giraddi Govindaraj expressed serious reservations about popular women's writing as lacking in seriousness and depth. He also commented on the stereotypical characters, predictable plots and the substructure of sentimentality in women's writing. Though he does not use the pejorative term 'kitchen literature', he sees it as confined to the circumscribed lives of middle-class women (Govindaraj 2012). During the earlier phase of writing by women in Kannada (from the early decades of the twentieth century), Masti Venkatesha Iyengar had harshly criticised Tirumalamba's writings. This attitude continues in the later phases. G. S. Amur is also sceptical about the quality of the writings by women. As Triveni's popularity established women writing as a distinctive part of Kannada literature, attempts were made to equate its popularity with superficiality. It was only much later that serious attention began to be paid to it.

The popularity of women writers was helped by two phenomena from the 1970s. One was the serialisation of novels in popular weeklies and monthly magazines such as *Sudha* and *Mayura*, and later in *Taranga*. Such was the popularity of serialised novels that some of the magazines ran four or five simultaneously. This boosted the subscription beyond expectations. The other phenomenon was the establishment of circulating libraries in urban localities, which lent books and magazines at an affordable per-day fee. The neighbourhood circulating libraries became a part of urban middle-class life and meeting places in the evenings. These libraries mainly stocked novels by women writers, and soon 'serious' writings disappeared from the shelves. Popular films based on women's novels further boosted their popularity. Critics began to take note of the phenomenon and the immediate reaction was to brand women's writing as 'kitchen literature', derogating it as a confined, repetitive, stereotypical writing, drawing freely on sentimentality. Some of these charges were justified because the genre of the domestic novel had been transformed into a superficial fictional form which substituted stereotypes for reality. The plots were predictable and the characters flat. There was a deceptive focus on 'women's issues' which lacked in depth. However, some of the criticism was nasty and suffered from over-generalisation.

The modernist (*Navya*) school of criticism had inherited from Arnold and F. R. Leavis a critical, dismissive perspective on popular literature as escapist and merely entertaining. This school had come down heavily on Aa. Na. Kra. and Ta. Ra. Su. as representative writers of popular fiction. A little later, both popular literature and films were dubbed as 'products of culture industry' without any serious theoretical engagement with popular culture. One of the most influential of such critical essays was by U. R. Ananthamurthy, on the popular film *Naagarahaavu* based on Ta. Ra. Su.'s novel. Ananthamurthy also critiqued S. L. Bhyrappa's novels as 'popular' in the negative sense. (This will be discussed in the last section of this chapter.) Shankar Mokashi Punekar was probably the only serious critic to defend popular fiction in Kannada. It was in the *Navya* phase that a wedge was driven between mainstream serious literature and popular literature. As discussed above, Giraddi Govindaraj was also dismissive about women's writing. Unfortunately, some good novels bore the brunt of this critical debate and were deprived of the critical attention they deserved. It was only decades later that feminist critics began to discover some of the 'lost women's texts' and to subject them to critical scrutiny. The more serious consequence was that the majority of the common readers began to see serious writing as the product of a small ultra-sophisticated elite group. It was only in the late 1990s that a cultural studies perspective on popular literature and culture began to develop. Meanwhile the powerful critique of modernist fiction launched by Poornachandra Tejaswi and his own later writings had opened up different fictional modes which drew on some of the sub-genres of popular fiction. The *Bandaya* movement also rejected modernist fiction and moved towards a new orality and began to use the creative resources of folk and popular literatures. The new generation of fiction writers today is reaching out to an urban readership, with some writers like Vasudhendra establishing an impressive and wide readership. The categories like 'serious' and 'popular' are problematic in the present context.

***

We will conclude this chapters with a discussion on the most prominent practitioner of contemporary popular literature in Kannada. S. L. Bhyrappa (1931–2025) has not been identified with any of the literary movements in Kannada. He began to write in 1961. Though two of his earlier works have been published recently, they have not received much critical attention; nor have they enjoyed the popularity of his other novels. So one could say that his career as a novelist began in 1961 with the publication of *Dharmashri*, a novel in which the main theme is the protagonist's conversion to Christianity and eventual return to the Hindu fold. In narrative style, language and characterisation the novel belongs to the genre of the domestic-social novel in the realistic mode. It could easily pass for a novel by Ta. Ra. Su. with its regional ambience and the quotidian life it depicts. The central crisis of the novel relates to the protagonist Satya's decision to convert to Christianity in order to marry the woman he loves, Lily. This causes him intense agony and a sense of guilt. In his typical analytical style, Bhyrappa probes into the motives driving the protagonist and the ambivalence surrounding his decision. He realises that he would be unhappy and feels fragmented with his conversion. The crisis is resolved when he returns to the Hindu fold through the Aryadharma rituals. What could have been an interesting love story ends up justifying the saying from the *Bhagavad Gita*, 'It is better to die in one's own *dharma*; it is death to choose another *dharma*'. In this early novel, Bhyrappa demonstrates his considerable talent in authentically recreating a realistic ambience and credible characters. But the novel also shows how the novelist in him yields to the desire to assert a certain interpretation of an ideological kind. The lively narrative with interesting characters like Shankara (an RSS member), Rachamma and Lily, becomes a little programmatic at the end. Satya's conversion to Christianity is not very convincing. The novel has seen over fifteen reprints and is still in circulation.

Bhyrappa's *Vamshavriksha* (1965) appeared in the same year as Ananthamurthy's *Samskara*, and is an uncanny foil to it. *Samskara* is about Praneshacharya, the epitome of brahminical tradition, going through the angst of realising that the dharmic beliefs he had relied on are inadequate in confronting the primordial drives of human nature. His individual existentialist search is all the more painful because he also has to find a solution for the pending last rites for the dead Naranappa who had given up brahminical customs to lead the life of a depraved sensualist. In *Vamshavriksha*, Shrotri, who had adhered to the values of self-abnegation and the sanctity of the family, in the end discovers that he himself was born to an adulterous relationship. Meanwhile the wife of his dead son, Katyayani, falls in love with her teacher Raja Rao, marries him and is forced to give up her son Sheeni. In this vast novel with several complex characters, Bhyrappa attempts to probe philosophically into serious issues such as abstinence and indulgence, and interrogates the family as an extra-individual value but also as a curb on individual choices. The novelist also introduces the themes of *dharma* and *prakriti*. There are powerfully written episodes in the novel. But the attempt by the author to valorise Shrotri as an ideal figure and to punish the transgressors like Katyayani and Raja Rao, brings an unnecessary imbalance to an otherwise powerful work.

Daatu (1973) is a novel about the caste system and untouchability. Satyabhama, the daughter of the village (brahmin) priest falls in love with the son of the local politician, a shudra. The politician father is wily, self-centred and treats the scandal of the proposed inter-caste marriage as a game of caste politics, weighing the possible benefits for his career. Satyabhama's father thrashes her inhumanly, but she decides to follow him to the village. Her lover oscillates and is persuaded to marry an influential person's daughter from his own caste. Satyabhama becomes an ascetic and recluse. Her brother, a budding politician and a businessman, plays a crucial role in all the happenings. Throughout the narrative, questions are raised not only about the caste system but about the sincerity of those who claim to follow it. The portrayal of the local society, the politics of caste, and the protest against caste by the local youth are the mainstay of the novel. Bhyrappa raises uncomfortable questions about the resistance to the caste system. The hurried and somewhat contrived ending of the novel is a weak point. Satyabhama's transformation is ambivalent and hardly answers the questions the novel raises.

Two major retellings—of the *Mahabharata* and the *Ramayana*—are Bhyrappa's remarkable achievements. *Parva* (1979), a vast novel, is an extraordinary retelling in which the puranic, symbolic and transcendental aspects of Vyasa's *Bharata* are stripped to the bones. Bhyrappa rewrites the epic from a starkly naturalistic point of view (some critics have described it as an anthropological perspective) where all actions are results of the earthy, worldly passions and primordial drives of human beings. The Pandavas are born not by godly boons but out of co-habitation with men for the purpose of begetting male children. Such a denuded, existentialist perspective is bound to shock the received perceptions of the readers. The result is a vast narrative with extraordinary characters and the drama of many conflicts.

Uttarakanda (2017) is a retelling of the *Ramayana* from Sita's point of view. It turns out to be a no-holds-barred, scathing critique of Rama, palace politics and patriarchy. Bhyrappa, who has been criticised for his misogynist and anti-feminist novel *Kavalu* (2010), creates in this novel a Sita who walks out of Rama's grand ceremonial ritual and returns to Valmiki's ashrama to will her own death, sleeping in the furrow of the land. Once again, the style is realistic and anti-puranic. There are no gods and Rama's *dharma* is shown to be merely masked politics. *Uttarakanda* is a devastating novel and it is difficult to believe that the author of *Kavalu* and *Avarana* (2007) has written this.

The critical consensus in Kannada however is that *Gruhabhanga* (1970) is Bhyrappa's finest work. From a reading of his autobiography, *Bhitti* (1996), one can see that this novel draws heavily on Bhyrappa's own experiences. The novel is about a region Bhyrappa is familiar with, and he reconstructs it as it could have been in the pre-independence period. It is the story of a family and a village crowded with powerful characters. There are no philosophical questions or ideological discussions. The novel, to use a cliché, is a piece of life. It is about human beings who have to struggle against circumstances beyond their control and against their own nature which controls them. There is no redemption and no possibility of transcendence. But even in this unfree world, human emotions and relationships thrive. There is also a powerful sense of the community which is not idealised, and there is no way the characters can ignore it.

S. L. Bhyrappa is a phenomenon in Kannada literature with a huge and loyal readership, and most of his novels have sold in phenomenal numbers. He would seem to be an exemplary popular writer of fiction. However, his prolific writing is capable of interrogating the use of the category 'popular'. Bhyrappa's novels explore vastly different experiences; and his innovative, creative imagination is impressive. No modern writer in Kannada has attained the popularity that he has. For his innumerable devoted readers, Bhyrappa is a cult figure, a sage and a philosopher; on the other hand, no other Kannada writer has so consistently received negative criticism from mainstream Kannada critics. It has been an adversarial relationship with Bhyrappa missing no opportunity to condemn the literary establishment, especially the *Navya* school, as elitist and imitative of the Western models. He has been scathing in criticising them as blind followers of Camus, Kafka and Sartre. Controversially, he has openly supported right-wing ideologies and made interventions justifying even the most anti-democratic actions of right-wing politics. What then explains his extraordinary popularity? What are the main charges made by serious critics against his fiction? What is his position in contemporary popular Kannada fiction?

Readers have found his novels accessible. Bhyrappa has rarely deviated from the realistic narrative mode, which assures the readers that the novels are about them. The ordinariness of the characters facilitates the reader's emotional identification with them. Though Bhyrappa is capable of a vast range of registers and styles, he has remained steadfast in employing a style of writing which remains close to the everyday spoken language. Though his major novels employ metaphors and motifs, they remain unobtrusive, and he consciously eschews a dense symbolic style. He introduces a certain weightiness to his novels by using the narrative to raise philosophical questions. One may doubt their profundity and question whether they force a wilful bending of the narrative to support 'a thesis' (U. R. Ananthamurthy's comment). But the readers are impressed by the seriousness which they feel imbues the narratives. Even his most loyal readers have never described him as entertaining. This makes his popularity enigmatic. It would be difficult to compare him with any of the popular writers discussed earlier in this chapter.

THIRTEEN

Folk Literature and Performance

Any study of folk literature in Kannada has to necessarily look at three major trajectories which constitute the discipline of folklore studies. The first two began almost simultaneously. One was the interest shown by Christian missionary scholars who introduced print culture in the then *Kannadanādu* and used printing technology to collect and anthologise folk literature. This was an enterprise which ran parallel to their work of 'discovering' the literary texts of the Kannada tradition and publishing scholarly modern editions of these texts. In lexicography, especially in Reverend Ferdinand Kittel's work, the description of the Kannada language also included proverbs and puzzles which were later included by scholars under 'folk literature'. The major contribution came from Hermann Mögling and Kittel (Havanur 2021). Literary historians have attributed the interest in folk literature among European scholars and missionaries to the effort to understand the common people, their belief systems and values. As indicated in several chapters, this was not just a part of their proselytising mission. There was a genuine interest in Kannada folk literature as a distinctive expression in the Kannada language. (Mögling, for instance, collected and published about 300 proverbs in Kannada which are quoted in Havanur's *Hosagannadada Arunodaya*.) It is also possible to explain the interest in folk literature as part of the European Romantic movement with its interest in folk and cultural expressions beyond the literary and urban modes.[1] The relationship between the German philosophers of the eighteenth and nineteenth centuries and British Romanticism is well established. Most of the missionary scholars were from Germany and presumably were familiar with these developments.

Mögling collected and published several texts, some of which were recognised as canonical works and were widely popular. These include *Jaimini Bharata* by Lakshmeesha and Kumara Vyasa's *Bharata* (also known as *Gadugina Naranappana Bharata*). He also published *Basava Puranamu* and a *Yakshagana* text. He edited and published one hundred *kirtanas* (poetic compositions by the *Dasa* poets which were rendered musically

[1] Critics have commented on the influence of Bishop Percy's collection of folk poems on William Wordsworth and others. The interest in folk literature was part of the German scholarship in the eighteenth century.

and/or recited). His edited works also include folk poems. Mögling published a book of 300 Kannada proverbs under the title *Lokokti Vidhānā*. German missionaries also collected and translated *Tulu Paddanas*, folk songs and riddles.

Kittel contributed articles to *The Indian Antiquary* (1873) on the belief systems in Coorg. As pointed out earlier, his dictionary of the Kannada language includes proverbs and colloquial expressions which are part of the folklore.

Kittel's contemporary J. F. Fleet wrote in detail about Kannada ballads and published seventeen historical ballads.[2] A. C. Burnell and C. Manor also made useful contributions to the study of folklore (Paramashivaiah 1979; Havanur 2021).

The other trajectory has much to do with the rise of a Kannada consciousness from the last decades of the nineteenth century, which led to the *Navodaya* (Kannada renaissance) movement in the early decades of the twentieth century. The work of the missionaries, scholars and administrators had laid the foundation of a Kannada subnationalism by creating a sense of the Kannada literary tradition and of *Kannadanādu* of the past, the latter owing to the collection of epigraphs and *kaifiyat* by Colonel Colin Mackenzie and others. The printing of the canonical works reinforced the idea of an ancient Kannada literary tradition. This in turn also led to a serious interest in folk literature, especially in North Karnataka. The literary group *Geleyara Gumpu*, established by Bendre, included members from Halasangi led by Madhura Chenna (Halasangi Channamallappa). While Bendre was rooted in folk traditions and therefore participated in the collection and publication of folk poetry, Madhura Chenna presented a paper on folk literature at the Kannada literary conference in 1923. This is considered as the first major statement on the relevance of studying folk literature in Kannada. Another member of the group, Betageri Krishnasharma was instrumental in the publication of *Garatiya Haadu* (1931), one of the most influential anthologies of folk poems, in this case using the three-liner *tripadi* stanza form which itself is considered a folk poetic form in contrast to the classical metrical forms derived from Sanskrit poetry. From the 1920s, field work, collection and compilation of folk literature continued uninterrupted, though folk literature had to wait till the 1960s to be recognised as an academic discipline in the universities. In most cases, it was first recognised as one of the courses at the postgraduate

---

[2] Fleet published the Kannada ballads he had collected, in *Indian Antiquary* from 1885 to 1890 (quoted in Paramashivaiah 1979, 2016).

level in Kannada literature, and then as a separate discipline. This phase of academic and institutional recognition led to significant research and theorisation in the study of folk literature. Several scholars such as D. Javaregowda, J. S. Paramashivaiah and P. K. Rajashekhar came to be associated with the academic discipline. The discipline expanded itself to include historical, anthropological and cultural studies of folklore. Folk performative arts, artefacts emerging from folk practices, rituals, dance and musical forms constituted the material for folklore studies. As J. S. Paramashivaiah (known as Jee. Sham. Pa.) points out, the shift was from folk literature to folklore under the influence of theoretical frameworks of Western scholarship.

The inception of folk studies as a discipline also energised discussions of the 'absent presence' of folk literature as an alternative tradition in Kannada literary tradition. Scholars point out that from the first extant book of poetics in Kannada, *Kavirajamarga*, there are references, albeit negative and sometimes dismissive, to folk traditions in poetry and performance. There has been a long and inconclusive discussion regarding the genres '*Chattana*' and '*Bedande*'. While the consensus is that they are distinctly folk forms and different from the known classical forms derived from Sanskrit, there is no agreement on what exactly they were. Most critics are inclined to treat them as forms of *Haadu Gabba*, literally 'poetry for the ear', that which is sung accompanied by music. Other references by Rajashekhara and Madhurakavi are negative, describing such traditions of composition as '*gramya*' (with connotations of 'unsophisticated' or 'non-literary'). They even hint that these compositions are 'vulgar' (Seetharamaiah 1994). On the basis of such references, it has been argued that mainstream Kannada literature patronised by kings and noblemen, and circulating only among the literati, either refused to acknowledge folk traditions or derided them as unacceptable to a refined sensibility. This is also seen as an instance of the marginalisation of 'minor' or subaltern literary-cultural traditions by the dominant mainstream culture. However, another argument is that the mainstream Kannada literary tradition appropriated these traditions to enrich its resources. For example, the concept of *Desi*, so crucial to the Kannada tradition, also involved the process of creative appropriation of regional folk traditions. Pampa, the first great poet, affirms that good poetry makes its passage through both *Mārga* and *Desi* modes (K. V. Narayana in Shivarudrappa 2016). He does not see them as adversarial. The poetic practice of Pampa, Ranna and Andayya is evidence of the openness to the local and regional modes of composition. There is also evidence that folk songs, dance, music and performative arts were popular among the masses. The reference to *Pagarana* (*Hagarana*) is certainly to a comic or farcical form of folk performance (Seetharamaiah 1994). D. R. Nagaraj's (2012) concept of regional *Desi* is useful in negotiating with the presence of folk traditions.

The moot question is, can we reconstruct the history of Kannada literature on the basis of the major texts of folk literature made available through the work of the modern scholars? Serious questions have been raised regarding the validity and authenticity of literary histories which do not acknowledge the need to reconstruct these histories based on the canonical texts recognised as 'literary' (including the present one!). Two major folk epics, *Manteswamy Kavya* and *Male Madeshwara Kavya*, both now available in scholarly editions, have led to a radical questioning of the experiences, value systems and the world view considered as reflecting the Kannada sensibility merely on the basis of canonical works. Ignoring the problem of essentialising the Kannada tradition, one could seriously ask why the folk epics represent a counter-culture and wholly different ways of experiencing and understanding the world. The following section examines the folk epics in some detail before returning to these questions.

***

Manteswamy Kavya is an epic narrative about a folk hero named Manteswamy, or Manteda Lingappa and *Dharege Doddavaru* (*The Great One*). He is said to be a historical personage, probably of the fifteenth century, but goes through deification characteristic of cumulative oral epics. There are also extraordinary shifts in historical time and space because in the major episode he goes to Kalyana for a trial of 'the truth of Basavanna', the twelfth-century leader of the *Vachanakaras* and founder of the Lingayat religion. He is also referred to as Allama himself or as a spiritual guru resembling Allama. It is clear that the oral epic creates the powerful figure of Manteswamy as a symbolic interlocutor of Basava's religion which had later lost its vision of radical equality and was dominated by the powerful priest class of the *Jangamas*. In the epic, these later developments are worked backwards into Basava's own times by portraying the fake *Jangamas* feasting at Basava's *Mahamane*, the legendary home in Kalyana. Manteswamy deliberately enters Kalyana as a leper with puss oozing from his open wounds, covered in filth and carrying the carcass of a calf on his shoulder. He is refused admission by the guard who also beats him. Manteswamy lies down in a trash heap. Meanwhile the 'bell without the tongue' tied up at the entrance begins to ring and the drum begins to beat on its own announcing that a guru greater than Basava himself is in Kalyana. Basava and his wife Neelamma recognise Manteswamy, The Great One, and invite him to their home. He refuses and when they tug at his arms and feet to force him to go with them, the limbs fall apart and they carry them in a bag along with the carcass of the calf. The *Jangamas* are horrified and, accusing Basava of blasphemy, leave the *Mahamane*. Manteswamy performs a miracle when all their *istalingas* (the *lingas* worn on the body by Lingayats) disappear. The episode exposes the false pretentions of the *Jangamas* to Basava. Manteswamy now appears to him as an emanation of holy light. The extraordinary episode in the epic syncopates centuries of spiritual and religious history relating to Basava and the Lingayat religion. It has been argued somewhat convincingly that Manteswamy belongs to the Madiga caste, an 'untouchable' caste. The epic presents the cultural and spiritual resistance of the downtrodden communities which had in Basava's time converted to the Lingayat religion. The texture and language of the epic evidences the close connections of these communities with the Lingayat religion and more particularly the *Siddha* mystical traditions (Nagaraj 2012). Manteswamy is portrayed as a hero who conquers several persons only to make them his disciples. Some of these individuals, like Rachappaji, belong to the *panchala* group of communities who are artisans and blacksmiths. Many critics interpret this as an allegory of the major shift in agrarian practices where iron implements played a key role. The epic recounts the journeys and conquests of Manteswamy until he decides to repose. Most of the episodes follow the pattern of resistance, conquest and discipleship of individuals Manteswamy encounters. The narrative unravels complex social worlds wherein patriarchy co-exists with women's resistance and powerful religious centres are seen as hierarchical institutions which attempt to harass Manteswamy himself. Nagaraj (1999) describes Manteswamy as a spiritual rebel emerging from the subaltern classes.

What stands out in the epic is the way in which the composers and singers of the epic show an intimate knowledge of the Shaiva mystical traditions, the Lingayat religion and the spiritual traditions which were very different from the mainstream Vedic religious traditions. While the *Kalamukha* and *Kapalika* Shaiva traditions preceded the *Vachanakara* movement, the non-Vedic spiritual–mystical traditions, whose influence is strong on this epic, were an all-India phenomenon. The oral epic steers clear of the major religions of the medieval period. The 'structure of feeling' in the epic also differs from that of the Bhakti traditions. The significance of these factors is that they raise questions about the relationship between the major religions in Karnataka and the vast communities which celebrate deified folk heroes such as Manteswamy, Male Madeshwara, Junjappa and Beerappa. The major religions patronised by royal dynasties and fiefdoms do not seem to have affected these communities at any depth. Contemporary popular religious culture in Karnataka is not very different despite the political hegemony of religions such as Lingayatism.

***

Do the oral epics present a counter-cultural world? Are the differences substantial enough to challenge our existing notions of 'Kannada Culture', though the essentialist term itself is problematic? In the reading of the present author, the epics as well as many folk poems do represent a set of experiences, beliefs and values which are marginal to the mainstream culture. What is taboo and considered 'impure' in mainstream culture is accepted and at times celebrated. Consumption of meat, an animistic–ritualistic world view, the deep intimacy with nature, etc., are adhered to. There is a deliberate resistance against institutionalised religion and royal regimes. If one remembers that the major Kannada literary texts of the medieval period are centred around major religions and that subaltern communities are almost absent in these narratives, it is this life-world which is foregrounded in the oral epics. Their way of life manifests itself in rich detail in these oral epics. Close attention is paid to the material aspects of life, especially the world of labour and of making things.

However, it is not a pristine world of egalitarian values. There is clear indication that the egalitarian values of tribal life are compromised by the feudal agrarian social world. Along with rebellious women, there are many who wish to conform to the cultural stereotypes of womanhood. Patriarchy seems to be gradually usurping the women-centric life style.

The cosmos of the oral narratives, which is very different from the one depicted in the canonical Kannada works, is revealed in the creation myths with which they begin. In contrast to the puranic creation myth of Brahma creating the world, the folk epics transform the hero himself into the creator. For example, Manteswamy, in the creation myth section, is described as divine or eternal light who bifurcates the cosmos into 'below and above' and then goes on to create the puranic gods of the Indian tradition. Yet, when he decides to descend from Kailasa to the earth he becomes a mendicant in search of disciples. In complete contrast to the later puritanic Hindu traditions, he is depicted as entering into a 'blue' trance by smoking '*bhangi*', a species of opium. Food styles and modes of worship tabooed in later Hinduism are not only accepted but celebrated in the epic. His carrying the carcass when he visits Kalyana is a symbolic way of questioning the stigma attached to professions practised by certain Dalit communities. Interestingly, in several *Vachanas* Basava claims that he is born to a servant couple and his ancestry is of the Dalit *sharanas* such as Dohara Kakkayya. Manteswamy himself is respectful towards Basava and tells him that he is innocent and cannot distinguish the genuine *sharanas* from the fake ones. Most scholars agree that the Manteswamy tradition exhibits an impressive amount of intertextuality with canonical literary works of the Lingayat tradition, especially *Prabhulingaleele* of Chamarasa and the *Shunya Sampadane* (edited or compiled by different individuals from the fourteenth to sixteenth century). Among the many contentious interpretations of the epic, the present writer would subscribe to the view that the Manteswamy epic works through cultural memories of the *Vachanakara* movement, but is also strongly rooted in the *Natha*, *Kapalika* and Shaiva *Tantra* traditions. In addition, it reconstructs cultural memories through the lens of Dalit communities. An amazing example is that the priest class, *Jangamas*, who believe in *Kattu Linga* (that is, in the iconic *linga*) itself are shown as false followers. Those who refuse to equate the two and assert their faith only in the *linga* worn on the body are true followers of Basava and are named as such by Manteswamy. Interestingly, all of them belong to the untouchable communities. This has also been interpreted as evidence of the resistance from the subaltern communities against the decline of egalitarian values in the Lingayat religion.

The conquests made by Manteswamy are only aimed at adopting the conquered as *sisumaga* (child/son) or disciple. This is symbolic of the effort to make the Manteswamy cult expansive and inclusive. Banjagere Jayaprakash interprets this as referring to the conversion of some of the artisan communities which had not come within the fold of the Lingayat religion earlier. The interpretation is based on the premise that the Manteswamy cult, though resistant and critical, was still a part of the Shaivite religion.

The narrative proceeds to record Manteswamy's sojourns, and the episodes portray him as possessing magical powers and not hesitating to impose severe trials on those who ultimately swear allegiance to him. The narrative, with many variations and cumulative additions, provides thick details of the social world, and an equally powerful depiction of human emotions and relationships. Episodes from the epic are sung in many all-night sessions even today. The oral epic has to be understood only in the matrix of ritual, performance and orality in which we find it even today. From a literary point of view, one finds an extraordinary poetic texture, repetition and knitting together of motifs and symbols, and the energy of a performative–narrative mode.

Manteswamy confronts the collaboration between the *Jangamas* and the royal power in one of the episodes. When Manteswamy, according to the *Jangamas*, desecrates the communal dinner, they advise the king to send him poisoned food which is accidentally eaten by the two princes. The king repents his deed and the princes are brought back to life. In such episodes, Manteswamy is unrelenting till he wins over disciples, but never causes any harm to them. These are different from the martial values celebrated in the medieval Kannada texts. As Purushottama Bilimale (1997) comments, the hero in such folk narratives is not divine-born, is an ordinary individual who faces persecution and suffering, and is generally a victim who dies early while trying to fight for his people.

Though it is nearly impossible to date oral/folk epics and narratives, the values and belief systems celebrated in them are counter to those in the literary texts. This continues in the folk ballads of the early modern period and later. The famous ballad on Tipu Sultan (*Bheshak Tamasha, Tiger Nishana*) portrays him as a brave tragic hero who 'shook the British Crown'. There is no mention of his alleged religious bigotry. An Urdu ballad probably composed in the Malnad region compares him to Karna. Ballads on Kittur Chennamma, one of the first queens to take on the British, and on Sangolli Rayanna, her follower, are powerful anti-colonial compositions. This is in contrast to the *stuthi* poems (tributary poems) composed by well-known *Navodaya* poets on British kings, queens and officers.

***

Male Madeshwara Kavya is sung and performed by singers who are called *guddas* (disciples). They belong to a group of castes, and young men from these castes are dedicated to the worship of Madeshwara through a ritual. They become part of the itinerant group of singers who are dedicated to the singing of the epic especially during the season of the pilgrimage to the shrine associated with Madeshwara. He is also said to be a historical personage from an untouchable caste and there is similarity between his and Manteswamy's confrontation with religious institutions and feudal power.

In one of the episodes, Madeshwara is referred to as a Madiga (an untouchable caste). He is also described as a *sharana* (a devotee, or a Shaivite follower, and more specifically a follower of Basava's religion) who makes a journey from the 'North' to the 'South'. This is interpreted as the journey of a *sharana* to the southern regions of Karnataka, to the hilly and forest areas, home to wild animals and to two major tribes, *Soligas* and *Jenu Kurubas*. By making tribal men and women his disciples, Madeshwara establishes his own cult. The epic of Madeshwara is also a cumulative oral narrative which is many-layered like an archeological site, with layers belonging to several phases of civilisation and history. Hi. Chi. Boralingaiah argues that some sections of the epic, especially the one relating to Sankamma, are about the transition from the hunting and food-gathering nomadic phase to primitive agriculture (Boralingaiah 2018). In his opinion, this transition is accompanied by the gradual establishment of a patriarchy with its emphasis on the woman's fidelity and chastity. For example, in Sankamma's episode, it is Neelayya, a *Soliga*, who is attracted by the beautiful Sankamma and marries her. The couple is forced to leave his family, as she is harassed by the relatives for being barren. They construct a *podi* (hut, or 'dwelling place') in the middle of a thick forest. When it is time for Neelayya to go away for nine months for hunting and food gathering, he is troubled by thoughts of other men seducing Sankamma in his absence. He, like a patriarchal male, suspects that she would be susceptible and yield because, 'You can never trust a woman'. When he asks her to take an oath of fidelity and chastity she bluntly refuses; and she asks him to take back the bride price he had given to marry her and let her go. This is an extraordinary assertion of freedom. But Neelayya subjects her to extreme cruelty by denuding her, tying her down with creepers and writing seventy-seven charms and a magic circle which no one can cross alive. He then leaves.

Madeshwara, who has settled down among the seventy hills, comes to the hut and releases Sankamma. She begs him to relieve her of barrenness with the gift of a child. He tries to warn against this. She does not budge and declares that she shall refuse to lie and claim that it was Madeshwara who has saved her from barrenness. The most extraordinary line spoken by Madeshwara in this conversation is, 'Do you think I am Brahma, Vishnu or Ishwara to give the boon of instant motherhood!' The narrative has a symbolic ritualistic description of the cure for her barrenness, which is open to many interpretations.

Other episodes describe Madeshwara's wanderings and acquiring of disciples, ultimately leading to the conquest and destruction of the Shramana king. Madeshwara's arrival at the seventy hills and forests is preceded by his failed attempts to find refuge in the three Lingayat monasteries. In each of them, he is treated as a bonded labourer and humiliated. He curses them before leaving. Like the epic of Manteswamy, *Male Madeshwara Kavya* also represents the disillusionment of the lower castes and the untouchables at the transformation of a radical egalitarian religion, which had received them into its fold but has now become a hierarchical institution of oppressive power. Manteswamy and Male Madeshwara are rebels who register their protest and go on to establish their own cults among the oppressed communities. As argued earlier, it is difficult to read a chronological history into the cumulative epics, but it cannot be denied that they encode the cultural memories of what happened after the *Vachanakara* movement of the twelfth century.

In the early section of the epic, Madeshwara is described as 'Puttalinga' who falls down to the earth when Lord Shiva shakes his long tresses. Thus he descends to the earth carrying an element of Shiva's power. Despite his depiction as a lonely wanderer with no known parentage, the epic deifies him as god. In fact, in one episode, to escape from the humiliation of being a nameless orphan born of unknown parents, he enters into the womb of one Uttarajamma and takes birth again! As Boralingaiah points out, Madeshwara is imagined as a non-Vedic god who is adept at magic and charms. He can perform tricks as well as miracles. The epic is a symbolic narrative about the establishment of a cult that takes into its fold tribal and primitive agrarian communities.

Another famous and popular episode is about Bevina Hatti Kalamma, a self-respecting stubborn woman who is the matriarch of a powerful agrarian family. When Madeshwara comes to her dwelling and asks for *kwaranya* (gift of food), which would symbolically mean surrender to him, she refuses and vows never to yield to him. Madeshwara uses his magical powers to destroy her wealth and her home, and for even making her helpless and nude. As many commentators have pointed out (Boralingaiah 2018), the episode allows Kalamma to emerge as the assertion of strong womanhood and shows Madeshwara in a poor light as a misogynist.

The Shravana Dore episode also encodes a historical memory. 'Shravana' is 'Shramana', indicating that the king is a Jaina. He is a tyrant who has kept in captivity even gods. Madeshwara not only conquers him but orders footwear made of his skin and wears them. Obviously, the episode looks back to the violent clashes between the Jainas and the Shaivites in Karnataka's history.

***

The radical difference embodied by folk epics and poetry was not recognised in Kannada criticism and literary histories for a long time. One of the reasons for this is the uncritical valorisation of folk literature as the expression of the 'innocent, unlettered minds', without paying attention to the critique it offered. Under the sway of the nationalist movement and the Kannada subnationalist movement which converged, folk poetry, especially those associated with the daily chores of rural women, was celebrated as *Garatiya Haadu*, songs of the ideal wife and homemaker. In Tanika Sarkar's analytical framework, the anonymous women folk poets were the ideal Hindu women—devoted wives, loving mothers, and self-effacing sacrificers. That the folk songs were also sites of resistance and raised uncomfortable questions about patriarchal norms was ignored. As Shailaja Hiremath argues, critics and folklorists expressed the fear that modernity and autonomy would destroy the ideal of the '*garati*'. Protecting Indian (read Hindu) culture was to protect this pristine innocence of women (Hiremath 2022).

The other form of the valorisation of folk literature was to treat it as the main 'mother root' (*Tayiberu*) and nourisher of mainstream literature without examining the nature of the relationship between the two. There is evidence that there was mutual exchange and that the boundaries between the two were porous. For example, *Yakshagana* freely appropriated from canonical Kannada texts. Until recently, the *arthadhari*, the interpreter in the *Talamaddale* folk form, would draw on his intimate knowledge of classical Kannada texts. Equally important is that some of the canonical texts like Naranappa's *Gadugina Bharata*, *Jaimini Bharata* and *Channabasava Purana* were familiar to the rural people through recitation and *gamaka*. So were the compositions of the *Dasas*. There were vibrant rural communities which listened to and learnt by heart the compositions of poets like Shishunala Sharif. In fact, the vocative mode of these compositions presumes an intimate relationship between the composers and the community.

Another aspect of the appropriation of folk literature was to marginalise the sociocultural fault lines revealed in it. For instance, *Kerege Hara* (Sacrificed to the Pond) contains the motif of the sacrifice of a woman (sometimes a child) to save the village pond or to beseech the blessings of gods to send rains to fill the pond. In the famous folk narrative poem, a powerful family decides to sacrifice the daughter-in-law in order to save a pond when the son is away. Neither is she consulted nor is she informed about it till very late. Her own natal home refuses to intervene. The helpless victim is valorised in Kannada criticism as the ideal noble woman who saves the honour of the family and the pond. That her husband after his return also follows her is treated as a tribute to her womanhood. Even an astute critic like K. V. Subbanna praised this poem as a celebration of 'Kannada values'. Feminist critics have read the folk song as revealing the cruelty of the patriarchal order masked by notions of ideal womanhood. It has already been pointed out how one episode in *Male Madeshwara Kavya* describes the extreme cruelty of the husband Neelayya. The wife exhibits extraordinary courage in refusing to take a vow of fidelity and is even prepared to walkout of marriage. Thus, Kannada folk literature contains a contradictory mix of patriarchal victimisation of women and expressions of her autonomy. Scholars like Boralingaiah and Venkatesh Indwadi argue that such contradictions reflect the transition from food-gathering pastoralism and hunting to agriculture. The transition meant a shift from a woman-centric world view to a male-centric one. As the residual cultural elements do not altogether disappear, one finds a curious mixture of contradictory world views. The major folk epics in Kannada also record the marginalisation of mother goddesses along with the deification of the male hero. Increasingly, mother goddesses appear negatively as '*mari*', and are treated as slaves to the heroes or the male gods (as in *Male Madeshwara Kavya*).

On the other hand, the folk songs provide expression to the personal lives of women, although there is a tendency to idealise and stereotype them. In the poems, the woman is not just the idealised mother but also a daughter who has lost her natal home, a wife oppressed by the in-laws and the invisible labourer. She is a devotee, a dreamer and a figure of subdued protest. She emerges on her own in the domestic sphere and in the social world which has little space for her. The codes of ethics and sexual morality are far less rigid than they are in the literary texts, and many songs are about transgression of the social norms. There is also a close intimacy between women and the world of nature. Some of the passages in which women describe the beauties of nature are unequalled in the canonical literary texts. What are hastily described as 'songs of unlettered housewives' are in fact replete with extraordinary metaphors and images.

There are several poetic and narrative forms in Kannada folk literature—*lavanis* (ballads), *tripadis* (three-liners with fixed number of feet), lullabies, and songs associated specifically with chores such as grinding corn on the grindstone, pounding on the stone mortar, sowing and threshing corn.

There are also songs related to festivals and rituals. Chandrashekhar Kambar has provided an exhaustive categorisation of such songs (Kambar 2011). There are songs for every occasion, generally sung by a group of women. Together, they describe a quotidian world which is colourful, robust, and full of rituals and festivals. Despite a deep devotion to the supreme reality, the world view expressed is earthy and this-worldly. It is almost impossible to relate this world to the Vedic way of life. Gods and goddesses from the puranas and puranic religion do enter this world, but are immediately transformed and nativised: Parvati can abuse Lord Shiva and Shiva can lie to her and cheat on her; Tirupathi Thimmappa can advise the folk hero not to bring another wife home; Parvati and Shiva chat chewing betel leaves and betel nuts all the time. Folk epic heroes can cast spells, make men die and then revive them. Junjappa, a folk hero who turns into a god, can wander around as a poor helpless orphan. In this sense, folk literature deconstructs the world portrayed in the major literary works.

The two long folk epics discussed above also record the peregrination of folk heroes and deities from one linguistic cultural space to another. For instance, Mylara, worshipped by many communities, is known as Khandoba in Maharashtra. Dhere and many other scholars argue that the pastoralist shepherd communities constantly wandered from region to region, carrying cults and deities with them (Dhere 2011). There were both confrontations and comingling among these communities. Suresh Nagalamadike and Purushottama Bilimale argue that these communities strictly maintained the hierarchical division into several endogamous groups. But in the process of pastoral wanderings they gradually intermingled, especially because of the need to produce and market their produce (Bilimale 1997). The songs and narratives provide mythical discourses on the historical memories of such transactions. Another curious phenomenon is of the *Kadugolla* community which was Shaivite in its worship but crossed over to the Vaishnavite religion, and worshiped gods from both the religions. Their folk epic, *Junjappa*, freely shifts from one religious deity to another and also constructs situations for the deities to interact.

When read together, the folk epics seem to narrativise the civilisational phases from hunting, food gathering, primitive agriculture, pastoral cattle and sheep rearing, leading to barter and marketing. Parallel to this but at a later period, they trace the history of Shaivism, Veerashaivism of the twelfth century, the decline of the radical religion, hegemony of the priests and the spiritual revolt of the marginalised communities. This is followed by, or accompanied by, the establishment of cults under the leadership of the wandering gurus such as Madeshwara and Manteswamy.

In *Halumatha Kavya* a series of mythological narratives are built into the larger narrative to deify Beerappa of the shepherd community and to eulogise the profession of shepherding itself (Paramashivaiah 1979). In the section relating to the creation myth, demons are transformed into sheep and the gods, Vishnu, Brahma and Mahadeva, do the shepherding by turns. When it is Parvati's turn, she sends away the sheep to the earth and then hides them under a hollow beneath the earth. While furrowing the soil they are discovered, and thus begins the profession of shepherding. The epic is immersed in details referring to the profession and the social world constructed around it. Cattle rearing is introduced and cows are held sacred. The folk hero Beerappa is transformed into a deity and Shiva himself pays homage to him. However, the deification does not change his everyday life within his community. There are various episodes featuring many fully realised characters. What is extraordinary about the folk epics is their adherence to common everyday life. There is an enthusiastic celebration of labour, work, food, music and dance; and folk deities are active participants in the celebration. There are sorrows and suffering, but then they are treated as part of human existence.

The folk hero and deity Mylara Linga is worshipped in Karnataka and Maharashtra under different names. In Karnataka, the community of Goravaru has kept the Mylara tradition active with the recitation of the poetic narratives about him. Like the Neelagaras and Guddas, Goravas have a distinctive style of clothing, musical instruments and style of singing. They also undergo dedication to the deity and become itinerant singers of the songs about Mylara. The annual fairs held in his honour in Mylara near Hoovina Hadagali and near Nanjanagudu are attended by several lakhs of devotees even today.

Kannada scholarship in the last two decades has been paying close attention to the various folk traditions and cults. The vast field-work-based research by Rahamat Tarikere is persuasive in its argument that the spiritual, philosophical and ritualistic traditions of *Natha*, *Aaroodha*, Shakta and Sufi are strongly entrenched in Karnataka's rural society and that their followers are large in number. This is in complete contrast to the image of Karnataka as a modern, urbanising state dominated by a cosmopolitan capital and its hybrid culture. Cults and rituals with a probable history of several thousand years exist as strongly as they did in the past. There has been a continuous tradition of the *tatwapadakaras*, rural composers of spiritual and philosophical poetry. The Government of Karnataka has brought out nearly forty volumes of *tatwapadakara* compositions. It seems as though the epicentre of original creativity in Karnataka's culture lies outside the canonical literary tradition. There is a distinctive poetics supporting this creativity, though it is not theorised or articulated elaborately. It has to be constructed from the poetic practices themselves. While is can be assumed that there was constant exchange between the literary and folk domains in themes, motifs and verse forms, it would be difficult to specifically describe the chronology and processes involved in this exchange.

***

The folk performative forms have a long history though their exact beginnings are a matter of conjecture. Among several such forms, *Yakshagana, Bayalata, Talamaddale* and *Parijata* are the major ones which continue to be performed. They have regional origins and the performances are also distributed regionally. While *Yakshagana* and *Talamaddale* are dominant across the coast in Dakshina Kannada and Uttara Kannada districts, *Bayalata* and *Parijata* are dominant in the North Karnataka region. These forms are continuously evolving and changing with traditionalists mourning the loss of their purity or distinctiveness. The huge demand for their performances—it was reported that one leading *Yakshagana* troupe (the Idagunji Mahaganapati Yakshagana Mandali) has been booked for several years—is evidence of the undiminished popularity of these forms. The phrase 'culture as material practice' is eminently suitable for describing these performative forms. They are inalienably rooted in the local and regional seasonal cycles and agrarian activities. They are performed locally in the midst of a community of spectators; and, in the past at least, all stage props were made of locally available materials. Before the emergence of the professional performing troupes, the village community itself would perform these forms with the available local talent. Novels, short stories and autobiographies in Kannada describe how these local productions and performances were a significant communitarian activity. Legendary performers and singers were celebrities with huge following. The performances are not only based on epics and puranic material. Their 'scripts' borrow freely from literary texts. The script writers and major performers demonstrated mastery over the Kannada literary tradition. Though not all, many 'scripts' have survived and have entered print culture. Scholars like Muliya Thimmappaiah have commented elaborately on them. Muddana, the herald of modern Kannada literature, himself wrote a number of *Yakshagana* scripts. Shivaram Karanth introduced many innovations in *Yakshagana*, transforming it at times into a ballet. He not only directed a troupe but also performed in some *Yakshagana* plays. He also wrote a scholarly work, *Yakshagana Bayalata*.

***

Apart from being popular in Karnataka, *Yakshagana* is performed across the world. Its increasing popularity and following is an interesting cultural phenomenon. Scholars have provided detailed analyses of the various elements of *Yakshagana* such as text, costume, music, performance, stage and props. Only a brief description is attempted below.

Chandrashekhar Kambar places *Yakshagana* in the category of *Bayalata* because it is performed on an open, public stage. The stage is bare except for the performing space, and also includes a slightly elevated portion for the chorus of singers and musicians. The traditional costumes and makeup are colourful. There are two major styles of performances, namely *tenka tittu* and *badaga tittu*. According to Mohan Kuntar (2013), the stage consists of three distinct spaces including *poorvaranga* where the ritualistic worship is offered as a prelude to the performance. Many commentators including Shivaram Karanth have suggested that the worship reveals traces of *Nagaradhane*, an ancient form of worship. It is also suggested that *Yakshagana* as a form originated from ritualistic worship though there is no definite evidence to support this. However, there is no doubt at all that the origin of *Yakshagana*, like many other forms, was in a ritual in which the community participated. Kuntar describes the *Mummela*, the chorus occupying the front space, as Shaivite in its expression and confined mainly to song and dance. The *Himmela*, on the other hand, is clearly Vaishnavite and provides an intellectual framework to the performance. However, Kambar finds that *poorvaranga* worship is quickly performed without elaborate steps in the *Bayalata* performances. It is at times perfunctory. What is interesting is the coexistence of three modes (*Nagaradhane*, Shaivite expressions and Vaishnavite elements) which refer to the manner in which the popular form was gradually appropriated by the major creeds. It was only much later that the taboo among brahmins against attending *Yakshagana* performance was given up. The performances also depended on local patronage by the landlords, until they began to be performed inside 'tents' (like commercial dramas) and an entrance fee was introduced. Thus, the acceptance of this popular 'plebian' form has a complicated history. *Yakshagana* has now become an iconic cultural art, distinctively regional and finding enthusiastic support from the urban and even non-resident populations.

Each performance is based on a *prasanga* or episode from the epics and puranas. The original plot and characters are retained but the performance interprets the episode in a free and uninhibited manner. Talented actors can add dialogues, make interventions and deviate from the original script. Comic characters have absolute freedom to shift the time frame from the puranic to the contemporary, and introduce witty commentary on the present sociopolitical scenario. The extraordinary flexibility of the form is evidenced in the fact that there were *Yakshagana* performances on Adolf Hitler and the nationalist movement. Stage realism is unheard of, and therefore, the performance is not constrained by notions of realism. The dramatic action is also interrupted by music and dance—in fact, it is a song-and-dance performance which also includes dramatic action. This flexibility is possible because the trio of audience, performers and the *Bhagavata* are thoroughly familiar with the epic or puranic material which can be stretched and reinterpreted in every performance. Kambar has argued that every performance in folk theatre is instantaneous and the 'meaning' of the performance is what the audience experiences during the performance. There is no pre-determined 'meaning' (Kambar 2011).

Though the role of a 'text' or 'script' is apparently marginal in *Yakshagana* performances, a performance is necessarily a variation on a text. Fortunately, many of these texts have been collected and printed. There have been legendary writers of *prasangas*, such as Parthi Subba from Kasaragodu and Muddana. The tradition has been kept alive by contemporary writers such as Amrutha Someshwara. Karanth of course wrote his own scripts. The texts being written for performances, many familiar features such as prosodic forms, use of different registers and characterisation had to be retained. Recent studies have pointed out the originality of the script writers despite the constraints of the performance requirements. This was true of the *Bayalata* performances also. As discussed earlier, the famous *Sangya Balya*, said to be based on true events, was written by one Pattar Master; and the family about which the script was written brought an injunction against the performance under the colonial DPA act. M. M. Kalburgi wrote his own 'true version' in his *Khare Khare Sangya Balya* (2005, The True *Sangya Balya*). Several autobiographies by well-known script writers provide insights into the making of the *Yakshagana* texts.

The relationship between the performers and the audience has certainly changed with the improved sources of stage lighting. From flame torches to lamps to electric lighting, there have been profound changes which have affected this relationship. They have also changed the style of acting. However, *Yakshagana* has withstood the challenges of commercial theatre, films and television by its innate flexibility and adaptability.

A modified form of the *Yakshagana* is *Talamaddale* which is performed without costumes and dance. It is more of a poetic debate than a performance. The focus is on the *arthadharis*, those who participate in the elaboration, exegesis and interpretation of what is given by the *Bhagavata* to prompt the debate. This may be a dialogue or an incident or a verse. The *Talamaddale* can extend over hours depending on the resourcefulness of the participants and the response of the audience. Some of the debates are of complex philosophical nature and draw on vast scholarship.

***

Thus, the folk theatre was a site for entertainment, performance of several art forms and also sharing of knowledge. It was also essentially a public ritual, participatory in nature. According to Shankar Mokashi Punekar, even company drama (commercial theatre) possessed this feature of communitarian participation (Mokashi Punekar 2012). He argues that the shift to amateur realistic drama which was urban-centric and catered to the educated middle class, broke this communitarian tradition. K. V. Subbanna also argues on similar lines (in Akshara et al. 2018). K. V. Akshara (2018) is also critical of the disruption caused by modern amateur, realistic theatre. Ironically, in the 1970s and 80s, under the influence of the 'Theatre of Roots' movement sponsored by the Sahitya Akademi, playwrights like Karnad and Kambar returned to the techniques of folk theatre.

The major folk epics have survived mainly because they are associated with specific cults. Through the ritual of initiation, the singers of the epics are assigned the task of reciting, singing and performing them. There are also fairs and festivals which attract huge crowds who listen to the singing of the epics for several nights. These singers are also invited to households because of the belief that the recitations bring good fortune. One can conclude that folk literature has survived and flourished despite the momentous changes taking place since the colonial period. But scholars are of the view that the more secular folk poems and narratives have been disappearing as they are not related to surviving cults. It is the dedicated work of recording, collecting and publishing, especially by university departments, which has helped preserve folk poetry. Some of it has also been taken over by the music industry. The victim in the process has been the folk poetry produced by rural women which was meant to be sung while performing the daily chores or rituals and worship. With urbanisation and changes in the life styles in rural societies, these songs do not anymore survive outside of print culture. What is difficult to assess is the loss of creativity by women, which is astonishing in the extant texts of folk poetry collected decades ago. Where can that creativity find an expression now, is a moot question. Kambar is of the opinion that with modernity, urbanisation and print culture, folk literature ceases to exist. It becomes the past, however invigorating it may be to the practitioners of literature.

Bibliography

Adiga, Gopalakrishna. 1959. *Bhoomigeetha*. Bengaluru: Sharada Prakatanalaya.

———. 1977. *Mannina Vasane*. In *Samagra Gadya*. Bengaluru: Sakshi Prakashana.

———. 1999–2000. *Samagra Kavya*. Bengaluru: Sapna Book House.

Akshara, K. V. et al., ed. 2018. *Kannada Theatre History 1850–1950: A Source Book*. Manipal: Manipal UP.

Alanahalli, Srikrishna. 1978. *Parasangada Gende Thimma*. Bengaluru: IBH Prakashana.

———. 1982. *Bhujangayyana Dashavataragalu*. Bengaluru: IBH Prakashana.

———. 2016. *Kadu*. Bengaluru: IBH Prakashana.

Amur, G. S. 1983. *A. N. Krishna Rao*. Delhi: Sahitya Akademi.

Ananthamurthy U. R. 2014a. *English Brahmana Mattu Kannada Shudra*. In *Prajne Mattu Parisara*. Bengaluru: Kannada Sahitya Parishat.

———. 2014b. *Karanthara Authentic Prapancha*. In *Prajne Mattu Parisara*. Bengaluru: Kannada Sahitya Parishat.

———. 2014c. *Prajne Mattu Parisara*. Bengaluru: Kannada Sahitya Parishat.

Ashadevi, M. S. 2004. *Mahile, Basavannana Niluvugalu*. In *Basavannana Vachanagalu: Samskritika Mukhamukhi*, ed. Amaresh Nugadoni. Hampi: Kannada University. 56–69.

B. M. Sri. (Srikantaiah, B. M.) 1921/2013. *English Geetagalu*. Bengaluru: B. M. Sri. Pratistana.

Bannadi, Sabita. 2010. *Alayavu Bayalagi*. Kundapur: Tingala Belaku Prakashana.

Basavanal, S. S. 1968. *Basavannanavara Shatsthalada Vachanagalu*. Bengaluru: Department of Kannada and Culture.

Basavaraju, L., ed. 1969. *Shivaganaprasadi Mahadevayyagala Shunya Sampadane*. Chitradurga: Sri Bruhanmatha.

———., ed. 2001. *Allamana Vachana Chandrike*. Bellari: Lohia Prakashana.

———., ed. 2002. *Pampana Sarala Aadipurana*. Mysore: Abhiruchi Prakashana.

Bendre, D. R. 1932a. *Hakki Haarutide Nodidira*. In *Gari*. Hubli: Srimatha Prakashana.

———. 1932b. *Tuttina Cheela*. In *Gari*. Hubli: Srimatha Prakashana.

———. 1960. *Gari*. Dharwad: Samaja Pustakalya.

———. 1974. *Sahityada Virata Swaroopa*. Dharwad: Samaja Pustakalaya.

Ben-Herut, Gil. 2018. *Siva's Saints: The Origin of Devotion in Kannada according to Hariharana Ragalegalu*. Oxford UP.

Bhusanurmath, S. S., ed. 1958. *Goluru Siddhaveerannana Shunya Sampadane*. Siddhalingeshwara Matha.

Bhusanurmath, S. S., M. S. Sunkarpur, and Armando Menezes, trans. 1965–72. *Shunya Sampadane: Vol. I–V.* Dharwad: Karnatak University.

Bilimale, Purushottama. 1997. *Koodukattu*. Malladihalli: Anandakanda Granthamale.

Boralingaiah, Hi. Chi., ed. 1997. *Male Madeshwara Maha Kavya*. Hampi: Kannada University.

———. 2018. *Karnataka Janapada Mahakavya*. Hampi: Kannada University.

Boratti, Vijayakumar M. 2012. *The Discovery of the Vachanas: Halakatti and the Medieval Kannada Literature in Colonial Karnataka.* Hampi: Kannada University.

Budal, Nataraj. 2016. *Kannada Kavya Mimamse.* Hampi: Kannada University.

Champakalakshmi, R. 2011. *Religion, Tradition and Ideology.* Oxford UP.

Chandrashekhar, S. 2005 *Ekikarana: Ondu Kathana*. Bengaluru: Kannada Pustaka Pradhikara.

———. 2006. *Vasaahathu Kaleena Karnataka*. Bengaluru: Department of Kannada and Culture.

Channaiah, H. M. 1974. *Jijnase*. Mysore: Saruchi Prakashana.

Chenni, Rajendra. 2004. *Vachana Chaluvali Mattu Basavanna*. In *Basavannana Vachanagalu: Samskrutika Mukhamukhi,* ed. Nugadoni Amaresh. Hampi: Kannada University.

———. 2009. *Traditions of Modernity: A Comparative Study of T. S. Eliot and Gopalakrishna Adiga*. Bengaluru: Ruvari.

———. 2011. *Rashtriyate Mattu Kannada Sahitya.* In *Ayda Vimarsha Lekhanagalu*. Bengaluru: Department of Kannada and Culture.

Chidanandamurthy, M. 2000. *Veerashaiva Dharma: Bharatiya Samskruti.* Bengaluru: Minchu Prakashana.

Chinnaswamy, Mudnakudu. 2004. *Chandirana Kanasu, Ingalarada Hunu.* Bengaluru: Manava Dharma Peetha.

———. 2018. *Geddalu Huluvige Bidda Marada Kanasu.* Bengaluru: Kannada Pustaka Pradhikara.

Chittala, Gangadhara. 2004. *Yeppatteradu Kavitegalu.* Bengaluru: Prism Books.

Chittala, Yashawanta. 1964. *Mooru Darigalu.* Dharwad: Manohar Grantha Mala.

———. 1983. *Chittalara Kathegalu.* Bengaluru: Praja Printers Private Limited.

Dabbe, Vijaya. 1989. *Mahile, Samaja Mattu Sahitya.* Mysore: Rachana Prakashana.

Dani, Surendra, and Ritti Srinivas, eds. 2020. *Aluru Venkatarayara Samgra Krithigalu. Vol. I.* Dharwad: Alur Venkata Rao Pratishtana.

Daniel, Susan, trans. 2015. *Kusumabale.* New Delhi: Oxford UP.

Desai, Shantinath, ed. 1987. *Gangadhar Chittalara Kavya Srishti.* Ankola: Raghavendra Prakashana.

Devadevan, Manu V. 2016. *A prehistory of Hinduism.* Warsaw, Berlin: De Gruyter Open Limited.

Devy, G. N. Chief ed. 2014–25. *People's Linguistic Survey of India.* Hyderabad: Orient BlackSwan.

Dhere, C. N. 2011. *The Rise of a Folk God.* New York: Oxford UP.

Dodamani, Sadashiva. 2014. *Dharwad Mattu Halasangi: Geleyara Gumpu Ondu Samskritika Adhyayana.* Hulakoti: Chandrabhaga Prakashana.

Ekkundi, Su. Ram. 2006. *Ayda Kavitegalu.* Heggodu: Akshara Prakashana.

Galaganatha. 1913/2014. *Eshwari Sutra.* In *Galaganatha Samagra Sahitya.* Vol.5, ed. M. M. Kalburgi. 2014. Dharwad: Manohar Grantha Mala.

Ganesh, Mogalli. 2008. *Kali.* In *Mogalli Kathegalu.* Bengaluru: Sapna Book House.

Garuda, Prakash. 2015. *Company Natak Arthath Vritti Rangabhumi.* Bengaluru: Bhoomi Prakashana.

Govindaraj, Giraddi. 2012. *Samagra Vimarshe.* 3 vols. Bengaluru: Sapna Book House.

Govindaraju, C. R. 2006. *Karnatakada Ekikarana Chaluvali Mattu Kannada Sahitya.* Bengaluru: Department of Kannada and Culture.

Guha, Ranajit. 1983. The Prose of Counter-Insurgency. In *Subaltern Studies II: Writings on South Asian History and Society.* Oxford UP.

Halakatti, P. G. 1926. *Sri Basaveshwarana Vachanagalu.* Bijapur: Shivanubhava Granthamale.

Hanumantayya, N. K. 2016. *Mamsangadiya Navilu*. Gadag: Ladai Prakashana.

Hanumanthaiah, L. 2018. *Samagra Sahitya, Vol. I*. Bengaluru: Kannada Pustaka Pradhikara.

Hanur, Krishnamurthy. 2006. *Eithihasika Kathana Geethegalu*. Bengaluru: Department of Kannada and Culture.

Harish, G. B., ed. 2012. *Vastu Vinyasa*. Bengaluru: Abhinava.

———., ed. 2014. *Mumbelagu*. Bengaluru: Sahitya Parishat.

Havanur, Srinivasa. 1974/2021. *Hosagannadada Arunodaya*. Bengaluru: Kannada Pustaka Pradhikara. (orig. pub. 1974)

Hegde, Rajaram. 2001. *Vaddaradhane: Loukika Adhikara Matthu Madhyakalina Jainamatha*. In *Vaddaradhane: Samskruthika Mukhamukhi*, ed. B. M. Puttaiah. Hampi: Kannada University.

Hiremath, Mallikarjun. 2001. *Havana*. Malladihalli: Anandkanda Granthamale.

———. 2021. *Havali*. Dharwad: Manohara Grantha Mala.

Hiremath, R. C., ed. 1972. *Gummalapura Siddhalingayathiya Shunya Sampadane*. Dharwad: Karnatak University.

Hiremath, Shailaja. 2022. *Nirupaneyachege*. Gadag: Sangam Pustaka.

Howe, Irwing. 1967. *The Idea of the Modern in Literature and the Arts*. New York: Horizon Press.

Indwadi, Venkatesh, ed. 2022. *Male Madeshwara Kavya Akshara Lokada Anusandhana*. Hampi: Kannada University.

Joshi, G. B. 1963. *Kadadida Neeru*. Dharwad: Manohara Grantha Mala.

Kaikini, Jayanth. 2003/2011. *Jayanth Kaikini Kathegalu*. Bengaluru: Ankita Pustaka.

Kailasam, T. P. 2018. *Kailasam Kannada Natakagalu*, ed. B. S. Keshavarao. Bengaluru: Ankita Pustaka.

Kalburgi, M. M. 1970. *Shashanagalalli Sharanaru*. Dharwad: Prasaranga, Karnatak University.

———., ed. 1993. *Samagra Vachana Sampura*. Vol. 3. Bengaluru: Directorate of Kannada and Culture.

———. 1994. *Karnatakada Kaifiyattugalu*. Hampi: Kannada University.

———. 2001. Introduction. In *Aradhana Karnatateeka*, ed. Shanthinatha Dibbad. Bengaluru: Sahitya Parishat.

———. 2005. *Khare Khare Sangya Balya*. Bellari: Lohia Prakashana.

———., ed. 2011. *Hariharana Ragalegalu*. Bengaluru: Department of Kannada and Culture.

Kambara, Chandrashekhar. 2009. *Siri Sampige and Other Plays*. Bengaluru: Provoke India.

———. 2011. *Desi Chintane*. Bengaluru: Ankita Pustaka.

Kanavi, Chennaveera. 1975. *Chiranthana Daha*. Bengaluru: Department of Kannada and Culture.

Karanth, Shivaram. 1941/2001. *Marali Mannige*. Bengaluru: Department of Kannada and Culture.

———. 1993. *Ten Faces of a Crazy Mind*. Bengaluru: Bharatiya Vidya Bhavan.

Karnad, Girish. 1971. *Tughlaq*. Delhi: Oxford UP.

———. 1980. *Aadadta Ayushya*. Dharwad: Manohar Grantha Mala.

———. 2013. *Taledanda*. Dharwad: Manohara Grantha Mala.

———. 2018. *Collected Plays*. 3 volumes. New Delhi: Oxford UP.

Kattimani, Basavaraj. 2011. *Jwala Mukhiya Mele*. Bengaluru: Department of Kannada and Culture.

Kittel, Ferdinand. 1968–71. *A Dictionary of the Kannada Language*. Madras: Madras University.

Krishna Rao, A. N. (Aa. Na. Kru.). 1983. *Sahitya Mattu Kama Prachodane*. Sagar Prakashana.

Krishnamurthy, M. G. 1970. *Adhunika Bharatiya Sahitya Mattu Itara Lekhanagalu*. Heggodu: Akshara Prakashana.

———. 1994. *Kritisamskriti*. Mysore: Rujuvathu Prakashana.

Krishnarao, A. N. 1943. *Veerashaiva Sahitya Mattu Samskruti*. Bengaluru: Padmashri Prakashana.

Krishnashastri, A. R. 1949. *Bhashanagalu Mattu Lekhanagalu*. Mysore: Venkannanavara Smaaraka Granthamale.

Kulkarni, R. V., ed. 1998. *Sahasa Bheema Vjayam*. Bengaluru: Sahitya Parishat.

Kum, Vee. 2010. *Bari Kateyallo Anna*. Bengaluru: Sapna Book House.

Kunhi, Bolwar Mahammad. 2017. *Swatantrada Ota*. Bengaluru: Kamadhenu Pustaka Bhavana.

Kuntar, Mohan. 2013. *Yakshagana Sthtityantara*. Bengaluru: Yaji Prakashana.

Kurtakoti, Kirtinath. 1962. *Yugadharma Hagu Sahitya Darshana*. Dharwad: Manohar Grantha Mala.

———. 2015. *Navya Kavya Prayoga*. Dharwad: Kurtakoti Memorial Trust.

Kuvempu, and Masti Venkatesh Iyengar, eds. 1958. *Karnata Bharatha Katha Manjari*. Bengaluru: Mysore Samsthanada Kannada Mattu Samskriti Ilakhe.

Lankesh, P. 2010. *Kranthi Bantu Kranthi*. Bengaluru: Lankesh Prakashana. (orig. pub. 1971)

———. 2010. *Nanna Tangigondu Gandu Kodi, Teregalu*. Bengaluru: Lankesh Prakashana. (orig. pub. 1965)

———. 2011. *T. Prasannana Grahasthashrama*. Bengaluru: Lankesh Prakashana. (orig. pub. 1964)

———. 2012. *Sankranti*. Bengaluru: Lankesh Prakashana. (orig. pub. 1973)

———. 2015. *Gunamukha*. Bengaluru: Lankesh Prakashana. (orig. pub. 1993)

Malagatti, Aravind. 1988. *Karya*. Mysore: Allama Prakashana.

———. 1994. *Government Brahmana*. Mysore: Chethana Book House.

———. 2016. *Ma Kavya: Kavya Samagra*. Mysore: Rachana Prakashana.

Masti (Masti Venkatesha Iyengar). 2011. *Samagra Kathegalu*. Bengaluru: Jeevana Karyalaya Trust.

Meera, L. G. 2003. *Hariharana Ragalegalu: Samskritika Mukamukhi*, ed. Shivanand S Viraktamata. Hampi: Kannada University.

Mokashi Punekar, Shankar. 2012. *Vastu Vinyasa*. Bengaluru: Abhinava.

Mugali, R. S. 2018. *Kannada Sahitya Charitre*. Mysore: Geetha Book House.

Nagalamadike, Suresh. 2018. *Halavu Bannada Hagga*. Bengaluru: Deepankara Pustaka.

Nagaraj, D. R. 1994. *Sahitya Kathana*. Heggodu: Sagara Prakashana.

———. 1999. *Allama Prabhu Mattu Shaiva Pratibhe*. Sagar: Akshara Prakashana.

———. *Listening to the Loom*, ed. Prithvi Datta Chandra Shobhi. Ranikhet: Permanent Black.

Nagaraj, Ki. Rum. 2012. *Tereda Pathya*, ed. Nataraj Huliyar. Bengaluru: Kannada Pustaka Pradhikara.

Nagarajaih, Hampa. 1992. *Vaddaradhane*. Bengaluru: Kannada Pustaka Pradhikara.

Nagaveni, H. S. 2004. *Meeyuva Ata*. Bellari: Lohia Prakashana.

———. 2011a. *Gandhi Banda*. Shivamogga: Aharnishi.

———. 2011b. *Suryanigondu Veelya*. Bengaluru: Prejas Prakashana.

Nandakumar, Pratibha. 2007. *Pratibha Nandakumar Avara Ayda Kavitegalu*. Sagar: Akshara Prakashana.

Nandi, R. N. 1975. Origin of Virasaiva Movement. *Indian Historical Review* 2.2: 32–46.

Nandimath, S. C. 1942. *A Handbook of Virasaivism*. Dharwad: The Literary Committee, L. E. Association.

Narasimhachar, D. L. 1971. *Pampa Bharata Deepike*. Mysore: Mysore University.

Narasimhacharya, R. 1961. *Karnataka Kavicharite*. Bengaluru: Kannada Sahitya Parishat.

———. 2020. *Karnataka Kavi Charite*. In *History of Kannada Literature*. Gyan Books. (Orig. Kannada Work published by Kannada Sahitya Parishat, 1961)

Narayan Rao, Hattiyangadi. 1919. *Angla Kavitavali*. Mumbai: Published by the author.

Narayana, K. V. 1997. *Beru. Kanda. Chiguru*. Bengaluru: Pragathi Graphics.

———. 2018. *Nudigala Alivu*. Shivamogga: Aharnishi Prakashana.

Narayana, P. V., ed. 2018. *Basavannana Vachanagalu*. Bengaluru: Ankita Pustaka.

Nayak, G. H. 1985. *Preface to Hosagannada Kavya*. Bengaluru: Kannada Sahitya Parishat.

———. 1989. *Nirapekhsha*. Sagar: Akshara Prakashana.

———. 2006. *Krithi Pareekshe*. Bengaluru: Kannada Pustaka Pradhikara.

———. 2018. *Kannada Sanna Kathegalu*. New Delhi: NBT.

Niranjana, Seemanthini. 1994/2014. *Janapriya Sahityadalli Streevadada Pratibimba: Triveniavara Kelavu Kadambarigalu*. In *Streevadi Sahitya Vimarshe*, ed. Tejaswini Niranjana and Seemanthini Niranjana. Bengaluru: Abhinava.

Niranjana, Tejaswini, and Seemanthini Niranjana, eds. 1994. *Streevadi Sahitya Vimarshe*. Bengaluru: Abhinava.

Nugadoni, Amaresh, ed. 2002. *Shunya Sampadane: Samskritika Mukhamukhi*. Hampi: Kannada University.

———. 2014. *Tatwapada-Sahitya Adhyayana*. Hampi: Kannada University.

———. 2016. *Neeru Tandavaru*. In *Tamandhada Kedu*. Channapattana: Pallava Prakashana. (third reprint)

———. 2019. *Kathegala Kattu*. Bengaluru: Desi Pustaka.

———. 2023. *Daivakke Modalu Sharanembevu*. In *Savari*. Bengaluru: Vasanth Prakashana.

Ollett, Andrew. 2017. *The Language of the Snakes*. Berkeley: U of California P.

Padikkal, Shivarama. 2001. *Nadu Nudiya Rupaka*. Mangalore: Prasaranga, Mangalore University.

Pai, Gopalakrishna. 2011. *Swapna Saraswatha*. Bengaluru: Bhagyalakshmi Prakashana.

———. 2017. *Swapna Saraswatha*. Trans. Sumati Shenoy et al. Manipal: Manipal UP.

Palkuriki, Somanatha. 1990. *Basava Purana* (translated as *Siva's Warriors*), trs. Narayan Rao Velcheru and Gene H. Roghair. Princeton UP.

Paramashivaiah, Jee. Sham. 1979/2016. *Dakshina Karnataka Janapada Kavya Prakaragalu*. Bengaluru: Abhinava.

Patil, Chandrashekhar, ed. 1993. *Pragatisheela-Navya-Dalit-Bandaya*. Dharwad: Sankramana Prakashana.

———. 2012a. *Appa*. In *Champa Natakagalu*. Vol.1. Bengaluru: Sapna Book House.

———. 2012b. *Kunta Kunta Kuruvatti*. In *Champa Natakagalu*. Vol.1. Bengaluru: Sapna Book House.

———. 2018. *Tinger Buddanna*. In *Champa Natakagalu*. Vol.1. Bengaluru: Sapna Book House.

Pollock, Sheldon. 2006. *The Language of Gods in the World of Men*. Berkeley: U of California P.

Puttappa, K. V. (Kuvempu). 2024. *Bride in the Hills*. Tr. Vanamala Viswanatha. Penguin Books.

Radhika, P. 2006. unpublished PhD thesis. Manipal Academy of Higher Education.

Raghavendra Rao, H. S. 2009. In *Nirdiganta*, ed. Shantha Imarapur, Dharwad: Sundara Prakashana. 143–54.

Rajashekhar, P. K., ed. 2006. *Maleya Madeshwara*. Bengaluru: Department of Kannada and Culture.

Rajendra, D. K. 1983. *Shri Sahitya*. Mysore: Institute of Kannada Studies, University of Mysore.

Ramachandran, C. N. 1999. *Triveni*. Sahitya Akademi.

———. 2014. *Kumaravyasa Bharata Haagu Janapada Mahabharatagalu*. In *Kumaravyasa Bharata: Samskruthika Mukhamukhi*, ed. Rahamat Tarikere. Hampi: Kannada UP.

Ramachandran, C. N., and B. A. Vivek Rai, ed. 2015. *Classical Kannada Poetry and Prose: A Reader*. Hampi: Kannada University.

Ramanna, Besagarahalli. 2011. *Bettada Melondu Maneya Madi*. In *Kanaja*. Ballari: Lohia Prakashana.

———. 2011. *Gandhi*. In *Kanaja*. Ballari: Lohia Prakashana.

Ramanujan, A. K. 1973. *Speaking of Siva*. Penguin Books.

Rangacharya, Adya. 2006. *Listen Janamejaya and Other Plays*. Translated by G. S. Amur. New Delhi: Sahitya Akademi.

———. 2007. *Shadows in the Dark: Four Plays*. Translated by Usha Desai. Bengaluru: Unisun Publications.

Ranganath, H. K. 2011. *Karnataka Ranga Bhoomi*. Bengaluru: Hemantha Sahitya.

Rao, Anupama. 2009. *The Caste Question: Dalits and the Politics of Modern India*. Berkeley: U of California P.

Rao, Gopala H. S. 2017. *Karnataka Ekikaranada Ithihasa*. Bengaluru: Navakarnataka.

Rao, Gulavadi Venkata. 1899. *Indira Bai*. Bengaluru: Department of Kannada and Culture.

———. 2019 (1899). *Indira Bai*. Tr. Vanamala Viswanatha and Shivarama Padikkal. Oxford UP.

Sadashiva, K. 1998. *Nalliyalli Neeru Bantu*. In *K. Sadashivara Samagra Kathegalu*. Bengaluru: Prism Books.

Sagar, Mamata G. 2007. *Mahila Vishaya*. Bengaluru: Ila Prakashana.

Samaya Pareekshe. 2013. Bengaluru: Sahitya Parishat.

Saraswathi, Du. 2001. *Eegen Maadeeri*. Bengaluru: Manasa

———. 2006. *Jeeva Sampige*. Bengaluru: Abhinava.

———. 2018. *Sanna Timmi Purana*. Bengaluru: Navakarnataka.

Sarkar, Tanika. 2003. *Hindu Wife, Hindu Nation*. Ranikhet: Permanent Black.

Satyanarayana, K., and Susie Tharu, ed. 2003. *Steel Nibs are Sprouting*. New Delhi: HarperCollins.

Seetharamaiah, M. V. 1994. *Kaviraja Margam*. Bengaluru: B. M. Sri. Pratishtana.

Settar, S. 2003. General President's Address: Footprints of Artisans in History: Some Reflections on Early Artisans of India. *Proceedings of the Indian History Congress* 64: 1–43.

———. 2007. *Ruvari*. Bengaluru: Abhinava.

———., ed. 2017. *Halegannada*. Bengaluru: Abhinava.

———. 2018. *Prakrita Jagadvalaya*. Bengaluru: Abhinava.

Shanbhag, Vivek. 1992. *Langaru*. Heggodu: Akshara Prakashana.

———. 1995. *Huli Savari*. Heggodu: Akshara Prakashana.

———. 2007. *Ondu Badi Kadalu*. Heggodu: Akshara Prakashana.

———. 2013. *Ghachar Ghochar*. Heggodu: Akshara Prakashana.

Shanteshwar, Veena. 1990. *Mullugalu*. Dharwad: Sankramana Prakashana.

Shekhar, M. S. 2010. *Garike*. Channapattana: Pallava Prakashana.

Shivaprakash, H. S. 2010a. *I Keep Vigil of Rudra.* Penguin Classics.

———. 2010b. *Kavite Indina Tanaka*. Mysore: Vismaya Prakashana.

———. 2023. *Mahachaitra, The Great Spring, and Other Plays*. Calcutta: Seagull.

Shivareddy, K. C., ed. 2003. *Kuvempu Samagra Gadya: Vol. I.* Hampi: Kannada University.

———., ed. 2004. *Kuvempu Samagra Gadya: Vol II.* Hampi: Kannada University.

Shivarudrappa, G. S., ed. 1974. *Samagra Sahitya Charitre*. Vol 1. Bengaluru University: Department of Publications and Extension Lectures.

———., ed. 1975. *Kavi Bendre*. Bengaluru: Bangalore University.

———. 1993. *Samagra Gadya*. Bengaluru: Kamadhenu Pustaka Bhavana.

———., ed. 2016. *Pampa: Ondu Adhyayana*. Bengaluru: Sapna Book House.

———. 2017. *Samagra Gadya. Vol 1*. Bengaluru: Priyadarshini Prakashana.

———. 2020. *Samagra Kavya*. Bengaluru: Sapna Book House.

Shobhi, Prithvi Datta Chandra, ed. 2012. *Listening to the Loom: Essays on Literature, Politics and Violence.* Ranikhet: Permanent Black.

Shrikanthaiah, B. M. 1985. *Kannada Maatu Taleyettuva Bage*. Dharwad: Karnataka Vidyavardhak Sangha.

Shubhachandra, ed. 2012. *Nayasena Deva Virachita Dharmamrutham*. Bengaluru: Kannada Book Authority.

Siddabasavaiah, Lalita. 2009. *Dari Nenta.* Tumkur: Chinmayi Prakashana.

Siddaiah, K. B. 2017. *K. B. Siddaiahnavara Khanda Kavyagalu*. Tumkur: Student Book Company.

Siddalingaiah. 1975. *Holemadigara Hadu.* In *Nanna Janagalu.* Bengaluru: Department of Kannada and Culture. (reprinted 2010)

Sitaramaiah, V., ed. 1994. *Kavirajamarga*. Bengaluru: B. M. Sri Smaraka Pratishtana.

Srinivasa. 2011. *Sanna Kathegalu Samagra. Vol. I*. Bengaluru: MVJK Trust.

Sriranga (Jagirdar, R. V.). 2006. *Sahitiya Atma Jijnase*. Partly translated by Shashi Deshpande as *Opening Scene: Early Memoirs of a Dramatist and a Play,* Penguin Books.

Srivalli, T. C., ed. 2015. *Giribale Sannakathegalu* (Short stories of Saraswatibai Rajwade). Mysore: Samskruti Book Agencies.

Subba Rao, T. R. 1987. *Chandavalliya Thota*. Mysore: Kavyalaya.

Subbanna, K. V. 2000. *Kavirajamarga Mattu Kannada Jagattu*. Heggodu: Akshara Prakashana.

Sumitrabai, B. N. 1994. *Kannada Mahila Sahitya Mattu Streewada Shodha*. In *Streevadi Sahitya Vimarshe,* ed. Tejaswini Niranjana and Seemanthini Niranjana. Bengaluru: Abhinava.

———. 2009. *Sarahaddugala Aache-Eeche*. Bengaluru: ILA Prakashana.

Sundaram, R. V. S., and Deren M. Patel. 2017. *Kavirajamargam*. Delhi: Manohar.

Swamy, O. L. Nagabhushana, ed. 2007. *The Sign: Vachanas of the Twelfth Century*. Hampi: Kannada University.

Tarakeshwar, V. B. 2006. *Vasahatushahi Mattu Bhashantara*. Hampi: Kannada University.

Tarikere, Rahamat. 1998. *Karnatakada Sufigalu*, Hampi: Kannada University.

———., ed. 2004. *Kumaravyasa: Sanskritika Mukhamukhi*. Hampi: Kannada University.

———. 2006. *Kattiyanchina Dari*. Bengaluru: Abhinava.

———. 2011. *Illi Yaru Mukhyaralla*. Gadag: Ladai Prakashana

———. 2014. *Karnatakada Moharam*. Hampi: Kannada University

———. 2017. *Karnatakada Shakta Pantha*. Hampi: Kannada University.

———. 2019. *Raja Dharma*. Hampi: Kannada University.

Tejaswi, Poornachandra. 1973/2014. *Abachurina Post Office*. Mysore: Pustaka Prakashana.

———. 2009. *Vimarsheya Vimarshe*. Mysore: Pustaka Prakashana.

Tirumalesh, K. V. 2011/2007. *Ayda Kavitegalu*. Heggodu: Akshara Prakashana.

———. 2015/2010. *Akshaya Kavya*. Bengaluru: Abhinava.

Vaidehi. 2006. *Gulabi Talkies*. New Delhi: Penguin Books.

———. 2011. *Shivana Meeyisuva Hadu*. In *Hoova Kattuva Kayaka*. Bengaluru: Christ University.

Vastare, Nagaraj. 2019. Preface to *Sakhi Charusheele*. Bengaluru: Chanda Prakashana.

Vasudhendra. 2016. *Hampi Express*. Bengaluru: Chanda Pustaka.

———. 2017a. *Mohanaswamy*. Bengaluru: Chanda Pustaka.

———. 2017b. *Vishama Bhinna Rashi*. Bengaluru: Chanda Pustaka.

Veeranna, C. 1986. *Kannada Sahitya: Charitrika Belavanige. Vol. I*. Bengaluru: Nava Karnataka.

———. 2011. *Kannada Sahitya: Charitrika Belavanige. Madhyakaalena Sahitya. Vol. II.* Bengaluru: Nava Karnataka.

Venkateshamurthy, H. S. 2021. *Hakki Mattu Rekke.* Bengaluru: Sapna Book House.

Vidyashankar, S., and G. S. Siddhalingaiah, ed. 1998. *Halageyaryana Shunya Sampadane.* Bengaluru: Priyadarshini Prakashana.

Visaji, Vikram. 2008. *Dharmamruthadalli Desi Swaroopada Hudukaata*. In *Dharmamrutha Samskrutika Mukhamukhi,* ed. Puttaiah B. M. Hampi: Kannada University.

Viswanatha, Vanamala, tr. 2017. *The Life of Harishchandra*. Murthy Classical Library of India.

———., tr. 2024. *Bride in the Hills*. Penguin Books.

Index

H

O

Forthcoming in ***Critical Histories of Indian Literatures***

A Critical History of Marathi Literature
Sachin Ketkar

A Critical History of Malayalam Literature
E. V. Ramakrishnan and P. P. Raveendran

A Critical History of Punjabi Literature
Akshaya Kumar and Jaidev Bishnoi